Monetary Scenarios

By the same author

Money Matters: A Keynesian Approach to Monetary Economics,
   with Sheila C. Dow (Martin Robertson, 1982)
*The Economic Imagination: Towards a Behavioural Analysis of
   Choice* (Wheatsheaf Books, 1983)
The Corporate Imagination: How Big Companies Make Mistakes
   (Wheatsheaf Books, 1984)
Lifestyle Economics: Consumer Behaviour in a Turbulent World
   (Wheatsheaf Books, 1986)
Psychological Economics: Development, Tensions, Prospects, editor
   (Kluwer Academic Publishers, 1988)
Behavioural Economics (2 Volumes), editor (Edward Elgar Publishing
   Limited/Gower Publishing Company, 1988)

Monetary Scenarios
A Modern Approach to Financial Systems

Peter E. Earl

Senior Lecturer in Economics
University of Tasmania

EDWARD ELGAR

Published by
Edward Elgar Publishing Limited
Gower House
Croft Road
Aldershot
Hants GU11 3HR
England

Gower Publishing Company
Old Post Road
Brookfield
Vermont 05036
USA

British Library Cataloguing in Publication Data

Earl, Peter E.
    Monetary Scenarios: a modern approach to financial systems.
    1. Monetary system
    I. Title
    332.4

    ISBN 1-85278-149-1

Printed and bound in Great Britain at
The Camelot Press Ltd, Southampton

Contents

Contents

Contents

Contents

Contents

List of Figures and Tables

Figures

Tables

Preface

This book is an attempt to make sense of modern financial systems by integrating Post Keynesian macroeconomic and monetary theory with recent microeonomic analysis drawn from the rapidly emerging literature of behavioural, 'new institutional' and transaction cost economics. It is a successor to *Money Matters: A Keynesian Approach to Monetary Economics*, which I co-authored with Sheila Dow while I was in the early stages of trying to put together a coherent alternative set of foundations for macroeconomic analysis, and is intended to complement strongly both Sheila's own more recent (1985) work *Macroeconomics: A Methodological Approach* and Victoria Chick's superb (1983) study *Macroeconomics After Keynes*.

Though written mainly between March 1988 and April 1989, the theoretical side of the book was taking shape from late 1984, long before the the Crash of 1987. Some of the ideas from Chapters 3, 8, 12 and 13 were tried out in seminars I delivered at the University of Adelaide in 1986 and Monash University, Melbourne in 1987, and at the 1987 'New Directions in Post Keynesian Economics' and 1988 'Review of Political Economy' conferences at Malvern. I am grateful for comments made on those occasions as well as to John Pheby for dreaming up and organising the splendid Malvern gatherings. My 1988 Malvern offering, which provided the basis for Chapter 8, was made more widely available as an Occasional Paper by the Information Research Unit at the University of Queensland: thanks are due to Don Lamberton for organising this and for his encouragement; particularly useful comments on it were provided by David Williams and Jo Runde. The expertise of my colleague Michael Brooks was useful when I came to include a public choice perspective in Chapter 5. Once again, the inspirational role of George Shackle's subjectivist view of economics and Neil Kay's pioneering work on industrial organisation should be obvious. Needless to say, I take sole responsibility for any errors and omissions that remain.

xi

Given my distaste for animal experiments, I hestitate to say that the real guinea pigs during the gestation of this book were members of my CEC201 Money and Banking classes at the University of Tasmania from mid 1984 to the end of 1987, and Mark Kerslake, Mark Jolley, John Madden, Robert Mallick, Tom Rohling and Rosalie Viney (especially Tom and Rosalie), who found themselves unexpectedly having to contend with Post Keynesian economics after being assigned or unwittingly volunteering to act as tutors on the course. However, I have no doubt that some of them may have felt at times that the experience of having me try my ideas out on them was indeed akin to that of torture. I am grateful for all their efforts and comments, for these have made it very clear where the difficulties lie in getting the message across. I guess I should be particularly grateful to the class of 1984 for not lynching me after I took over in mid-stream and, still suffering from jet-lag, stunned them with the announcement that they would no longer be learning from their beloved *IS-LM* text and would instead be expected to start coping with journal articles and monographs. Julie Waldon helped keep the mob from my office door by ensuring that typed copies of my notes for each lecture were rapidly made available. By 1987, these notes had grown to about 100 pages. During my 1988 study leave they were transferred to my Apple Macintosh and with the aid of Macwrite and Macdraw I began to expand and remould them to form the present book. For the painless way in which it has been possible to sculpt the book and then typeset it directly from my own Macintosh output via a Laserwriter II NTX, I must thank the boffins of Cupertino, California, though I must admit to having cursed them when unable to write for a couple of weeks as a result of the power supply module failing just after the Macintosh warranty had expired.

Finally, my biggest thanks must go to Sharon Axford for putting up with me not merely while I was preoccupied in writing this book but also during work on the others that I have produced in the seven years since *Money Matters*. By getting me to leave the computer alone and take a break occasionally, she probably helped hasten this book's completion as well as leading me to acquire a stronger taste for travel and for lazing around on Tasmania's wonderful beaches. I hope she will not be alarmed at my growing interest in the possibility of studying tourism from the behavioural perspective.

1 Introduction

1.1 Monetary Economics in a Turbulent World

The 1980s were an exciting time in which to be studying monetary economics. The decade saw major structural changes in the financial services industry, hastened by policies of deregulation and technological innovation, and accompanied by a growing belief that the way to get rich quickly was to work in the financial sector and to speculate. While these changes were undermining relationships that economists had estimated from previous data, many governments turned to monetarist policies for tackling inflation — policies which assumed that there was a stable relationship between monetary growth and the supposedly dependent variable, nominal expenditure. Inflation rates fell even though attempts by governments and central bankers to meet favoured monetary targets were often dismal failures, but unemployment rose dramatically and showed little sign of being merely a transitory phenomenon. With the collapse of stockmarkets in October 1987, some of the greedy joined the needy in the ranks of the unemployed.

This book has been written with a view to making sense of the 1980s and on the expectation that much of the monetary history of the 1990s could be similarly turbulent and speculation-driven. A new kind of monetary economics is needed in this kind of environment, one that is much less oriented toward econometric estimations and much more concerned with the effects of complexity and ambiguity on economic processes and with the ways in which institutions adapt to changing circumstances. Policymakers would be unwise to base their decisions on the extrapolation of existing trends in an environment where financial whizz-kids are prone to dream up new schemes that simultaneously boost their earnings and affect the structure of the system. Until things settle down — if they ever do — those who continue to pursue the traditional, highly quantitative approach to monetary economics, and who labour to produce yet more estimates of the supply and demand for money, are likely to be similarly foiled by the absence of stable parameters. As Cuthbertson

1

(1985, pp. 219-220) points out in his superb study of the mainstream literature, 'With innovation in financial markets, exactly what constitutes money becomes problematic', while the recent behaviour of demand for money functions in OECD countries makes it a 'pious hope' to argue that the pace of structural change is not rapid enough to necessitate a change in the definition of money. The failure of economists to agree even about the likelihood of a major downturn after the 1987 crash in share prices illustrates still more vividly how difficult it is to anticipate with much precision the pathways that economies will carve for themselves once they have evolved into complex systems that are full of interdependencies, subject to innovations and prone to arrive at 'crossroads' situations in which slightly different minor shocks have the capacity to provoke large movements in very different directions.

Although it is difficult to say with much precision what *will* happen when events such as major stockmarket crashes or financial innovations occur, I have written this book in the belief that monetary economists can at least make a contribution by exploring what *could* happen, including sets of events that might stop other events from happening. So long as such explorations do not leave one in the hopeless position of believing there are no bounds whatever on the courses that events may take, they may serve to raise awareness concerning the uncertainties associated with any particular set of policy measures and hence foster caution and careful debate about the wisdom of particular decisions. Though it is never costless to hedge one's bets, it may be better to be prepared to deal with a variety of possibilities than to take narrow-minded decisions and continually find that life is full of unpleasant surprises and/or opportunities that one is not in a position to grasp.

The title of this book is intended to convey that its approach to monetary economics has much in common with techniques of 'scenario writing' or 'futures thinking' employed in corporate planning. Although I was originally led to this style of thinking by the work of Shackle (1979) and Jefferson (1983) in the UK, such an open-ended approach to economic issues is unpopular in the Anglo-Saxon world, particularly with students who expect to emerge from their courses not with heightened perceptions of how little their teachers know but with a set of tools — such as skills in macro-econometric modelling — which they can apply with confidence. The French have felt much more at ease with the untidiness of this non-deterministic mode of analysis, which they call 'la prospective', and have revelled in the scope it offers for creative thinking. Like Godet, France's leading scenario planner, I recognise that

> there is *a multiplicity of possible futures* at any given time and that the actual future will be the outcome of the interplay between the various protagonists in a given situation and their respective intentions. How the future evolves is explained as much by human action as by the influence of causalities. The future should not be seen as a single predetermined line, an extension of the past; on the contrary, it is plural and indeterminate. The plurality of the future and the scope for freedom of human action are mutually explanatory; *the future has not been written, but remains to be created* (Godet, 1987, p. 5, emphasis in original).

But unlike Godet, I will not be trying to show how one can assemble a database of appropriate variables pertaining to the system being studied and then construct quantitative scenarios. My intention is to explore in general terms the decision dilemmas faced by protagonists in monetary systems and to examine theoretically the possible outcomes of various choices. However, examples from recent monetary history in the UK, the US and Australasia will often be used as a basis for discussions of how seriously particular rival possibilities should be taken.

1.2 The Conventional Wisdom: An Overview and Critique

This book may also be seen as a 'Post Keynesian' challenge to the kind of teaching literature that has followed Hicks' (1937) attempt to construct a simplified model of Keynes' (1936) *General Theory of Employment, Interest and Money*. Most students learn their economics from textbooks which try to set out in simplified form the essence of primary contributions to the discipline. They do not actually read the primary sources until they take graduate courses, and what they then see is coloured by what they have been warned to expect. Though many learn macroeconomics via expositions based on Hicksian '*IS-LM* analysis', few will realise that, later in life, Hicks (1976, 1980b) himself concluded that his portrayal may have led many economists astray and warned that it should not be used for significant discussions of policy. (I count myself lucky to have had a very different background: in my first week as a first-year undergraduate at Cambridge in October 1974, I was given a reading list which made it readily apparent that one could not even do the weekly essays without having 'read Keynes' in the original. Fortunately, the list suggested that one also read an introductory guide written in 1937 by Joan Robinson, who had been part of Keynes' circle during the writing of the *General Theory* and who subsequently coined the phrase 'bastard Keynesian' to describe contributions to macroeconomics that purported to be based on his ideas but which employed *IS-LM* analysis.) Given this, it seems appropriate for me to present an overview and critique of *IS-LM* analysis. Although my critical comments are theoretical in nature, this must not be taken to imply that macroeconomic models built on *IS-LM* foundations leave little to be desired in empirical terms: as Eichner (1983, 1987) ably demonstrated, the usual 'as if' justification for adhering to grossly simplified models does not stand up in this context. The discussion below draws heavily on contributions by Chick, Shackle and Weintraub to a symposium in the 1982 *Journal of Post Keynesian Economics*. Readers who have not previously encountered *IS-LM* may find that Figure 1.1 makes things easier to follow.

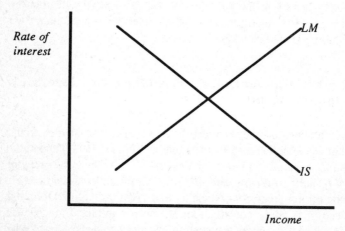

Figure1.1 *Equilibrium of Income and Employment*

The crucial simplification in *IS-LM* analysis is its use of the device of equilibrium to avoid any complications caused by the fact that history is an irreversible sequence of events. The methodology involves the comparison of alternative steady states in which events are replicated. Given a set of exogenously specified conditions, the positions of the *IS* and *LM* curves are fixed and the particular configuration of income and rate of interest implied by the intersection of the curves is assumed to be self-perpetuating. If an exogenous variable is changed, one or both of the curves will shift and the economy is assumed to move to the new configuration of income and the rate of interest implied by the new intersection of the curves. The new position is assumed to last until the system receives another exogenous shock. What happens during transitions from one equilibrium configuration to another is given scant attention, on the presumption that the transition period is brief. If the transition period is lengthy, or if the economy is prone to suffer frequently from external disturbances or to generate surprises internally, then the wisdom of treating macroeconomic systems 'as if they are in equilibrium' becomes questionable.

The *LM* curve depicts the combinations of flows of income and rates of interest that are compatible with holders of stocks of wealth not wishing to adjust the composition of their wealth holdings. If the level of income falls, the volume of transactions will drop and a smaller 'float' of instantly accessible money will be required in the economy. Those who have money balances in excess of their transactions needs will consider turning these into assets that offer higher rates of return. In so far as they bid for other assets the prices of the latter will rise and their effective yields will fall. Hence the upward slope of the *LM* curve: a fall in income reduces the transactions demand for money and the switch into other assets lowers the rate of interest.

A problem is rapidly encountered when consideration is given to the reasons adduced to explain the extent of the upward slope of the *LM* curve. It is suggested that some people may hold on to spare money rather than buying other assets with it, because they fear that the prices of these assets could fall and they will suffer a capital loss in excess of the extra interest income they will earn during the time they wish to hold the assets. Such expectations will limit the steepness of the *LM* slope. However, other people clearly are holding the non-money assets on the expectation that these will not suffer a significant fall in value. Both groups cannot be right, so we would expect them to change their behaviour before long: for example, if the rate of interest fails to rise, the money holders may decide to buy bonds after all and, in so doing, drive bond prices up and the rate of interest down. In other words, the *LM* curve may continually shift around even if the money supply is static (though there is good reason to expect the supply of finance to shift as a result of expectational shifts even if the authorities are taking no measures to adjust it).

Whereas the *LM* curve concerns a stock equilibrium (stocks of money and other existing stores of wealth in portfolios), the *IS* curve refers to a flow equilibrium. The idea is that certain components of aggregate demand depend on the rate of interest (in particular, investment) while others are exogenous (exports and government expenditure) or stable functions of income received (consumption expenditure on domestically produced goods). For each possible rate of interest, it is suggested that there will be a unique level of income at which expectations are realised. Given the rate of interest, investment is determined as a steady flow of expenditure. If government expenditure and export demands are fixed also as stready flows, then if planned savings by consumers (plus leakages to import spending and taxation) do not equal the injections flows arising from investment, public sector and export demand, firms will adjust their production levels and factor payments — up if there is an excess of demand (leakages less than injections), down if there is a deficiency of demand. Since the marginal propensity to consume is assumed to be less than one, any rise (fall) in income will lead to a smaller increase (decrease) in consumption demand than the change in income, so the system will tend to converge — at least, so long as there are no changes in the rate of interest, in the investment and consumption functions, and in government and export demands. Planned withdrawals will come to equal planned injections, so if income payments are then held steady no one will be surprised and events will repeat themselves. The higher the rate of interest, the lower is the level of investment and the lower is the equilibrium level of income. Hence the *IS* curve slopes downwards.

Post Keynesians argue that, because of uncertainty about future outlays and earnings, investment is likely to be affected more by shifts in confidence than changes in the rate of interest. Shifts in confidence will make the *IS* curve move around, often at precisely the moment when the *LM* curve is on the move. It then becomes doubtful whether we can really speak of separate functions concerning equilibrium in the money markets (*LM*) and goods markets (*IS*). A general change to a feeling of pessimism, for example, may cause a simultaneous shift in favour of money and away from assets whose capital values might be open to doubt; this could mean firms invest less than they would otherwise have done, given a particular rate of interest (*IS* shifts left) and do not use idle funds to buy bonds, and many bond holders try to shift into cash (*LM* shifts left). If both kinds of curves are normally on the move it seems questionable to speak of them as existing at all, for they are concerned with possible end results that are never attained.

Shifts of confidence can take place very suddenly: Shackle (1974) has compared them with the dramatic changes of pattern one observes while looking into a kaleidoscope and slightly twisting its casing. They may well occur before the system has had time to come anywhere near to reaching equilibrium in the aftermath of the last 'kaleidic' shift. It may be unwise to try to get round this possibility by assuming that adjustments to equilibrium are very rapid. Firms will often take six months or more to decide what to do about their employment levels. In the meantime, they can change the amount of overtime working they offer and/or adjust their waiting lists or stock levels. Expenditure can thus change without employment changing. Moreover, the system could only be said to have achieved equilibrium well after any decisions to increase employment and output have been taken, for until firms start observing sales levels they cannot be sure of the accuracy of their demand forecasts.

Instability in the *IS* function may arise because expectations are invariably falsified by the working through of the multiplier process following an injection of aggregate demand. For example, suppose that an increase in government expenditure comes as a pleasant surprise to firms supplying the government. Not only may income recipients working for government contractors spend some fraction of their marginal unexpected incomes, but the firms themselves may decide to step up their investment programmes. So, too, may firms who receive increased consumption and investment demand, and so on. We have the beginnings of a kind of 'super-multiplier', the working through of which runs counter to the attainment of a steady flow of income and different kinds of expenditure flows. Implicit in the 'super-multiplier' idea is a dual role for investment: in the short run, it generates aggregate demand; in the long run, it affects aggregate supply by augmenting capacity or displacing workers in favour of machines. The full employment level of output thus changes through time, as do the structure and volume of demand necessary to bring it about.

1.3 Risk-Taking and Employment: The Post Keynesian Vision

In the chapters that follow, I make no presumption that the economic system tends towards a state of general equilibrium. Instead I concentrate on studying choices and possible sequences of events that may follow them. My perspective is greatly influenced by Keynes' short-period analysis, as developed by Townshend (1937), Shackle (1973, 1974), Davidson (1978a, 1978b) Bausor (1982, 1984), Chick (1983) and Dow (1985) with an emphasis on the contracts and conventions that link the past, the present and the future in ways which sometimes promote orderly behaviour but which may on other occasions promote chaos. This section describes in a highly compressed way the essence of this view of a monetary system.

A scenario begins with financiers, wealth-owners, non-financial firms and would-be workers (and sometimes the public sector policy-makers) poised ready for action, looking into an as yet undetermined future, with history behind them. History is an important reference point in expectation formation, even though the future is not an extrapolation of the past. Relative prices have a strong 'conventional' element: if we all woke up tomorrow with amnesia and all price stickers and catalogues had vanished, we would be very confused, for what we are prepared to pay for things depends in large part on what we have got accustomed to paying in the past, not upon some underlying set of preferences we possess at birth. Lending policies of financial intermediaries also depend on conventions that have been selected in the course of history, not because they are the best ones available, but because they have seemed to work satisfactorily. Expectations about wage relativities, too, are historically rooted and difficult to adjust. In transactions, what constitutes an acceptable means of payment is again conventional: money itself is an 'institution'.

History also leaves economic actors with some formal contracts that are still in operation, which it would be costly to break and renegotiate. These cover things such as finance (for example, interest obligations on debentures, monthly contributions to life assurance policies), supplies of raw materials and other physical factors of production (for example, via leasing agreements), and wage rates for particular job slots. Some of these contracts specify fixed prices in money terms; some specify quantities as well. Taken together they imply a complex of constraints which will impact on the spending decisions that firms are willing to make, given their assessments of sales prospects and the fossils of past decisions that they possess in the form of fixed factors of the usual sort (corporation-owned buildings and machinery) and stock levels. Household 'production systems', likewise, will be trammelled by past commitments.

In an economy riddled with such contracts, finance is essential to production processes, for the contracts will not all expire at once or involve payments all being made at once. If workers are paid before their outputs are paid for, their employers need finance to get the process going. If workers are paid after products have been sold, they must have financial reserves or credit cards that they can use as means of payment or else their employers will never get the revenue from which to pay them. (A similar problem would exist in an economy of workers' cooperatives.) But committing oneself to financial out-payments in advance of knowledge that one's expected income/revenue is on its way is a hazardous business. (Formal general equilibrium theory often removes such hazards, along with any need for finance, by assuming the existence of a complete set of forward markets and allowing no futures contracts to be agreed upon until a price/quantity configuration has been found which clears all markets. Thereby it abolishes the significance of historical time, any need for money and any possibility of unemployment. See Debreu, 1959.)

The scale of finance required by a decision-maker for a particular level of activity will be affected by the terms she negotiates in respect of any new contracts she is free to make. In some markets, conventions will preclude any bargaining, thereby economising on transaction costs at the risk of leaving buyers and sellers dissatisfied. Elsewhere, bargaining will be conventional practice, but negotiations may break down or the need to reach a decision by a particular deadline may lead one party reluctantly to accept an offer made with the suggestion that they 'take it or leave it'. Attempts to avoid the costs of continuing to haggle for as long as it takes to find a set of transactions which leaves everyone satisfied thus entail a cost: the risk that some markets may fail to clear and some people's expenditure hopes will be dashed due to a lack of income. (It should be noted that bargaining stances will also be tied up with history and anticipations of the future. Past weakness at the bargaining table may suggest a future proneness to make concessions and encourage adversaries to be aggressive, but aggression will also be dependent on the state of the news concerning one's opportunity costs: see Shackle, 1949, Ch. 6.)

9

Introduction

The volume of factors a firm wishes to hire, in addition to its previously contracted inputs, will depend on its expectations of revenue, once its success at the bargaining table has more clearly defined its cost situation in respect of human, material and financial inputs. Firms' revenue expectations, summed together for the period in question, comprise the level of 'effective demand' in Keynes' analysis. 'Effective' demand here is not the same as 'effective' demand in modern work by neoclassical employment theorists following from reinterpretations of Keynes by Clower (1965; 1967) and Leijonhufvud (1968). All it means is the level of demand that firms in the aggregate are hoping to see materialise. (In the Clower/Leijonhufvud work it means the actual level of demand that has materialised, as distinct from 'notional demand', which is what people would like to spend, if only they could realise their desired employment offers.) This forward-looking concept is the decisive thing as far as employment determination right now is concerned. Next contract-making period, firms will have the debris of the past to deal with, and another, possibly different, set of expectations about the net revenues they might realise if they try to produce and sell particular volumes of new output (and dispose of unsold stock from previous periods).

Whether or not firms' expectations are realised depends upon consumption decisions and investment decisions, both in overall monetary value and in structural composition. There is no reason whatsoever why such an incompletely prereconciled set of decentralised decisions should result in plans being realised, even given the extent of viscosity imposed on patterns of behaviour by conventions and by contracts from the past. The level of employment selected by such decisions certainly need not have a functional relationship with the extent of any mismatch that could subsequently occur between expectations and outcomes. If employment has been reduced after previous periods of disappointment, it is by no means guaranteed that the gap between expected sales and actual sales will also be reduced, despite the reduction in expected revenue. Even if some workers cut their expenditure by less than any fall in their income, such tendencies for reductions in the wage bill to produce convergence may be offset by the unwillingness of firms to carry on investing as output stagnates, or by a growing unwillingness to spend on the part of those workers who remain in employment but who observe the worsening state of the economy and worry about losing their jobs. (They can carry on using existing durables that have not yet worn out, when otherwise they might have replaced them.)

Firms may argue that what stops them from hiring all those volunteering for work is the set of money wage rates that exists historically or that it seems possible to negotiate within an acceptable timeframe. But the problem is better seen as arising from their inability to raise enough finance or from their unwillingness to risk producing output that they may be unable to sell without incurring a loss. What stops a full employment level of demand emerging (even if there is not a full employment level of production) is not the level of factor payments being 'too low' in any objective sense, but the unwillingness of people to risk borrowing or lending. In other words, the unemployment problem is a problem of liquidity preference. People who would like to work to earn money are deprived of employment because liquidity — something whose supply private enterprise may be unable to enhance by hiring workers — is demanded by people who possess financial surpluses. Lower liquidity preference would encourage higher levels of employment in the present, but it might involve people in entering into obligations (such as loan repayments) that they would be unable to fulfil in future without there being a further lowering of liquidity preference. Changes in attitudes towards liquidity may thus produce patterns of obligations that first promote economic recovery but later generate grave disappointments.

1.4 An Outline of the Rest of the Book

The structure of this book broadly follows the Post Keynesian perspective just outlined, and the vision embodied in the earlier quotation from Godet. After a detailed discussion of the nature of liquidity preference and the speculative dimension of choice (Chapter 2) we move on to consider the portfolio choices of the four main groups of protagonists: consumers (Chapter 3), firms (Chapter 4), the government (Chapter 5), and the overseas sector (Chapter 6). These chapters make extensive use of the literature of behavioural economics wherever mainstream theory seems of doubtful validity and Post Keynesian thinking has so far failed to develop satisfactory alternative constructs. Though many behaviouralists are still largely ignorant of the work of Post Keynesians, and vice versa, there is nothing particularly *ad hoc* about this analytical strategy; the 1980s marked a growing advocacy of the notion that Post Keynesian and behavioural ideas exhibit strong complementarity — for example, see

Kay (1984), Foster (1987), Hodgson (1988) and Pheby (ed.) (1989).

In Chapter 7, the first steps are taken to examine interactions between the four groups: this short chapter explores intersectoral flows of funds. Since those with financial surpluses can fund the deficits of others without necessarily using the services of financial intermediaries, questions naturally arise concerning the rationale for intermediaries and their impact on the total volume of borrowing and lending. Chapters 8 and 9, which deal with these issues, are the core chapters of the book: it is here that we simply cannot avoid facing up to the problems of indeterminacy caused by processes of financial innovation in an increasingly complex system. In contrast to much of the textbook literature on money and banking, these two chapters portray financial intermediaries as firms operating, like many manufacturing businesses, in an oligopolistic environment. Chapter 8, the longest chapter in the book, makes extensive use of recent attempts by behavioural economists to explain the evolution of corporate strategies with reference to the transaction costs associated with contractually different ways of arranging economic activities.

By the end of Chapter 9 we are in a position to start looking at possible system-wide consequences of choices made by the various protagonists. Chapter 10 explores the workings of the Keynesian employment multiplier as a process, noting, amongst other things, how outcomes are contingent upon what income recipients decide to do with any additional savings that they make. Chapter 11 is an attempt to clarify and adapt to the present context some of the key themes that orthodox economics has persistently managed not to grasp from Keynes' work on unemployment and the determination of the price level. Chapter 12 examines, once again with considerable inputs from behavioural economics, the origins and policy implications of episodes of financial instability. Chapter 13 highlights various destabilising bottlenecks and stabilising sources of slack in economic systems that are both difficult to quantify and dangerous to ignore when monetary and macroeconomic policies are being formulated. Finally, Chapter 14 draws many earlier themes together in a discussion of the conduct and role of monetary policy in a deregulated environment.

2 Portfolio Choice, Markets and Liquidity Preference

2.1 Introduction

Perhaps the most appropriate way to begin a Post Keynesian analysis of how a modern financial system works is with an endorsement of the following words of Shackle (1982, p. 438):

[M]y repudiation of the equilibrium frame of analysis can best be summarised by saying *all markets are in some degree speculative*. There is hardly anything outside of perishable food or ephemeral entertainment whose price today is not influenced by ideas of what its price will be tomorrow, next week, next year. But these ideas are figments, suggested, not determined by our observation of the present (emphasis in the original).

Even this strong statement, which echoes sentiments expressed by 'Austrian' economists such as Menger (1971) and Mises (1966) and the most radical of Keynes' early interpreters, Hugh Townshend (1937), could be stronger in its departure from the mainstream vision. Shackle's two examples of residual non-speculative markets are questionable. The advent of the domestic deep-freezer has opened up opportunities for households to speculate in their timing of food purchases. Similarly, while entertainments may in themselves be ephemeral there is much scope to speculate about when is the best time to purchase the right to see them: I well recall arriving at a Led Zeppelin concert in 1972, with tickets that a friend had queued to get some weeks before, only to find desperate ticket touts selling tickets below their face value; more recently, innovative marketing by promoters of opera and orchestral concerts has frequently presented me with the dilemma of having to choose between purchasing at a discount a subscription series ticket for performances so far into the future that I could not be sure of being able to attend, or waiting and having to pay more.

Guesses about the future worth of a transaction undertaken today will affect choices not merely because things not purchased today may be more expensive in future, but also because things may be purchased today with a view to their possible resale value in the future. Before people get around to making new choices to buy and sell, a number of welcome or damaging events can take place, including the following:

(i)   Unexpected obsolescence may produce disproportionately poor resale values for physical assets whose owners have planned to trade them in before they had been fully worn out.

(ii) Something may happen to damage physical assets, causing them to fall in value.

(iii) A change in the chooser's financial circumstances (for example, a person loses her job and can no longer keep up repayments on loans she had contracted) may mean that dates at which assets are returned to the market are brought forward (or postponed) unexpectedly — possibly forcibly so.

(iv) A change in personal circumstances may mean that particular physical assets are no longer required (for example, a new job may bring with it a company car and little point is keeping one's own vehicle).

(v)   Assets may change in value due to changes in supply and demand conditions consequent on expectational shifts.

(vi) Financial assets may turn out to be relatively worthless if debtors default, or such assets might pay unexpectedly high dividends and appreciate in value.

These possibilities should be kept in mind throughout this chapter, as we examine the kinds of commitments that decision-makers can enter into in a modern financial system and some of the factors that can affect how easy it is to undo them without loss.

Before we proceed to the main body of the chapter, a note of clarification is in order. The word 'portfolio' is used in this book to signify the set of assets and liabilities to which a decision-making unit — be it an individual, a household, a firm or a government agency — chooses to make a commitment. Readers should interpret the term in a very broad manner. For example, a commitment to a particular employment opportunity is an asset in the sense that it is expected to yield a flow of income payments, but it is a liability in the sense that once the worker has signed the job contract she is obliged to meet certain commitments. An employment choice concerns what to do with one's human wealth, but the rest of an act of choosing a new portfolio involves more than just a decision about what to do with one's previously acquired possessions and financial wealth (whether to turn financial assets into goods for immediate consumption or whether to get out of one class of financial asset and into another). It also involves decisions about whether or not to get into debt and the kind of debt to get into. Although the ability to borrow is often a function of the would-be borrower's previous accumulations of financial and physical assets, it may also be possible to raise funds if the asset to be purchased with them is used as collateral, or simply because the borrower's earning capacity is judged adequate, given her other commitments, for her to be able to meet the required payments even though her 'non-human' wealth is presently very limited.

In addition to seeking to avoid an undue focus on financial wealth as a determinant of borrowing and spending, I also wish to stress that portfolio choice involves decisions about whether to rent or lease assets rather than to buy them outright, and whether to purchase flows of goods and services in the market rather than to produce them in-house (in other words, 'do it yourself' choices of households, vertical integration choices of firms and the socialisation/privatisation choices of governments); these decisions can have major impacts upon asset holdings and payments commitments. A portfolio that involves extensive borrowing and/or renting makes it possible for someone who has not previously accumulated large holdings of financial and physical assets to give the impression that she is wealthy: she can consume conspicuously but borrow and rent things in privacy, so long as she can keep up her repayment obligations and not suffer the ignominy of having her expensive durables repossessed or being declared bankrupt.

2.2 Contracts and Commitments

The legal status of the speculative commitments that a person chooses to enter into can vary in a number of ways. Many transactions are speculative in the sense that the seller and/or buyer do not know at the outset precisely the full extent of the quantity to be delivered or the price that will eventually be charged. In these kinds of cases parties to the transaction usually have at least an implicit contract in mind to limit the bounds of possibility: there will be expectations on both sides about what constitutes reasonable conduct. Neoclassical unemployment theory has often made this point in relation to wage flexibility and layoffs: one reason for workers not attempting to push down wages to overturn their employers' layoff decisions may be their recognition that the wage rates offered by the employers are inflated by a risk premium because of the likelihood of orders not arriving at a steady rate and the employers' desire to avoid the costs of price wars in their product markets and of renegotiating wages with their workers. Such workers would be expected to ensure that they had enough liquidity to enable them to weather periods when they were stood down by their employers. (As we shall later see, in contrast to neoclassical presumptions, there is no necessary reason to believe that if they did push successfully for wage reductions they would succeed in preserving their jobs.) But implicit contracts have a much broader usage than this: they seem to be a commonly employed device for enabling participants in turbulent markets to take decisions.

For example, a restaurateur who allows a couple to occupy a table may find at one extreme that they linger over a small snack and at the other that they ravenously eat a three course meal. However, since an initial detailed inquisition about their proposed schedule and eating intentions will hardly be conducive to a satisfactory atmosphere, the restaurateur may attempt to avoid having to turn potentially worthwhile business away by operating on average with a margin of excess capacity and relying on hovering waiters to exert tacit coercion on those who overstay their welcome. Usually, though, such coercion is not necessary since the diners will feel under some social pressure not to abuse their claim on the table.

Sometimes buyers can choose whether to engage in an implicit contract or opt for the relative security of a guaranteed price. For example, many people are willing to allow their cars to be serviced, or to engage lawyers to undertake conveyancing whilst buying new homes, on the basis of a very vague estimate of the likely bill. They accept that the idiosyncratic nature of these tasks makes it difficult to specify a price in advance but they make sure they have some surplus financial resources to meet any excess and expect that they will be warned if it turns out that an unexpectedly large amount of work has to be done. However, fixed-price conveyancing and servicing are increasingly being offered for those who prefer to avoid speculating.

Similar kinds of contractual informality are to be found in inter-firm contracts in societies where business thrives more on trust than on the basis of expensive legal advice. Akio Morita's description of his role in setting up the US branch of Sony is particularly instructive in this regard:

We had to translate all of our contracts into English and explain the company on paper in minute detail. The first thing that puzzled the lawyers and accountants was that many of our contracts specified that, if during the life of the contract, conditions changed in such a way that affected the ability of either side to comply with the terms, both sides would sit down and discuss the new situation. This kind of clause is common in Japanese contracts, and many companies do much or even most of their business without any contracts at all. However, it looked alarming to people who did not understand the way business is conducted in Japan (Morita, 1987, p. 94).

Morita goes on to recall the even greater alarm expressed by his American colleagues when they discovered that Sony was financed through a large number of renewable ninety-day loans. It was understood in Japan that banks making such loans would not exercise their rights to call them in, for very careful inquiries would have been made prior to the loans being made in the first place. The Americans did not accept that such trust could exist and wanted written guarantees that the loans would be renewed.

Despite the American enthusiasm for getting everything in writing, it has become increasingly common even in the US for borrowers and lenders to sign contracts with little idea of their ultimate financial implications. In the past, fixed-rate lending was the conventional form of transaction, even for long-term loans such as housing mortgages. Nowadays, however, few housebuyers would be able or willing to enter into such contracts. It has become accepted that gyrations in other interest rates, consequent on the vagaries of monetary policy and inflationary processes, make it unduly risky for financial institutions for fix their revenues for long periods during which their outpayments to depositors are difficult to predict. Nor would many housebuyers be keen to bind themselves to a particular rate of interest reflecting current market rates if they believed the long-term trend in interest rates was downwards. However, both parties to a mortgage seem to make the tacit assumption that monthly repayment figures will not lurch around discontinuously. Usually, when interest rates in general rise, repayment periods will be extended and/or housing interest rate increases will be limited even at the cost of creating a queue for new loans, in order to prevent existing borrowers from experiencing unduly severe disruptions to their current lifestyles. It is also usually understood that borrowers will not seek to refund their loans with an institution that is temporarily leading the market in cutting interest rates. A mortgage thus involves goodwill on both sides.

Transactions involving pre-agreed prices and quantities come in three broad forms. Physical and financial assets can be purchased or sold on a 'spot' basis, in other words, for immediate delivery at a price agreed to now, though it may be agreed that payment is required before, at the time of or some time after delivery. Secondly, there are 'futures' contracts, which specify that a particular item is to be delivered on a particular date at a price agreed to now, with an agreed timing for payments by the party to whom the asset is delivered. Thirdly, there are 'options', which come in two forms. A 'call' option gives the holder the right, but not the obligation, to purchase a particular item — which may even be a futures contract — from the original seller (the 'writer') at a previously specified price (the 'strike' or 'exercise' price) on or before a specified date. By contrast, possession of a 'put' option gives one the right to sell the specified asset to the writer of the option at the strike price. The price at which an option is sold by its writer is known as its 'premium', and this will then fluctuate in value in so far as there are changes in expectations about value of the asset that is the subject of the option. If the option is not exercised, the writer's profit is the premium, less transactions costs involved in marketing the option.

Though these different kinds of deals are usually illustrated with respect to markets for primary commodities and financial assets, they arise frequently in the broader run of consumer activities. An airline ticket, for example, is a futures contract in that it is often bought many months prior to the date of the journey, at an agreed price which is guaranteed so long as payment is made on or before a particular date. Likewise, we can note that it is quite common for one to be able to rent, say, a piano with an option to buy within a specified period at a particular price. Options are even starting to affect car markets: in 1988 the Australian importers of Renault cars introduced a scheme whereby purchasers would have the option to trade them in at a Renault dealer after five years for a predetermined proportion of their purchase prices.

Futures markets originally grew up as insurance devices whereby commodities dealers could protect themselves against falls in prices of their stocks, and commodity users could guard against rising costs of inputs. The term 'premium', for the price of an option, is likewise indicative of the original vision of options contracts as serving an insurance role, providing another way for people to hedge against possible changes in relative prices which would affect their portfolios in an adverse manner. For example, prior to the 1987 Crash, many pension funds would have been hedging against losses on their equity holdings by buying put options in the equities that they held, or even options in baskets of shares such as those making up particular stock exchange indices. The higher the strike prices in their options, the greater were their incentives to try to ride the bull market right up to its peak; this activity tended to push the market to a higher level still, ensuring that when the crash came share prices had further to fall (cf. Dale, 1988, p. 9). So long as the market continued to rise, these options were not be exercised and those who had written them were making attractive earnings from premiums. When the crash came, millions were lost by those who had written put options on the expectation that the market would continue to rise.

One of the most expensive errors of this kind was made by a major Australasian casualty of the 1987 crash, the Ariadne investment company. Six weeks prior to the crash, Ariadne's chairman Bruce Judge had attempted to dispel doubts in the financial community about the soundness of his company's assets by selling 58 million of its shares in the ailing New Zealand investment company Renouf Corp to the high-flying insurance firm FAI. The insurance acumen of FAI's founder, the late Larry Adler, was perhaps reflected in the fact that the deal included a put option on these shares, with a strike price of $NZ3.00. This option was kept secret from the market at large. Shortly after the crash, Adler and FAI 'neatly slipped out of a $A100 million paper loss and Judge was stuck with shares that promptly dropped 35 cents to $NZ 1.18 following the revelation' (McManamy, 1988, p. 125). This deal played a large part in Ariadne having to announce in March 1988 the biggest half-yearly loss in Australian corporate history ($A509 million).

The insurance role of these kinds of contracts has become increasingly obscured by the growth of trade in futures and options, in which people enter into such deals purely with a view to making money on changes in the market value of the contracts. For example, in his role as Bursar of King's College, Cambridge, Keynes did not buy grain futures on the expectation that he would hold them to maturity and then have to take delivery of sacks of wheat; if he bought them, he expected to sell them to someone else at a higher price. They might pass through many hands before ending up the portfolio of, say, a milling company that had actually decided it wanted to guarantee the price of the inputs it would need to receive on the maturity date. Likewise, many of those who nowadays buy equity options have no intention of ever exercising them; they are merely trying to exploit the scope that such deals provide for making a lot of money in return for a smaller outlay than would be necesssary if they speculated directly in the underlying assets. Suppose that, say, ICI shares are not expected to rise in value over the next three months. If so, it may today cost me next to nothing to buy call options in ICI shares with an expiry date three months hence and which specify a strike price equal to today's spot price. But if expectations change and ICI share prices rise substantially, the options will become valuable assets and I will be able to take my profit simply by selling them; I will not have to raise the cash to exercise the options and then incur the costs of disposing of the shares to realise my capital gain. On the other hand, if ICI shares fall substantially, the most I can lose is the sum I have paid for the options, which may be far less than the capital loss I would have suffered had I actually bought the shares.

When purchased with such motives, options become akin to lottery tickets or bets placed on gaming tables. More so even than speculative spot trade in equities and foreign exchange, options trading of this kind symbolises the era that Susan Strange (1986) has labelled 'casino capitalism'.

2.3 The Reversibility of Speculative Choices

The connections between contractual obligations, financial speculation and individual lifestyles were epitomised by a newspaper headline which appeared shortly after Black Monday (19 October 1987), when it became apparent that the failure of share prices to continue to rise was causing difficulties for some stockbroking firms and individual market players. The headline read: 'Yuppies' Armageddon — Oh, no, not the Porsche!' But it overlooked the fact that most of the erstwhile financial whizz-kids had leased their vehicles. Only at the end of the leasing period, after they had made a final 'balloon' repayment (for example, 'a 60 per cent residual'), would they actually have legal title to their cars and be in a position to sell them. Many of these leases would not end until the early 1990s. Some leasing deals that had once looked like sure-fire ways of making even more money (owing to the tendency of prices of secondhand exotic cars to appreciate) thus turned suddenly into financial millstones. Yuppies who needed cash in a hurry but could not find anyone willing to take over the leases on their cars were forced to off-load their art collections, antiques and even their real estate. If they had not considered 'forced sale' risks when choosing their portfolios, they were in for a harsh lesson on the case for doing so in future.

Such risks are by no means the preserve of people whose lives centre on the ups and downs of exchange rates and share indices. To be sure, by choosing a portfolio that leaves a good deal of room for manoeuvre, a decision-maker who is aware of the scope for turbulence in her life can try to sidestep the possibility that she will have to return her assets to the market and in doing so incur losses. For example, she may choose to keep a large margin of financial slack in the form of readily accessible deposits and make sure she has plenty of scope for running up additional charges against her credit cards. When choosing physical assets, she may seek to purchase ones which adapt to a wide range of requirements (a station wagon is more flexible than a sports car) or which are modular in design (a separable hi-fi system can be upgraded far more easily than an integrated music centre). She can also limit the extent of her commitments by making short-term contracts, not merely when placing funds with financial institutions and other borrowers but also by renting consumer durables and real estate rather making outright purchases. She can further reduce the need for change by keeping out of turbulent economic environments as far as possible. These kinds of strategies are discussed at length in Earl (1986, pp. 68-79) and Toffler (1970), but they will not be without their costs: for example, it may not be possible to purchase a station wagon that provides the exhilaration of a sports car, while tenancy laws may not prevent landlords from surprising their tenants with eviction notices. Hence decision-makers often choose to risk finding themselves in situations where they will want to change course.

Scope for taking a new direction or turning the clock back is not merely a function of the kinds of contractual clauses that condemned some of the newly-impoverished urban professionals to carry on driving their Porsches. Some choices, such as those made prior to the reactor explosion at Chernobyl, are *crucial* in the sense that they may cause changes in the environment that are for all intents and purposes permanent: even as this chapter was being written, precisely this point was being raised by the Wilderness Society as the Australian Government tried to decide whether or not to prevent the logging of the unique temperate rainforests of south west Tasmania. At the level of the individual, career choices may be similarly daunting: mistakes can leave a decision-maker too old to change course and start all over again. Even if these kinds of constraints are not expected to be present and nothing happens to change the market's rating of the relative worth of durable assets, a decision-maker's choice may be shaped by her assessments of the relative *liquidity* of assets that she could wish to sell or be forced to dispose of in the future.

Like Casson (1981, pp. 67-8), I think it is useful to distinguish two kinds of liquidity, even though they are affected by similar factors. First, we may say that an asset is liquid because it is easy to turn it into cash — in other words, because it has 'low transaction costs on a forced sale'. Transaction costs include the need to commit resources to the (re)negotiation and enforcement of contracts, as well as the costs of acquiring information about the characteristics of buyers and their whereabouts (or of demonstrating one's own product and whereabouts to potential buyers via advertisements, etc.). It should be noted that the ease of selling an asset will also be affected by the presence of such costs on the buyer's side of the market, along with stamp duties and other government levies on changes of ownership.

Secondly, an asset may be said to be liquid if little capital risk is involved in owning it because it is possible to predict quite accurately the price it will fetch in the future. For example, a three-month Treasury Bill is more liquid than a long-dated government security because the certain redemption value of the former in the near future places narrow bounds on possible fluctuations in its immediate worth: if the rate of interest offered on new issues of Treasury Bills were doubled, existing ones would hardly have to fall in price to offer a comparable yield over the remainder of their existence; whereas if a new issue of perpetuities were made offering double the present long-term rate, prices of existing perpetuities would have to halve for them to match the yield of the new ones.

Taken together, these two kinds of liquidity imply that when a person thinks about what she might be able to realise if she came to dispose of a particular asset, she should be thinking in terms of a *range* of possible net proceeds and their associated degrees of likelihood, given the particular time horizon over which she might want to sell: as Menger (1871) pointed out long ago, it is misleading to speak of *the* price of an asset if the asset in question does not enjoy perfect marketability.

2.4 Outputs, Carrying Costs and Liquidity Premia

If decision-makers are worried about the losses they might incur by recomposing their portfolios, then it initially seems more obvious for the economist to focus on their expectations of how much they stand to lose, rather than on liquidity *per se*. As far as physical assets are concerned, we would want to avoid confusion between a loss in value due to normal depreciation associated with wear and tear, and a loss incurred because one had to sell at short notice. However, while physical deterioration might be taken account of by a simple straight-line depreciation, we still have to contend with potential for variability in the amount of cash that it might be possible to raise by hurriedly trying to sell a particular asset. This forces us to consider how decision-makers are likely to frame 'variability' in mental terms.

Some might simplify the problem by considering only one habitually preferred selling routine and the 'most likely' net return. Others may try to think along the lines assumed in much of the literature on choice under uncertainty and consider 'the expected value' of net proceeds: that is, the average of imagined possible net sale returns, each weighted by their degrees of likelihood. Yet others may recognise that the first two approaches could be dangerous bases for making portfolio decisions, for in promoting a focus on a particular value they encourage the neglect of much lower realisation values which presently seem unlikely but which could be very inconvenient if they were actual outcomes (see Hart, 1940, 1942, 1947). Such decision-makers might consider the distribution of possible forced sale values in terms of its variance and skewness rather than just its mean (Hicks, 1967, p. 104) or, instead of treating rival possibilities in any statistical fashion, might size up liquidity by focusing in one of a variety of different ways on particularly attention-arresting pairs of imagined high and low realisation values (see Earl, 1986, Ch. 8; Ford, 1987; and the penultimate paragraph of section 3.4 below).

The liquidity premium concept introduced by Keynes (1936, pp. 226-9) provides us with an analytically convenient means for discussing the impact of liquidity considerations on portfolio choice without worrying about how decision-makers conceptualise uncertainty. Keynes argued that a person choosing a portfolio will appraise each asset by weighing up its overall performance in terms of:

(i) Its output, q. Examples of this would include the aesthetic appeal of a painting, or the expected profit stream from a factory.

(ii) Its carrying cost, c. This can include the costs of servicing any loans taken out to finance owning the asset in question, along with any costs of insuring and caring for it (or the amount by which the value of the asset will depreciate if it is used and these costs are not incurred). It is my experience that students seem prone to confuse carrying costs with transaction costs: they should remember that the former are holding costs, whereas the latter are costs associated with switching to another asset.

(iii) Its liquidity premium, l. This is the *value* a person places on it for the feelings of convenience or security she feels she can achieve by owning it and therefore being in a position to dispose of it. For example, other things equal, a person would be expected to feel rather uneasy about holding her wealth in the form of an asset that historically had a wide variance in forced sale prices, where she stood to lose a lot when she wanted (or had) to sell it in future; she would be prepared to pay more for an asset which, as far as she was concerned, promised a similar output and burden of carrying costs but was more readily marketable. It is through this focus on the worth of liquidity that Keynes escapes the need to worry about how decision-makers might conceptualise the uncertain losses that a forced sale could involve.

An asset's total prospective return is the sum of its $q - c + l$.

Keynes set out this essentially simple idea in a most disconcerting manner: he expressed the q, c and l of each asset not in terms of monetary equivalents but in amounts of the asset itself. For example, one might consider the case of a hire-car company contemplating the purchase of a fleet consisting of a hundred vehicles of a particular kind. The fleet's q would be the number of additional vehicles of this kind the firm could purchase at the end of the period in question from the fleet's rental earnings less advertising and administration costs. Its c would be the difference between the number of vehicles in the fleet at the start of the period and the number of brand new replacements that they could be traded against at the end of the period, after maintenance costs had been deducted. (I must confess to having found it difficult to decide under which heading to put maintenance, advertising and administration costs: there is a case for subtracting all three from gross output and instead treating q as a net revenue concept, so that c refers purely to depreciation; alternatively, one might treat them all as carrying costs along with depreciation, on the ground that if they were not incurred the firm would earn no revenue. In the latter case, q becomes simply the number of vehicles of the kind in question that could be purchased from gross earnings.) The fleet's l is not observable, but it would be the prospective output, again measured in terms of vehicles, that the company thinks it would be worth foregoing purely because of the ease of raising cash by selling its fleet if the need arose. If in terms of these vehicles the q, c and l were, respectively, 30, 17 and three, then the fleet's rate of return would be 16 per cent. In Keynes' terminology, this would be the fleet's 'own-rate of own-interest'.

This all sounds needlessly complicated, for normally we think of rates of return in money terms. However, there is no reason why we have to do so and, indeed, in times of inflation when we start thinking in 'real terms' we are no longer using money as our reference point, our standard of value. The key consideration, whichever standard of value is being used, is whether there is anything to be gained from having more or less of a particular asset in one's portfolio, and this depends on the relative rates of return one attaches to particular assets at the margin.

To convert own rates of return into comparable units, it is necessary to add to each asset's yield a factor, which Keynes labelled as a, to signify the expected change in price of the asset relative to whichever other asset is being used as the numeraire. Usually the numeraire will be money, so a is the expected change in the money price of the asset over the time horizon being used by the decision-maker. In the hypothetical case of the hire-car fleet, if the vehicles were expected to increase in price by 10 per cent by the end of the period, then the subjective money rate of return as seen by the company would be 17.6 per cent. Such a fleet would not be purchased if a higher yield seemed possible on altogether different assets or by, for example, purchasing rather fewer of the vehicles in question and purchasing other types of assets (such as some campervans to rent out).

It is much easier to imagine decision-makers normally conceiving of q, c and l as money values, with a being incorporated in l. In this schema, an asset's liquidity premium would be a function not merely of the value placed upon its marketability but also of the value of output the person is prepared to forego to obtain the asset, given her expectations about its future money price. By considering what decision-makers believe possible price changes to be worth, we also avoid any need to refer, as Keynes did, to 'the' expected change in the price of an asset in situations where decision-makers conceive of ranges of possible price changes.

With most consumer durables or industrial plant and machinery, one is holding them for q, despite their poor performances in respect of c and l. With financial assets, c is usually insignificant, but l might be highly positive or negative, depending on the way one expects prices to move and which asset one is using as a reference point. Money, in the sense of pure currency (as distinct from an interest-earning or even zero-interest deposit in a bank that might default), provides no q and incurs no c (unless one has to guard against robbery or the loss of one's wallet), but is supremely easy to dispose of for what one has given up to get it — unless we have inflation or relative price movements amongst rival monies, as in foreign exchange markets. By holding it we may feel highly secure against risks of nasty trade-in losses and relative price shifts, but in doing so we are speculating that it is worth giving up chances of obtaining q. Unless long-term interest rates are expected to fall, the yield available on short-term securities will tend to be less than on long-dated bonds, since the former will have a larger l owing to their smaller risk of capital loss in the event of a general rise in interest rates.

2.5 Factors Affecting Asset Marketability

The physical characteristics of an asset will determine the ease with which it may be sold and the likelihoods of particular prices being achieved if sellers choose to incur a given set of transactions costs. It will normally be easier to find buyers for general purpose assets than for highly specific ones, while the less complicated an asset is, the smaller will be the costs associated with demonstrating it to buyers and overcoming any fears they have about its likely performance. Disposal costs may also be affected by the asset's financial divisibility, for though there are normally economies of scale in arranging transactions, the chances of persuading someone else to purchase an asset will depend on the total asking price of what one is trying to sell. In principle, any physically indivisible asset can be sold to a large number of individual buyers, but in practice problems involved in defining property rights often get in the way of doing this (see Kay, 1983).

Consider the case of a company that is short of cash and is thinking of trying to raise money by selling the office block it uses as its headquarters and then leasing it back from the new owners. If the building is placed on the market as a single item, its purchase may be an act that only managers of really large portfolios will be able to contemplate without fearing they are putting too many eggs in one basket or without having to incur the costs of forming a purchasing consortium. An alternative strategy would be to offer individual rooms for sale to a large number of purchasers, each of whom could engage in leaseback deals with the seller. However, if high transactions costs were anticipated for the latter deal, and if it were expected to be difficult to achieve a satisfactory price/leaseback arrangement by selling the building to a single purchaser, then the firm might prefer to keep the building and instead make a new debenture or equity issue to raise the cash. (Given the costs of relocation, a further problem with selling the building as an entity would be the risk of being held somewhat to ransom by the monopolistic owner when the leasing agreement came up for renewal — cf. the discussions of opportunistic behaviour in sections 4.4 and 8.5.)

Characteristics such as idiosyncrasy and indivisibility will affect the variability of the number of buyers and sellers in the market. This in turn will impact upon how long it is likely to be necessary to wait before an acceptable price can be achieved for a particular asset, and whether or not there is scope for avoiding both waiting and transaction costs by trading it in to a dealer for a worthwhile amount of 'spot cash'.

The more idiosyncratic and indivisible an asset is, the more likely it is that buyers and/or sellers will be very thin on the ground, even if the asset comes into a broad market category which is typically well populated on both sides. For example, any car whose production run was shortlived owing to its being widely classed as a 'lemon' is likely to have a very erratic secondhand market. Someone trying to sell such a vehicle may usually expect to find that buyers looking for a car in the category into which it falls will view its 'non-price' attributes with disdain or suspicion. Hence they will fail to be drawn to it even if far less is being asked for it than for its more successful rivals. On the other hand, one might be lucky enough to enter the market as the only seller at the same time as it is being frequented by an enthusiast who will stop at nothing to get exactly what she wants (cf. section 3.4) and whom one feels little compunction about exploiting in the absence of rival sellers.

The more idiosyncratic a product is, and the thinner its market, the greater is likely to be the mark-down between the price that dealers will on average expect to get from selling it and the trade-in value they are prepared to place on it. There are two main reasons for this. First, any dealer may expect to have to incur substantial carrying costs (both in terms of working capital and storage/display space foregone from other uses) until an enthusiast comes along looking for precisely the product in question. Secondly, competition from other dealers will be limited by the extent to which a dealer has to make an investment in knowhow in order to be able to appraise the worth of the assets she chooses to hold, and has to accept the risk of being sold a defective or (particularly in the case of antiques) fake product against which she might be liable to subsequent purchasers. There are some products which no intermediaries are prepared to buy and hold in stock pending the arrival of a potential customer. In most cases, housing epitomises this category, even though it is by no means obvious that most used houses are less marketable than, say, used cars or antiques. One obvious transaction cost reason why estate agents rather than 'used house dealers' are the normal order of the day is the length of time it takes to settle the transfer of ownership of real estate and the legal costs this entails. The carrying costs entailed in holding stocks of houses are even more difficult to ignore, as anyone who has had to take out a bridging loan will attest. However, it is interesting to note these factors did not seem to prevent some property companies (such as Barratt Developments in the UK) from pioneering marketing schemes whereby people who had previously bought one of their homes could trade them in and move up very rapidly to new ones on the same estate or in their developments in other areas.

2.6 Alternative Means of Payment

Money is often said to be an essential lubricant to processes of exchange in complex economic systems because difficulties of achieving a double coincidence of wants arise when traders have specialised tastes and can offer specialised skills in return. This view plays down the possibility that attempts to turn non-money stores of wealth into other assets may be made to work, even in the absence of a double coincidence of wants, by making the assets that one wishes to dispose of suitably cheap in terms of the asset one wants to obtain (so long as the principle of 'gross substitution' holds — which may not always be the case, as we shall see in sections 3.4, 3.5 and 11.4). In principle, any durable physical or financial asset could serve as a means of payment and store of wealth, but some assets are better suited to serve this role than others. Bulky physical assets would not have to be transported from place to place if traders were prepared to accept titles to them, which guaranteed their condition and whereabouts. A person seeking to avoid risks would naturally try to hold her wealth in terms of an asset which normally enjoyed stable supply and demand conditions and a 'thick' market, and such an asset would therefore command a premium price in terms of other assets.

Contrary to the picture traditionally given by monetary theorists, barter deals are very common in modern economies, both in the context of trade between individuals in a social grouping (see Pahl, 1984) and in international transactions. In the latter context barter deals of various kinds have become popular with socialist and third world nations as means of promoting exports without driving their prices down or lowering their exchange rates; some estimates suggest they account for over 30 per cent of the total value of trade (see Tschoegl, 1985; Verzariu, 1985; and Cohen and Zysman, 1986). Social barter often uses an implicit contract involving credit where there is no immediate double coincidence of wants, the more so the better the transacting parties know each other (see the work on friendship by Duck, 1983). By contrast, international barter deals usually involve one party in accepting as a means of payment something which is not desired for its use value. The hazards of trading in this way are illustrated well by the following two examples from the early 1980s.

The first concerns the Swedish pop group ABBA, who bartered fur hats and other commodities with COMECON nations that were reluctant to part with 'hard currency' to pay for ABBA records. Attempts to turn these commodities into desired currencies led to a disastrous venture involving spot trading of oil on the Rotterdam market. Poloil, the trading company subsidiary of ABBA's Polar Music International, lost $US7 million in 1980 when 'it got saddled with a tanker full of oil which it couldn't sell on a falling market' (*Economist*, 10 October 1981; see also *Sunday Times* 16 March 1980). After at one point being on the verge of losing much of their personal fortunes, the group sold Poloil, only to face allegations that the disposal involved a huge act of tax evasion (*Times*, 21 July 1984).

The second case also involves oil, but this time on a \$US1 billion scale. In 1984 Saudi Arabia bartered 34 million barrels of oil for a fleet of 10 Boeing 747s. Since the contract was made only a few months after the Saudis had pledged to the other members of OPEC that they would limit their production to 5 million barrels a day, rumours about the Saudis temporarily increasing their daily production of oil by 1.1 million barrels a day to pay for the Jumbo jets were enough to send the world oil market into turmoil for four weeks and depress world prices (*Sydney Morning Herald*, 17 August 1984).

The hazards of accepting payment in fur hats or oil certainly contrast with the advantages of exchanging goods and services for money: notes and coin are particularly attractive for their divisibility, portability and cognisability, although even their acceptability may vary from context to context (for example, traders may be reluctant to accept payment in terms of huge amounts of coin or foreign currency but, in times of domestic hyperinflation, foreign currency can become the preferred means of payment). However, we would be making a great mistake if we were to think of money only in terms of notes and coin. Financial and technological innovations have ensured that nowadays only a tiny fraction of the total value of payments are made by cash. These innovations have caused the monetary authorities to come up with a plethora of ways of quantifying the volume of funds that could be mobilised to purchase other assets.

Initially, the increasing willingness of sellers to risk accepting cheques as means of payment promoted a focus on *M1*, in other words, money defined as currency plus cheque accounts at banks. But this is now known as 'narrow money', and views of what constitutes 'broad money' have been revised repeatedly. *M3*, the most commonly targetted monetary aggregate, includes savings deposits with banks, which have become increasingly easy to access at short notice. Moving up to *M6*, the authorities have included deposits with building societies, finance companies and money market corporations. This makes eminent sense, given the emergence of phenomena such as building society cheque accounts, and the linking of building society accounts to automated teller machines.

In the UK, recognition that many non-deposit financial assets can easily be turned into predictable volumes of bank deposits even led to the creation of statistical series for yet broader monetary aggregates, such as *PSL2* (*M3* plus 'all comparable liquid assets'), whose titles no longer mentioned money as such. This development must have pleased the older Post Keynesians such as Kaldor. As least as far back as the time of the Radcliffe Report (1959), they had been arguing that as more and more liquid substitutes for bank deposits appear, the task of defining 'the money supply' in an operational manner becomes all the more impossible, so that the focus for the monetary authorities should therefore be on the 'whole liquidity position', and on the willingness of decision-makers to part with some of their liquidity in exchange for possible interest earnings or physical goods and services (see Kaldor, 1982, especially Lecture 1). However, *PSL2* was renamed *M5* in late 1987 as part of yet another attempt at reclassification, while a new measure, *M4*, was introduced for slightly less broad-minded economists who were at least willing to treat building societies as if they were banks.

With the growing use of computers for keeping records of the ownership of financial assets, some of the more far-sighted neoclassical monetary economists have been led to imagine scenarios in which buyers are able to pay for their purchases without even going to the bother of turning their liquid assets into bank deposits (see Black, 1970; Fama, 1980, 1983; Greenfield and Yeager, 1983; Hall, 1982; Harper, 1984). The most extreme scenario is one where all transactions involve electronic barter, and bank deposits and cash have became obsolete, not merely as means of payment but also as stores of value. A widely accepted unit of account would still be needed to simplify decision-making in such a world: to neoclassical theorists who hanker after a return to the days of the gold standard, the obvious solution is to value everything in terms of grams of gold.

In an electronic barter economy, individuals would hold their liquid reserves in terms of bonds, debentures, equities, futures claims, liabilities of mutual funds and property trusts and so on. When shopping, they would simply have the shopkeeper call up on the shop's computer the current price of whichever asset they wished to dispose of and, if this were acceptable to both parties, the change of ownership of the necessary number of units of the asset would then be wired to the appropriate ownership register. From a neoclassical standpoint, where one does not expect prices to gyrate wildly on a minute to minute basis, shops would seem to have little reason to insist on payment in terms of a diversified bundle of claims or to quibble about any particular financial asset that was offered by their customers. This is because as soon as assets had been accepted as means of payment they could be sold, via the computer system, for others that were considered more desirable as stores of value. A

31

Shacklean perspective, however, suggests that there could well be times when fears of discontinuous kaleidic shifts in relative prices made people very fussy about the assets they accepted as means of payment (for an excellent discussion of the nature of liquidity in relation to discontinuities, see the correspondence between Townshend and Keynes, reproduced in Keynes, 1979, especially pp. 291-2).

2.7 Speculation and Economic Welfare

Now we have considered factors that affect desired portfolio compositions and methods by which assets may be exchanged, some general remarks are in order concerning the aftermath of speculative choices. Changes in portfolios may simply involve changes in the distribution of existing assets (for example, if I purchase some existing shares and run down my bank deposits to do so) or the exchange of new assets for other new assets or for pre-existing ones. Trade in newly created physical assets may have a direct impact on whether or not current employment levels are maintained, whereas an exchange of existing assets only affects employment directly in so far as a dealer receives a margin for acting as an intermediary between buyer and seller. However, purchases of existing assets may indirectly promote an expansion of output and employment if trade takes place at prices in excess of their production costs, if indeed they are reproducible. The creation of new financial assets does not necessarily imply increased levels of output and employment. For example, although a new bank loan might enable a borrower to finance the purchase of a new consumer durable, it might instead be used to make speculative purchases of existing shares.

Frustrated would-be housebuyers could be forgiven for questioning the morality of a financial services industry which refused to grant them credit because it looked more attractive to lend money to people who planned to use it to fund financial speculation. However, the recent explosion in the volume of financial speculation was accompanied, at least until the Crash of 1987, with a growing conviction on the part of speculators that their greed was a good thing for the economies in which they operated. From the Post Keynesian standpoint, the latter view is questionable, for it seems based on an outdated view of the nature of speculation. The classical picture of the speculator is of an expert trader who helps keep prices in a particular market from falling by accumulating buffer stocks and helps prevent prices from rising by unloading previously purchased stocks. On this view, then, the commodity dealer or stockmarket speculator performs a socially usefully function by smoothing away temporary supply and demand mismatches in much the same way as a used car dealer or an antique trader. The Post Keynesian economist, by contrast, sees most speculators as 'movement traders' (the term is that of Irwin, 1937), who seek to buy whichever asset is rising most rapidly in price and, the moment that it looks like it is going to be displaced in this role by something else, sell out in favour of the latter (for an empirical study, see Bird, 1981). Financial success for these operators thus depends not on a detailed knowledge of the long-term ('real') supply and demand conditions, but on their ability to predict the behaviour of others. Their herd-like behaviour tends to promote self-fulfilling expectations: for example, a widespread belief that gold is about to displace property as a hedge against inflation will, if acted upon, result in a collapse of the price of property and spiralling gold prices.

Much activity by movement traders consists purely of 'paper-shuffling' in futures and options that needlessly enhances the scope for major chain reactions to occur in the event of the bankruptcy of those who have made personally disastrous forecasting errors. However, most speculation in financial and commodity markets is socially undesirable not merely because of the kinds of conspicuously disruptive effects that it can have on the rest of the economy (these are examined at length in Chapter 12). It also involves more insidious distortions in the processes of resource allocation and may promote social divisions.

Consider what went on prior to the Crash of 1987. During the long bull run, many speculators did well on average purely as a result of the general rise in equity prices. Had there been a unanimous change in expectations, the rise could have happened without any trade taking place whatsoever. In fact, massive sums of money changed hands because of differences in expectations. Much of the turnover came from people attempting to make money by movement trading across assets within the generally rising market. But for every movement trader who bought or sold at just the right time, there had to be another who had made a mistake. The liquidity of the market also led to attempts by some wealth holders to reduce their holdings of deposits and increase their stakes in equities, futures and options. This clearly increased turnover, too, but since every purchase of a financial asset involves the sale of a financial asset, those increasing their stakes in the market could only succeed in doing so if others got out of the market or 'wrote' new assets. If the latter occurred and the new assets happened to be equities issued to finance expenditure on new physical capital, the stockmarket could be said to be performing an obviously productive function. All too often, however, asset writing concerned yet more contracts for options, motivated by a desire to gamble rather than to insure against price movements.

Many orthodox economists, I suspect, would be tempted to play down effects of this whirlpool of essentially unproductive speculative activity on the economy at large, for the rational expectations literature encourages them to argue that few of the speculators would have been systematically either right or wrong in their hunches. However, even if there were only a few who on average gained and lost and if these responded symmetrically, there would still have been significant impacts on total sales in other sectors. The sheer volume of speculative trade in financial assets was such that those who arranged the transactions could make fortunes from commission-based bonuses and from 'golden hellos' as they tranferred between companies, taking their established clienteles with them (for details of the pay explosion in the City of London, see Reid, 1988, Ch. 4).

In the economies in which speculative activity boomed, the impact of the spending of these highly concentrated incomes on the overall volume of demand for new, domestically produced goods and services was probably less than would have been generated by an identical expansion of incomes that was shared out more evenly. Stereotypical financial whizz-kids were big spenders on status goods, whose supplies by nature were difficult to expand (cf. Hirsch, 1977). Thus, in the Greater London area and increasingly far beyond, lavish spending by City employees helped to inflate sharply the price of housing (the supply of which could not easily be expanded due to the shortage of land with planning approval) and, via the import of exotic cars, Italian suits, footware and so on, worsened the UK balance of payments. In the south of England, and in areas in which City high-fliers bought holiday homes, first-time buyers then found themselves having to cut back sharply on other forms of spending in order to save up for house deposits or meet mortgage payments.

Finally, there is a possibility which greatly troubled Keynes (1936, pp. 158-61): speculative activity may pose a threat to genuine entreprenerial endeavour. Wild instability in prices makes it very difficult to assess the likely yield of long run commitments to particular assets, while it is possible that employment will suffer if enterprise investment is crowded out by the diversion of finance and 'the best brains of Wall Street' (Keynes, 1936, p. 159) to speculation about the price of existing assets. Similar fears have been voiced more recently, by Eltis (1976) and Grant (1977) in the UK and by Marzouk (1987) in Australia, who have argued that, in their respective economies, explosions in the supply of financial assets have been followed by burgeoning speculative activity which exacerbated tendencies towards deficient levels of investment in plant and machinery. Even if the sucking of financial and mental resources into a whirlpool of foreign exchange, property and securities speculation does not actually make it difficult to raise venture capital and recruit able employees, investment may suffer simply because managers conclude that it is easier to make money and meet short-term reporting goals by buying and selling currencies and used companies rather than by developing new products and struggling for market share.

The obvious policy to counter speculative paper-shuffling is to increase/introduce taxes on capital gains and impose substantial stamp duties to make it very costly for people to move from one asset to another. Keynes himself advocated a transfer tax but was afraid that problems would arise if one went too far in the direction of making financial commitments difficult to dissolve: if the liquidity of equities were greatly restricted people would be much less inclined to take on risk by purchasing them, and hence new enterprise capital could become more difficult, rather than easier, to obtain. Nowadays, however, it seems likely that such a problem would largely be cirumvented by institutional adaptations: rather as in Japan at present, banks would tend to become major shareholders in manufacturing enterprises, transforming maturities on behalf of their depositors and being in a strong position to safeguard their long-term interests, while firms would probably tend to lease even more equipment from banks, rather than buying it with finance raised via equity issues.

2.8 Conclusion

Mainstream economists see liquidity preference as synonymous with 'the demand for money', and as interesting because it affects the slope and position of the *LM* curve that they hope statistically to discover. The Post Keynesian view outlined in the chapter is much broader. It does not see monetary and real forces as separable and raises doubts about the scope of finding an operationally relevant definition of money (see also Kregel, 1980; Rotheim, 1981; and Wells, 1983). Given this, the main title of this book might be said to be inappropriate: perhaps I should have chosen 'Liquidity and Speculation' instead.

'Contracts, Liquidity and Speculation' might have been better still. Many issues concerning financial instability and the nature of financial firms that are discussed in later chapters of this book arise because contracts are costly to enforce and because many portfolios in a modern financial system are linked together and/or contain potentially dangerous mixes of formal and informal obligations, pertaining to assets whose liquidity is not particularly stable. Whether or not a choice of portfolio will lead a decision-maker to default on her obligations is not simply a function of whether or not it causes her net worth to become negative. Much will depend upon the timing of payment obligations, income flows from assets and the scope for turning assets into something which will satisfy one's creditors. Those who end up in bankruptcy courts may do so essentially because they have run into short-term cashflow problems, even though their portfolios have positive net values when seen from a long-term perspective that their creditors are unwilling or unable to take. Conversely, someone whose net worth is negative may avoid being declared bankrupt so long as she can keep up her payment obligations by selling off assets or deceiving others into lending her even more.

3 The Size and Allocation of Household Savings

3.1 Introduction

This is the first of a series of chapters in which I explore processes of decision-making by the various protagonists in a monetary economy. Though my focus here is on household behaviour, it is important that readers should study this chapter before turning their attention to what I have to say, in Chapters 4 and 5, respectively, about the behaviour of firms and governments; for since all kinds of decision-makers have to confront basically the same kinds of problems, many of my comments about the choices made by households have a much broader applicability. In particular, I will be introducing some themes from the literature of behavioural and psychological economics that may be unfamiliar to many readers and which will surface repeatedly in later chapters wherever decision-making is being discussed. Those who find these ideas appealing and wish to learn more about this rapidly rising research programme should find it useful to investigate books by Kornai (1971), Nelson and Winter (1982) and Hodgson (1988); many seminal articles on behavioural economics are reprinted in Earl (1988).

It is curious that Post Keynesian and behavioural economics were not integrated long ago, for they seem to be strongly complementary. As was stressed in the previous chapter, liquidity preference is the core concept in Post Keynesian monetary theory. In the behavioural research programme the core notion that decision-makers suffer from bounded rationality: their mental capacities prevent them from seeing problems in all their complexity and working out optimal solutions to them. The link between the two research programmes arises because of the logical difficulties involved in any attempt to incorporate liquidity in an optimising analysis. These difficulties have recently been discussed by Boland (1986, pp. 148-54), who argues that in taking up positions of liquidity — or more generally, of flexibility — decision-makers are choosing to operate inside the boundaries of their capabilities. Saving is not undertaken just to earn interest as part of a long-run consumption optimisation plan. Much of it represents an attempt to 'leave a little room for error or for the unexpected' (Boland, 1986, p. 149). Recognising their own fallibility as decision-makers, wealth-owners hold back from commitment, hoping to avoid pushing their luck too far. In doing so, they reduce the supply of funds to others or curtail demands for goods and services. In the language of behavioural economics, then, we might state the basic message of Keynes as follows: the more (less) that decision-makers worry about the possible consequences of their own bounded rationality and the more (less) they feel the future is full of imponderables, the more (less) they will retreat into positions of liquidity, of flexibility.

It is doubtful that Keynes himself would have had any objections to a marriage of these two research programmes. Recent work by Dow and Dow (1985) has highlighted Keynes' own rejection of the 'pretty, polite' techniques of orthodox decision theory in favour of a psychological approach to portfolio choice, hinted at through his stress on the roles of 'animal spirits' and of rules of thumb as devices by which choosers delude themselves into thinking they know more about the future than they justifiably claim to know. Unfortunately, most Post Keynesians have kept well clear of the literature on the psychology of decision-making despite being willing to make use of Keynes' comments about 'animal spirits' as a basis for challenging those who assume that macroeconomic relationships are stable. This has left them vulnerable to the kind of objection voiced by Coddington (1983), namely that their entire view of macroeconomics seems nihilistic if fluctuations in aggregate expenditure are said to be rooted, not in changes in objective economic circumstances, but in 'the spontaneous and erratic workings of individual minds' (Coddington, p. 53). The popularity of this critique is such that it seems appropriate to begin by showing how behavioural ideas and research methods offer a way of developing liquidity preference theory in a constructive manner.

3.2 Bounded Rationality, Confidence, and Creativity

An examination of the logical problems of choosing under uncertainty does appear initially to open the sort of analytical

Pandora's box that so troubled Coddington. Whenever a decision needs to be made, it is impossible to know what will happen if a particular plan is selected. At best, the decision-maker can try to construct a list of states of the world that might eventuate. Oversight could mean that this list includes neither the event that actually happens, nor the possibility of the decision-maker finding herself surprised because an unanticipated event occurs. Those possibilities that *are* imagined may vary in their implications for the chooser but there may be costs associated with seeking to hedge against all of them. Mindful of such costs, the decision-maker may prefer to adapt her portfolio quite closely to those possibilities which seem difficult to dismiss, and leave herself uninsured against those events that seem harder to take seriously as prospects (cf. Heiner, 1983, pp. 576-7). (Some events that are difficult to imagine may, of course, be taken very seriously and insured/hedged against, because they would be ruinous to the chooser if they did actually happen.) The next task, then, is to decide how hard it is to dismiss each imagined possibility.

In mentally rehearsing rival scenarios, the decision-maker may well follow the logic used by Shackle (1979) and take the view that she has no ground for dismissing a possibility unless she can see something which could block its occurrence. If she can see all manner of things that could get in the way of a particular happening, then she may feel justified in labelling it as 'practically impossible', or 'unbelievable' in prospect. On the other hand, if she can think of nothing which could happen to stop a particular outcome, then she may label it, along with any other rivals against which it is proving equally problematic to argue, as 'perfectly possible'. But here the thoughtful decision-maker may well realise that she has not really solved her problem of deciding what to believe. The event- blocking possibilities themselves can only be taken seriously if nothing seems likely to get in *their* way: in other words, a problem of infinite regress stands in the way of attempts to form the judgments upon which confidence may be based.

The infinite regress problem seems potentially paralysing for the decision-maker who tries to think carefully about how the future could look. Indeed, the more creative the person's style of thinking, the wider the range of states of the world she may find herself worrying about and the harder she may find it to make even slightly conclusive arguments against anything.

Now, of course, there are some occasions in which uncertainty does seem to exert a paralysing force and people retreat into positions of especially great liquidity. But most of the time people seem to be able to place boundaries of some kind on what they believe could happen if they attempt to allocate resources or engage in particular forms of social interaction. Though the world could behave in an endlessly kaleidic manner and lurch around wildly if decision-makers formed their beliefs and choices at random rather than avoiding commitment to anything at all, this is not what one usually observes. In practice, something gets in the way of the infinite regress and random choices: this 'something' needs to be introduced into Post Keynesian analysis in order that unduly nihilistic conclusions are not drawn from attempts to analyse the nature of choice. The behavioural theorist's notion of bounded rationality seems perfectly suited to play this role.

A decision-maker can be said to suffer from bounded rationality when her limited cognitive hardware and the time pressure under which she has to choose prevent her from grappling with the full complexity of the decision problem she faces. Although it might seem that modern computer systems overcome some human information-processing bottlenecks, it is far from obvious that they contribute to a net lessening of the decision-maker's difficulties. This is particularly so in the world of high finance where computers have facilitated all-day trading in financial assets on globally integrated markets. The age of information technology has increased the need for instantaneous decisions and may have replaced one kind of information overload (raw data) with another (larger volumes of processed data).

The limitations in the decision-maker's ability to dream up and keep vast numbers of conflicting possibilities in mind will ensure that she is blind to many possible events. To avoid getting bogged down in philosophical worries, a decision-maker, like an economic scientist, will use some kind of system — or *methodology* (in the sense of a body of methods rather than the science of methods) — for dealing with inconsistent ideas and reacting to recognised anomalies. In other words, she will use a collection of rules that reject some ideas as unbelievable and allow others, out of the limited set she bothers to consider, to seem in some degree credible (see Earl, 1986, Ch. 6). A core of basic assumptions about the world will be used to provide some kind of dogmatic starting point for the formation of other images.

A significant implication of decision-makers using *systems* of rules to guide them in the gathering and interpretation of economic information is that it would *not* be appropriate to see them as forming their expectations, and hence their choices, in a spontaneous and erratic manner. This is so even though their images of the world are subjective, personal constructs that may bear little resemblance to 'rational expectations' which neoclassical economists, with access to identical information sets, would choose to construct. Furthermore, it should be recognised that the possibility of decision-makers using 'objective' information in different ways does *not* necessarily mean that market behaviour is going to be impossible to anticipate with tolerable accuracy. What it *does* mean is that, to form such expectations themselves, economists will need to start studying the actual belief-forming methodologies used by decision-makers. In doing so, they must get used to thinking of markets as institutions populated by traders whose opinions differ, just as opinions of economists differ, because they are using different rules for making sense of the complex world with which they have to contend.

The idea that economic analysis should be based on a single type of hypothetical 'representative' decision-maker is, of course, an aspect of neoclassical methodology that Keynes himself abandoned: this is clear from his analysis of how differences in opinion about possible price movements play a vital role in reducing market instability. But so far his lead has not been followed — even in Post Keynesian economics — to produce anything comparable with the marketing literature's taxonomy of multiple lifestyle categories; it is therefore most encouraging to see Boland (1986) recently urging neoclassical economists themselves to study the incidence of different expectation-forming methods.

Obviously, the bounded rationality of economists will make it impossible for them to take account of all the idiosyncratic ways of thought that traders use to make sense of financial markets. Like market researchers, they will be forced to do sample survey studies and use simplifying stereotypes, segmenting their populations of market participants into groups with approximately similar ways of thinking (for example, 'chartists' and 'fundamentalists', or people who base their decisions on the behaviour/advice of a particular individual) and of gathering information about the 'state of the news'. Inevitably, these segmentations will in some respects be rough and ready: it will be necessary to force-fit some sampled individuals in order to keep the number of segments manageable. But this need to make abstractions should not be a worry so long as it leads to acceptable predictions. Economists should remember that during internal debates in their own profession they habitually perform such pigeonholing operations, confident that they can make satisfactory predictions of the behaviour of particular kinds of economists who seem at least to share major analytic building blocks and who tend to employ similar routines for dealing with criticism and anomalies. (For example, a neoclassical economist may label me as a Post Keynesian, may use Joan Robinson as a Post Keynesian stereotype, and then may quite often — though not always — accurately anticipate how I construe economic phenomena.) All I am suggesting here is that economists should start paying attention to the methodologies used by their diversely-minded subjects for coping with economic problems, and not just to those used by their peers.

3.3 Portfolio Characteristics and Portfolio Preferences

Having used the behavioural/psychological literature to analyse the formation of expectations, some Post Keynesians might well want to go no further in the direction of integrating the two research programmes. They might suggest that, given her expectations, a wealth-holder's choice of portfolio could be explained in terms of her initial endowment of assets, the set of options open to her, and her preferences. Post Keynesians could borrow tools from modern neoclassical economics to show how, on the basis of these four elements, wealth-holders could come to choose how much to spend and what to spend it on; how much to borrow, how long to borrow it and where to borrow it from; and how much to save and what to do with new and previous accumulations of wealth.

An obvious strategy is to present portfolio choice in terms of Lancaster's (1966, 1971) 'characteristics space' analysis of demand, which highlights the multidimensional nature of choice. After all, in Chapter 2, liquidity preference theory was treated as being concerned with a variety of dimensions of choice, including asset marketability, carrying costs and risk of loss in value, as well as the outputs of goods and services that particular assets may have the capacity to deliver. Similarly, financial institutions differ not merely in terms of rates of return and riskiness but also in terms of ease of access (number of branches, locations, opening hours, number of autotellers, chequeing facilities, electronic funds transfer at point of sale facilities); in the extent to which one needs to establish a record as a depositor in order to borrow later on; the kind of interest payment (for example, it may be based on one's minimum balance in each month or be worked out on a daily basis); in their complexity and the friendliness of their personnel; in the charges they make for cheques; in their penalty clauses for premature withdrawals; in the availability of complementary services such as travel or insurance; and so on.

Obvious though it may be to model portfolio choice in these terms, economists have preferred to confine their analysis portfolio choice to a simple two dimensional risk/return model of financial payoffs, and have left the study of non-price competition in the financial services industry to those in marketing (such as Anderson *et al.*, 1976). In this section I will present a brief illustration of portfolio choice from the Lancastrian standpoint but, for reasons of diagrammatic convenience, I will follow my fellow economists in limiting myself to two dimensions of choice.

Suppose a person has chosen to save a particular amount per month towards her retirement, and that she can place this with institutions that seem to differ in their riskiness and past rates of return. Figure 3.1 shows the mixes of characteristics she perceives to be associated with three institutions.

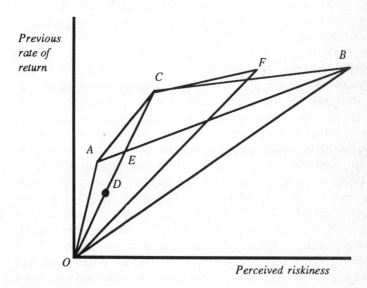

Figure 3.1 *Hypothetical Risk and Return Possibilities*

If the consumer puts all her money in A she gets to the end of the ray OA. If she puts all her money in B, a much less secure-looking institution but one which has previously offered a much higher rate of return, she gets to the end of ray OB. She can also choose to put some money in A and some in B, thereby changing the characteristics mix produced by her portfolio. Depending on the relative size of her deposits in A and B, she can be at rival points along the line AB. Will she wish to put any money in a third institution, C? If she could only reach point D by putting all her money in C she would not put any money in it unless she had other characteristics in mind in respect of which C offered a better deal than A and B. With only the two characteristics, she can do better than D by choosing a mix of deposits with A and B that leaves her at point E. However, if the person could get to point C by depositing all her money with insitution C, then it would stand a chance of picking up her custom even in the two characteristics case. Efficient choices for her would now lie along the frontier BCA, instead of AB.

We now come to the question of how the person comes to select a particular mix of assets. If we make the conventional assumption that the person is prepared to trade off characteristics against each other at ever-decreasing marginal rates, her preferences can be represented by a set of indifference curves which slope upwards to the right at an ever-increasing rate. (The rightwards upward slope arises because, other things equal, riskiness is a counter-desired characteristic of a portfolio.) Depending on where we were to draw such curves on Figure 3.1, we would find that the consumer would do best by choosing to put her wealth either all in A, or all in B, or all in C (these are all non-tangential corner solutions) or part in A plus part in C, or part in C plus part in B (these are both tangency results). She would not choose a mixture of all three in this two characteristics case, nor would she choose a mixture that involved her only in placing part of her wealth with A and part with B.

(It is important to note that the ability of this analysis to generate unique choices can only be taken for granted if, as Figure 3.1 implicitly assumes, the 'wealth holding technologies' are all linear and a doubling of holdings in a particular institution thus doubles the characteristic outputs one gets from that institution. This may not be the case — for example, bigger deposits often earn higher rates of interest — and if so we no longer have straight lines all the time. If so, strange things can happen to the shape of the 'efficiency frontier', causing multiple points of tangency on some indifference maps and leaving the consumer apparently in two or more minds about what to do: see Watts and Gaston, 1982.)

Lancaster's analysis provides a neat way of explaining why people may hold a variety of deposits in different kinds of financial institutions. It can also be used to analyse the effects of changes in the products offered by these institutions. For example, suppose B maintains its high rate of return and as a result is given a better credit rating by the financial press, such that our hypothetical chooser now believes she can reach point F if she puts all her wealth with B. The 'efficiency frontier' then becomes FCA. If she were previously depositing with C and/or A, somewhere along CA, she would not change her portfolio, but if previously she were somewhere along BC, she could improve her position.

The analysis becomes less workable in diagrammatic terms if we start trying to include characteristics that have a binary nature (for example, a particular bank either has a branch on the campus of my university, or it does not), or if asset diversity is itself a desired characteristic of a portfolio. In the latter case, unlike the one considered above, a portfolio containing more than two types of assets might be selected even if the decision-maker only had one other characteristic (such as previous yield) in mind. The two-dimensional case depicted in Figure 3.1 saw the consumer as weighing up the average riskiness of her portfolio (in whatever terms she construed 'riskiness'), but she might well be willing to trade an increase in riskiness against a reduced likelihood that she could suffer losses on all fronts simultaneously. In other words, an individual wealth-holder might be prepared to shoulder high risks so long as she has 'hedged her bets' by 'putting her eggs in many baskets'. Her attitude would be like that of a firm which is willing to operate in turbulent market environments, where products are prone to be rendered obsolete overnight by new technologies or changes in fashion, because it has a large number of at least partly separated activities and will not be ruined by the sudden demise of any one of its existing highly profitable activities or by the failure of one of its new products to win market acceptance (see Kay, 1982, 1984, and sections 4.5 and 8.6 below). If we added this third dimension, and increased the list of assets, diagrammatic analysis would become problematic, but one can see intuitively that, depending on what the various assets seemed to offer in prospect, the decision-maker might well find it efficient to put together a portfolio containing more than three assets, with much higher average riskiness and higher average earnings records than in the two characteristic, three asset example. (For a somewhat different attempt to present a Post Keynesian model of portfolio diversification, see Joaquin, 1988.)

3.4 Information Overload and Portfolio Choice

At the start of the previous section a behavioural economist would have been put on guard immediately by the lengths of the lists of components of a household spending/borrowing/saving plan and of the characteristics associated with financial packages and institutions. In information processing terms, the consumer's task is to evaluate a substantial data matrix, in which each row (or column) pertains to a particular characteristic and each column (or row) represents a particular physical or financial asset or an item for immediate consumption. If there are many rows and columns, the consumer could find herself overwhelmed by the task of choosing a mixture of consumption assets, consumer durables, financial assets and loan obligations if she tried to consider all possible trade-offs by weighing up the pros and cons of particular asset mixes along the lines of the Lancaster theory, until she found the best package. This would be particularly likely to happen if she was uncertain about abilities of particular choices of assets to produce particular characteristics. The behaviourally-inclined Post Keynesian would expect portfolio choosers to try to reduce their task to a manageable one by a variety of simplifying strategies and tactics. These turn out to be not without relevance to policy issues.

The scale of the decision problem can be reduced enormously by initially approaching it at quite a high level of abstraction, for example by thinking in terms of basic needs and wants, broad categories of expenditure and savings in general. From this simplified view of things, a set of budgets can be worked out, and then detailed attention can be given to one expenditure category, or to the allocation of a selected volume of saving (for a more detailed discussion, see Earl, 1983, pp. 150-60; 1986, pp. 66-7). Figure 3.1 implicitly presumed something like this had happened. Such budgeting procedures are widely used in organisations, but we should expect many households to employ them too, though their forms will differ among households. In some cases saving may be treated, as Keynes (1936, p. 97) suggested, as a residual category, comprising anything left over after allocations to maintain one's habitual standard of life. In other cases, the consumer may be sufficiently concerned with her future situation, and sufficiently affluent, to make a definite commitment about how much she will put by each period to add to her total stock of financial wealth.

At whichever level of abstraction a decision-maker is using, she may further attempt to overcome information overload by abandoning any attempt to find an optimal mix of assets. Instead, she may simply look at a set of possible portfolios one after another until she encounters one which she judges to score sufficiently highly according to a set of personally-chosen criteria. At that point she may stop search and appraisal and make a commitment, unless she employs some kind of subsidiary rule such as 'examine two more packages, just in case..., and then choose the best so far discovered'. Herbert Simon, who won the 1978 Nobel Prize in Economics for his work on behavioural analysis, coined the term 'satisficing' to describe this way of choosing (see Simon, 1957, 1959; Wright, 1975).

Such appraisals would probably involve the investigation of discrete combinations of assets, rather than marginally different sets. In contractual savings deals, for example, one would expect nicely rounded figures — £100 per month in A and £100 a month in B versus £150 a month in C plus £50 per month in D. Widespread use of such rounded numbers in contractual savings arrangements could produce discontinuous movements in aggregate consumption expenditure whenever changes in incomes were seen by savers as enabling themselves to move up to a larger rounded figure for the amount they could afford to squirrel away. For people thinking about getting into debt, rounded numbers could also play a trigger role, which, given the divisibility of loans, one would not expect from the standpoint of conventional theory: for example, a person might only actively start trying to fix up a loan once she feels she can afford £200 per month, with the result that a pay increase triggers a change away from consuming many low value goods and towards an indivisible loan-financed item she has been looking forward to buying for a long time.

Somewhat implicit in the discussion immediately above is a third method of simplification: decision-makers can reduce the volume of information they need to handle by using particular attributes of a case as proxies for many more. One alarming example of such a proxy was displayed by a bankrupt Australian couple in an interview for a television programme (*Sixty Minutes*, 17 May 1987) prompted by the news that households nowadays make up 70 per cent of

Australian bankruptcy cases: the couple said they had judged that they would be able to cope with the burden of adding successively to their debts on the basis that the banks and finance companies would not have been prepared to let them do so if it was unlikely that they could keep up their payments; they appeared not to have done the necessary budgeting calculations themselves, nor to have realised that the lenders may have knowingly accepted a high default risk on the expectation that sales of repossessed durables could recover most of any outstanding funds. Some financial institutions also use rather worrying proxies: Crapp and Skully (1985, p. 85) stress that established credit ratings may often displace the use of a scoring system in loan appraisals; these can fail to take account of recent or highly conceivable changes in a person's financial position (see section 9.6 below for a further discussion of satisficing by loan managers).

A fourth method for dealing with information overload in multidimensional portfolio choice problems is to use decision heuristics that avoid the need for weighing up the pros and cons of possible bundles of assets and liabilities, and which instead treat the problem of choice one dimension at a time, in a filtering manner. For example, there is what I have elsewhere (Earl, 1986, Chs. 7-9) labelled the 'behavioural lexicographic' or 'characteristic filtering' routine. Here, the wealth holder sets a target for an acceptable level of attainment in respect of each of the characteristics she has in mind. She then ranks these targets in order of priority and sees how her possible choices shape up in respect of them. Figure 3.2 concerns a hypothetical consumer whose first priority is to obtain a financial portfolio the variance of whose value is not expected to exceed V. Her second priority is to find a portfolio which she expects to deliver an interest/dividend yield of at least R. Any portfolio which permits her to get into the region bounded on the right by the line perpendicular to V and bounded below by the line perpendicular to R is perfectly satisfactory in respect of her top two priorities.

Suppose the consumer can choose between three kinds of financial assets, or combinations of them. Point H shows how she expects to fare if she places all her savings with a reputable bank: she may feel their nominal value is absolutely guaranteed, but she may not expect to get a satisfactory rate of interest. If she uses all of her savings to purchase 'blue-chip' equities, she may expect to reach point I, whereas point J may seem feasible if she puts together a portfolio consisting solely of 'junk bonds'. Any combination on or inside HIJ

is feasible, but only those portfolio combinations represented by points on or inside *IMNP* are satisfactory for her first two priorities and are thereby deemed worthy of consideration in respect of her third priority. The filtering process continues down the list of characteristic targets until only one portfolio combination is left or until a target is encountered that none of the so-far-unelimiated combinations can meet. In the latter case the portfolio mix that comes closest to meeting the target is selected. (It is possible that the person runs out of targets before getting to a decision, in which case she will have to employ some kind of tie-break procedure.)

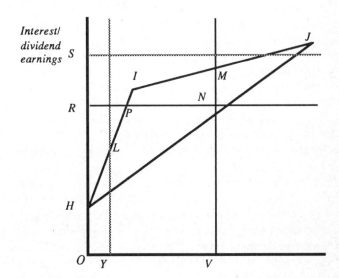

Variance of portfolio value

Figure 3.2 *Priorities and Portfolio Choice*

If the person set more demanding standards for either of these tests, she could find herself arriving at a somewhat frustrating choice even before she worked further down her list of wants. For example, suppose her target for her portfolio's earnings rate was not *R* but *S*. In this case, the least unsatisfactory option would be to select the portfolio implied by point *M*, for she although she does not have the prospect of meeting her target earnings rate, she has got as close to it as she can without compromising her tolerable variance level. Alternatively, suppose she set an even more demanding variance limit, indicated by Y. In this case, the best she can do is to choose the mix of bank deposits and 'blue-chip' shares implied by point L. This is so regardless of whether her earnings target is R or S.

As with the Lancastrian analysis presented in the previous section, the model I have just outlined does not adequately address the question of uncertainty. In each case one of the characteristics has been concerned with the risks of possible capital losses or gains, but uncertainty on the other dimension has been totally ignored. In reality, it may often be the case that a decision-maker judges herself to be taking a chance on a particular target because she takes rival possible outcomes on either side of it quite seriously. In this sort of situation, satisficing seems to involve a more complex test of adequacy: for example, the decision-maker may ask, with respect to each scheme that does not seem guaranteed to meet her target for the characteristic she is considering, 'does it look *sufficiently unlikely* that this will produce an outcome which falls *too far below* my target, and does it look *sufficiently likely* that it could produce an outcome *sufficiently better than* my target to make it worth taking the risk?' Such a method for reaching a decision handles uncertainty without involving what Shackle has for many years argued to be the logically questionable act of combining rival, mutually exclusive possibilities to form single measures of variance or or a single expected value or 'certainty equivalent' score for each characteristic in terms of which a scheme of action offers an uncertain prospect. But of course, this is not to say that no one in practice prefers to use a decision rule that collapses ranges of possibilities to single values, as in the cases illustrated in Figures 3.1 and 3.2. (For a more detailed discussion, see Earl , 1986, Ch. 8.)

The characteristic filtering approach offers an interesting picture of substitutability, or the lack of it, in response to changes in market conditions. A financial firm that is doing badly because it fails to meet high priority targets in the minds of many potential customers (not all of whom will set identical targets or priorities) will be wasting its time if it tries to improve its position by improving its performance on characteristics that are commonly accorded low priority. Given the possibility that filtering routines may be responsible for behaviour at odds with the principle of gross substitution, studies of their frequency of use may shed a good deal of light on debates about the transmission mechanisms of monetary policy and the possible existence of gaps in the chains of substitution between assets of various kinds (cf. Karacaoglu, 1984).

3.5 Attitudes, Principles and Self-Control

Lexicographic kinds of decisions need not arise only as results of attempts by portfolio choosers to make multidimensional problems more manageable. It may be the case that decision-makers are simply building their lives around particular broad principles, which they rank hierarchically. Economists seem to be coming to recognise this even more slowly than Barclays Bank recognised that it might pay to distance themselves from the apartheid regime in South Africa. Prior to their disinvestment, Barclays had, according to the *Guardian Weekly* (30 November 1986), 'lost a number of bank accounts from Labour councils and some charitable business. But the most serious damage that the South African connection has done to the bank has been the relatively small number of young graduates and undergraduates who have opened accounts at Barclays.' Rather more alert to the implications of wealth-holders with consciences have been the growing body of entrepreneurs who have set up ethical investment funds, achieving competitive returns despite their policies of avoiding putting money into companies involved in unranium mining, environmental destruction, the production of weapons, tobacco, alcohol, toxic wastes, and so on. The emergence of such funds was noted even by Toffler (1970) and now about $2 billion is invested in ethical mutuals in the United States. The first ethical fund in the UK was launched in 1984 by the Friends' Provident Life Office, which started a similar fund in Australia in 1986. Interestingly enough, the modern tendency towards cross-shareholdings among companies has made it very difficult to buy completely 'sound' shares, so the mangers of the Friends' Provident funds — which have been among the top performing equity-based trusts — have adopted a satisficing rule: they will invest in an otherwise sound company that holds shares in a prohibited one provided that its interest is less than five per cent.

The role of principles in portfolio choice is just one aspect of a much bigger topic: how people's attitudes, 'hang-ups' and views of their own strengths and weaknesses affect the kinds of consumption and savings behaviour in which they engage. Changes in the use of consumer credit may reflect shifts in long term attitudes, as well as innovations in the supply of credit instruments. Such a psychological perspective suggests that attitudes, rather than interest rates, could have been a decisive barrier to increases in the rate of expenditure. For many people in the past, the idea that they might borrow probably carried implications which raised excessive feelings of guilt — confusion over self-identity (for example, 'I thought I wasn't the sort of person who...') — that could be quelled by acting out a role consistent with their self-expectations (that 'I'm a patient, prudent sort of person'). Now attitudes are different. As *The Economist* (6 April 1985) has observed, 'The big spenders of today were born in the baby boom that followed the second world war. They are not constrained by the cautious attitude to credit that their parents carried with them from the 1930s, epitomised by the Lancashire housewife who did not use the washing machine until the last instalment had been paid'.

On the side of market innovations we can note Maital's (1982, pp. 138-9, 143-5) psychological analysis of how credit cards have enabled people to buy things on credit without having to display themselves to onlookers (or themselves) as the sort of people who have to borrow, and without having to go through the anxieties of facing up to mysterious and until recently stern-faced bank managers. At the time of purchase, it is unclear whether the credit card is going to be used as such or merely as a debit card, with payment to be made in full when the next statement arrives. This may allow the shopper to convince herself at the time of purchase that she is doing the latter, while the sales campaigns of the credit card organisations encourage their customers to think of their credit cards as smoothing devices, not as somewhat pricey substitutes for personal loans (cf. the discussion of cognitive dissonance theory in section 12.2). 'Access, your flexible friend, the card that helps you keep your balance!' is a slogan that presents the UK version of Mastercard as a substitute for a precautionary demand for money, but the fact that Access statements do not distinguish between contingently necessary purchases and longer term borrowings enables users to shunt to the back of their minds any unease they feel about the latter types of items.

The integration of psychological perspectives and institutional material allows question marks to be raised about whether financial deregulation is to be encouraged or whether there is a growing need for watchdog agencies. Once we recognise the limited capacities of consumers to formulate and solve long-run household management problems, and once we note the possible malleability of consumer perceptions in the face of images from advertisements, credit cards can seem potentially dangerous pieces of plastic, that distract weak-willed and financially myopic individuals from the task of providing for their future expenditure needs. The extent to which consumers need to be protected from themselves is something one cannot pronounce upon in this context until there has been some assessment of how far consumers recognise their own fallibility as financial managers and accordingly set themselves constraints in the form of contractual savings schemes (cf. Thaler and Shefrin, 1981). Certainly, the existence of such devices as Christmas Club accounts — that pay lower rates of interest than some easy-access accounts but lock funds up, away from temptation — implies that banks and some of their customers both recognise the problem of a lack of self-control.

3.6 Alternative Theories of the Consumption Function

The complex role of social and psychological forces in shaping long-term aggregate savings behaviour was recognised by Keynes (1936, p. 109) in his pioneering discussion of the consumption function. However, despite his emphasis on the ability of shifts in confidence to produce an erratic pattern of investment demand, he did not seem to recognise the scope for psychological factors to generate instability in the short-term consumption function. He simply argued (1936, p. 110) that

Since, therefore, the main background of subjective and social incentives changes slowly, whilst the short-period influence of objective factors is often of secondary importance, we are left with the conclusion that short-period changes in consumption largely depend on changes in the rate at which income (measured in wage units) is being earned and not on changes in the propensity to consume out of a given income.

The wisdom of generalising Keynes' investment theory to encompass investments by consumers in durable goods was soon recognised by Townshend (1937), whose article provided much of the inspiration for Chapter 2. If people typically replace durable goods long before they are completely worn out, and if it is a matter of their discretion as to when they replace them and whether they commit themselves to altogether new products, then we should not be surprised to find that their willingness to commit themselves to credit or exhaust their savings accumulations will depend on their confidence as well as on their current incomes and interest rates. In fact, the short-run demand for consumer durables has exhibited considerable instability, and behavioural investigations using questionnaire-based indices of consumer sentiment (pioneered by George Katona at the University of Michigan's Survey Research Center) have repeatedly shown that a significant part of this can be accounted for by shifts in confidence: see, for example, Adams (1964), Shapiro and Angevine (1969), Katona (1975), Smith (1975), Pickering (1977) and Williams and Defries (1981). These studies vary in their degrees of success in using indicies of sentiment to predict expenditure on durables, but they share the same conclusion: a strong influence on buyer behaviour is *not* exerted by economic variables which reflect an *ability* to make purchases.

Work on the role of confidence in explaining savings behaviour has received scant attention from mainstream economists, as is evidenced by the absence of Katona's name from the index of almost every orthodox macroeconomics textbook. Instead, the profession has concentrated on examining other kinds of modifications and alternatives to Keynes' portrayal of consumption as a simple function of absolute income. Given the ready availability of good detailed textbook treatments of such theories, it seems necessary only to give brief sketches of some of them here, containing the essential themes to which reference will be made in later chapters (see also the classic survey article by Farrell, 1959).

Ando, Brumberg and Modigliani (Modigliani and Brumberg, 1955; Ando and Modigliani, 1963) highlighted the fact that society is made up of people at different points in different consumption lifecycles. For example, a college graduate might get herself in debt while studying, and then go through a period in which her income increased greatly at the same time as she cleared her debts and started saving up a deposit for a house. On buying a house she might also commit herself to flows of expenditure on consumer durables (such as a washing machine, a television, a car, and so on). A lot of her income would then go on servicing this debt. The years when she borrowed would be recorded as ones in which she engaged in substantial dissaving, and these would be followed by years of repayments in which her income exceeded her spending on new consumption items. With rises in her real disposable income aided by the erosion of the real value of her debts by inflation, she could find herself in middle age accumulating more money than she wanted to spend. However, in retirement, she would become a dissaver once more and, if she had judged things correctly, would die leaving only those net assets she desired to bequeath to others.

A lifecycle view of savings behaviour opens up the possibility that a person's marginal propensity to consume will be less than her average propensity to consume, for her income may rise as her desire to spend declines. This is a very different route to such a result compared with the Galbraithian suggestion that consumers may run out of innate expenditure needs as they get richer. However, the sizes of a person's marginal and average propensities to consume will change throughout her lifecycle. For example, if her consumption is falling more slowly than her income (as in retirement, perhaps), her marginal propensity to consume is positive and less than unity. If her consumption is falling but her income is still rising (as her retirement approaches, perhaps), her marginal propensity to consume is negative, and could be fractional or less than minus one, even though her average propensity to consume for that year is a positive fraction.

In the lifecycle analysis, changes in savings behaviour in the aggregate will largely depend upon changes in the size of population, its composition (earning patterns and age structure), as well as factors such as the ages of marriage and retirement. These are not sudden shifts but, as already noted, the propensities to consume have displayed a good deal of short run instability. Friedman's (1957) 'permanent income hypothesis' is a long-term analysis which seeks to explain short-term movements without reference to shifts in liquidity preference. Consider the situation of a farmer (or anyone else whose income is prone to fluctuate). It will often seem desirable to smooth one's consumption flow out over time instead of adjusting it in line with jerky income flows. Hence, Friedman argues, such a consumer will take a long-term view of her prospects, a view which she will only adjust if she detects changes in long-run market conditions (such as the agricultural policies of the European Community with respect to sugar imports, as opposed to low earnings from a sugar crop due to unusual weather conditions). Her consumption will than be a function of her long-run view of her income prospects. A temporary increase in income above trend may be associated with a rise in consumption, but purely because of the rising trend, implying a marginal propensity to consume which is a positive fraction for that individual in that year. But a temporary reduction in income may also be associated with a rise in consumption, giving a negative marginal propensity to consume.

Duesenberry's (1949) 'relative income hypothesis' had earlier introduced something of a social psychology perspective and argued that what matters for a consumer is not absolute income but her income relative to other people. If incomes fall, consumers will reduce their savings rates, and even run down past accumulations of wealth, in order to carry on consuming roughly as before and maintain their social standing. When incomes once more begin to increase, consumers who are saving with a view to the longer run (for example, for lifecycle reasons) will increase their consumption rather slowly at first, catching up on their savings. But as they observe others expanding their consumption, they too will start to spend more. On average, the typical consumer may be following a simple proportional relationship between consumption and long run income, but her short-run behaviour is temporarily cyclical or seems to involve a ratchet effect if she is never forced to cut her consumption when her income falls below its most recent peak. We could think of her as having short-run consumption aspirations determined by the attainments of her 'reference group' and that these adjust rather sluggishly as her income fluctuates, producing a kind of ratchet effect. As consumers achieve major promotions (or demotions), their reference groups will shift. However, they may find it difficult initially to decide how much they can safely spend and how much they need to spend on conspicuous consumption to maintain a new position in the social pecking order: demand may thus be held back by those who err on the side of caution or given a temporary filip by those who let their achievements 'go to their heads' (see section 12.2).

3.7 Effects of Changes in Interest Rates on Household Saving and Borrowing

Interest rates have so far only figured in this chapter in relation to choices concerning the composition of portfolios of financial assets. The sizes of such portfolios have either been taken as given or have been explained with reference to other factors. However, in the formation of monetary policy, it is usually presumed that changes in interest rates can be used to induce changes in aggregate consumption expenditure. In this section it is argued that the efficacy of this mechanism should not be taken for granted; sometimes interest rate increases may have great power, but at other times people may just carry on (or refrain from) spending regardless of the higher (lower) price of loan finance and/or the higher (lower) opportunity cost of using up previously accumulated interest-earning deposits.

Before we move on to these discussions it seems worth noting that the tendency of the consumption function literature to play down the role of interest rates in shaping aggregate savings behaviour contrasts sharply with the tendency of pre-Keynesian thinkers to portray interest rates as the key determinant of choices concerning the timing of consumption. The reorientation seems to have occurred because Keynes objected to the view of his predecessors in a number of ways. He doubted whether savings decisions were much influenced by the costs of intertemporal substitution and pointed out that interest was not a 'reward for waiting' but a reward for parting with liquidity — it is perfectly possible to refrain from spending income without increasing one's holdings of interest-earning financial assets (see further, section 10.6). Rather more importantly, he challenged the idea that a rise in interest rates would result in higher levels of saving even if people did respond by trying to save more. His 'paradox of thrift' scenario suggested that such efforts could be self-defeating unless investment demand happened to increase, which it was hardly likely to do if interest rates had risen. The fall in consumption expenditure would reduce income levels and although people might save a higher proportion of their incomes they could fail to save more in total (however, see section 10.7 for some problems with this argument.) Indeed, if their reduction in spending discouraged investment expenditure, they might well end up saving less overall.

In so far as people are accumulating or spending funds as part of some long-term attempt at smoothing out consumption and/or producing a particular lifecycle sequence of expenditures, and if they do not see interest rate changes as permanent, we may doubt whether attempts to use interest rates as a regulator of aggregate consumption demand will have much success. Politicians should take careful note of this: it is foolhardy to announce that one is increasing interest rates to reduce aggregate demand and in the same breath tell voters that, if all goes well, it should be possible to bring interest rates back down before very long. (Precisely this error was made by the Australian government in 1988-9.)

The impact of an increase in interest rates is likely to be similarly muted in respect of demand in, say, the car market in so far as the demand is arising because consumers, locked into particular lifestyles, are experiencing problems with worn out vehicles that are threatening to generate major repair bills or have suffered terminal failures in roadworthiness tests. Interest rate increases are unlikely to form insuperable barriers to these essentially non-discretionary purchases: many consumers who have 'had enough' of their existing vehicles may be able to absorb higher interest charges without increasing their monthly commitments simply by borrowing over, say, four years rather than three; other consumers who need to replace their cars may decide to borrow a little less than they otherwise would have done, but they will still make their presence felt somewhere in the market.

Attempts to use higher interest rates to reduce consumption demand may be expected to work rather better during periods in which speculative and social factors are exerting a major influence on expenditure decisions. Here, too, the car market is instructive, for when an economy is booming, many applications for car loans are likely to involve status-related discretionary upgradings of vehicles that still function adequately as means of transport. In this case, the importance of bandwagon effects (see Leibenstein, 1950) means that a major contraction of demand in the vehicle market may arise from a relatively small initial cutback in spending that results from a negative impact of higher interest rates on consumer confidence. But whether or not a sharp increase in interest rates *is* associated with a decline in confidence will again depend upon how long consumers expect the higher rates to last and upon how they judge the relative significance of other pieces of economic news: if the economy is booming and policymakers are saying that higher interest rates are necessary to eliminate overheating, this does not have to imply that they are trying to engineer a recession.

In the reverse case, when reductions in interest rates are being used to stimulate demand, it is unlikely that there will be much of a change in spending unless the change of policy leads to an improvement in confidence. Cheaper loans and poorer returns on financial assets may fail to induce substitution in favour of less liquid physical assets if people are pessimistic about their employment prospects and are not running down their liquidity because they think it is 'too dangerous' to do so (cf. Blatt, 1979, and the discussion of the work of Katona in the previous section).

A rather more deterministic verdict can be reached in respect of the likely powers of a tight money policy as a tool for stopping a boom in the housing market. The key factor here is that during a frenzied property boom it is common for housebuyers to borrow as much as they can over as long a period as possible. In this situation they intend to accumulate equity in their properties not by repaying the principal but via capital gains, for when home loans are scheduled for repayment over periods of twenty years or more, interest charges initially account for almost their entire monthly cost. People thus borrow on the expectation that their money incomes will rise along with the value of their property and their mortgages will therefore only prove to be temporary millstones. An interest rate increase poses a problem for these would-be borrowers largely because it limits the amount of debt on which they can cover the interest bill, rather than by making it more difficult for them to begin repaying the loan principal. To put it simply, an extended term mortgage in practice is little different from an interest-only bridging loan: if the interest rate rises by a quarter, a given monthly sum will only finance about four fifths of the pre-increase figure. A would-be house buyer will only be able to borrow as much as she had planned prior to the increase if she can find room to increase her monthly repayments by about a quarter or greatly extend the repayment period of the loan.

A sharp rise in home loan rates will therefore be a very effective way of bringing a property boom to an end. Once thirty year mortgages are being taken seriously there is little slack remaining to take up in the form of an extended loan period unless inter-generational loans are introduced (as appears to be happening in Japan) or the lending body (or, more likely, the parents of the buyer) takes out an equity share in the property. Failing these rather desperate-sounding measures, there will be a reduction in fresh housing loans either because intending buyers themselves recognise they cannot enter or move up the housing market without compromising their basic priorities — such as paying for food, electricity, existing hire purchase obligations and so on — or because suppliers of finance force that recognition upon them by refusing to let them increase the proportion of their monthly budgets taken up by housing expenses. Hence intending first-time buyers will hold on to funds earmarked for deposits and remain in rented accommodation whilst waiting for interest rates and/or property prices to fall to affordable levels. Those who would otherwise have moved up-market will sit tight in their present homes, particularly once they discover the impact of the interest rate increase on the marketability of their property. This is precisely what happened in the UK in late 1988/early 1989.

3.8 Wealth Effects on Consumption Demand

When people are surprised by unexpected changes in the marketability and relative prices of goods and financial assets that they possess or would like to possess, their perceptions of their wealth may change. To the extent that their spending is a function of their perceived wealth, they may then change their rates of expenditure. These changes in expenditure are known as wealth effects, and should be distinguished from effects of shifts in liquidity preference on consumption. The former arise from relative price changes that have happened; the latter arise from anticipated movements in relative prices.

Consider a situation in which the rate of inflation rises unexpectedly. People who have deposits in financial institutions will find that these have fallen in value. To someone saving up for retirement, this may be an event which forces her to cut back her current consumption so that, when she retires (and now she might also plan to postpone the event), her consumption stream is not severely curtailed. Such a person may cut back consumption in real terms even if her salary has kept pace with inflation, for her past savings have taken a drop in value. But if her salary is not indexed, she has suffered even more and may be expected to cut back consumption in real terms by an even bigger amount.

Now consider someone who has large borrowings and an inflation-indexed salary and who is pleasantly surprised by the high rate of inflation. The value of her indebtedness in real terms is less than expected. If the asset against which she has borrowed is a house whose value has risen in nominal terms the ratio of nominal debt to the value of the house will have fallen, so she could sell the house, pay off the debt and have money left over as a deposit for an even more expensive house, and scale up her mortgage in line with her salary. Or she could take a 'second mortgage' against the capital gain and use the money to increase her expenditure (for example, by buying a holiday home, or a home extension).

In the example just given, we have 'back-to-back' effects: the creditor loses and spends less, whereas the debtor gains and steps up her expenditure. If there is to be an impact upon aggregate demand (as distinct from the structural distribution of spending), the two kinds of wealthowners must have different marginal propensities to consume out of their wealth. Otherwise, the two effects simply cancel out. The various models of savings behaviour considered in section 3.6 should make it clear that there is no obvious reason why everyone should have identical marginal propensities to consume, or why the weighted average of gainers' marginal propensities to consume should equal that of losers (cf. Tobin, 1980, Ch. 1). The main group of losers might be 'small savers', who have little room to increase their saving even if inflation is getting in the way of their plans to accumulate a house deposit. Gainers might be young professionals whose present expenditure is constrained more by borrowing capacity than by current income. In this case, inflationary surprises would be followed by an increase in overall expenditure. It should be added that people may also increase expenditure as a result of unexpected inflation causing them to revise their expectations of the future course of inflation. This would not be a wealth effect but a shift in liquidity preference; however, it could be difficult to untangle wealth effects and liquidity preference shifts. Some 'one-sided' wealth effects may also be envisaged, but any discussion of these is best left until Chapter 11, since they are at the centre of disputes between Post Keynesian and mainstream economists on unemployment and inflation (see section 11.4).

3.9 Conclusion

The evolutionary paths traced by financial systems are constrained by what wealth-holders and income recipients are able to believe about their financial circumstances and about the payoffs to various sets of commitments into which they might enter. Whether or not a major change in a person's net worth actually does have any impact upon her rate of spending will depend very much on her attitudes to such a change. For example, some people who suffer major losses due to a fall in share prices might carry on spending if some or all of the following conditions hold: (a) they feel they must do so in order to maintain their social status; (b) they are both able and willing to increase their borrowing; (c) they had not come to see their now evaporated unrealised capital gains as part of their 'permanent wealth'; or (d) the judgmental rules they employ make it impossible for them to believe the market will not recover before long. Others might make major cutbacks because they see things differently.

In this chapter I have examined the kinds of processes by which such beliefs are formed and methods by which people choose what to do with their wealth and borrowing power. I have tried to show how an acceptance of the analytical significance of bounded rationality and the consequent use of decision rules and satisficing routines would enable Post Keynesian economists to take a subjectivist stance without laying themselves open to charges of nihilism. My analysis complements the broader thesis put forward by Heiner (1983), who has argued that the possibility of prediction in economics *only* arises because people use routine methods for coping with problem events that are, strictly speaking, unique occurrences.

To rebut fully the assertions of those, such as Coddington, who have accused Post Keynesians of nihilism, it is unlikely to be enough just to show that, in principle, economic modelling is compatible with a subjectivist view of expectations once a behavioural perspective is introduced. The sceptics will demand to see such modelling undertaken in practice. To narrow down the directions in which monetary systems may evolve in response to *particular* changes in the state of the economic news or innovations by financial entrepreneurs that change the set of options open to consumers and savers, Post Keynesian economists will have to begin to engage in studies of *how* decision-makers *actually* make up their minds about what could happen and what might be adequate courses of action for them to select. If they only add a behavioural perspective to their work by incorporating *theoretical* insights from behavioural economics and from psychology, they will still be left able only to discuss what Coddington (1983, p. 99) called the 'texture' of events. But, even then, they should be in a stronger position than hitherto in some policy debates — for example over the need for the prudential control of financial institutions and the regulation of consumer credit.

While advocating that behavioural research methods become part of the toolkit for applied work by Post Keynesian economists, I remain enough of a follower of Shackle's wise words to want to make it clear that I hope such behavioural investigations will not be used as a basis for claims that one can precisely foretell the future. Whenever Post Keynesians seek to draw from such investigations aggregative implications about possible responses to changes in the 'state of the news', they should be explicit about scope for error due to the use of simplified stereotypes. Following Shackle, they also should always warn that creativity in the minds of decision-makers has the potential to prompt choices vastly different from those so far observed. Hence policy recommendations based on behavioural studies should themselves contain room for manoeuvre, in case portfolio choices take surprising turns (cf. Hart, 1945, 1947). Post Keynesians could do much to help restore the tarnished public image of economists if, instead of trying to divert attention away from debatable assumptions underlying their conjectures, they presented their policy advice in a way which highlighted the uncertainties that have proved difficult to dismiss and explained why, therefore, inflexible or finely tuned policies could be dangerous.

4 Pricing and Investment Decisions

4.1 Introduction

An understanding of corporate pricing and investment decisions is a prerequisite for the study of monetary economics. The investments that firms choose to undertake can have many forms, which may differ in the extent to which they augment the supply potential of the economy or merely involve a change in the ownership and control of existing assets. They may also vary considerably in the financial demands they make upon the banking system. Corporate requirements for external finance are in turn dependent on the prices that firms have chosen to charge for their existing products and the sales volumes they have been able to achieve. Corporate pricing decisions, when weighed together by official statisticians, determine the reported rate of inflation in the economy. Inflation is not something that happens in an impersonal, mechanistic way as a result of excessive aggregate demand or rising factor costs: firms need not choose to take advantage of buoyant markets and, if they cannot negotiate their way out of paying higher costs for their inputs, they may not always feel it wise to pass them on to their customers through higher prices.

This chapter explores pricing first since expectations about revenues are logically prior to decisions to invest in new products and processes. Comparisons are made between the Post Keynesian 'normal cost' analysis of pricing and the recent neoclassical theory of contestable markets. A liquidity preference perspective is then introduced. Following this, there is a discussion of strategic aspects of corporate investment that involve less of a focus on what might be achieved by selling outputs in the market than on how far markets should be used as a vehicle for achieving the goals of those taking decisions. The chapter ends by considering the responsiveness of investment decisions to changes in the rate of interest.

4.2 Pricing and Competition

Prices are seen in neoclassical economics as market-clearing devices, that ensure a balance between the amounts producers are willing to supply and the amount customers wish to demand. Post Keynesian economists accept that this view may be a reasonable way of portraying the workings of markets for primary commodities — so long as due account is taken of the roles that speculators may play as buyers and sellers in these markets. However, in other contexts, Post Keynesian price theory is not a market-clearing analysis (see Andrews, 1949, 1964; Andrews and Brunner, 1975; Eichner, 1976; Lee, 1984; Lee *et al.*, 1986; Reynolds, 1987, Chs. 4-6). Producers of manufactured goods and services are seen as setting prices for their products and then waiting to see how many customers are attracted by their terms. Where buyers call for tenders, a would-be seller either wins the contract or loses out to a rival bidder who offers a more competitive bid. In other cases the seller does the calling and stands willing to supply as many or as few units as buyers come forward to make purchases at the marked price. Faced with uncertainty about their selling environments, firms tend to set themselves sales targets that seem both reasonable, given the knowledge that they do have, and likely to provide an adequate return. If unexpectedly few buyers show up, selling efforts will be increased and/or marketing campaigns given a rethink; possibly attention will also be given to modifying the product as a means of solving the problem. If sales figures are pleasantly surprising, decision-makers will have to work out whether they have been setting their sights too low, or whether they are dealing merely with a temporary spurt in the market.

To suggest that prices are set on a 'take it or leave it' basis is not the same thing as explaining how firms decide which prices to set. The Post Keynesian explanation of pricing choices centres on the kinds of relationships that firms have with their customers and the competitive environments in which they operate. When Post Keynesians speak of buyers or customers they do not only have consumers in mind: they recognise that the vast majority of trade concerns intermediate stages of production and is actually carried out between firms. Industrial buyers may be expected to possess more expertise than members of households, but we should not jump to the conclusion that boundedly rational individuals will necessarily end up getting a bad deal even if search and experimentation are costly activities. Buyers make their choices in a social world, so reputations have a big role to play in determining which firms they will approach as possible suppliers. Competition will be vigorous so long as existing producers have to battle with other producers or if they operate in fear of potential competition from new entrants who could undermine any attempts at policies of explicit or implicit collusion.

Potential competition might not immediately seem to be a very powerful force limiting the prices that firms can charge: new businesses starting from scratch may have a hard time getting established, particularly if a sizeable investment in capital and marketing is required to get production and sales volumes up to the minimum efficient scale of output. However, a much more powerful threat comes from well established firms on the lookout for markets which they can enter on the basis of their established knowhow and capital investments (see Moss, 1981, and section 4.5). Such a basis for entry, if strong, would mean that few costs would have to be sunk in an experimental foray into a market where existing suppliers seemed to be incompetent or to be pushing their luck. In the limit, a firm might be able to engage in 'cross-entry' by using its existing sales force and capital equipment, both of which might be underemployed, and have no need to invest in anything except for advertisements and working capital.

If existing producers in a market are looking out for expansionary opportunities elsewhere, they are likely to be living in fear that raiders from other markets might find it attractive to invade their own territory. For firms that wish to preserve their existing market positions one simple pricing rule should stand out as rational: prices should be set just below the levels that would appear to make cross-entry viable, given the conjectured opportunity costs of potential producers. Since firms may find it difficult to assess which alternative lines of activity are being assessed by potential rivals, even if they have a good idea whom the latter might be, they will tend to use their own production and marketing expenses per unit of output as a guide to the opportunity costs of potential producers. Incumbent producers' prices thus become based on their average variable expenditures per unit at their target sales rates for their planning periods (commonly called 'normal costs' by Post Keynesians), plus a mark-up from which capital outlays and overhead expenses may be recouped and profit streams generated. If the power of competition is such that a firm believes it cannot set the mark-up high enough to cover all outlays and provide a satisfactory rate of return, then it will not remain in the market in the long run if it is already a producer, or bother to enter the market if it is presently only a potential producer. Incumbent firms will only be setting mark-ups that generate supernormal profits if they believe that their experience in the market gives them an advantage over potential producers.

In emphasising that potential competition is an important force in many markets, Post Keynesian price theory overlaps somewhat with the modern neoclassical approach to oligopoly, namely the theory of contestable markets associated with the work of Baumol *et al.* (1982). However, Post Keynesian analysis does not take very seriously the idea of a *perfectly* contestable market in which there are no sunk costs and both entry and exit are costless. In this hypothetical situation, which contestability theorists have suggested might be a not unrealistic 'as if' way of viewing many markets, the ability of firms to stage costless 'hit-and-run' raids concentrates incumbents' minds wonderfully against any temptation they might have to pursue socially indesirable pricing policies. Prices then become parameters that incumbents have to live with, rather than discretionary variables chosen in the light of sometimes imperfect judgements about the likely behaviour of other firms (for a detailed Post Keynesian appraisal of the contestability literature, see Davies and Lee, 1988). Throughout the rest of this book it should be understood that, although I may speak of markets as 'hotly contested', I do not have in mind a state of perfect contestability as a reference point. Any situation in which marketing costs have to be incurred violates the costless exit condition — advertisements, for example, are a very obvious example of a non-recoverable expense. Exit is also hardly likely to be costless if entry involves expenditure on new physical equipment — assets will only be perfectly marketable if they are not at all idiosyncratic (see section 2.5).

Marketing considerations actually receive considerable attention in the Post Keynesian/behavioural analysis of corporate behaviour. The notion of perfect contestability would be more acceptable if formal contracts between buyers and sellers could be specified in detail and then enforced without significant costs being involved by parties on either side. Doubts about standards of service would be eliminated, and if customers wanted to make sure of future deliveries for which their needs were presently uncertain they could do so via contingent claims contracts. In reality, of course, transaction costs are often difficult to ignore and with some products it is intrinsically difficult to set out in detail what is going to be delivered. (For example, it is hard to imagine a fully-specified contract for the delivery of a hairdo, given the number of hairs involved and the fact that while a hairdresser may be conscious of how a hairstyle works, this information is normally supplemented by tacit knowledge and would not in any case be easily spelt out to the customer.) In this sort of situation, unlike that which prevails in primary commodity markets, firms do not merely have to decide how much to invest in physical equipment. To ensure that their physical equipment does not run at disastrously low rates of capacity utilisation they must also make decisions about the kind of investment in marketing that may be needed to overcome any doubts that potential buyers have about their products and standards of service. For any hypothetical combination of physical and marketing investments, the key question is therefore whether a price that covered the full costs of production and marketing would be likely to be low enough to generate the sales volumes required for profits targets to be met.

Marketing costs do not arise only when firms seek to enter markets or expand their interests in their existing markets by launching new products. Attempts to build up market share, either from scratch or as an addition to previous attainments, may prove very costly unless the market population is changing and/or incumbents enrage their regulars by letting their standards slip below satisfactory levels, thereby provoking them to search for a better source of supply. Certainly, some degree of flux is to be expected in markets, even in the absence of changing macroeconomic conditions, due to geographical shifts of customers, the progression of consumers through lifecycles that involve different patterns of choice, and the rise and fall of industrial buyers' requirements as they develop new products or the fortunes of their existing ones change. If new customers or disaffected former clients of rival producers are not to arrrive on a purely random basis, marketing expenses will obviously be necessary.

To build up sales still further will require an investment in marketing to overcome goodwill relationships that exist between incumbent firms and those buyers who would otherwise see no point in changing their purchasing routines. These relationships, which figure nowhere in Baumol *et al.*'s (1982) treatise on contestable markets, may be seen as implicit contracts that emerge as alternatives to costly fully detailed and/or contingent claims contracts. They play a particularly important role in determining relative market shares when firms are selling ranges of products or items that customers purchase time and again. If buyers are satisfied, they will tend to return on future occasions even if there are other firms claiming to offer an identical deal. They thereby avoid the risk of paying the same price for what might turn out to be an inferior non-price deal with an untried alternative supplier, and if they are recognised as 'regulars' they may get preferential treatment on occasions when they are in urgent need of supplies. The risks associated with a disappointing standard of quality or service may be such that a 'better the devil you know' consideration will not just keep buyers away from alternative suppliers who quote an identical price; it may also deter them from switching to unknown suppliers that are offering cheaper deals.

Where there is scope for cultivating a goodwill relationship, suppliers may be expected to take a long-run view on pricing and capacity decisions. They will avoid inconveniencing their regular customers by moving prices around to reflect changing market conditions, particularly since supernormal profits achieved through exploiting customers will encourage the latter to consider the offerings of existing rivals and may encourage the entry of others or promote intervention by government agencies. They will also tend to operate with some spare capacity even when the markets in which they operate are not in a state of depression. If new customers arrive on the scene, firms with spare capacity can service them without having to disappoint their regular clienteles. In other words, incomplete capacity utilisation in normal times may often represent an investment aimed at building up goodwill, though naturally the scale of such investments is limited by the costs of maintaining a margin of slack. In boom times waiting lists may have to be used to ration supplies. However, so long as a firm does not find its waiting lists getting longer than those of its rivals, it should be possible for an individual supplier to acquire further goodwill even despite not being able to satisfy new customers on the spot.

Figure 4.1 is an attempt to sum up these arguments in graphical form. *OS* represents the firm's sales target. The price it charges, *OP*, is formed by adding a mark-up to *AVC*, its average variable costs. The firm's average total costs (*ATC*) are the sum of *AVC* and *AFC*, its average fixed costs, and its planned net margin is the difference between *ATC* and *OP* at *OS*. The horizontal line *PP* is not a horizontal demand curve of the kind found in the theory of the perfectly competitive firm. It simply represents the firm's average revenue possibilities at the price *OP*, but whether actual sales are equal to the target *OS* will depend on how successful the firm is in marketing its product relative to its rivals, on stochastic factors and on the general state of demand.

Because firms typically operate with a margin of slack and are concerned about keeping the goodwill of their customers, changes in the strength of orders will normally lead to changes in their rates of output and/or stockholding levels, rather than in the prices that they charge. When increases in the rate of inflation are associated with buoyant market conditions, the Post Keynesian approach to pricing sees them as arising because of changes in normal costs and in the risk of entry. Booming conditions in final product markets may be associated with shortages in factor markets and hence an inflation of factor costs. These are most likely to be passed forward into higher prices if they are expected not to reverse later in the business cycle, which is more likely for wages than for primary commodity inputs.

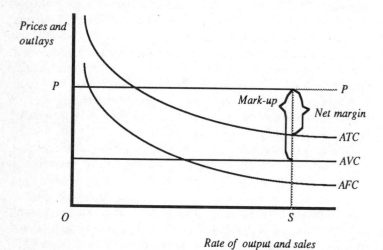

Figure 4.1 *The 'Normal Cost' Approach to Pricing*

In times of normal or depressed trade, inflation can arise due to increases in normal costs, such as higher payroll taxes and prices charged by public utilities, as well as debt servicing charges and higher wages that arise either through cost-of-living clauses in existing contracts or through new concessions in the face of union pushfulness aimed at restoring relativities (see also section 11.6). However, whether their markets are booming or relatively depressed, companies facing increased outlays will only have a limited ability to shift them forward to their customers if their actual and/or potential competitors at home or overseas are having an easier time in factor markets.

Incumbent firms may be expected to be less afraid of cross-entry by established producers if business conditions generally are booming. In contrast to periods of slack business when excess capacity due to a lack of orders will tend to concentrate managers' minds on the possibility that they might try to break into related lines of activity, managers are more likely to be preoccupied with the task of meeting orders in their regular markets by bringing new investment projects on stream at their scheduled times. Consequently existing producers in each industry may recognise that they can charge higher margins and exploit inelastic market-level demand conditions without provoking cross-entry. Once the boom comes to an end these firms would then absorb further cost increases and allow their margins to shrink back to 'normal' levels. The main factor working against such policies of engaging in implicit collusion and 'making hay while the sun shines' is that a condition of *general* overheating is rare, particularly in economies open to competition from overseas producers; there will usually be some firms, somewhere, on the lookout for ways of making use of spare potential by carving new markets for themselves.

4.3 Pricing as Speculation

Pricing choices are always speculative, since managers in one firm cannot read the minds of their counterparts in rival organisations. As events unfold and provide further clues about competitive conditions, many guesses about what constitutes wise prices to charge will be revised, and with them the prices in question. Sometimes errors have consequences that are practically irreversible: for example, overly arrogant pricing stances by incumbents may provoke market invasions that lead consumers to change their non-price demands in the light of experience with the somewhat different products offered by interlopers. In this section, attention is drawn to some of the risks that may be *deliberately* taken by those who have to work out which prices to set and whether to change existing prices.

In some lines of business managers have frequently to weigh up whether to make a deal with a potential customer today or instead to hold out for a rather better deal in the near future. Such a dilemma arises in two kinds of situations. The first is when firms cannot replace used-up inventories instantly and without cost. An obvious instance of this concerns the pricing of used cars, even though the ease of entry and exit make the used car market appear highly contestable. If a dealer lowers the price of a vehicle today it may be possible to clinch the sale and free up scarce space and working capital. But if replacement stock with good potential profitability is not being offered as a trade-in or cannot immediately be found in the wholesale market, it may be better to lose today's potential customer to a rival. Tomorrow it may be possible to sell the vehicle to a person who is less inclined to haggle and/or has a more marketable trade-in to offer, or who has missed out on the broadly similar product that today's lost customer has purchased from a rival car yard.

Secondly we must consider the predicament of firms operating in an industry that suffers from patterns of demand that are so erratic as to deter incumbent firms from investing in enough capacity to satisfy peak demand levels. This case will be illustrated with reference to the construction industry (see Andrews and Brunner, 1975, Ch. 5); another obvious example concerns the supply of electrical engineering equipment for power stations (see Richardson, 1969). Building firms typically put in tenders for more work than they can handle, expecting only to win a proportion of the contracts. How low they will go in making any bid for a contract is constrained by their perceptions of their own opportunity costs: if they win a particular tender battle, they forego the use of the committed resources from servicing other contracts which might be won at a later date. When they place their bids, they cannot be sure how low they need to go to win, for they usually cannot be sure quite how desperate their rivals are to get the business: the opportunity costs of their rivals are private, subjective constructs. (It should perhaps be added that although the cheapest tender will normally win, a firm that *is* known to be *really* desperate for business could fail to get a contract despite promising to undercut all other tenders: the customer might justifiably fear that this firm could be forced into liquidation before the job is finished.)

It is in the nature of the construction industry that jobs are typically non-standardised, one-off tasks. A building firm that is not adaptable will rapidly go out of business owing to the thinness of demand for narrowly defined kinds of work. However, many firms will pick up experience and equipment which suits them particularly well for certain kinds of jobs, for example, concreting rather than bricklaying. Hence although firms in the industry are normally able to undertake a great variety of contracts, they will be keener to win some contracts than others, just as used car dealers are not normally confined to selling a particular model of used car and yet nonetheless prefer to trade in a particular part of the market. If a building firm is finding a lack of work in its preferred area it can try to get contracts for other kinds of work, but if its managers take the view that their preferred kind of contract is likely to emerge before too long, then they would be foolish to tie up its resources elsewhere for very far into the future unless they do so on exceptionally good terms. In putting in bids for the jobs that are currently available, they may specify higher prices than they would quote if they took a more pessimistic view of future prospects and were keener to win these contracts. If rivals are also taking the view that better contracts will be available in future for firms that have the capacity to handle them, they may likewise put in tenders that reflect these opportunity costs and the firm in question may still stand a chance of winning enough of these contracts to fill its order books.

In the latter case we do not have the pure form of 'normal cost' pricing discussed in the previous section, for prices move around as incumbents' opportunity costs change with the strength of demand, failing to cover full costs in depressed times and involving supernormal margins in peak periods. Nonetheless, if incumbent firms wish to discourage cross-entry they must not allow their long-run earnings to rise above the opportunity costs of would-be rivals. The same is true for the earlier case illustrated with reference to the used car market.

A rather different kind of speculative pricing is central to work by Post Keynesian economists who have focused their attention on large, growth-oriented corporations — Eichner called them 'megacorps' — run by management teams that are confident of their capacities to undertake major investments in diversification. Their retained profits provide a means for financing research and development and the purchase of new plant and machinery without incurring the underwriting fees charged by merchant banks or the risk of embarrassment associated with the flotation of a new issue in an unpredictable stock market (see Wood, 1975; Eichner, 1976, 1985). Alternatively, they may be used to finance portfolio investment or takeover raids against other firms. The management team of a megacorp may therefore be expected to consider the impact of their pricing decisions on the funds that are available for investment, and here they are likely to recognise an important trade-off.

Such managers will not expect their firms to suffer an immediate catastrophic loss of market goodwill if they set prices somewhat above 'normal cost' levels. Although some sales may be lost quite quickly to existing rivals if the latter do not follow suit, this kind of substitution will be limited in so far as products are differentiated in 'non-price' terms and prices are not taken outside the budget ranges of target customers (see further Earl, 1984, pp. 142-8; 1986, Ch. 10). Although cross-entry may be provoked, new producers may take a considerable period of time to accumulate the additional physical and intellectual resources needed to produce comparable outputs and build up market credibility, even if, in broad terms, the market into which the latter are moving is rather similar to their original area of interest. (An obvious example is how, after its initial diversification away from a dependence on motorcycle manufacturing, the Honda company has taken practically a quarter of a century to come anywhere near to posing a serious threat to European manufacturers of prestige motorcars.) In these situations the costs of attempting to keep competitors out of their markets indefinitely may be judged to be substantial in terms of foregone shorter-term profits, particularly since such cost might be incurred without even producing the desired result. So managers may decide to risk reductions in the long-run sales of their existing products by pricing them so as to generate larger profit flows in the short run.

How far the management team of a megacorp will try to push up its profit margin will depend upon the time horizons that its members keep in view: if the firm will become a likely takeover target or unable to raise external funds from its bankers unless it can demonstrate strong profitability right now, its top managers will be more likely to risk damaging the long-run prospects of its current products by greedy short-run pricing.

The dynamic nature of the market environments in which such pricing choices have to be made helps to ensure that these decisions are every bit as hazardous as those concerning portfolio investment: the timing of competitive entry and the magnitude of an entrant's threat cannot be known in advance with certainty; nor can strategists be sure that the higher profits that their firms earn in the short run on their existing products will be sufficient to enable them to carve a secure position for their firms further down the track. If entry is more rapid than expected, incumbent producers may not have had sufficient time to plough their supernormal profits back into superior new products, more cost effective production processes, or portfolios of financial assets that give them security against would-be takeover raiders.

4.4 Transaction Costs and Internalisation Decisions

The volume of external finance that a firm requires for investment purposes may vary according to the kind of strategic move it is attempting to make, as well as being affected by the risks that it is taking in pricing of the products it currently produces. Industrial economists have highlighted the fact that much expansion is undertaken through merger and takeover activities, rather than by the purchases of new plant and machinery and expenditure on new marketing campaigns. The former strategy clearly requires less by way of skills in innovation and marketing flair, but relies heavily on organisational and financial skills. It has often been possible for large firms to purchase other companies simply by creating extra shares and exchanging them for shares in the company that they are acquiring: in effect, their stock market standing means that their shares are seen to be as good as cash (see Meeks and Whittington, 1976). Since the share-exchange method for financing takeovers dilutes the equity of existing shareholders, managers will be less inclined to use it to make really large purchases of existing assets if they are afraid of alienating existing major shareholders who at present can easily muster majority voting power. In these situations complete or partial takeovers may be undertaken only after the raider has borrowed heavily, leaving its balance sheet vulnerable in the event of a major downturn in shareprices.

Economists have paid far less attention to the monetary implications of the fact that firms involved in similar product markets vary considerably in the extent to which they use in-house facilities for the production of raw materials and semi-finished inputs or do their own distribution. Take, for example, the business of publishing. Some firms subcontract the copy-editing, typesetting, printing and binding of the books that comprise their catalogues and pay other firms to distribute them to retailers; rather than owning the physical assets that they use, they may be leasing them from finance companies. Other firms employ more staff and invest in the technology necessary for the production of books (though rarely do they own logging concessions and papermaking factories), and

75

maintain warehouses or even a chain of retail stores in which they sell a good part of their output as well as the products of other companies (as with Barnes & Noble in the US or Angus & Robertson in Australia). Some publishers seek the advice of outside referees on the merits of works that authors have submitted; others employ full-time editors to read manuscripts and decide for themselves which ones will be worthy additions to their firms' catalogues. Some may even employ staff writers. As far as overseas markets and authors are concerned, we can observe a similar variety of strategies. It is common for one publisher to get another to act as its overseas agent and distribute its books on a commission basis (it is also common for Australasian academics to bypass these agents and local bookstores and buy their books by mail-order direct from British or American publishers or from major overseas bookstores, such as Heffers of Cambridge). A popular alternative is to sell a batch of books outright to an overseas company, along with sole distribution rights over particular territory. But fully multinational publishing houses are also common.

The existence of such diverse ways of setting out to achieve a particular end result — in the case of our publishing example, profits from the sale of books to libraries and consumers — implies a wide range of possible financial scenarios. Firms that make extensive use of downstream and upstream subcontractors may be able to engineer huge volumes of production without themselves having recourse to large-scale borrowing from the external capital market or without having had to accumulate internal sources of funds from years of previous profitable operations. In the event of a downturn in its market, such a firm is financially less vulnerable than one which has committed itself to a strategy of 'internalisation' involving vertical integration and which has prefered to own rather than rent its capital assets. The obvious question arising from this observation is how we might explain why 'some firms do, but some firms don't' prefer to make extensive use of external contractors. This phenomenon has only recently received from economists the attention that it really deserves, as part of a body of new literature known as 'Transaction Cost Economics'. The key contributions are by Williamson (1975, 1985) and Kay (1982, 1984); all have been inspired by a paper by Coase (1937), the broader implications of which were not seen at the time of its publication.

Coase argued that the firm is a device for dealing with change without a need to rewrite contracts to cover the impact of changes on affected parties. The firm has a rationale only because there are costs associated with getting things done in the market. Consider a situation where a publishing company finds one of its books selling unexpectedly well and therefore wishes to increase its supplies to its distribution network. If the book is one of many that it prints and binds in-house, and if the contracts with its workers do not tie them to the production of particular books, then it is, in principle, a simple matter to get production increased: a manager just has to request that more copies are produced, either by taking up spare capacity or by cutting back on the production of other books. If the company had adopted the strategy of subcontracting the printing and binding of its books, matters could be more difficult; for unless a contract already existed to cover the contingency, it would be necessary to negotiate with an outside supplier for the production of extra copies. Valuable sales could be lost in the interim. If the runaway success of the book had been totally unexpected, it is unlikely that the management of the publishing company would have previously negotiated arrangements for production on a greatly enlarged scale at a later date, for negotiation may involve a lot of time spent in drawing up and haggling over fine print.

The essence of the firm is that it is an institution designed to facilitate production or exchange whilst avoiding some of the costs that would arise if business were conducted through activity-specific market contracts: in a firm, activities are undertaken by people engaged via rather loosely-specified contracts and directed by managers who decide what they would like to see done in the light of changing conditions. The costs of maintaining the management team are substituted for the costs of arranging and implementing more detailed contracts. Entrepreneurs with different sets of experiences and/or different ways of forming expectations may come to very different conclusions about the merits of internalisation versus market contracting even when they are engaged in similar lines of business.

The parallels between the Coasian view of the firm and the Keynesian view of money and liquidity presented in Chapter 2 should be obvious; in fact, what first prompted me to read Coase's paper as an undergraduate was a footnote in Goodhart (1975, p. 4) in which this was pointed out. Loasby (1976, pp. 165-6), too, has briefly explored this theme, commenting that 'Money and the firm both imply a rejection of the concept of general equilibrium in favour of a continuing management of emerging events' (p. 165). Like cash in hand, workers whose employment contracts are short on specific details can normally be redeployed with the minimum of fuss to take account of the employer's needs. At the other end of the liquidity spectrum, commitment to highly detailed contracts for the supply of labour or other goods and services is more like house ownership in terms of the costs of change. However, just as it is difficult to specify precisely what differentiates money from other assets, so it is by no means easy to define precisely the boundaries of a particular management team's span of control, its ability to change its mixes of inputs and outputs as and when it wishes. Some employment contracts are more watertight than others, and employees and other suppliers of inputs may vary from time to time in their interpretations of what their side of the bargain entails. Full internalisation may not be necessary if one wishes to influence one's suppliers and distributors: Richardson (1972) notes the scope for achieving such results via minority shareholdings and by engaging in customary forms of market behaviour (for example, regular customers of a firm may expect preferential assistance in a crisis and often receive it even though nothing more than an implicit long term contract exists). Similar sentiments are voiced by Harrigan (1983), who coins the term 'quasi-integration'.

Recent extensions of Coase's work by Williamson (1975, 1985) have been concerned with implications of the possibility that parties to a transaction may behave in an 'opportunistic' manner: that is to say, they may guilefully exploit the ignorance of parties on the other side of the transaction. This theme is closely related to our earlier discussions concerning pricing and contestability. A firm is unlikely deliberately to charge a mark-up in excess of the minimum it needs to justify its continuing involvement in a particular line of business unless it believes it has some kind of competitive edge over other producers, both actual and potential; for if the market is easy to enter, attempts to charge 'rip-off' prices are likely to be discredited by rival firms offering duplicate products. The possibility of potential and actual competitors with similar bases of experience being able to discredit those who try to behave with opportunism may tend to curb such behaviour even when contracts are incompletely specified and/or costly to enforce. However, there is no guarantee that this will happen. Would-be entrants with a partial knowledge of what incumbents are up to may not be able to expose them convincingly without incurring considerable research costs and even those with a detailed knowledge of the set-up might need to incur substantial marketing costs before they could succeed in selling a cheaper duplicate or a superior product for a similar price. The more intrinsically difficult it is to specify in advance what a customer is supposed to be getting, the harder it is for someone else to prove that a better deal could be obtained elsewhere.

Williamson argues that the incentive to make guileful use of one's private knowledge will vary according to the transactional environment in which one is acting. This claim may be illustrated if we refer once again to the publishing example. The important thing to bear in mind during the course of the discussion is that none of the problems raised would arise if relationships between transacting parties were specified fully in costlessly enforceable contracts.

Suppose a publisher uses an intermediary to distribute its books in overseas markets. If that intermediary is part of another publishing firm that produces rival products, then it has to trade off the earnings it can make from pushing its client's products to the best of its ability, against the earnings it can make from concentrating on pushing its own products at the expense of those of its client. It could try to explain away poor sales of the client's books with reference to the difficulties of selling in this market, difficulties which it knows better than the client. How could the publisher prove otherwise, thousands of miles away from the scene?

If the publishing firm is aware of these risks, it is likely to consider the pros and cons of some transactional alternatives. For example, making commission contingent on the distributor selling a minimum number of books may look a bit better to the publisher than a sum per book, so long as a distributor can be found who will accept such a deal. Something which might produce an even better selling effort would be a deal in which the distributor actually bought a minimum number of books for resale from the publisher. Yet another strategy for the publisher to consider is vertical integration, which would involve setting up a distribution network from scratch or taking over an incumbent firm. This option might well be blocked by imperfections in the capital market and the limited capabilities of the firm's management team (in the sense of Penrose, 1959). Otherwise, though, it might look attractive since those involved in the distribution side would know that if they failed to work effectively they would be helping rival firms at the expense of their employers. There would be some incentive for all employees to pull together and follow management's exhortations, even where the latter could find it difficult to prevent shirking by the former within the compass of their loosely-specified contracts of employment. But it might not escape the attention of those involved in distribution that their's was something of a captive market, unlike that enjoyed by an external contractor, so they could feel able to take things more easily without their employers deciding to write off the sunk costs of their investments in distribution. Worse still, if there were economies of scale in distribution, it could be difficult to find an outside market for any surplus capacity owing to a lack of faith on the part of would-be clients. So even if in-house distribution employees could be expected to do their best, the questionable services of outside contractors might look preferable to the unit costs of avoiding the market. Vertical integration, in short, is not a sure-fire way of disposing of risks of opportunism. No wonder 'some firms do, but some firms don't!'

4.5 Diversification

The internalisation decisions so far considered have concerned vertical relationships between stages of production and distribution processes. However, much investment concerns horizontal diversification, for example from book publishing into magazines and newspapers, and from print media into electronic media. This kind of diversification has been analysed from the transaction cost perspective by Kay (1982, 1984). One of his main themes is that many such strategic moves involve attempts to exploit existing corporate strengths in new contexts (cf. the Post Keynesian analysis of 'cross-entry' in section 4.2). Their intentions are to achieve 'synergy' or 'economies of scope' by exploiting complementarities and making better use of underutilised corporate resources (not merely physical capital but also management skills, knowhow, marketing connections and even brand names and market images). Thus a company involved in, for example, both print and electronic media may be able to achieve profits greater than the sum of profits that could be achieved by separate print media and electronic media companies. However, unlike earlier writers such as Ansoff (1968), Kay considers whether it may be possible to achieve synergy without internalisation: by trading with others the rights to use its and/or the others' underutilised resources, a firm may be able to exploit economies of scope without investing in new assets or merging with another company.

Many firms in fact do seek to achieve synergy via market transactions — far more, in fact, than Kay acknowledges. There is much evidence that strategists have become aware of the scope for their firms to make money as providers of design consultancy services rather than by committing themselves to huge capital investments that would be necessary were they to go it alone in a new area: for example, instead of attempting to move into the market for cheap family cars, the makers of Porsche sports cars have provided engineering inputs for SEAT and Lada, whilst instead of developing their own technological solution to the problem of vibrations in large capacity four-cylinder engines Porsche have themselves used under licence the 'silent shaft' technology developed by Mitsubishi. Joint venture arrangements likewise are becoming a popular way for companies to exploit complementarities and reduce their needs for investment funding (see Mariti and Smiley, 1983).

Although more and more firms are using such arrangements to broaden the scope of their operations without incurring the financial and managerial costs of investing in new designs, production processes and market goodwill, many other companies still prefer to diversify by taking on more resources. To explain this, Kay notes how the possibility of opportunistic behaviour in the face of incompletely specified contracts may make synergy-trading strategies seem unacceptably dangerous. For example, if a technology is not specific to a particular product and has yet to be widely applied, knowledge gained via a licensing deal concerning the product might lead the licensee to develop unforeseen spin-offs on which no royalty has to be paid; it might even enable the licensee to become a competitor. Similarly, firms which purchase technology inputs may fear that visiting consultant engineers could gain access to some of their corporate secrets. These kinds of considerations need not lead potential synergy traders each to incur the costs of 'going it alone'. In many cases, the problem will be addressed by one of the firms making a takeover bid for the other, or through an amicable merger. Whether or not this happens, the costly decision to bring more resources within the boundaries of the firm is a consequence of problems in using markets.

Many firms have also become avid users of capital markets because the ways in which their management teams have sought to exploit their existing resource bases have been shaped by a desire to avoid 'putting too many eggs in too few baskets'. When a firm seeks to use up scope for achieving both production and marketing synergy by increasing its ranges of activities, the least demanding strategy in terms of the pressure it places on management and on the firm's financial resources will be one which involves producing additional

81

products that are similar to those it already makes and which sell in much the same markets. If the firm's planners feel that they are not operating in an environment prone to 'muggings' in the form of technological innovations and adverse changes in tastes or in government policy, then they are likely to feel under considerable competitive pressure to adopt this strategy — if the firm spreads its talents across a variety of fields, it risks being undercut by rivals that are ruthlessly pursuing the advantages of specialisation. However, Kay would argue that if the planners believe their firm's environment is one in which catastrophic muggings are likely, they will probably hedge their bets by choosing a strategy that makes only a limited use of potential syngergy links between activities. They might therefore undertake investments which realise potential for production synergy but involve making a commitment to a new kind of market, and/or which expand their firm's range of offerings in its existing market but require it to acquire new kinds of production equipment and managerial knowhow.

These hedging strategies could involve taking over other firms and then achieving the various synergies by policies of rationalisation. This route has the advantage of giving the firm access to established markets, equipment and managerial expertise. It is also a way for the management team to make the position of their firm less vulnerable almost overnight, so long as the acquired resources can be digested without too much trouble (which often is not the case: see Earl, 1984, pp. 184-7) and have not been purchased at an inflated price with borrowed funds, leaving the firm with a dangerous gearing ratio.

Centred as it is on fears concerning the possible sudden truncation of the lifecycles of products and/or production processes, Kay's hedging analysis is something of a departure from the conventional approach to diversification. In the orthodox analysis the various activities in which the firm is involved are assumed to be prone to exhibit some variance in their earnings through time but they are not portrayed as likely to suffer a terminal downturn or, in the case of new products, to die in their infancy. Rather, the idea is that corporate earnings and cashflows can be smoothed out by putting together a diversified portfolio of activities that are not expected simultaneously to go through temporary bad patches.

There are obvious parallels between both of these views of corporate diversification and the analyses of portfolio choices of individuals in Chapter 3 (cf. the discussions in sections 3.3 and 3.4 surrounding Figures 3.1 and 3.2). In fact, the parallels are so great as to lead one to ask whose interests these kinds of corporate diversifications are actually intended to serve. If shareholders wish to insure themselves against erratic earnings and/or the possible failure of some companies whose shares they own, they can do so by buying diversified portfolios for themselves. Given this, they might be expected to be interested in new or established firms that are trying to reap the advantages of specialisation. When managers of such companies generate higher profits than they feel they need to reinvest to maintain an acceptable rate of return in their existing line of business, they can dispose of surplus earnings without diversifying by distributing them to shareholders as dividends. The shareholders can then use these dividends as they choose. If shareholders do not wish to use dividends to finance consumption, they can either place them on the money market or use them to buy small shareholdings in other companies. Alternatively, they can choose to invest in specialised companies that tend to retain their surplus earnings but which use them to fund portfolio investment on behalf of their shareholders — *not* to satisfy the shareholders' hedging and/or earnings-smoothing motives, but to help them to reduce their tax liabilities (if marginal tax rates on dividends are higher than on capital gains) and give them indirect access to economies of scale in making deposits or buying shares. (The latter only became important in economies such as the UK in the 'Big Bang' of the late 1980s when fixed-rate commissions on share purchases were abolished.)

The appeal of shares in diversified companies seems to arise because financial markets are characterised by information problems and transaction costs. One simple fact is that if people hold shares in only a few large diversified companies, they may find it easier to keep an eye on how the companies are doing. Much more important are considerations associated with the limited abilities of small shareholders to control the companies in which they have a stake.

A small shareholder who is dissatisfied with an existing management team may face considerable personal costs if she initiates moves to call an extraordinary general meeting and/or get a large assembly of similarly disaffected shareholders together to vote in a new board. Hence individual shareholders may grudgingly choose to continue to tolerate an unsatisfactory situation or quietly sell their holdings. Even if a zealot does decide to shoulder these costs, public choice problems mean it is also likely that many small shareholders will choose not to incur the costs of showing up and voting. Each will realise that their own votes, taken in isolation, are unlikely to be decisive, so voting is something they will choose to do only if they see it as a matter of principle — in other words, because they expect to derive psychological, not pecuniary, benefit from showing up and expressing their feelings (cf. Brooks, 1988, pp. 184-5). An incompetent or opportunistic management team may therefore continue to reign.

By purchasing shares in a limited number of diversified companies a person does not necessarily achieve any increase in her ability to influence the performance of the companies in which she has a stake. However, the person may be choosing to purchase shares in firms whose incumbent management teams have reputations for being able to extract superior perfomances from their assets. Some may be running high-profile conglomerate holding companies that specialise in buying smaller firms, rationalising (asset-stripping?) them and then selling them at a profit. Others may divide their operations into a series of mini-companies, make performance comparisons amongst them and then allocate funds for new investments to those that do well: in effect, the head office of such a company acts as an internal capital market and provides more powerful performance incentives than dispersed individual shareholders could hope to impose on collections of smaller companies in which they choose to hold shares (see Williamson, 1970, 1971, 1975).

Hedging and earnings-smoothing diversification strategies may also be in the interests of teams of senior managers, enabling diversified firms to attract such staff whilst offering less generous terms than specialised firms. But here, too, the basis for such strategies is initially open to question. This is so even though, for a senior manager of a specialised company, the price of a catastrophic mugging in its product market is likely to be the need to find a new job, and despite the possibility that this may also be the price of being a manager in a specialised firm which just goes through a temporary bad spell — an imperfectly informed stock market may undervalue the firm's assets and prompt a successful takeover raid, leading to changes being made in respect of senior personnel. Such managers would be justifiably afraid of losing their jobs, given that they could expect to find themselves competing for alternative positions against others who still had high-ranking positions and would not be asked to explain why their firms failed or why they were 'let go' during a post-takeover rationalisation. A well-conceived strategy of diversification reduces the likelihood that a firm will suffer a major setback to its overall earnings unless there is a general downturn in activity. Hence it is a means by which managers can try to make their positions less vulnerable. However, since such a strategy also has its risks — things may go badly wrong as the managers move into unfamiliar territory —, it is by no means the natural solution to their problem.

In principle, senior managers might conceivably hedge their employment bets in turbulent market environments by dividing their working weeks between several firms, as sometimes happens with non-executive board members and 'blue collar' operatives. In practice, however, employers would be likely to be wary of increasing the sizes of their management teams by hiring senior staff on a part-time basis: this policy could open up considerable scope for managerial confusion unless staff sharing a particular role spent a lot of time making detailed records or briefing each other about what had happened on their latest shift; worse still, a company could suffer as a result of opportunistic behaviour by managers whose loyalties were divided between the various (possibly competing) companies between which they divided their time.

Alternatively, a management team might concentrate on extracting an impressive performance from a specialised set of activities in the hope that they could later raise new funds to tide them through a temporary bad patch or to finance the development and marketing of a new product if they are unlucky enough to be hit by a catastrophic mugging in their present product market. However, they are likely to encounter a problem similar to that which leads those screening job applicants to be biased in favour of those who are presently employed. If the company seeking to raise money is a specialised one that has just suffered catastrophic mugging in its product market, potential suppliers of funds are likely to experience difficulties in deciding whether the company's current misfortunes are the result of bad luck or a lack of foresight on the part of management. Were the latter the case, the company might be one to avoid, for though its management team may profess to be basing their proposals on specialised knowledge they may also be tending to see potential costs and revenues through rose-tinted spectacles. A similar problem arises in respect of companies that are performing poorly at present despite being involved with products whose lifecycles have not entered an obvious stage of terminal decline. Faced with uncertainties about management capabilities, those with funds may prefer to steer clear of such companies and concentrate on ones that are making less grand claims about the potential of their investment plans but which are not presently in difficulties.

In other situations the problem may be that it is difficult to raise venture capital on the open market with out giving too much of one's plans away to potential competitors. By borrowing from bankers instead of raising equity capital managers could achieve greater confidentiality, but this has a cost in the form of higher risks of bankruptcy because interest payments are rather harder to suspend than equity dividends in times of crisis.

Since diversification internalises part of the capital market it provides a means by which a management team can sidestep the need to persuade sceptical new sources to provide funds (or the cost of persuading a merchant bank of doing the persuading on their behalf) and preserve secrecy without taking on additional gearing risks. A diversified firm is able, in the language of strategic marketing theory, to 'milk' its mature 'cash cows' to fund the development and marketing of cash-hungry new products, some of which may take off, turning from 'question marks' into 'star performers'. Management's task is to make sure that enough stars appear and get turned into new cash cows as older cash cows and some question marks turn into 'dogs' and have to be liquidated. If they succeed at this, they can escape a forced return to the labour market (see Earl, 1984, Ch. 1).

However, we must not forget the other strategy by which senior managers can avoid the risks of losing their jobs and the costs of going to the capital market to raise funds each time they run into trouble. As noted earlier, if a specialised firm is earning profits in excess of those required for investment in its existing area of interest, it can use the surplus for portfolio investment rather than paying out larger dividends or diversifying into unfamiliar territory. Then, when it subsequently finds itself needing to change direction or deal with a temporary cashflow problem, it can liquidate some of these investments. Most firms do practice this policy on a limited scale, though few are inclined to accumulate huge mountains of cash — the obvious exception is GEC in the UK (see Williams *et al.*, 1983, pp. 153-7) — because the possibility of achieving higher returns on equities or physical investment may make those that do so seem attractive takeover targets. Their reluctance to use surplus funds to accumulate susbtantial minority equity investments 'for a rainy day' is probably partly because shares have unpredictable values and (much less importantly) because transaction costs must be incurred to dispose of the shares when the rainy day comes. But they may also fear that they could be seen as potential majority shareholders by the companies whose shares they purchase and thereby invite retaliatory corporate acquisitions of their own shares.

It is interesting here to note that in Japan unique institutional circumstances have actually led giant companies to make extensive use of equity holdings as pools of reserve assets. Prior to 1945, the Japanese business scene was dominated by a handful of giant conglomerates — the Zaibatsi — that owned about forty per cent of industry. These firms were broken up by the occupying forces. In their places have emerged loose industrial groupings of related firms that are not formally tied under a particular corporate holding company but which nonetheless see themselves as sharing risks with each other (as in the case of Mitsubishi Manufacturing and the Mitsubishi Bank, which are nowadays separate companies). The share ownership structure involved in these groupings is one that probably would be deemed illegal if practised elsewhere, for 70 per cent of Japanese shareholdings involve one firm owning shares in another and many of the cross-shareholdings are highly incestuous in nature. This unusual concentration of ownership makes it very difficult for outsiders to engineer takeover raids via open market purchases of shares, so management can get on with the business of overseeing the development and marketing of better products without having to worry about short-term profitability. In effect, the companies diversify by holding shares in each other, rather than by diversifying in product markets. When a company needs funds for a major restructuring it sells some of its shares to other companies in its ownership nexus, usually via direct negotiation rather than by placing them on the general market. In this way a Japanese firm can try to conquer its overseas rivals by doing particular things really well and then regrouping to invest in something new if its product comes to the end of its lifecycle or other producers catch up and the going gets too tough.

4.6 Effects of Changes in Interest Rates on the Volume of Investment

In his *General Theory* Keynes (1936, Chs. 11 and 12) presented a pair of seemingly incompatible descriptions of the processes whereby investment decisions are made. On the one hand, he offered his 'animal spirits' view, centred on the overwhelming importance of confidence and dogmatic commitment in the face of irreducible uncertainty. On the other hand, he offered his 'marginal efficiency of capital' view, which seems closely akin to modern techniques of dicounted cashflow and internal rate of return analysis. The former view did not allow changes in the rate of interest to exert much leverage unless they could lead to changes in the states of mind of those involved in investment decision-making. But the latter view has been seen by many economists as pointing to pretty much the same conclusion as its modern counterpart: an investment scheme must offer a rate of return at least as great as the firm's opportunity cost of finance and if its expected value is unattractive at a high rate of interest it may come to seem a gamble worth taking if a lower rate materialises.

Pioneering studies of the impact of interest rate policies on investment were conducted in the late 1930s/early 1940s (the classic project was undertaken by the Oxford Economists' Research Group, many of whose findings are reprinted in Wilson and Andrews, eds, 1951, Ch. 1; see also Andrews and Brunner, 1951). Like subsequent investigations in the 1950s and 1960s they raised doubts in the minds of the first generation of Post Keynesian economists about the impact of interest rate changes on investment. Further doubts arose from studies which revealed how many firms tended to use prospective 'payback periods' of three to five years as criteria when deciding which investments to undertake (see for example Neild, 1964). Such criteria implied exceedingly high discount factors, which firms tried to justify with reference to the risk of their projects only having short lifespans as a result of the rapidity of technological change.

The Post Keynesian belief in the unimportance of interest rates in investment decisions grew stronger still in the 1970s as the emerging literature on the theory of the megacorp stressed the importance of internally generated funds and the importance of new product development as a means of ensuring the long-run survival of these firms. This complemented the findings concerning the shortness of payback periods. If firms aimed to be expanding at, say, 15 per cent a year and faced profits tax rates of 50 per cent, they would need to be earning a rate of return of 30 per cent on their internally generated funds, which would imply a payback period of shortly over three years (see Eichner, 1985, p. 34). If they could dream up investment schemes that offered such returns, they would have no need to enter the external capital market and hence changes in the external cost of funds would exert no direct influence on their investment decisions. In the 1980s the corporate sector in the UK was actually a net lender, failing to undertake enough physical investment to absorb its profits surplus and instead engaging increasingly in portfolio investment.

A strikingly different reason why interest rate changes may have little impact on some investment decisions seems to be implied by studies of differences between strategies of Japanese firms and their rivals in the US and the UK. Whilst many US and UK megacorps have been busily repackaging existing products and processes to generate the short payback periods that will enable them to meet their growth goals without recourse to the external capital market, their Japanese counterparts have been borrowing heavily on a long-term basis to outmanoeuvre them. The Japanese approach rejects both conventional discounted cash flow and payback period methods of investment appraisal on the grounds that they are biased against large scale strategic investments that may take ten years to become a commercial business and then take a further ten years to recoup their original investments (see Williams *et al.*, 1983, pp. 25-7, 72-3). With time horizons as long as this, they will attach little significance to temporary increases in the cost of rolling over debts incurred to permit the pioneering of radically new products or manufacturing processes. The same will hold for firms in other countries that seek to do likewise and can persuade the banking community to give them the kinds of loan horizons that are normally reserved for real estate borrowing.

Despite arguing that both long-term strategic investments and more risk-averse rapid-payback projects may be isolated from changes in the opportunity cost of finance, I think Post Keynesians would be wise to recognise that corporate planners who work with short time horizons may well be lured away from investing in new plant and machinery when real interest rates reach the kinds of levels observed in the 1980s. Where firms do not appear to take a Japanese-style long-term view of investment, it is easy to understand why, like GEC, they may choose to build up cash mountains instead of using their profits streams to finance investment in new assets and technologies: if it is possible to earn a relatively risk-free return of well over 10 per cent in the money market and at a later date use the proceeds to buy into processes that others have pioneered, and if physical investment would have to involve moves into unfamiliar territory, then why bother with the latter?

Post Keynesians should also now be more willing to concede that interest rate changes may exert a considerable indirect influence via their impacts upon firms' assessments of their potential markets or upon the cashflows that their existing investments are generating. Even if higher interest rates do not lead to a reduction in consumer spending (see section 3.7), firms may still find that the amount of cash they have available for investment is reduced because of the greater cost involved in servicing any existing corporate borrowings. This may lead to some projects being delayed if firms are afraid of increasing their gearing ratios and hence resist the idea of borrowing more to cover the investment funding shortfall caused by reductions in their retained earnings. Worse still, rises in interest rates may lead to a strengthening of the country's exchange rate and hence make it more difficult for domestic manufacturers to price their goods at viable levels in the face of foreign competition. This factor is difficult to ignore given the squeals of anguish from corporate sector representatives in the UK (1980-1), the US (1984-6), New Zealand (1984-8) and Australia (1988-9) when high interest rate policies were pursued regardless of their impacts upon exchange rates.

4.7 Conclusion

This chapter has had little to say on the processes whereby managers form their expectations about the possible outcomes of their complex pricing and investment decisions. I have been assuming that readers will be keeping in mind the material from Chapter 3, particularly the idea that decision-makers cope with life with the aid of systems of rules. (I have elsewhere provided more detailed accounts of the role of such systems in the context of corporate decision-making: see Earl, 1984, 1987.) However, the chapter has been rather unusual in the amount of attention that has been devoted to corporate decisions concerning vertical integration and horizontal diversification. Partly this is because the material will be employed in Chapter 8 in an investigation of the economics of financial intermediation and recent structural changes in the financial services industry. But I also believe it is important to focus attention on the various strategies by which corporate managers may seek to meet their goals because these alternatives have different macroeconomic implications.

There is an unfortunate tendency amongst economists to discuss investment decisions as if they affect only the level of aggregate demand through the purchase of new plant and machinery or expenditure on research and development. In so far as managers choose policies of expansion that involve combining their operations with those of other companies they may be raising external finance — possibly at the expense of less well-established firms that would dearly have liked to be able to borrow money to finance expenditure on brand-new assets and research programmes — without doing anything directly to add to employment. They may even end up shedding labour if they subsequently engage in policies of rationalisation to achieve synergy. Other methods of expansion involving the exchange of existing assets can only exert an indirect influence on the demand for labour, one that may take longer to materialise if indeed it does. When firms finance takeovers by borrowing from the banking system, much of the money that they spend on purchasing shares in their victim companies may get respent elsewhere in the stockmarket, helping to drive up share prices in general. The higher that share prices rise, the less attractive become internalisation schemes involving mergers, so some firms may be induced to expand by purchasing new physical assets instead. Some of those who sell shares as their prices increase may chose to spend capital gains on consumption.

5 Portfolio Choices of Governments

5.1 Introduction

As they form their spending plans, decision-makers in the private sector would often be wise to try to take account of likely changes in government policies — just as public sector decision-makers would be wise to try to anticipate changes in the behaviour of those in the private sector. For example, if a sharp and sustained rise in interest rates seemed imminent, it would be rather foolish for consumers to commit themselves to mortgages that they could barely afford and whose terms could not be increased in the event of higher interest rates to keep monthly payments constant. Nor would one want to be holding long-dated government securities if interest rates rose, because a capital loss would be entailed. But public sector decision-makers would be unwise to go about engineering such a rise in the price of money if they knew that the private sector was starting to have doubts about the wisdom of continuing to spend at the current rate. Both groups would also be wise to take account of foreseeable changes in any other variables that would affect the desirability of their choices. In so far as they recognised that they could be surprised by the the behaviour of these variables and by the actions of other decision-makers, they would have a reason for leaving themselves some room for manoeuvre.

Neoclassical economists have tended in recent years to construct their models around the 'as if' assumption that private sector decision-makers generally do take account of likely changes in government policy and are successful in their attempts to infer from past observations how governments tend to react to particular kinds of unexpected exogenous shocks or in the face of surprising private sector behaviour. Having made this assumption, they have found it hard to avoid the implication that government policies only have any impact upon the system if they cause surprise to people in other sectors. For example, suppose the members of the private sector have

92

discovered that there is a particular functional relationship between increases in the monthly balance of payments deficit and increases in interest rates. Unexpectedly bad balance of payments figures will be a cue for the private sector to expect a particular increase in the rate of interest and, in so far as their willingness to spend is a function of the rate of interest, they will adapt their spending plans accordingly. Spending will fall before the government actually gets around to raising interest rates. When the increase actually happens, there will be no change in private sector behaviour unless the magnitude of the increase is different from what has been expected.

The extent to which private sector decision-makers do in fact seek to predict government behaviour and make their own choices contingent on these predictions is an empirical question to which behavioural research may help provide an answer. So too is the question of the accuracy of private sector predictions of government behaviour. In so far as neoclassical assumptions do *not* hold one would expect changes in government policy to be followed by changes in private sector behaviour.

In some respects, the task of predicting the choices of government ministers is easier than that of predicting the behaviour of consumers and firms, for in their efforts to win votes political parties espouse aspects of the philosophies that they have developed as means of coping with a complex world. They debate their views publicly at conferences and their members give interviews with journalists who seek to uncover any hidden agendas in their speeches and manifestos. Sometimes, they even make public the forecasting models that their advisors are using (for example, the UK Treasury model). They often state their goals, along with the methods that they plan to use to attain them and the methods that they intend not to use. However, they tend to be wary about spelling out their aims in numerical terms, since by specifying something precise they may leave themselves open to criticisms of failure if the outcome falls short of the target.

This chapter examines factors that complicate the making of government policy and which should therefore be borne in mind by anyone attempting to predict government behaviour. It begins by looking at the effects of bounded rationality and then moves on to consider the role of the 'vote motive', the relationship between a government and its reserve bank, and debates about the extent to which public expenditure increases displace private sector expenditure rather than promoting increases in output and employment.

5.2 Bounded Rationality and Public Policy

In neoclassical theories of public choice, a government is typically portrayed as trying to maximise a particular utility function that involves trade-offs between particular social and economic indicators in which voters are thought to be interested. Behavioural theory, by contrast, sees the political arena as one in which carefully considered acts of constrained optimisation are particularly unlikely to be the order of the day. It is a turbulent environment in which there is constant pressure for the rapid resolution of complex problems, a place in which a week is a long time and which should be avoided by those who cannot stand the relentless heat. Those who choose to inhabit it must compete not merely with members of rival parties but also with members of their own party who aspire to positions of greater power. In doing so, they face acute problems of bounded rationality — hence the claim of Steinbruner (1974, p. 327) that 'Decision processes based on fundamental operations of the human mind are critical to understanding the behaviour of governments and consequently the determination of political events.'

Whilst out of office, politicians may be unable to obtain much of the information that they require for planning the implementation of their party's policies. Their overriding concern is with winning power, so they will tend to spend the bulk of their time criticising the incumbent government. If their party wins an election and they are given ministerial responsibilities they will find themselves being criticised by their peers if they do nothing to alter the policies of their predecessors, and criticised by the opposition for any policies they do implement. Given that they are likely to be moved to other positions after a relatively short period, they have an incentive to pursue policies that have a conspicuous short-term effect, rather than ones which bear fruit over a much longer period in a more subtle way and for which they will find it harder to obtain recognition. But, as the satirical BBC series *Yes Minister* has emphasised, they may have to contend with public servants who are supposed to be their advisors but who resist changes because they are working with longer time horizons and wish to avoid upheavals that may be reversed by a subsequent change of government. Once ministers are promoted or demoted to another portfolio they may find that their hard-won experience is of limited further use.

Bounded rationality makes the segmentation of government into ministerial departments necessary as a means to overcome information overload. However, information overload is reduced only at the cost of a failure to take account of feedback linkages between the activities of rival ministries: for example, one department may be subsidising transport costs of commuters while another is trying to encourage out-of-town office relocation. Problems continually surface owing to the tendency of ministers to engage in 'fire-fighting' behaviour in their own domains rather than getting together to work out a coordinated set of microeconomic policies.

When government ministers get together in cabinet to discuss matters of economic policy, they will normally be arguing about the implications of figures referring to events several months before that have only recently become available. In discussing changes in macroeconomic variables, they are likely to follow the tendency of theorists to keep things simple by failing to consider the sectoral patterns that underlie aggregate figures. Matters can be further simplified if, instead of defining a welfare function with specific policy trade-offs, they talk in terms of separate targets for the variables in question — for example, an acceptable inflation rate, unemployment rate, growth rate and balance of payments deficit (cf. the characteristic filtering approach to choice, discussed in section 3.4). In some situations, policy instruments may get treated as if they are ends in themselves — note, for example, the obsession of some politicians with targets for the public sector deficit or the growth of particular monetary aggregates. The relative sizes of targets are the outcome of bargaining between different groups in the policy-making circle, who have conflicting interests and/or different perceptions of the electoral implications of aiming to meet particular goals.

Satisficing theory predicts that such decision-makers will adopt the attitude that 'if it works, don't mess with it' in respect of any variables that are not judged to be falling short of their targets. Instead, their focus will be on any targets that are generating cause for concern because they have not been met sufficiently recently and/or seem unlikely to be met in the near future. Rather different standards may be demanded by opposition politicians and by the media, leading to claims that the government is failing to recognise that a crisis exists. How long ministers will take to face up to the need to do something may depend on whether they see action as involving a threat to their credibility because of past statements they have made that rule out the use of particular policy weapons. (One might call this the 'sacred cow syndrome' — a famous example of it was the reluctance of the Wilson government to face up to the need for a devaluation of the pound in 1967.) As time passes, it may become easier to go back on one's word, owing to the short memories of voters and the opposition.

When action has been delayed so long as to produce an atmosphere of crisis, one would not expect a careful consideration of interdependencies between the crisis variable and those that are presently performing satisfactorily. Nor would one expect policy instruments to be applied in a particularly subtle manner. Rather, as Mosley (1976, p. 60) has pointed out, there is likely to be a tendency to adopt a sledgehammer approach. He notes the following comment from the Radcliffe Report (1959, pp. 150-1, para. 434):

When restrictive action has been thought necessary, the inclination [of the British authorities] has been to make a general call for restraint, and to announce several restrictive measures together, or almost together, normally a rise in Bank Rate, stern words on bank advances, hire purchase controls and a pruning of capital programmes in the public sector — all at once.

Hence measures may be taken to bring one target variable back on course despite their adverse spill-over implications for other targets. Through this procedure of 'giving sequential attention to goals' (as it is termed by Cyert and March, 1963), a government may lurch from one focus to another and seem to go round in circles.

The appeal of a doctrine such as monetarism is easy to understand in a world in which complexity makes it difficult to fathom how to use discretionary policies successfully to resolve conflicting economic objectives. Monetarist thinking portrays price stability as a prerequisite for investment in productive capacity and denies the existence of any trade-offs between unemployment and inflation in the long run. Working on the presumption that economies are stable unless disturbed by government intervention, and that inflation is always the result of growth in the money supply being induced to run ahead of growth in physical capacity, monetarism involves the application of a simple rule relating monetary growth to the underlying growth of productive potential in the economy. It greatly simplifies the task facing policymakers and provides a means whereby they can justify focusing on other issues in the face of mounting unemployment. Monetarists could even try to justify their policies by stressing that since adherence to a money-growth rule enables them to reach decisions without processing the much larger volumes of information required for policies involving discretionary intervention, they will be less likely to make information processing errors (cf. Heiner, 1986, pp. 328-9). Unfortunately, as is shown in later chapters, monetarism achieves its simplicity as a result of being built on some very naive foundations.

5.3 Politics and Macroeconomic Management

The possibility that politicians may choose fiscal and monetary policies with an eye to their electoral consequences has been raised on a number of occasions (for example, Nordhaus, 1975; Lindbeck, 1976; and Macrae, 1977). This section presents a behavioural view of political business cycles, centred on a consideration of parallels between the processes involved in winning votes and the right to govern, and the process of competition between oligopolistic firms.

An incumbent party must maintain the goodwill of the voting population if it is to stay in office. The opposition will usually be asking voters to switch in favour of a 'new, improved', set of policies, having revamped its platform following a post mortem on its previous defeat, whereas the electorate will have experience of the results of the governing party's policies. This is important, since voters cannot compare rival political offerings on a trial basis and then make up their minds. Rather, they are asked to make reasonably long-term commitments to competing 'products' that are complex — so complex that not even experts will normally agree on their abilities to live up to their proponents' claims. Hence so long as voters do not feel dissatisfied with what they perceive to be the impact of the incumbent party's policies they may be difficult to seduce via promises from the opposition that they could do rather better.

How badly the economy as a whole will have to be performing before a government will wreck its chances of re-election may be expected to depend very much upon the distribution of economic misery and the means by which voters in general set their aspirations. Consider an economy in which unemployment has been rising and a government preaching the long-run benefits of a policy of economic rationalism has been slashing expenditure on social services. Even mass unemployment is usually a problem facing the minority. For the majority who have jobs, the experience of life in such a period of macroeconomic stagnation may be one of rising living standards because they are not feeling the effects of cutbacks in social programmes and are instead enjoying the benefits of reduced marginal rates of income tax that have been introduced supposedly to improve the incentive to work and take risks. Fear of joining the ranks of the unemployed may make them moderate their pay demands, but so long as their relations and close friends are not out of work and some kind of safety net exists for the poor and jobless, they may feel little compunction as they vote for a continuation of such policies.

The unemployment rate that a government achieves may of course be seen as indicating something about its general competence in economic management and therefore be of concern to voters even if they do not feel their own jobs are particularly at risk. But the benchmarks that voters use in judging the performance of their elected representatives are likely to vary through time, partly because their aspirations will tend to adjust into line with what seems feasible. For example, in the UK in the early 1970s the figure of one million unemployed was viewed with alarm; by the 1980s, however, people seemed to have grown used to recorded unemployment of three times this size and it was difficult to find even the opposition parties suggesting that there was much hope of bringing the figure down to one million in the short-term. Meanwhile, in Australia, the Labor government could concede that late 1980s unemployment rates in excess of 7 per cent were far worse than the 1.5 to 3 per cent rates of the 1960s and yet claim to be doing rather well by comparison with even worse figures being recorded in the UK and New Zealand.

When attainments change for the worse, aspirations will take time to adjust into line with them unless there is immediate agreement that there are good reasons for believing it would be very difficult to do any better. A sharp downturn that has only lately materialised may therefore pose more of a problem than continuing stagnation to a government with an approaching election deadline: voters will not yet be resigned to a decline in their prosperity. This may tempt the ruling party into pursuing policies that will lead to a rapid improvement in the fortunes of the economy despite being inconsistent with what the party would regard as good long-term management. So long as the harmful effects of policies aimed at generating a pre-election boom do not become conspicuous until after the election, and so long as the bounded rationality of voters is such that they fail to 'see through' the strategy, the government may be able to get its victory, after which it can rein in the economy.

There are a number of aspects of democratic systems which make it rather dangerous for a government to engineer a political business cycle. It is clearly in the interests of the opposition parties to alert voters to any opportunistic moves that the government is making. (Margaret Thatcher's success might be taken to imply that there are even votes to be won from a demonstration that one *is* choosing policies for their supposed long-run advantages despite their conspicuous short-run costs.) Working against this, and in favour of implicit collusion by major parties, would be any worries held by major opposition parties that they could be exposed as having pursued precisely such strategies when they were in office. In the long-run, however, opportunistic policies of alternating major parties are likely to be exposed by emerging minor parties whose reputations are untainted in this way because they have never been in office. Minor parties have the same role in the market for votes as that served by potential entrants in industrial markets: as the then senator and leader of the Australian Democrats Don Chipp once observed, their presence serves 'to keep the bastards honest'. In countries with coalition governments there is a further competitive restraint on the pursuit of opportunistic macroeconomic policies. The point here is that 'since coalition members will be competing against each other in the next election, at least one of them stands to benefit by blaming any undesirable development on one of its partners. Usually the larger partner will be responsible for economic policy. In this situation the smaller party (in Germany the FDP) could only gain by informing voters about its partner's "unsound" behaviour' (Dinkel, 1981, p. 228).

Such considerations make it unsurprising that, in his study of the making of macroeconomic policy in the UK and the US, Mosley (1984, Ch. 7) did not find much evidence of *overt* pre-election policies aimed at raising disposable income: a tax-cutting budget close to election time could be expected to be seen as an insult to the intelligence of voters. Nonetheless Mosley did find evidence that incumbent parties tended to adopt more invisible kinds of approaches to macroeconomic stimulation in the run-up to an election. This, too, should not be surprising. Given the disagreements amongst professional economists and other commentators about the effects of any macroeconomic stance, governments could vigorously deny that their policies were aimed at securing electoral success regardless of longer-run consequences for the economy. As Mosley (1984, p. 190) observes, 'Amidst such a cacophany of discordant voices, it is crazy to expect voters, however educated, to come to a unanimous or "rational" judgement about what the effects of a pre-election boost will be and punish the government for its "irresponsibility".' The case of Australia presents a contrasting picture, of governments acting with blatant electoral cynicism via policies aimed at 'the hip pocket nerve' of the potential floating voter. The work of Gruen (1985) rather suggests that governments in Australia have seen the typical voter as myopic, materialistic and politically unsophisticated; they have often given tax cuts in August, to come into effect in November, apparently hoping that their generosity would be remembered in December elections. Given this, it is not surprising that minor parties such as the Democrats have recently emerged.

Whether expansionary maroeconomic policies are engineered for political reasons or out of a genuine belief that they are needed to prevent unemployment, they will normally be more popular both with voters and with ministers holding non-financial portfolios than will policies aimed at reducing aggregate demand. Buchanan and others have extended this line of thought to argue that a Keynesian approach to economic management is unworkable in a democratic system: political pressures will ensure it is applied asymmetrically, producing a bias toward budget deficits, monetary expansion, public sector growth and inflation (see Buchanan and Wagner, 1977; Buchanan *et al.*, 1978). The removal of a balanced budget constraint enables politicians to avoid confronting some difficult trade-offs. Ministers with non-financial portfolios will welcome expansionary fiscal policies, for these will provide opportunities for them to increase their commands over resources and hence enhance their reputations and influence. But those with non-financial portfolios will steadfastly resist cuts in their budgets when finance ministers are looking for ways of dampening down expenditure growth without increasing taxes. (A good illustration of these pressures occurred in Australia while this chapter was being written: in March 1989, the finance minister, Senator Peter Walsh, asked to resign because he was finding it too exhausting trying to get his colleagues to agree to expenditure cuts.) In so far as finance ministers win neither expenditure cuts nor tax increases, and in so far as a tight monetary policy proves a relatively ineffective substitute for restraining aggregate demand, the failure to eliminate macroeconomic overheating may lead to inflation and/or balance of payments difficulties. In so far as the public sector deficit is reduced by tax increases rather than by cuts in public expenditure, the economy may suffer in the long run due to distorted patterns of incentives, while if workers successfully push for higher money wages in an attempt to resist the reductions in their real wages, inflation may persist despite the reductions in aggregate demand.

Since Buchanan and Wagner published their critique of interventionist macroeconomic policy many politicians have sought to win votes by preaching policies of 'sound finance' that have often been built around simple balanced budget rules. Though such a switch of opinion first seems at odds with the predictions of 'public-choice' analysis, the message is one to which voters have been encouraged to relate in terms of parallels with their own financial positions. (Here, Charles Dickens' fictional character Mr Micawber may have a lot to answer for!) In the US, moreover, in contrast to the UK and Australia, the successful preaching of such policies in the 1980s was followed in practice by record budget deficits — much as Buchanan and Wagner would predict.

A somewhat similar but more complex scenario concerning the difficulties of reconciling demand management policies and democratic pressures was independently developed in the UK by Bacon and Eltis (1978). Their focus is on how the kinds of reflationary packages that governments tend to prefer lead to a cumulative decline in the ability of a country to generate a satisfactory balance of payments performance. They argue that ministers prefer to see unemployment tackled not by cuts in taxes but by expansions of public sector employment which raise both the socal wage and the resources at their command. Reflationary packages thus tend to increase the share of non-marketed output in the economy, absorbing workers who demand imports but are now no longer readily available to the marketed goods sector to produce exports and import substitutes. The reduced availability of resouces to the market sector ensures that, as incomes rise, imports are sucked into the economy in far larger volumes than were recorded during the previous upturn. To deal with the balance of payments crisis, the government curtails demand by raising taxes rather than by cutting public sector non-market employment. Workers resist this threat to their living standards (after failing to make any allowance for the enhanced social wage), and attempt to pass the burden on to firms. Unfortunately, the pressure of foreign competition prevents firms from retaliating fully with higher prices. The resulting profits squeeze leads to a cutback in investment, reduced international competitiveness and smaller domestic capacity growth. Rising unemployment brings with it some improvement in

101

the balance of payments that disguises the declining long-term position. The government then reacts with a reflation that further increases the size of the non-market sector, and so on.

The Bacon and Eltis thesis has been criticised with respect to its neglect of the way in which some so-called 'non-market' activities, such as education, may affect the performance of the 'market' sector. Empirical question marks have also been raised: for example, in the case of the UK during the 1960s/early 1970s, female 'non-market' employment increased while male 'market' employment declined, and although pre-tax profits had fallen substantially the same could not be said of post-tax profits. Despite these criticisms, and despite the willingness of right-wing governments to set about cutting the social wage during the 1980s, the Bacon and Eltis scenario seems to warrant serious attention as a pointer to what could happen in the event of a leftward swing in political preferences.

5.4 The Reserve Bank and the Financing of Public Sector Deficits

Whether or not public sector deficits arise through the pursuit of political self-interest, they somehow must be financed. Governments have three financing modes at their disposal. Like consumers and firms, they can raise money by selling some of their existing assets; they can create new claims on themselves and sell these IOUs; or they can borrow from their bankers.

The first option, labelled as 'privatisation', has attracted much interest in recent years owing to the rightward shift in political preferences. In the UK and New Zealand, privatisation provided a major source of funds for public sector spending while income taxes were being reduced in the second half of the 1980s. Since it is difficult to sell state-owned assets to the private sector unless they seem to have a positive present value, it is easy to construe such policies as short-term political expedients in terms of their ability to reduce government borrowing. However, governments in both countries may have taken the view that, after a short lag, tax revenues would rise due to the incentive effects of lower marginal rates and may have believed that these revenues would more than offset the foregone returns from the sale of profitable state enterprises. Further grounds for taking a rather less cynical view are contained in the transactions cost analysis of vertical integration discussed in section

4.4. It may be possible to float loss-making state enterprises as private companies because it is expected that such a redrawing of legal boundaries will have a positive effect on incentives, attenuating tendencies towards opportunistic behaviour. For example, people may be prepared to buy shares in the newly privatised enterprises in the belief that changes in work practices will be introduced, bringing productivity improvements that otherwise would have been politically impossible to achieve. They may also expect that management will be much more likely to develop new markets and products once they have to ensure that their organisations can 'stand on their own feet'.

The other, more frequently employed options both involve the reserve bank of the country in question. Such a bank is in many respects identical to a commercial bank; indeed it might not even be a nationalised institution — the Bank of England, for example, was founded as a private company in 1694 and it was only in 1946 that its ownership was transferred to the UK Treasury. One conspicuous difference concerns the composition of a typical reserve bank's assets and liabilities, since it does not deal with consumers (aside from its employees) or non-financial firms and even limits its loans to the financial sector to only a select few institutions. Its assets consist of government securities, loans to other banks and other securities that it has purchased from them, its holdings of gold, its net claims on its overseas counterparts — in other words, the country's official foreign exchange reserves — and its physical capital. Its liabilities consist of what is commonly called the 'supply of high-powered money' (or the 'monetary base'), in other words, notes and coin in the hands of the public and vaults of financial institutions, various kinds of deposits made by banks and other financial institutions, and claims on it by its overseas counterparts. Its net assets or 'reserves' are funds that it has accumulated on its own account from its retained profits. These can be written up or down in the event of gains or losses in respect of the value of any of its assets (the significance of reserves in bank balance sheets is discussed in detail in section 8.2).

If a reserve bank wishes to purchase government securities on the open market in a bid to keep their prices from falling and interest rates from rising, it pays for the additional assets with cheques drawn on itself. If the securities have been sold by members of the non-bank private sector, they will deposit these cheques with their banks and the latter will then present them to the reserve bank. Alternatively, the banks themselves may receive the cheques directly as a result of selling assets to the reserve bank. Either way, liabilities of the reserve bank will rise by an amount equal to the value of the securities it has purchased as it honours the cheques by crediting the accounts of the commercial banks that have presented them for payment.

When the government borrows funds from the private sector, the role of the reserve bank is akin to that of a merchant bank acting on behalf of a company that wishes to float a new share issue. It handles the sale of the new securities, either at a pre-specified price or by calling for tenders. In the former case it stands ready to purchase those which do not find a market at the offer price. In the latter case it may undertake 'open market' purchases of government stock on its own account if the tender bids are disappointing and the effective yield required by the market is too high to be compatible with its policy on interest rates. If the demand for government securities from wealthy individuals, firms and private sector financial institutions is such that the reserve bank does not take on any extra government securities, the financing of the government's deficit has no direct impact upon the supply of high-powered money. Those who are purchasing government securities will write out cheques drawn against their bank accounts; these will be paid into government accounts at the reserve bank and debited from the accounts of the security purchasers' banks at the reserve bank. When the government spends the proceeds, it will pay by issuing cheques drawn against its accounts at the reserve bank. Recipients will pay them into their bank accounts, leading to a transfer of deposits at the reserve bank from government accounts to bankers' balances, or they will cash them, causing government balances at the reserve bank to fall and the volume of notes and coin in circulation to rise.

Some of the borrowed funds may originate overseas, as may some of the demand for shares in ventures that are being privatised. In both cases foreign currency holdings will be exchanged for domestic currency. This will not have a direct impact upon domestic bank deposits if the overseas lenders are trying to buy the domestic currency to pay for their claims on the government at the same rate as domestic traders are trying to sell an identical amount of it to raise foreign currency to pay for a surplus of imports over exports or to facilitate net lending overseas. However, if the overseas fund-raising by the government exceeds the private sector's overseas deficit in the period in question, then there will be an upward pressure on the value of the domestic currency. Matters then become more complicated: they are dealt with in section 6.3.

If the reserve bank does step in and purchase securities in its role as underwriter of a new government loan issue, then it is increasing its lending to the government just as surely as in a situation in which no attempt is made to sell new government securities to the private sector and it simply 'prints money' to finance the deficit. Its assets rise by the amount of the extra government securites that it accepts but so, too, do its liabilities: it credits the government's account with an identical amount of additional deposits, against which the government draws cheques to pay for transfer payments or expenditure on goods and services.

In the light of the discussion in the previous section, it seems appropriate to end this section by considering whether a reserve bank is likely to act as a bastion of integrity in the face of what its experts see as a politically motivated fiscal policy. In principle, for example, it could try to use a restrictive monetary policy to counter an overly expansionary fiscal policy. In practice, however, its management might find it difficult to act independently if they felt they were likely to be caught in the act and then punished by the government. Compared with thirty years ago reserve banks have little chance of pursuing independent monetary policies without being detected: the growth of expertise on monetary economics in finance ministries and academia makes it harder for them to argue that no one else has the practical experience to manage financial markets and make definitive statements on the impact of monetary policy on aggregate demand (Moran, 1984, pp. 26-7). This may make a government more inclined to exploit any constitutional powers it possesses to issue directions to the management of its reserve bank or dismiss the governor and other board members and replace them with its own nominees.

The conditions under which the reserve bank governor is appointed may be such as to prevent a government from disposing of a recalcitrant incumbent as and when it suits them. If the governor is appointed for a guaranteed term of, say, five years, as in the case of the Bank of England, an incoming government with new views on macroeconomic policy may have to live for quite a while with a governor appointed by its predecessors. Such a governor is particularly likely to uphold the independence of reserve bank policy if he or she is coming up to retiring age and has no intention of seeking a renewal of the contract. It should also be recognised that when a government exercises the opportunity to make a politically suitable appointment it may run into disagreements with the appointee once an initial honeymoon period is over. An excellent case study of the evolving relationships between Margaret Thatcher and

105

governors of the Bank of England has been provided by Reid (1988, Ch. 10): it makes clear that personality factors, and not just legal boundaries, played a crucial role in determining the influence of the Bank through time.

In some countries it is difficult for the government to give directions without taking the risk that it will end up in a very public debate about its motives. In Australia, for example, the Federal Government can only force a policy upon the Reserve Bank after going through the formal procedure of tabling both its order and the Reserve Bank's reply in Parliament. No government has ever taken this step. This was something that both the Government and the Reserve Bank could point out to defend themselves early in 1989 when the Bank was accused by members of the parliamentary opposition of delaying necessary interest rate increases in order to assist the chances of the ruling Labor party in impeding elections in 'mortgage belt' constituencies.

Despite the presence of such checks on government interference, those who make policy decisions at a reserve bank may sometimes find it hard not to take careful note of the possibility that the government may opt to change the law if its existing powers seem insufficient to guarantee the kind of monetary policies desired by the majority of politicians. It is therefore no wonder that in their 'public choice' critique of the practice of Keynesian demand management policies Buchanan and Wagner (1977, pp. 122-3) looked with horror at proposals to reduce the independence of the US Federal Reserve Board: early in 1976 the House of Representatives passed a measure which, if it became law, would make the term of the Board chairman coincide with that of the US president, add 'public' members to boards of regional Federal Reserve Banks and direct the Board to adopt the objectives specified in the Full Employment Act of 1946.

5.5 Crowding Out

Many of those who have advocated balanced budgets have begun their cases by raising the possibility that increases in government expenditure may displace private expenditure that otherwise would have taken place. They have jumped from this starting point to the conclusion that fiscal policy is not an effective device for dealing with unemployment. The alleged displacement effects of deficit-financed public spending have been the subject of an extensive theoretical and empirical literature that goes under the heading of 'crowding out' (for an excellent review, see Arestis, 1985).

The crowding out of one sector's expenditures by the expenditures of another sector can arise in respect of financial and/or physical resources. The Bacon and Eltis theory, discussed in section 5.3, involves both forms, though the kind of financial crowding out it entails is rather unusual: it arises when the government seeks to *deflate* the boom it has engineered and workers bring about a profits squeeze through their attempts to maintain their real incomes in the face of tax increases. During the depression of the 1930s, a fear of financial crowding out was widespread in official circles in the UK. It led Keynes to experience much resistance to his proposals for creating more jobs. The 'Treasury View' held that public works programmes could not increase prosperity because there was a fixed amount of saving (given the level of interest rates) from which investment could be financed, public investment would either displace private investment or private consumption. In his critique of this analysis Keynes (1937a) pointed to a fundamental confusion between the concepts of saving and finance. If an increase in public sector investment could somehow be engineered without crowding out private sector expenditure it would of necessity create an equal flow of savings that might be used to finance subsequent rounds of spending (see section 10.3 for a numerical example). However, Keynes conceded that government spending might cause 'congestion' in financial markets if people were unwilling to part with liquidity by exchanging their bank deposits for public sector securities. If people could be induced by a rise in interest rates to use their spare bank deposits to purchase government debt, there was a risk that private sector expenditure might be reduced owing to some of the demand for such securities coming from people who otherwise would have used their money to purchase goods and services or securities issued by the corporate sector.

Financial crowding out is unlikely to be very important unless the economy is characterised by the kinds of conditions which make it likely that private sector expenditure will be very responsive to increases in interest rates (see sections 3.7 and 4.5). Nor should we predict it to be significant if the financial community does not expect increasing borrowing by the public sector to be associated with a rise in interest rates. If increases in interest rates are expected by those who hold long-dated government securities, they would be wise to switch into deposits with financial institutions, while those who might otherwise have been willing to purchase government securities to obtain a higher yield than is available on deposits would be wise to stay where they are. If acted upon, such expectations will tend to be self-fulfilling. When no such fears are harboured, higher volumes of public sector borrowing are unlikely to be associated with substantial increases in interest rates: the Post Keynesian analysis of the working of financial markets (discussed in Chapter 9) suggests that any diversion of funds away from the financing of private sector expenditure is likely to lead to alternative sources of finance being tapped for a relatively low increase in borrowing costs.

When financial crowding out does appears likely to dampen the impact of an expansionary fiscal policy, it may be countered by a variety of means. The government could undertake a bigger net increase in expenditure, or finance a larger part of its deficit by borrowing from the reserve bank. Policy-makers could also think seriously about financing a larger part of the public sector deficit with short-term bonds: these should be easier to sell than long-dated stock because they involve minimal capital risks and corporate treasurers are likely to treat them as very close substitutes for deposits in money markets. It may even be possible to manage the expectations of speculators by announcing that the reserve bank will be standing by to counteract any tendency for interest rates to rise as a result of the government deficit. Those who believe the announcement will be able to purchase or continue to hold long-dated government securities without fear of possible capital losses despite the impending increase in their supply. If the announcement is widely believed, there should be no need for the reserve bank actually to step in and purchase unwanted government stock to prevent interest rates from rising.

A more sophisticated critique of the expansionary power of public sector deficits was offered by Barro (1974), as a modern day reincarnation of an old idea from Ricardo with an added rational expectations twist. He suggested that people would notice that higher levels of government expenditure were being financed by government borrowing and infer that taxes would be higher in future to permit repayments. People who drew such inferences would then cut back current consumption so that their living standards did not fall so much in future: they could run down their savings as taxes increased. Some people might indeed behave like this, but so far little evidence has been produced to suggest that this is what most do. The lack of empirical support comes as no surprise to Post Keynesian economists who doubt that everyone uses a neoclassical macroeconomic model when forming their expectations, and who dispute the assumption that consumers normally have a good idea of the fiscal stance of their governments. If many people are unaware than an expansionary fiscal policy has been implemented, it is possible that that consumption expenditure will actually be crowded in: consumers may observe greater prosperity and start assuming that their living standards are going to be permanently higher or that their chances of losing their jobs in the near future have fallen. Here is another debate whose resolution may be aided by behavioural research on how people make up their minds.

5.6 Conclusion

The development of macroeconomic theory and model building techniques led early Keynesians to expect that governments would be able and willing to eliminate business cycles by 'fine-tuning' their net expenditure levels and financing modes to offset changes in corporate and consumer behaviour at home and in international markets. The modern Post Keynesian, armed with ideas from behavioural theory and public choice analysis, has much less cause for optimism. Even if governments are not worried about impending elections, their policies are likely to differ substantially from those that an omniscient, disinterested economic advisor would recommend. They will be often be surprised by shifts in macroeconomic indicators and will be beset with acute and unavoidable bounded rationality as they try to make sense of data that they can only collect and collate with a lag. Hence any attempts they make at macroeconomic management will tend either to be essentially reactive and prone to exacerbate fluctuations or will involve something of a leap in the dark based on 'animal spirits'.

One way for economists to react to this is to follow subjectivists of the 'Austrian' school and urge the abandonment of interventionist philosophies. But this seems an inappropriate direction to take if one believes that macroeconomic systems lack self-stabilising tendencies and that economic advisors can use scenario planning to help reduce the frequency with which their political paymasters find themselves being surprised by economic events.

6 International Trade and Capital Flows

6.1 Introduction

What happens in the international accounts of a country depends on decisions taken by consumers, firms and public sector bodies in the country in question and elsewhere in the world. In a sense, therefore, much of what we need to know about the underlying causes of a country's evolving economic relationship with the rest of the world has already been dealt with in Chapters 3, 4 and 5. For example, theories of consumer choice employed to analyse savings behaviour might just as well have been employed to understand decisions about whether or not to spend money on imported products rather than items that have been made locally. Similarly, the transactions cost theory of corporate strategy may help us understand why some firms choose to set up overseas subsidiaries or purchase an existing company overseas rather than making contracts with companies overseas for the supply of imported inputs or the distribution of exported outputs (see also section 8.6, where these ideas are applied to multinational banking). Such decisions will entail capital outflows from the multinational firms' base countries and capital inflows for the host countries. In later years, if profits are repatriated to the multinationals' head offices, the 'invisibles' parts of host country current accounts will record debit entries.

Some of this chapter may certainly be construed as doing little more than stating implications of analysis in earlier chapters, but I hope this will be useful to readers who might not immediately be able to see for themselves the relevance of some of these ideas to, say, non-price and strategic aspects of international trade. However, much of the chapter is preoccupied with two other issues. One of these is the fact that international transactions normally involve more than one currency, and economists remain divided about what might be the most appropriate way to determine exchange rates. The other is that although international accounts are set up so that they always net

110

out to zero, it is not guaranteed that the means employed in one year to ensure this happens can be employed in later years, owing to interactions between current and capital accounts and changes in perceptions of the wisdom of extending loans to a particular economy.

6.2 The Determination of Exports, Imports and Capital Flows

It is conventional to portray the export revenues of a country as being unaffected by the strength of its domestic demand. Changes in export revenues are thus seen as being dependent on changes in the level of economic activity overseas and on changes in international competitive conditions. This view appears to ignore the possibility that a rise in domestic demand may mean that firms are not driven to try to expand their exports, when otherwise they might have done so in order to meet their sales targets. However, the conventional assumption looks more acceptable once we recall the discussions in section 4.2 concerning the role of goodwill as a determinant of market shares: export markets cannot usually be built up overnight — distribution networks must be established, 'red tape' overcome and customer confidence created — and they will not lightly be neglected merely because home demand has suddenly gone up.

Although it is possible that a history of depressed domestic demand could lead firms to attempt to meet their aspirations by making a sustained effort to build up their markets overseas, it seems more likely that, in the long run, growth in export revenue is actually positively related to growth in domestic demand. For example, if we contrast the sluggish performances of the UK and the US in the 1960s and 1970s with the dynamic ones of, say, West Germany and Japan, it is difficult to avoid the impression that the dynamics of international trade are largely independent of existing differences in comparative costs and are determined instead mainly by income elasticities of demand and international patterns of innovation. One of the first to perceive this phenomenon was Posner (1970), who proposed an explanation built around the following simple proposition: the rate of generation of new products by a country is roughly dependent on the growth of its gross domestic product. If a country has achieved a high rate of economic growth it will be developing more new products than its more sluggish rivals and these products will enjoy a high income elasticity of demand. Hence the booming export earnings of Japan and West Germany relative to those of the UK and the US.

Posner's perspective on international trade implies that a country will experience a rising marginal propensity to import if it has been suffering from stagnant domestic demand. Such a situation is conducive neither to domestic producers being able to develop improved products that will readily find overseas customers nor to domestic firms being willing and able to undertake major expansions of capacity that will leave them able to cope with increased orders when demand eventually recovers. Given this, it is unfortunate that countries with balance of payments problems frequently use demand-contracting policies in their efforts to cut imports. To the extent that deflationary pressures lead to smaller wage and price increases than would otherwise have occurred, people may reduce imports in favour of domestic output. Otherwise imports will only fall because aggregate expenditure has been reduced. This is a most inefficient way of obtaining such a result: if the marginal propensity to import is, say, 0.2, a reduction in imports by a particular amount will only take place if there is a fivefold reduction in income. When domestic demand is increased once again, the Posnerian argument leads one to expect that, for a given level of unemployment, the country will tend to record a higher deficit than before the squeeze. If the country can maintain the higher level of activity it will tend to generate more new products and its trade performance will tend to improve, but if it lacks a means of financing the trade deficit in the interim then the recovery may have to be brought to a stop. In the latter case, the economy seems trapped in a vicious circle, for it will suffer a further relative decline.

It is commonly assumed that a country suffering from an excess of imports over exports can close the gap by devaluing its exchange rate. Consider, for example, the fall of sterling relative to the Australian dollar between 19 December 1987, when £1.00 = $A2.54, and 17 December 1988, when £1.00 = $A2.15. If the border price of a particular British product was $A10 000, its manufacturer would have been receiving £3937 per unit at the end of 1987. If Australian border prices were not changed, the British firm would be earning £4651 per unit at the end of 1988, an increase in profit per unit of £714. The firm could cut its Australian price to $A8425 without earning any less than before in terms of sterling, and it might earn more if the price cut increased sales. But a price cut would only earn more foreign exchange for the UK if the Australian demand for the goods in question were price-elastic. If the Australian market for the product in question were an oligopolistic one, a price cut might seem to carry the risk of an unprofitable price war. On the other hand, if the £714 extra profit per unit were taken instead, neither the volume nor the Australian dollar value of the firm's exports would rise in the short run. In the long run, the extra profits might result in a better product being developed but there would also be the risk that the higher profit margin would encourage other British firms to look at Australia as an export market, along with firms from other countries whose currencies have also fallen against the Australian dollar.

The arguments in the previous paragraph can be reversed to see the possible effects of a depreciation of sterling on the cost of imports in terms of foreign currency. Producers of imports will lose profits if they cannot raise their prices in terms of sterling. In markets where UK manufacturers' prices have been limited by the fear of overseas competition, the depreciation of sterling creates a situation in which prices can be raised on the expectation that existing overseas producers will follow suit. If UK producers raise their local prices by the same percentage amount as the fall in sterling, importers can raise their prices by the full amount of the depreciation. In these cases, savings in the foreign exchange bill of the UK only arise if the UK demand for the products is price-elastic. However, if there is a substantial change in relative costs of domestic and overseas producers, it may be that potential competition from other UK firms becomes the anchor for pricing. Existing UK producers would therefore increase their prices by less than the increase in relative costs suffered by their overseas competitors. In the latter case, overseas producers that try to maintain something like their normal mark-ups on UK sales may find volumes of exports to the UK collapsing as their prices rise sharply relative to those of UK producers. They may find it more profitable to supply British importers at lower foreign exchange prices than previously, though there is only so far they can proceed with such a strategy before finding themselves open to accusations that they are engaging in 'dumping'.

As Kaldor (1978, Ch. 7) has shown, currency depreciations have often had a limited ability to turn trade deficits into surpluses. Countries that devalue tend to suffer an increase in inflation and its associated costs, such as the disruptive effects of industrial action taken by workers involved a wage-price spiral. Supply-side responses are unlikely to be rapid if there is little confidence that the real cost advantage initially produced by the depreciation will be maintained for very long. These poor responses may be exacerbated by a reduction in investment in manufacturing as investor attention is diverted in search of hedges against inflation. By extending Posner's argument about the role of innovation in shaping patterns of trade, we should also recognise that many goods are not purchased because of their cheapness but because of superior 'non-price' characteristics, such as design, finish and reliability. If so, increases in the relative prices of imported products may do little to reduce the devaluing country's import bill unless they are on such a large scale as to take the products out of the budget ranges of the local population. Meanwhile, if discerning overseas buyers see a product as unsatisfactory in non-price terms, it will fail to win extra sales even at a lower price unless it starts to fall within the budget ranges of 'down-market' groups of customers who are used to making do with something even worse.

Now let us turn to capital flows. Aside from the kinds of strategic considerations that may lead firms to purchase overseas subsidiaries, the major factor shaping international capital movements is the expected rate of return on portfolio investment in foreign firms and financial assets. For example, the strength of the US dollar in 1984-5 originated largely from confidence in the prospects for the US corporate sector as the economy recovered, and from the attractively high interest rates being offered on bonds being sold to finance the US government's budget deficit. These two sources of high returns caused many people to put their funds into America. While this happened America recorded a huge current account trade deficit, that was due partly to the strength of domestic demand, but which also resulted from the high cost of US exports and cheapness of imports caused by the rise in the US dollar sparked off by this exceedingly strong capital inflow.

Liquidity preference theory suggests that a country could have lower interest rates than the rest of the world and still attract capital inflows, due either to a more attractive risk situation (such as the security and, for those with funds of doubtful origins, the anonymity of a Swiss bank), or expectations of an upward movement in its exchange rate. If the latter is the case, deposits in that country in terms of its own currency may achieve a capital gain that overwhelms any loss of potential interest earnings. Of course, if speculators can make deposits in a high interest country denominated in terms of the

currency whose value is expected to go up, they might get the best of
both worlds. Note that if an expected rise in a currency's value does
take place and is expected to proceed no further, then there is no
longer an incentive to hold that currency if one is foregoing interest
or security; it is time to send one's 'hot money' elsewhere.

6.3 Monetary Implications of International Payments Imbalances

Balance of payments 'imbalances' can arise due to trade flows, capital
flows or a combination of these factors. If there is a surplus (deficit),
then the country's inhabitants and firms are gathering more (less)
foreign currency than they are sending overseas. In cases where the
country has a fixed exchange rate the difference must be made up by
the government running down (increasing) its indebtedness to the rest
of the world. This 'official financing' involves paying back (taking
out) loans from the International Monetary Fund and/or the reserve
banks of other nations, or building up (running down) holdings of
gold and foreign currency reserves. When there is a surplus (deficit)
what happens in essence is that the reserve bank of the country
increases (reduces) its claims on official bodies overseas, whilst
increasing (reducing) its liabilities to domestic firms and residents.
Deposits with banks will rise (fall) as net claims of (amounts owed
by) domestic consumers and firms in terms of foreign currency are
paid in (withdrawn), and consequently the balances held by banks at
the reserve bank will rise (fall). In a fixed exchange rate system it
thus appears at first sight as though balance of payments surpluses
lead to an increase in the 'supply of high-powered money', while
deficits reduce it.

It is too early in this book for us to discuss whether or not
changes in bankers' balances may bear any relation to changes in the
overall volume of lending and spending in the economy, and what the
direction of causation may be. Such matters are dealt with in Chapter
9. For the present we can simply note that if a government believes,
rightly or wrongly, that such a relationship exists, it might well want
to intervene to stop the country's balance of payments surplus
(deficit) from having a monetary impact: it can seek to do this by
instructing its reserve bank to sell (buy) bonds on the open market
equal in value to the inflow (outflow). This activity is called
sterilisation. It may run into trouble if people do not want to buy

(sell) bonds, for then the rate of interest would have to rise (fall) and this could cause yet more funds to flow in (out), thereby nullifying the policy. The Canadians ran into this trouble in the early 1950s when they had a balance of payments surplus; in the end the Canadian dollar was allowed to float upwards as a means of stopping it. However, sterilisation may sometimes proceed with little trouble: for example, a balance of payments surplus may be a result of an increase in the national propensity to save and the reduction in domestic demand for foreign currency to purchase imports might be mirrored by an increase in the desire to purchase domestic securities (this kind of possibility underlies some of the thinking in Chapter 7).

If exchange rates are floating, a surplus of foreign currency earnings over foreign currency payments does not necessarily lead to a rise in the value of the domestic currency: it is possible that decision-makers in the domestic economy (particularly firms and banks, but also expatriates) may simply choose to accumulate foreign currency deposits in banks overseas. However, if they wish to turn their foreign currency earnings into domestic currency they must find someone prepared to sell them domestic currency. To find buyers for their foreign currency they will need to lower its price. People providing the domestic currency at this price could be, amongst others, (a) speculators who believe its value is going to fall back at a later date; (b) new importers who now believe they can do viable trade if they bring goods in at cheaper foreign currency prices, and who will need to pay for their imports with foreign currency; or (c) people who now think it worthwhile to make a capital export — for example to set up an overseas factory to produce at the now more competitive exchange rate and then import its output. In these cases there is no obvious impact upon bankers' balances at the reserve bank, so long as none of the domestic currency was being held initially as an 'offshore' deposit. (However, by the end of Chapter 9 it should have become apparent that the composition and size of some broader monetary aggregates could be affected if the buyers and sellers of the domestic currency may have different tendencies to make deposits with the various kinds of domestic financial institutions.)

If the reserve bank decides to do a bit of 'dirty floating' to stop the currency from appreciating too much in value, it acquires overseas currency in exchange for claims upon itself. In cases where the sellers of foreign currencies deposited their newly acquired domestic currency claims in the domestic banking system, the monetary impacts in the domestic economy would be akin to those in the case of fixed exchange rates, for both the country's holdings of foreign exchange reserves and bankers' balances at the reserve bank would rise. However, if the domestic currency ended up in banks overseas, there would be no direct impact on the domestic volume of bankers' balances: the reserve bank would simply have increased its liabilities overseas in exchange for an equal increase in its claims on its overseas counterparts.

6.4 Alternative Methods for Dealing with Balance of Payments Problems

In the era of fixed exchange rates, from the famous 1944 meeting at Bretton Woods until 1973, currency parities were only changed infrequently. Countries that were experiencing international payments imbalances had to look at the possibility of using other policy instruments to confront these problems. As was noted in the previous section, the method of using reductions in domestic demand to reduce imports tends to misfire in the long run, as well as having a short-run cost in terms of unemployment and foregone output. The fact that many nations ended up using this approach led some economists to argue that the fixed exchange rate system had an inbuilt deflationary bias as far as output and employment were concerned. Unfortunately, those who achieved persistent surpluses, most notably West Germany and Japan, appeared to see them as no more problematic than did the 'mercantilists' of the seventeenth century (see Robinson, 1966), especially since the IMF did not punish them for failing to expand their economies simultaneously with the contractions of those in deficit. If the nations with surpluses had been willing to increase their imports, there could simply have been a change in the world distribution of consumption, rather than a loss of employment and output.

From the standpoint of neoclassical macroeconomics, seemingly obvious solutions to the deflationary bias problem are implied by open economy versions of the basic *IS-LM* model. These models suggest that combinations of fiscal and monetary policy can be devised to permit a country which is prone to a balance of payments deficit at full employment to eliminate it without there being any need to change the exchange rate.

The starting point for such models is the idea that, given the state of world demand, the exchange rate, and the marginal propensity to import, a particular current account deficit or surplus will be associated with each possible level of income that policymakers might seek to engineer. If a country has a trade deficit and wishes to avoid running down its overseas currency reserves, it must generate an offsetting capital account surplus. Such a surplus could be generated by ensuring that the country's interest rate was sufficiently high relative to overseas interest rates. The reverse would hold for situations in which there was a current account surplus. For each level of income that might, somehow, be attained, there would be an interest rate such that the current and capital account balances summed to zero. The locus of such interest rate/income combinations is usually portrayed as an upward sloping line, often called the *BP* line, as in Figure 6.1. The more highly mobile capital is, the smaller the interest rate differential needed to attract funds from overseas, so with perfect capital mobility the *BP* curve would be horizontal, its height determined by interest rates on world markets.

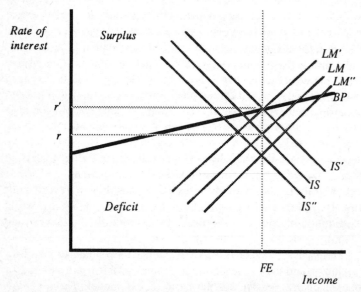

Figure 6.1 *Fiscal and Monetary Policy in an IS-LM Model of an Open Economy*

The task of the policy-maker is then seen to involve choosing an appropriate mix of fiscal and monetary policies so that the economy has an *IS-LM* intersection on the *BP* curve at the point corresponding

118

to full employment. The interest rate will then be such that any current account deficit (or surplus) is offset by a capital account surplus (or deficit). If the *IS-LM* intersection occurs at a rate of interest above (below) the rate of interest shown by the *BP* line at the level of income implied by the *IS-LM* intersection, then the balance of payments will be in surplus (deficit). An official monetary movement will therefore take place. If this is not sterilised, it will shift the *LM* curve to the right (left) in the case of a surplus (deficit). The new *IS-LM* intersection will lie nearer to the *BP* curve, but unemployment will have fallen (risen) as a result of the surplus (deficit). Eventually, unsterilised monetary movements will move the *LM* curve so that it cuts the *IS* curve at the point at which the latter intersects the *BP* line, but this intersection need not be at the full employment level of income.

In the example shown in Figure 6.1, the country in question starts out at full employment (*FE*) but has an external deficit. A policy mix that raises interest rates without changing domestic demand appears to be required. The right mix involves a tighter monetary policy, which shifts *LM* to *LM* ', and an easier fiscal policy, which shifts *IS* to *IS*'. The reverse change of mix — an easier monetary policy, *LM* to *LM*", and a tighter fiscal policy, *IS* to *IS*" — might be able to keep output at *FE*, but would worsen the balance of payments.

Unfortunately, this analysis is subject to precisely the same criticisms that were raised against closed economy IS-LM models in section 1.2. Its failure to take account of the passage of time is particularly serious, for it gives the erroneous impression that we are dealing with a series of curves whose positions are fixed. Each year that a country runs a current account deficit it increases its indebtedness to the rest of the world. Worse still, its current account will deteriorate through additional interest payments having to be made for every increase in its overseas indebtedness — whether this takes the form of borrowing from overseas governments and financial institutions or simply the acquisition of its income- and/or interest-earning assets (such as domestic equities or real estate) by overseas residents and firms. It therefore risks ending up needing to borrow more simply to pay the interest on its previous borrowings, and as it borrows more it is likely to find itself having to pay higher rates of interest. This is of course precisely the situation in which many developing nations have found themselves; it is also the situation that has been looming for Australia, that once unlikely candidate for 'banana republic' status.

If creditors are not disposed to tear up their claims on a country that has become trapped in a vicious circle of rising international indebtedness, the country can only get out of trouble if it achieves a balance of trade surplus. This point has been emphasised by debtor countries as they have sought to increase their borrowings: 'If you lend us more foreign exchange', they have often said, 'we can use this to purchase investment goods and then increase our exports or reduce our propensity to import'. Given the risk that such a loan might simply be used to finance consumption and that, even if it is not, any improvement in export earnings might be insufficient to swamp the rising burden of interest payments, one can see why the official agencies such as the IMF have tended to insist on austerity packages and devaluations as preconditions for lending. Given such preconditions, one can also see why the likes of Mexico, Argentina, Brazil and so on have preferred to raise funds from private sector international banks, who seem to have been reluctant to believe that these nations could ever end up having to declare themselves bankrupt.

Countries with balance of payments problems may have three other policy measures at their disposal if they wish neither to change currency parity nor to promote capital inflows via higher interest rates.

First, such a country may try to 'live' with the deficit by running down its foreign currency reserves or persuading the rest of the world to accept payment in terms of domestic currency. This method is clearly closed to many countries and is ultimately little different from that of using high interest rates to attract capital. Sooner or later reserves will run out and/or the rest of the world will wonder about the wisdom of accumulating more and more IOUs without cashing them in. The classic example is that of the US in the 1960s, which was able use its own dollars to pay for its net imports. Suppliers of goods imported by the US were confident enough in the value of the US dollar not to demand payment in their domestic currencies. If they did want domestic currency, their governments were often willing to accumulate US dollars as foreign exchange reserves. Those who did not bother to turn their US dollars into domestic currency could either use them to purchase goods and services from third parties who had similar confidence in the US currency or they could make deposits in terms of US dollars with banks that had branches outside of the US. These banks, located mainly in Europe, then lent out the 'eurodollars'. The proceeds of these loans might get deposited in banks in the US, but they could also be redeposited in eurocurrency markets or find their way into foreign currency reserves. Until 1971, the belief that US dollars could be converted into gold remained strong enough to make them generally acceptable despite the huge US deficit at the prevailing exchange rate. In that year there was a loss of confidence in the dollar, led by the French who had become worried that the value of dollars held outside the US exceeded the value of gold in Fort Knox. The strategy was then no longer tenable and instead the US dollar was devalued and the price of gold was increased in terms of dollars.

Secondly, a country in deficit could seek to use prices and incomes policy measures to bring its inflation rate below that of the rest of the world and thereby improve its trade performance at the existing exchange rate. Proponents of free markets would doubtless argue that prices and incomes policies distort market processes and may therefore produce resource misallocations. They would therefore suggest that flexible exchange rates would be a preferable tool to employ. (It might be better if they acquainted themselves with some of the market-based anti-inflation plans that have been proposed: see section 11.6.)

Finally, trading conditions could be changed by measures such as industrial subsidies, improved export credit guarantee provisions, tariffs, quotas, bureaucratic requirements, the direction of bank lending (for example, away from foreign car purchases, but towards enterprises that produce import substitutes for which the income elasticity of demand is high). Once again, proponents of free markets would be expected to claim that efficient resource allocation would be discouraged, either because protection from overseas competition would lead to a reduction in the pressure for domestic firms to innovate and adopt high productivity work practices, or because these kinds of measures are at odds with the principle of comparative advantage. In respect of the first objection, it should be noted that a depreciating exchange rate is just like, say, a tariff in making life easier for import-competing firms. In respect of the second, dynamic aspects of comparative advantage need to be considered.

Conventional trade theory is right to stress that it makes no sense to use a given volume of resources to save a particular amount in foreign exchange if a greater sum could be generated by using these resources to produce goods for export. However, the theory is cast very much in terms of current opportunity costs of producing a given set of products, rather than the the kinds of cost positions that could be achieved, and the new kinds of products that it might be possible to produce, given experience in particular lines of enterprise. The following parable from the work of D.H. Robertson (1954, p. 58) illustrates nicely the dangers of attempting to deal on the basis of current comparative costs with those who take a more dynamic view:

The simple fellow who, to the advantage of both, has been earning a living by cooking the dinner for a busy and prosperous scientist wakes up one day to find that his master has invented a completely automatic cooker, and that, if he wants to remain a member of the household he must turn shoeblack. He acquires a kit and learns the technique only to find that his master has invented a dust repelling shoe, but would nevertheless be graciously willing for him to remain on and empty the trash bins. Would he not be better to remove himself from the orbit of the great man and cultivate his own back garden?

From a short-run perspective it may indeed look counter-productive to use import controls to create artificial incentives for domestic firms to invest in import substitutes. Such incentives may lure resources out of presently 'efficient' exporting industries. In the long run, however, such sacrifices may pay off if improvements in efficiency are made in the import-substitution sectors, permitting higher net exports than would otherwise have been achieved. It should also be noted that if a country is simultaneously beset with unemployment and a balance of trade deficit, it ought to be possible to implement a policy of import substitution without any sacrifice in terms of foregone export earnings. The key issue is thus not really one of short-run efficiency but whether or not such policy measures provoke retaliation. But it should be noted that unless nations with surpluses are prepared to step up their imports, retaliation is a potential problem whatever measures are used to deal with balance of payments difficulties. Selective policies such as quotas and subsidies can at least be aimed only at nations with mercantilist tendencies, so that the positions of nations which are also struggling with deficits are not made worse.

During the era of fixed exchange rates the measures discussed in this section were rarely employed consistently or ruthlessly enough by governments whose economies suffered from balance of payments deficits. Consequently, the deficits failed to disappear and instead foreign exchange reserves ebbed away. Because exchange controls were imperfect, domestic speculators, as well as overseas holders of domestic currencies, would sooner or later seek to obtain foreign currencies on the anticipation of a devaluation. There usually followed a fruitless attempt by the domestic authorities to maintain confidence by spending reserves on meeting the speculators' demands. Eventually, a large enough mood of crisis would develop for it to be agreed that it was time for a change in the set of fixed parities.

6.5 Floating Exchange Rates in Theory and Practice

The Bretton Woods system was less than a decade old before Friedman (1953, pp. 157-203) set out what is perhaps the classic case for abandoning managed exchange rates and leaving things to market forces. His paper employed the appealing analogy of the justification for 'daylight-saving time'. As daylight hours change, some activities become inconvenient at their usual time. One way of dealing with this is to do them at different times, but a way of avoiding retimetabling (except across time zones) is to change all the clocks within a particular time zone by the same amount relative to some external reference point. In the balance of payments context, a deficit may have arisen because money wages have risen relative to those of trading partners. To restore competitive relative costs one can seek to reduce domestic wages in money terms, but this will involve considerable transactions costs. A flexible exchange rate could permit the adjustment to occur without there being any need to change wages in terms of domestic currency.

Friedman also argued that a free market in foreign exchange is likely to be associated with moves towards freer trade and that a floating exchange rate is a means whereby a country can seek to enjoy national sovereignty in economic policy. Both of these suggestions seem open to question. Friedman could certainly note how in the late 1980s Australia and New Zealand each removed many import quotas and reduced tariff rates after floating their respective currencies, but these policies stood in a sharp contrast to the emerging trade war between the US and the European Community. Moreover, in so far as capital inflows lead a country's currency to become grossly overvalued in purchasing power parity terms, then we should not be surprised to see its government coming under pressure from local manufacturers who see little chance of staying in business unless protection is increased.

The national sovereignty argument is supposed to work as

follows. If economies in the rest of the world are suffering from overheating, a country with a floating exchange rate need not suffer from inflationary pressures: if it wishes to avoid them, it can simply allow its exchange rate to rise to choke off any excess demand for its exports. Likewise, if a country is suffering from unemployment due to a lack of aggregate demand, it can reflate its way out of the problem without piling up the overseas debts that would otherwise occur as rising incomes lead to attempts to increase expenditure on imported products: it can simply allow its exchange rate to depreciate to switch demand back in favour of local production. In practice, governments may find that matters are not quite so simple. For example, consider the case of a country at full employment that is suffering from a number of capacity shortages (cf. Chapter 13). Its government may wish to deal with the capacity problem by promoting increased investment activity without increasing macroeconomic overheating. It decides to institute a tighter fiscal policy simultaneously with a less restrictive monetary policy, so as to encourage investment whilst leaving overall demand unchanged. But suppose governments of major economies elsewhere in the world are reacting to overheating by instituting restrictive monetary policies rather than by increasing taxes or cutting public expenditure. Policymakers in the country in question may then find their efforts confounded by a capital outflow in response to the emerging interest rate differential. In so far as the departing finance capital would otherwise have rested in domestic bank deposits, its exit will not involve any reduction in aggregate demand, but it will entail other parties ending up holding this amount extra as deposits with domestic banks. This will only happen if the exchange rate falls, thereby raising import prices and leading to an increase in demand for domestic output — so much for the country's independence of monetary policy.

Friedman's enthusiasm for freely floating exchange rates is by no means shared by all his fellow economists on the right of the political spectrum. Some have taken the view that one should only countenance such an exchange rate regime if labour markets are freely competitive. For example, Einzig (1970, p. 43) rather emotionally argued that under floating exchange rates there would be 'much less inducement . . . to restrain the obscene plundering of the community by trade unions'. In a system of managed exchange rates in which parities are only changed under duress, workers involved in the production of internationally tradeable goods risk pricing themselves out of their jobs if competitive conditions ensure that their employers cannot pass on higher labour costs in higher prices. If exchange rates adjust swiftly to changes in relative costs, this risk is largely eliminated and workers are encouraged to see how far they can increase their share of factor incomes at the expense of the real profit margins of the corporate sector: should they push their luck too far, a fall in the exchange rate may ensure they can remain in employment. Employers likewise may believe that exchange rate flexibility prevents real costs from getting out of line with those in other countries for any significant period of time. If so, they may be more willing to give in to aggressive wage demands than they would be under fixed exchange rates. Hence, in a world of organised labour, a switch to a floating exchange rate regime is thus seen as likely to lead to an increase in the rate of inflation.

This objection to floating exchange rates rather evaporates if they are introduced by governments that pursue pro-market policies in many areas and yet have the support of trade unionists because the alternative is government by a party with even less of an inclination towards socialism. An obvious case in point is that of Australia, which floated its currency, rather belatedly, in December 1983. The float of the Australian dollar was accompanied by a centralised policy of wage fixing known as 'The Accord', which esssentially involved a pact between the Federal Labor Government and the trade unions. The Accord held up remarkably well despite only allowing money wage increases partially to compensate workers against rising import prices consequent on reductions in the value of the Australian dollar.

Einzig was also worried about the possibility that freely floating exchange rates would be associated with 'self-aggrevating movements' arising in non-equilibrium situations in which speculators would be prone to oversell a depreciating currency, thereby generating inflationary pressures that would cause the equilibrium rate to decline (1970, Ch. 11). This is in sharp contrast to Friedman's faith in the ability of currency markets to uncover appropriate equlibrium values for exchange rates. Friedman contended that flexible exchange rates need not be unstable ones and that they would be unlikely to promote the kinds of destabilising speculation experienced with managed parities whenever changes seem likely. If underlying conditions are themselves changing gradually, decision-makers will find it far easier to cope with a succession of small changes than large infrequent changes. Any exchange rate instability observed in such a regime would be seen by Friedman as a symptom of instability in underlying real conditions and not the product of the flexibility *per se*. His paper portrays destabilising speculation as a most unlikely phenomenon on the ground that it could only happen 'if speculators on the average sell when the currency is low in price and buy when it is high' (p. 175), which would imply that they lose money.

From the standpoint of movement trader theory, discussed in section 2.7, it is Einzig rather than Friedman who looks on strongest theoretical ground. It should be recalled that this theory suggests that speculators seek to sell that which is falling and buy that which is rising most rapidly in value. Rates and directions of change, not absolute levels, are the things for speculators to watch: if the market looks set to overshoot a value that an individual speculator believes to be appropriate in the long run, there may be money to be made out of the market's folly and attempts to do so (for example forward sales of the currency in question) may help bring about the expected overshooting. Destabilising speculation need not carry the seeds of its own destruction unless movement traders tend to be systematically wrong or unable to meet their obligations on occasions when their expectations are horribly confounded. Mistakes were particularly to be expected in the early years of the age of flexible exchange rates, for managers with rules of thumb developed in the previous environment of fixed parities would be expected to take some time to develop routines for coping with the new regime. But it is difficult to argue that the weeding out of the more conspicuously unsuccessful speculators in the financial crises of the mid-1970s was sufficient to produce the extinction of movement traders as a species (on the contribution of currency dealings to bank failures in that period, see Dow and Earl, 1982, pp.152-60).

Some Post Keynesians may be rather surprised to discover that a case for not expecting floating exchange rates to become targets for destabilising speculation was also outlined by none other than Nicholas Kaldor, in a paper written in 1965 for the British Chancellor of the Exchequer (first published in Kaldor, 1978, Ch. 3). Unlike Friedman, Kaldor did not try to argue that speculation always tends to smooth things out. In particular, he cited primary product markets as ones in which speculators will tend not to take positions that help prices return to their average levels following supply- or demand-side shocks. The presence of inelasticities of supply and demand in these markets may mean that 'speculators do not expect the price to return to "normality" at all quickly; their short-period expectations concerning prices may run counter to their long-period judgment' (p.

57). However, his advice was that free market in sterling would not work like this, for the world elasticity of demand for the great variety of goods that the UK might export would be far higher than for an individual commodity input such as cotton or wheat. It should be quite easy for speculators to reach conclusions about what a reasonable value for a currency might be if they examine its purchasing power in terms of bundles of commodities and to make comparisons of unit labour costs across economies. Hence any zone of instability in a free market for sterling would be rather narrow — Kaldor (1978, p. 58) contended that 'it is most unlikely that this range should exceed 5 per cent on either side from the theoretical "equilibrium price"'.

In the event, short-term movements of exchange rates do not seem to have been those that one would expect from studying purchasing-power parities (for a study of eight major currencies, see Haache and Townsend, 1981). A particularly obvious example was the behaviour of the US dollar in the mid 1980s. In 1984-5 it was be very easy to argue that, given US labour costs, the US dollar was vastly over-valued, especially as the US did indeed have an enormous trade deficit. But corrective forces were swamped by the extent of inflows on the capital account due to demand for high-yielding US debt. If Kaldor were still alive today, he would no doubt recognise that his analysis suffered from an unduly narrow focus on relative costs in respect of traded commodities: in the world of today, international capital flows outweigh trade flows by about fifteen to one, while import and export sales of manufactured goods and services are heavily dependent on non-price attributes such as design excellence and delivery availability. One should also remember that Kaldor was making his case with respect to the UK, or more particularly the UK prior to its dependence on the performance of its North Sea oil fields. Given his recognition that primary commodity markets are prone to destabilising speculation, it is unlikely he would have come to the same conclusion had he been advising the treasurer of a country, such as Australia, that is very heavily dependent on a limited range of primary products for its export earnings.

6.6 Economic Forecasting Problems in Floating Exchange Rate Regimes

Observations of exchange rate gyrations do not necessarily imply that foreign exchange markets are suffering from destabilising speculation. Although such gyrations *might* have been smaller in the absence of speculative currency trading, it is possible that they would otherwise have been even more pronounced: speculators' purchases and sales of currencies *could* have been working in the right directions but not on a sufficiently large scale to smooth short-term exchange rate movements into line with their long-term trend values. Whatever their cause, the kinds of exchange rate fluctuations that have been observed in the past decade are a cause for concern because of the difficulties they cause for decision-makers. The result of the present system is that changes in relative competitive strengths of companies have come to depend less on having innovative products, marketing strategies and well organised production facilities and far more on luck or shrewdness in guessing exchange rate movements and adapting sourcing policies accordingly. This in turn is likely to have led industrialists to focus their efforts more on making money by trading currencies rather than by investing in physical assets and marketing campaigns (cf. section 2.7).

An incisive statement of this perspective from within the corporate sector is to be found in the autobiography of the co-founder of Sony, Akio Morita (1987, p. 282), who writes as follows:

What we didn't count on was that a factor other than the competitive power of our goods— namely, money traders — would begin to affect the value of world currencies. . . . This resulted in a constant changing of rates that had nothing to do with industrial competitiveness. For those of us engaged in worldwide trade, it was as though some bully had come swaggering onto the golf course and was changing our handicaps at every hole.

In this situation the price of our goods became a matter virtually beyond our control. To illustrate the problem, suppose, for example, we listed the price of a television set not at a specific dollar, yen, pound, franc or lira amount, but at whatever the price ten shares of Sony stock would be on the day you bought the set. Who would buy under such circumstances while the stock is being traded and the price is fluctuating each day? Who could manufacture under such circumstances?

Events in the Australian car industry in the turbulent half decade that followed the flotation of the Australian dollar provide an excellent case study of the strength of Morita's objections to the current system. Prior to its flotation, the Australian dollar had been pegged to a basket of world currencies weighted in line with their relative importance in Australia's trade; some fears about its potential instability certainly had been voiced, but these were based more on the view that the market for Australian dollars would be much thinner than those of the country's major trading partners. Even so, the vehicle maunfacturers seem to have been surprised by the gyrations with which they had to contend. Tables 6.1 and 6.2 give some idea of the topsy-turvy courses taken by the Australian dollar and the four main overseas currencies pertinent to the carmakers' plans.

Table 6.1 *Number of Units of Selected Overseas Currencies that could be Bought with an Australian Dollar*

	24Dec. 1983	15Dec. 1984	14Dec. 1985	13 Dec. 1986	19 Dec. 1987	17 Dec. 1988
$US	0.89	0.85	0.69	0.65	0.71	0.85
DM	2.48	2.62	2.32	1.32	1.16	1.48
¥	210	209	180	106	91	104
£	0.63	0.70	0.63	0.46	0.39	0.47

Differences in inflation rates between Australia, the US, the UK, West Germany and Japan can play only a minor role in explaining these exchange rate movements. Australia's inflation rate in this period was certainly higher than in the other countries, but not dramatically so, and the others certainly did not suddenly acquire double digit inflation during 1988 when the value of the Australian dollar recovered by well over 10 per cent. Rather, the vehicle builders had to contend with real changes in production costs that were dependent on views taken in currency markets on changes in world commodity prices; on relative non-price competitiveness; on the significance and future course of Australian, US and UK trade deficits, the US public sector deficit and relative interest rates; and on various unsettling political events. The role of speculative flows rather than trade as a determinant of the value of the Australian dollar since December 1983 has been such that whilst Australia is a classic example of a 'small open economy', its currency has been the fifth most heavily traded in the world in some periods since its flotation: so much for fears that instability would arise because the market for Australian dollars would be too thin.

Table 6.2 *Value of an Australian Dollar in Terms of Selected Overseas Currencies as a Percentage of its Value a Year Before*

	1984	1985	1986	1987	1988
$US	95.5	81.2	94.2	109.2	119.7
DM	105.7	88.6	56.9	87.9	127.6
¥	99.5	86.1	58.9	85.9	114.3
£	111.1	90.0	73.0	84.8	120.5

The 1985-6 fall in the Australian dollar and its 1988 recovery were mainly due to corresponding changes in the world prices of its major primary commodity exports. If speculation had been fully stabilising, the fall would have been smaller and Australia would have enjoyed a larger offsetting increase in capital inflows whilst its export revenues were depressed: the tendancy for the Australian dollar to fall should have led to a speculative demand for it on the expectation that its value would rise when commodity prices recovered. As it was, speculators seemed to have a great deal of trouble deciding how long it might be before such a recovery of export demand materialised. Many commentators and politicians raised the possibility that what was being observed was more than a temporary change in patterns of supply and demand in commodity markets. If so, a long term increase in the demand for the Australian dollar would only arise in the current account if resources were shifted into the production of other kinds of goods that could be exported or used as import substitutes. Without such a structural change, Australia would gradually move into a state of insolvency if capital inflows propped up the value of its currency year after year. It was necessary to ask whether the transformation could only be achieved if the value of the Australian dollar were lowered and, if so, by how far it might have to fall. The 'Lucky Country' had not previously been called upon to rise to such a challenge, so past track records of enterpreneurial and institutional evolution were not particularly conducive to answering these crucial questions in an unambiguous manner. Unlike those trying to respond to potential new export opportunities, speculators did not have to commit themselves in the long run: they could buy in and sell out as their opinons wavered about the likely direction of the currency's value.

While the value of the Australian dollar fluctuated, three other factors loomed large in the minds of strategists in the car industry. First, local content requirements: a failure to meet an 85 per cent local content target would result in substantial import duty charges being incurred on overseas content. However, these duties, and those on 'fully built up' vehicles would be made less onerous each year and all vehicle import quotas and licences were phased out. Secondly, there was the government's car industry rationalisation plan, which came into operation shortly after the flotation of the dollar. The plan allowed for credits to be given for export sales to allow the importation of components and fully finished vehicles. Thirdly, all cars manufactured after 1 January 1986 would have to run on low octane unleaded petrol.

The two major protagonists, Ford Australia and General Motors-Holden, in conjunction with their head offices in Detroit, came up with very different responses, particularly in respect of how to serve the key market segment for large, six-cylinder family cars. Ford continued a policy of making its ageing but top-selling Falcon model with an excess (around 95 per cent) of local content and successfully adapted its engine for unleaded fuel, meanwhile developing a new model and engine locally for launch in 1988. An export orientation for the company was only supposed to start to manifest itself in earnest in late 1988 with the launch of a small sports car built specially for the US market. Exports of this car, to be called the Mercury Capri, at the rate of 36 000 units a year would earn Ford Australia the credits it needed to keep its small and medium car ranges competitive by increasing its Japanese imports from Mazda (in which Ford US has a partial shareholding). Holden, by contrast, had built a large four-cylinder engine plant with the aim of earning export credits by supplying engines to Opel and Vauxhall, the West German and

UK subsidiaries of GM. Its six-cylinder engines could not be adapted to run on unleaded fuel, and Detroit did not provide it with the funds to develop a new engine which would do so. (Holden was in no position to dig into its own pockets to follow Ford and develop such an engine. In 1978, as part of GM's world-car strategy, Holden had replaced its large home-grown Kingswood with the smaller looking Commodore, an Australianised version of the Opel Rekord. The company then accumulated major losses as the Australian public gradually switched in favour of the bigger, reskinned Falcon and handed market leadership to Ford.) After a worldwide search, Holden decided to purchase six-cylinder engines and transmissions from Nissan in Japan for the 1986-8 model years and contracts were duly signed.

With the benefit of hindsight about exchange rate movements, both strategies appear somewhat unfortunate. The halving of the value of the Australian dollar in terms of the yen was a severe blow for the profitability of Holden's Nissan-powered Commodore in 1986-8. Holden enjoyed no offsetting benefit through its engine exporting activities, for the contracts with the European arms of GM involved transfer prices in terms of Australian dollars. As far as its Falcon model was concerned, Ford found itself nicely insulated against the collapse of the Australian dollar. Matters were rather different with small and medium sized models which depended heavily upon Japanese inputs: the price gap closed sharply between these cars and the Falcon, so much so that there was a collapse of sales of Ford's medium sized Telstar model (a badge-engineered version of the Mazda 626). As Holden's inclination to deal with Nissan Japan faded, Ford and Nissan Australia got together to produce a shared medium sized model for the local market, to be launched in late 1989/1990.

In 1988 the tables were turned. Early in the year Ford introduced its new Falcon and met with strong criticism because its local suppliers of automatic transmissions had not yet been able to produce a four-speed automatic gearbox to match the new engine. Meanwhile, following a major departure by GM from its world-car strategy, Holden was getting ready for production a new wide-bodied Commodore that shared little with its superficially similar European counterparts. Holden had decided to insulate itself against the strength of the yen by adapting one of GM's own six-cylinder Buick engines for the local market and initially importing them from the US, along with GM four-speed automatic transmissions. When the new, smoother and more economical Commodore appeared, Ford paid dearly for its local content strategy: the three-speed Falcon lost market leadership for the fourth quarter of 1988. Ford's position was made even worse by the collapse of the US dollar towards the end of 1988, which further helped Commodore profitability: the Mercury Capri — whose launch had been delayed by a change in US safety legislation which required it to be re-engineered to include an aircushion restraint — suddenly looked a far less profitable project. At the time the sports car contract had been awarded, an Australian dollar would buy little over $US0.60. In January 1989, as the Australian dollar rose towards $US0.89, Allan Gilmour, Ford's executive vice president of international operations, was quoted in the US magazine *Autoweek* as saying that cancellation of the contract was a possibility. Mexico was rumoured to be under consideration as an alternative production location. However, in March 1989, by which time the Australian dollar had fallen to around $US0.80, Ford decided to carry on with its original plan to make the Capri in Australia.

The exchange rate instability that makes forecasting so problematic for large firms also affects the broader community. This is not merely because investment may suffer if the bewildering uncertainty leads big business to build larger risk factors into its calculations. Internationally mobile consumers can find their fortunes changing sharply depending upon their own luck in predicting speculation-driven exchange rate movements. For example, overseas vacations or periods of academic study leave that have to fixed up well in advance can turn out to be unexpected bargains or financial millstones, while six months' delay in emigration due to unforeseen problems over a visa can produce substantial windfall gains or losses in the value of funds intended for use as a house deposit. Consumers may also benefit or suffer if managers of public utilities are pleasantly or unpleasantly surprised by exchange rate movements that take place after they have borrowed overseas to fund major construction projects: for example, the electricity prices I have had to pay whilst writing this book have been inflated by increases in the costs of servicing and repaying huge, low interest loans raised by the Tasmanian Hydro-Electric Commission in terms of Swiss Francs prior to the collapse of the Australian dollar. Similarly, the library and laboratory facilities available to university students are coming increasingly to depend on the speculative positions taken by university bursars with respect to the funds over which they have command and the timing of orders and payments for imported books, journals and scientific equipment.

Proponents of flexible exchange rates argue that decision-makers who are worried about possible adverse affects of exchange rate movements do not have to become active speculators, since they can seek to cover themselves by hedging in the forward exchange markets. To be sure, the use of forward markets, like any form of insurance, involves some cost, but at least decison-makers then do not have to face other kinds of uncertainties — such as, 'Will there be a fiscal squeeze?' or, 'Will import licences be available?' — that tend to arise when countries on fixed exchange rates run into balance of payments disequilibria.

Forward currency markets are indeed widely used as a form of insurance against exchange rate movements. Excellent discussions of precisely how this is done are to be found in Argy (1981, Ch. 19), Carew (1985, Ch. 12) and Lewis and Wallace (eds) (1985, pp. 374-88). Forward markets with delivery dates of up to a year from the date of contract are very useful for guaranteeing the local currency value of expected export revenues or import payments. The trouble is that markets with horizons of much more than a year tend either to be thin or non-existent, whereas the combined gestation and payback periods of most physical investment projects or the duration of long-term loans will often be five years or more. Consequently firms can still find themselves being hammered by exchange rate movements that fail to reflect changes in real costs or which suddenly inflate the cost of using overseas finance. And even to the extent that they can insure their positions, there is always the risk that parties on the other side of the deal may default on their obligations after making mistaken forecasts during in an attempt to use the markets for speculative purposes rather than for hedging.

6.7 Conclusion

In an age in which production is increasingly dominated by multinational enterprises and can be undertaken in more locations around the world, the traditional view of imports and exports as based on relative costs is by no means obsolete. Buyers may now choose very much on the basis of non-price factors between the products that come into their budget ranges, but patterns of trade depend increasingly on locational sourcing decisions of multinational firms. The more mobile production is, the more that exchange rates, incomes policies and government inducements will determine the outcomes of international sourcing decisions. Firms in countries whose currencies tend to appreciate over time, such as West Germany and Japan, have adopted two solutions to the problem of rising domestic labour costs. One is to move production offshore; the other is to concentrate on products at the leading edge of technology for which premium prices can be charged and which remain beyond the advancing knowhow of lower cost production centres. In so far as knowledge and innovation advantages are lost to rising stars such as Korea, Taiwan and Hong Kong, the shift of economic power in favour of West Germany and Japan could be relatively short-lived if it proves difficult to hold down domestic living standards. However, assets accumulated overseas during years of trade surpluses will provide something of an income-earning buffer against falling living standards in these countries. This is in sharp contrast to the bleak future facing high-wage debtor nations (the list of which now includes the US following the remarkable turn around of the Reagan era). In the absence of protectionist policies, it is difficult to see how they can maintain their living standards if they cannot compete on price with low-wage, newly industrialising countries; cannot ape the technological leadership of the West Germans and Japanese; and cannot enjoy a rising trend in prices of their primary commodity exports (if any) or attract ever-increasing numbers of international tourists and foreign currency-paying students. As for low-wage nations that have little by way of infrastructure to show for years of borrowing, it is difficult to see how they can make much economic progress and join the ranks of newly industrialising countries unless they can succeed in having their debts written off.

These scenarios are particularly distressing since the deflationary bias of the fixed rate system has not been eliminated by the adoption of floating rates. If anything, matters are now worse than in the 1950s and 1960s owing to the ease with which speculative currency switches can be made and the difficulties that floating rates cause for long-term planning. As Stewart (1983) has observed, a country that is sufficiently public spirited to pursue expansionary macroeconomic policies at a time when its trading partners are pursuing policies of austerity will tend to suffer from a capital outflow, for corporate treasurers and other speculators will expect it to suck in imports and consequently experience a depreciation in the value of its currency. If such an anticipatory flight of funds is overdone and the currency is pushed down below a level that the domestic policy-makers judge to be reasonable, there is precious little they can do on their own to push its value up unless they have very substantial foreign currency reserves to sell. They may therefore find themselves with an acceleration of inflation driven both by rising import prices and by macroeconomic overheating due to the tendency of the balance of trade to move into surplus. In such circumstances it is likely that they will have to turn back from their expansionary pathway. This is in sharp contrast to the position of countries that have been using high interest rates and expenditure cuts to deflate their way out of balance of payments problems and the associated cost-push inflationary pressures of a falling exchange rate: though such policies threaten returns to investment at home and overseas, the market tends to view them favourably, and demonstrates its approval through a capital inflow which further dampens demand by pushing up the exchange rate. If the market over-reacts, domestic policy-makers can either relax their policies somewhat or engage in 'dirty floating' by buying foreign currency with their now popular domestic currency. But they may be tempted to let the exchange rate rise beyond levels that local entrepreneurs find tolerable: a rising exchange rate reduces both inflation and the value of claims on the domestic economy in terms of foreign currencies.

If it seems impossible to overcome the deflationary bias and exchange rate instability through increasing international cooperation between governments and their reserve banks, then any nation that wishes to avoid having its economy disrupted by the chaotic workings of the international economic system may consider the strategic advantages of using import controls and industrial subsidies to manage its trading position in the long run (see Krugman, ed., 1986). As long ago as 1930 Keynes himself put forward a strategic case for departing from free trade. In a memorandum to the Committee of Economists of the Economic Advisory Council (reprinted in Keynes, 1973, p. 193), he argued that:

Any manufacturing country is probably just about as well fitted as any other to manufacture the great majority of articles. It is unlikely, for example, that there would be great advantage in all the motorcars in the world being made in the United States, and all the tin plates being made in South Wales, and all the steel rails being made in Belgium. On the other hand, now that nearly all the manufacturing countries of the world have decided on a certain measure of self-sufficiency, a country which does not follow suit may pay a much greater price in instability than it gains through specialisation.

The costs of sacrificing the advantages of specialisation may be especially worth incurring in today's turbulent economic environment. Small open economies that specialise according to their comparative advantage are particularly vulnerable to changes in strategic trade groupings: an obvious example is the long-term trauma suffered by New Zealand after the UK, its main export customer, joined the European Community. Similar ups and downs may be experienced for technological reasons by countries that do not adopt a strategic approach to the management of their international trading positions. They may do well for a time simply by being in front with a sought-after innovation and enjoy the advantages of having more experience of producing it than their rivals. But at other times they may suddenly find themselves running into trouble because technological leadership has passed elsewhere. This may happen even if their workers are as well trained as those of their rivals and their firms have invested in the most up-to-date manufacturing methods. In a world of surprises due to opportunism and innovation, nations as well as companies may find themselves in trouble if they put too many of their eggs in too few baskets or fail to engage in policies of vertical integration to safeguard their sources of supply and/or their downstream markets.

7 Intersectoral Flows of Funds

7.1 Introduction

After four chapters in which we have examined the portfolio choices of different kinds of individual decision making units, we can begin to consider how their choices are linked together and how this is facilitated by financial institutions. If, for the moment, we treat financial institutions simply as domestic or overseas firms, and do not separate the activities of the reserve bank from those of the government, we have four main groups to consider: households, firms, the government and the overseas sector. Each issues financial assets which are acquired by the other groups. For example, households purchase equities issued by the corporate sector and some of their deposits with financial institutions are used to finance the purchase of securities issued by the government, loans to firms and loans to governments and firms overseas. However, in any period the total value of newly issued financial assets, less the value of existing ones that are being retired as loan repayments are made, must equal the sum of net acquisitions of financial assets in the system. Though some groups are net borrowers (they issue more financial assets than they acquire), other groups are net lenders (they acquire more financial assets than they issue) and the *net acquisition of financial assets* (NAFA) by the system as a whole is, by definition, equal to zero. That is to say:

Personal Sector NAFA + Corporate Sector NAFA + Government NAFA + Overseas Sector NAFA $\equiv 0$

The identity has no causal content but it draws our attention to the fact that if the borrowing and lending intentions of decision-makers in the various sectors of the economy are incompatible then they will have to be reshaped until portfolios can dovetail properly together. Such accommodations will be induced by changes in relative prices and asset yields, which in some cases may involve changes in the volume of output and employment. Such is the perspective from which this chapter explores several aspects of NAFA interlinkages, to pave the way for detailed discussions in subsequent chapters concerning the role of financial institutions, the growth of monetary aggregates and the dynamics of aggregate demand.

7.2 Gross and Net Liabilities of an Individual

Before we look at the relationships between the various sectors of an economy, it is probably useful to explore the derivation of an individual's NAFA. Table 7.1, which was inspired by an example in Gowland (1985, Ch. 6), illustrates the hypothetical case of a person in the year in which she purchases her first house. Compared with her position at the start of the financial year, her financial assets at the end of the year are down by $5000 and her liabilities have increased by $56 000, so for that year her NAFA is -$61 000.

Table 7.1 *An Individual's Sources and Uses of Funds*

Sources of Funds		Uses of Funds	
Post-tax Income	$20 000	Expenditure on Current Goods and	$14 000
Sales of Shares (A-)	$4 000	Services	
Reduction in Building Society and Credit	$2 000	Purchase of House	$64 000
Union Deposits (A-)		Purchase of Car	$3 000
Mortgage (L+)	$50 000	Increase in Bank Deposits (A+)	$600
Borrowing from Parents (L+)	$4 000	Purchase of Savings Certificates (A+)	$400
Bank Loan (L+)	$2 000		
Total	$82 000	Total	$82 000

(Note: A+ denotes an increase in financial assets, A- a reduction in financial assets, and L+ an increase in financial liabilities.)

It will be observed that her gross liabilities are bigger than her net liabilities at the end of the year: if she wishes she can reduce her debts by $1000 by cashing in her savings certificates and running her bank deposits down to zero. However, if she does so, she will have no cash with which to make purchases until she receives her next paycheque, and no easily cashable financial reserve which she can draw upon in the event of, say, an unexpected repair bill for her car. In other words, her bank deposits meet her transactions needs and her savings certificates are earmarked to serve her precautionary needs. To the extent that savings certificates are in practice viewed in this way, it make it seems appropriate to view them as akin to money, as in the *PSL2* monetary aggregate.

Situations in which individuals and insitutions are each borrowing and lending simultaneously are very common, but financial innovations are removing some of the forces that underlie them. For example, penalty clauses with respect to premature repayments were once common features of financing contracts, particularly hire purchase deals, but now that the market for loans is becoming more hotly contested, financial institutions are increasingly using the absence of such clauses as a major selling point. Even more significant is the use of credit cards as devices to keep down the need to access cash in the periods between the receipt of income payments. However, it is by no means possible to make all purchases with credit cards, and even where credit cards are accepted, they may not be the particular ones that a person has. The rate of interest charged on cash advances by credit card companies is normally somewhat higher than on personal loans, and considerably higher than on mortgages. Hence it could prove rather expensive to use one's entire net income to reduce one's debts the moment it was received and then take out cash advances to cover cash-only expenditures incurred before the next payday.

Matters may be rather different for those wealthy enough to obtain a line of credit from their banks, against which they can draw cheques up to a pre-specifed maximum. The 'super-mortgages'/'home equity loans' that banks are starting to offer are actually marketed with an emphasis on their abilities to facilitate the minimisation of gross liabilities, and are particularly attractive to those who would otherwise pay high marginal rates of tax on interest received from their deposit balances. Such loans are essentially giant overdrafts secured against real estate — for example one may borrow up to 90 per cent of the value of one's home, less the amount still owed on a first mortgage — and though they involve a substantial establishment fee, they enable borrowers to purchase new consumer durables simply by using up slack in their credit lines rather than by negotiating new loans. While these packages may be powerful devices for winning creditworthy customers, it is obviously against the interests of the banks if those who take out home equity loans go too far towards minimising their indebtedness on a day to day basis. Hence the banks normally give their clients fairly high minimum credit limits: to stay above the minimum credit level if one cuts down on spending, it might even be necessary to use the line of credit to refinance some of one's first mortgage at a higher level of interest. Hence, unless one is the sort of person who persistently needs a lot of credit, such arrangements may prove little more inviting than conventional loan contracts.

In addition to these kinds of reasons for portfolio choices involving gross liabilities in excess of net borrowing, we should also note that sometimes shrewd operators even find it worthwhile to engage in 'round tripping' — borrowing in one market and then lending the money out for a higher yield in another market — because banks have failed to make simultaneous adjustments to their lending and borrowing rates.

Within any particular sector, some participants are likely to have positive NAFAs and others negative ones: for example, some firms may be borrowing to finance new investments while others are accumulating financial assets; middle-aged consumers may be saving for retirement while young couples are getting into debt and selling off asset holdings to finance consumption, as in the lifecycle theory of the consumption function. In aggregating individual portfolios into sectoral categories we can very easily end up overlooking the significance of *intra*-sectoral financial linkages and fail to spot the emergence of potentially dangerous NAFA patterns. It should never be forgotten that any particular NAFA total for a group of financial portfolios can be consistent with a variety of different current states of aggregate demand and subsequent evolutionary courses for the economy (just as the sum of NAFAs for the economy as a whole is always zero, no matter what the level of aggregate demand). For example, consider a sector consisting of just three portfolios, which has an overall NAFA of zero. If the first portfolio owner borrows cash from the second to buy something from the third, total spending may increase, but the NAFA of the sector remains zero: the NAFA of the first party will have fallen by the amount that the NAFA of the

141

third has risen, while the second party has simply changed the composition of her assets (she now has a claim on the first party but has less cash than before).

An exploration of linkages between firms within the financial sector is likely to be particularly worthwhile, even though financial firms and the banking sector as a whole are normally portrayed in flow of funds analysis as having NAFAs of zero. Such firms are assumed normally to have negligible net lending positions on the grounds that a bank is essentially an intermediary which by its very nature tends to expand (or contract) its assets and liabilities at the same rate (see section 8.2). However, an enormous volume of inter-institution lending has contributed to the development of an intricately layered system of institutions and obligations. Savings banks may lend to commercial banks; building societies and credit unions may keep their liquid assets deposited with banks; commercial banks borrow from each other or lend to overseas financial institutions, and have deposits with or borrow from reserve banks; and so on. The system is a terribly interconnected nexus, rather than a simple pyramid, but attempts to think of it in terms of rather more well defined layers have given rise to useful approximating terms such as 'wholesale' and 'retail' banking. Although such complexity is completely glossed over in the simplified analysis in this chapter, we shall later (particularly in Chapter 12) be devoting much attention to the events that can arise if defaults occur when portfolios are financially interconnected in this manner. Readers interested in even more detailed analyses of flows of funds in the financial sector should find it rewarding to consult Roe (1973) and Marzouk (1987).

7.3 A Flow of Funds Matrix

This section presents a numerical illustration of flows of funds in a hypothetical small open economy. Though it is highly aggregative in nature, the example at least goes beyond the original four sectors of the NAFA identity by separating out the banks and reserve bank as individual sectors. The six rows of Table 7.2 represent the six main sectors of the economy, while the seven columns concern six kinds of financial assets (we shall assume that no others exist) and the NAFAs of the various sectors. It is assumed that there are no non-bank financial intermediaries.

The personal and corporate sectors have both increased their borrowings from the domestic banking system, while the corporate sector has raised additional funds by selling equities to the personal sector and to overseas buyers.

Table 7.2 *A Six-Sector Flow of Funds Matrix*

Sector	Advances	Equities	Bonds	Bank Deposits	Deposits at Reserve Bank	Forex	NAFA ($ million)
Personal	-650	+200	+200	+525	0	0	+275
Corporate	-50	-500	+250	+475	0	0	+175
Banks	+700	0	+100	-1000	+200	0	0
Government	0	0	-1400	0	0	0	-1400
Reserve Bank	0	0	+350	0	-200	-150	0
Overseas	0	+300	+500	0	0	+150	+950

(Note: + indicates an increase in net holdings of these assets by the sector in question; - indicates a decrease in net holdings of these assets by the sector in question or an increase in liabilities of this kind.)

The government has a deficit of $1400 million which it has financed by selling bonds to the personal, corporate, banking and overseas sectors and by having the reserve bank take up $350 million of the increase in the national debt. However, the monetary base of the economy has, by the end of this accounting period, only risen by $200 million. This reflects the sterilisation of a $150 million balance of payments deficit by the reserve bank. The economy has a balance of trade deficit of $950 million which is only offset to the tune of $800 million by capital inflows ($300 million purchase of domestic equities by foreigners, plus $500 million purchases of government bonds by foreigners). Hence foreign exchange reserves (labelled as Forex) have been depleted by $150 million to close the gap: clearly, we have a country operating under a fixed exchange rate regime or with only a partially floating currency.

The reserve bank has purchased $150 million of government securities from the domestic private sector to ensure that the $150 million loss in foreign exchange reserves is not matched by a $150 million contraction in the monetary base. Despite the fact that the deposits of banks with the reserve bank have risen by only $200 million by the end of the accounting period, total bank deposits — in other words, *M3* as opposed to *M0* — have risen by five times this amount (on how this may have happened, see Chapter 9).

Although each of the columns of this matrix sums to zero, we would be unwise to suggest that the matrix depicts an economy that is in some kind of steady state equilibrium and that this pattern of portfolio changes could be expected to reproduce itself year after year. We must not forget relationships between stocks and flows in markets for financial assets. An obvious consideration here is that repayment of debts involves turning a negative NAFA into a positive one. Obvious though this may be, it rarely rates a mention in discussions in the mass media about the international debt crisis. Yet, if debtor nations are to reduce the scale of their debts, it is not merely necessary that creditor nations eliminate their current account surpluses; the latter must actually be prepared to begin to run trade deficits and allow the former to enjoy trade surpluses. As far as a debtor nation is concerned, a zero trade deficit simply means that its international liabilities are not increasing.

Secondly, it should be noted that although individuals within a particular sector may be accumulating financial assets with a view to spending in excess of their incomes at a later date, it is possible that the sector as a whole may persistently display a positive NAFA: for example, as incomes and populations increase, personal saving by some people will tend to exceed dissaving by others. This makes it easy to see how a government may be able to finance an ever-increasing 'National Debt'. It should also be noted that the table shows only net increases and decreases in asset holdings, but the ability of particular borrowers to keep on raising money will depend on their total net worth and their prospective flows of income (these factors will affect how they seem as credit risks) as well as on the general willingness of others to keep piling up financial surpluses. If a sector or an entire domestic economy is prone to record a negative NAFA and its income grows more slowly than its interest obligations, then, like an individual, it will eventually become unable to meet the interest charges on its debts. Its ability to carry on issuing financial assets will then disappear.

7.4 The Relationship Between Public Sector Borrowing and the Balance of Payments

The NAFA figures chosen for Table 7.2 may look somewhat anachronistic in an age in which a return to pre-Keynesian modes of economic thinking has led some governments to aim for public sector surpluses despite the presence of high levels of unemployment. They were in fact chosen with a somewhat nostalgic regard for my first encounter with the NAFA identity: the so-called 'New Cambridge' controversy of the mid 1970s. In 1974, members of the Cambridge Economic Policy Group estimated an equation for the volume of private sector expenditure in the UK in the years 1954 to 1972. This equation seemed to imply a higly predictable private sector NAFA that was very small, of the order of £1 billion, and that almost all money paid out by the government, regardless of what it was for, would fairly rapidly be spent. Though the Group had very little to say about the likely theoretical basis for this finding, they took it to have major significance for macroeconomic policy: if the public sector deficit increased, the UK current account deficit would worsen by approximately the same amount because the domestic private sector would hardly increase its purchases of government debt. Hence it was argued that a reduction in the size of the public sector deficit was the key to the reduction of the UK current account deficit. To stop cuts in net government spending from causing unemployment, the government should introduce measures to reduce the propensity to import (the Group favoured import controls). Fiscal policy thus became the Group's recommended means for controlling the balance of trade and international trade policy its means for controlling aggregate demand and employment (see Cripps *et al.*, 1974).

Unfortunately for its proponents, but fortunately for the rest of the UK economy, the predictive capacities of the Cambridge expenditure equation broke down dramatically: as the rate of inflation soared in 1973–5, there was a sharp rise in the private sector savings ratio. The equation, which had been specified in real terms, was soon respecified in terms of current prices and its performance then improved somewhat for the first two years outside its original estimation period (Cripps *et al.*, 1976), though its errors there were still much greater than within the original period. The performance of the Cambridge model thereafter continued to be subject to fairly wide margins of error (Cuthbertson, 1979, pp. 88–9). This was a formidable lesson in the dangers of drawing powerful policy conclusions from econometric

145

models based on a 'black box' view of the micro-determinants of aggregate data series.

Although the original Cambridge model grossly overpredicted the UK's current account deficits in the mid 1970s, these deficits were nonetheless bad enough to place the country in a position where an imminent drying up of the supply of finance from overseas savers and international banks led it to turn to the International Monetary Fund as the lender of last resort in 1976. In other words, despite the fact that corresponding to the UK deficit there must have been current account surpluses elsewhere in the world, it was by no means guaranteed that funds would be willingly recycled back to the UK on its capital account. The price extracted by the IMF for its loan included cuts in the UK public sector deficit and the acceptance of a limit on 'domestic credit expansion' (DCE). The latter concept is most simply defined as the increase in the $M3$ less the increase in the economy's foreign exchange reserves. (In terms of the economy represented in Table 7.2, we have a DCE figure of $1150 million: unlike a limitation on $M3$ growth of $1000, a DCE limit of $1000 would have forced the authorities in this economy to introduce measures to cut demand and limit the drain of foreign exchange reserves.) Given the possibility that the relationship between $M3$ growth and spending on imports may be more fluid than the monetarists at the IMF seem to imagine (see Dow and Earl, 1982, Ch. 16), we may be thankful that relatively little has been heard of DCE targets in recent years. Countries have increasingly preferred to keep well clear of the IMF and to try instead to weather their balance of payments difficulties with the aid of sharp depreciations in their exchange rates and/or by using unprecedentedly high interest rates to attract capital inflows. However, undergraduate readers would probably be wise to familiarise themselves with the DCE concept, for the time may yet come again when problems of sovereign indebtedness lead to a failure of the private international capital market and force more nations into the boa-like embrace of the IMF.

7.5 'Printing Money' Revisited

The NAFA identity tells us that if government runs a deficit of, say, $10 billion, the domestic private sector and the overseas sector between them must end up holding $10 billion worth of extra claims on the government *regardless* of how the deficit is financed. But the willingness of decision-makers in these sectors to hold additional claims on the government will depend on how they assess the prospective yields of these claims. According to Perrin (1984, p. 19), this raises doubts about viability of 'printing money' as a deficit financing option, since the domestic private sector may have little wish to hold increasing volumes of currency and may be reluctant to hold larger bank deposits *unless interest rates are increased*. Hence if an attempt is made to finance a public sector deficit largely by borrowing from the reserve bank, decision-makers will treat any addition to the monetary base as if it is a 'hot potato' until events occur which make them increase their demand for money.

In exploring Perrin's fears we can simplify things at first by considering the artificial case of a closed economy. In so far as members of the private sector are initially unwilling to accumulate the levels of additional bank deposits implied by the deficit that the government is running, there will be a search for higher-yielding assets, such as durable goods or equities and bonds, or an increase in current consumption. People may also dispose of unwanted bank deposits by paying off some of their bank loans and thereby providing banks with an incentive to join in the demand for bonds or attract new borrowers. Interest rates will therefore be lower than if the deficit had been financed by forcing more bonds on to the market. However, falling yields on financial assets other than cash may lead some potential lenders to expect that yields could rise in future and bring about a fall in asset values. Others may be disinclined to lend more to risky marginal borrowers. Both of these groups may therefore prefer to build up speculative deposits for the moment. This will limit the extent to which demand increases.

Since the economy is, by assumption, closed, any increase in demand must either be accommodated by an increase in the domestic output of physical goods and services — some of which may have been purchased because of the greater ease of raising money — or, unless decision-makers are willing to join longer waiting lists, an increase in prices. In the former case, the private sector ends up absorbing the public sector deficit even in the absence of a rise in the speculative demand for money: the rise in real incomes is associated with positive savings and an increase in the demand for transactions balances. In the latter case, which is essentially that envisaged by monetarists, the excess bank deposits would be soaked up by an increase in nominal demand for transactions balances. The case that eventuates will depend very much on the amount of slack in private sector firms and in the labour market.

In an open economy, the domestic private sector can dispose of unwanted assets by selling them to overseas residents or by inducing the reserve bank to reduce the nation's net claims on the overseas sector. In the following cases, there is no effect on the exchange rate:

(i)   Domestic residents may dispose of unwanted increases in their holdings of money balances by increasing their net imports of goods and services. The current account moves into deficit but, rather than let the exchange rate depreciate, the reserve bank runs down the nation's foreign exchange reserves: the deposits of banks at the reserve bank fall by the same amount as the reduction in foreign exchange reserves.

(ii) Domestic residents dispose of their unwanted bank deposits by increasing their net imports of goods and services but the exchange rate does not tend to fall as overseas residents decide to accumulate bank deposits in terms of the domestic currency.

(iii) Net imports of goods and services are increased but titles to real estate and/or financial assets such as bonds and equities are sold to the overseas sector. Unlike (ii), domestic residents end up continuing to hold larger volumes of bank deposits: they appear to think these are a better bet than the assets they have sold.

(iv) Net imports of goods and services are increased but domestic residents sell off some of their holdings of overseas assets. As in (iii), domestic residents as a group end up holding larger volumes of bank deposits than they held before the deficit was financed: some may have used the proceeds of their sales of overseas assets to purchase domestic securities, whose sellers are speculating that bank deposits are now a better bet; others may have moved straight into bank deposits.

Unfortunately, as the IMF would be only too keen to point out, none of these can be sustained indefinitely. In cases (ii), (iii) and (iv), moreover, something must be happening to make some agents take the view that yields in the domestic economy are going to be higher than hitherto relative to those available overseas.

It is quite possible that yields on domestic financial assets will rise even if the government finances its deficit by monetary expansion rather than by selling bonds: for example, the rise in activity may lead to greater confidence on the part of some domestic and/or overseas residents about earnings prospects for domestic equities, or to a boom in domestic investment demand which generates increasing competition for funds. If yields do not rise following the monetary expansion and if domestic residents are reluctant to accumulate additional speculative or transactions balances, the value of the domestic currency will fall until (a) the necessary improvements in prospects of domestic firms relative to their international competitors are produced; (b) some foreigners start to accumulate holdings of the domestic currency in the belief that its exchange rate is now so low it is likely to appreciate and give them a capital gain; (c) the reserve bank engages in 'dirty floating' and runs down foreign currency reserves; (d) expectations of a monetary squeeze are formed by some agents, which lead to an increased demand for speculative balances and a rise in domestic interest rates; or (e) the demand for transactions balances rises due to the expansion of real domestic activity and/or the inflation associated with higher import prices.

7.6 Conclusion

Though all individual NAFAs in the economy must always sum to zero, this in no way guarantees that those who wish to have negative NAFAs will find their demands readily accommodated by others. Interest incentives and other assurances may have to be offered to bring about such an accommodation, and would-be borrowers may prefer to curtail their spending rather than offer such terms. The result may be that fewer financial assets are created and hence aggregate demand is less than it might have been had less onerous terms been required by potential lenders. Unlike other sectors, the government can finance its spending by 'printing money' rather than by offering inducements for private sector decision-makers to lend it money. But even this may not be a costless method of financing public expenditure, as the government may be unable to stop private sector decision-makers from subsequently trying to dispose of additions to the monetary base in ways which compromise its targets for the price level, the value of the country's exchange rate (and hence real wages) and/or the size of its foreign currency reserves. How far these targets are compromised will depend on the international competitiveness of the economy and the degree of supply side slack to be taken up. The greater the supply of spare physical and human capital, and the lower the marginal propensity to spend on imports, the greater will be the rise in real domestic activity when public spending exceeds tax receipts and the less reluctant the private sector will be to absorb any increases in the monetary base engineered by the government.

8 Economic Analysis of Financial Institutions

8.1 Introduction

In trying to understand the behaviour of financial institutions, we can make profitable use of the literature considered in Chapter 4, that has been developed to analyse the behaviour of firms in general. In this chapter, my concern is with the division of financial activities amongst different kinds of institutions, rather than with their price setting policies. The latter will be dealt with in Chapter 9. The applicability of the literature on the theory of the firm to both of these aspects of the operations of financial institutions is perhaps hardly surprising, given that a typical financial centre has many things in common with a high technology industrial estate or a shopping centre; it will contain many firms of varying sizes, ranging from highly specialised financial boutiques to firms such as Citicorp — diversified financial supermarkets that permit 'one stop financial shopping' and have operations in many countries.

Behind the shopfronts and inside the computer-filled offices of a typical financial centre, three main activities will be going on, with different degrees of associated risk. Least threatened by unexpected market downturns is the business of providing information to those who have funds to place in the money markets or to those seeking to raise finance. Some firms specialise purely in this activity; examples here range from small high street partnerships offering 'investment advice', up to major credit rating agencies that appraise the risks associated with loans to large corporations and nation states. (In Australia, even the ordinary person in the street may be aware of the work of Moody's Investors' Services, for this New York firm made the headlines in 1987 — by downgrading the Australian national credit rating from 'AAA' to 'AA1' — and again in 1988 — by reducing the rating of Australia's largest company, BHP, after the latter embarked upon a $A2.7 billion share buy-back campaign.) If these bodies offer bad advice and cause their clients to lose money, they risk losing future business through their tarnished reputations.

But that is all, for they do not actually take on any of their clients' financial risks.

A second activity is that of bringing suppliers and users of finance together and arranging the legal paperwork. This, too, may be very much in the nature of a 'fee for service' operation (as was the case with with stockbroking in Britain before the 'Big Bang' ended the required separation between brokers and jobbers), unless the firm in question takes on some financial risks to fill in possible gaps between the arrivals of buyers and sellers in the market in question. For example, a merchant bank may underwrite a new equity issue that it is handling for a firm, but might not normally expect to have to take up unsold shares. However, these kinds of firms have increasingly been taking on considerable risks of asset price movements: as Hamilton (1986, p. 89) notes, the big league American investment banks Salomans or Merrill Lynch on any one night 'might "go to bed" with an overnight exposure on their books of bonds and stocks of between $3 billion and $5 billion'. In times of financial collapse, a firm that specialises in dealing in securities might be able to do very handsomely: one such scenario would be where a flight from the market brings lots of orders to sell. However, such a firm might get into deep trouble if it purchased shares that its clients (or other market participants) were selling and then held on to them on a mistaken expectation that their prices would recover rather than falling further before settlement became due. In the shakeout of securities firms following the Crash of October 1987, yuppie un-employment increased partly because of hammerings of broking firms due to their own misjudged speculations and partly because the switch from bullish to bearish sentiments led to a collapse in the volume of trade on which commissions might be earned once the markets had become more orderly.

Thirdly, there is the activity hitherto given greatest attention in works on money and banking, namely, *financial intermediation* — in other words, raising money from one group of agents and relending it to another group. If the latter group do not perform very well, the interest payments or dividends that can be transferred to the former group may have to be slashed, with a capital loss also being implied for them if their claims on the institution are marketable or if the encashment values of their claims are related (as with some superannuation funds) to the value of the institution's assets. It may even be the case that the financial institution itself becomes insolvent and cannot honour claims on deposits in full or, in the case of 'capital guaranteed' superannuation contracts, cannot meet its lump-sum repayment obligations.

In a world of incomplete and dispersed information, where many individuals have strong opportunity cost reasons for not spending much of their time studying and personally participating in financial markets, the existence of financial firms engaging in the first two kinds of activities is readily understandable. However, given the availability of these two kinds of financial services, careful thought is required before one can provide a rationale for financial intermediation. In the sections that follow the economics of intermediation will be explored, along with reasons for recent changes in the activities of financial firms.

8.2 Balance Sheets of Financial Intermediaries

The assets of a solvent financial intermediary are necessarily equal to claims upon it, from the moment it begins to set up operations and thereafter so long as it stays in business. In conventional texts on monetary economics, this statement is simplified to take the following form: 'the assets and liabilities of a solvent financial intermediary are necessarily equal'. An auditor, however, will conventionally divide the debit side of a financial intermediary's balance sheet into 'liabilities' and 'share capital and reserves', rather than treating as liabilities all the money that has been raised by the institution. This distinction between the two debit categories is important. The former comprise any money the intermediary has raised in the market, whether from depositors, or from loans by the reserve bank and/or other financial intermediaries, to which a particular claim — which may involve a detailed schedule of repayments or withdrawal under particular terms — is attached. The latter, which I shall hereafter call 'reserves' for short, refers to the intermediary's net assets. These are a residual, whose value will be adjusted to ensure that the two sides of the institution's balance sheet sum to the same amount. For example, when loans are written off as bad debts, or a rise in interest rates causes the intermediary to suffer capital losses on its holdings of securities, it will record a reduction in reserves of an equal amount. If the institution is wound up and ceases to exist as a going concern, depositors and creditors have first claim on its funds as assets are cashed in. Any funds that remain from liquidation will be paid to shareholders, pro rata to their shareholdings. In the case of a financial intermediary that is wound up in a state of insolvency, its liabilities will exceed its assets, so the shareholders will get nothing and those who have made deposits with it or otherwise lent it money will only receive back a fraction of the amount with which they have they have parted.

If they are at all worried about the risk of losing their money, any would-be lenders to a financial intermediary or subscribers to a new issue of its equities may wish to know about the size of its liabilities relative to its existing reserves (which they may prefer to call its debt/equity ratio), as well as about the composition of its assets and liabilities. Reserves will be relatively unlikely to become depleted if they are proportionately large and if the intermediary has a set of claims on clients with strong credit ratings, while the vulnerability of the intermediary to a run of claims for repayment will clearly depend on the kinds of deposits it has accepted and on its ability to recall loans at short notice. These matters will also be of interest to the monetary authorities, who may lay down regulations about the structure of balance sheet an intermediary is allowed to have if it is to come into a particular category and receive particular privileges such as access to lender of last resort loans from the reserve bank. We will come back to the issues of financial failure and prudential control in Chapter 12. The effects of restrictions on balance sheet compositions will also be discussed in some detail in Chapter 9, when the issue of credit creation is discussed. For the present, I wish merely to explore the development of a financial intermediary's balance sheet in general terms in order to set the scene for the rest of this chapter's discussions about the economics of the financial firm.

Suppose a new finance company is set up via the flotation of equity stock. This company is likely to appoint bankers and pay the cheques it receives from the equity buyers into its new bank account. It now has assets (the bank deposits) and 'reserves' (the claims of the equity holders). It may then purchase premises and pay by writing out a cheque on its bank account and passing this to the vendor of the premises. Its assets still equal its reserves, though its assets are now divided between bank deposits and the buildings it owns.

To become operational, our hypothetical finance company will need to spend money, hiring staff and paying for advertisements, which may seek subscribers to a debenture issue. These expenditures will initially run down both its reserves and its assets, as payments are made to staff and for advertisements. However, to the extent the firm markets itself successfully, it will receive cheques from debenture purchasers that it can pay into its bank account: it now has liabilities (claims of debenture holders for a stream of interest payments and, on a particular day, for repayment of principal), but its assets have risen by an equal amount. It is ready to make loans — for example, to members of the public who wish to purchase new and secondhand consumer durables — and indeed it is likely to need to do so simply to honour its obligations to holders of its debentures due to the interest rate on these being greater than what it earns by leaving the money in its bank account. Attempts to win borrowers away from other sources of finance will eat further into its reserves and its bank balance. So, too, will the processing and administration of the deals it strikes with borrowers and the interest payments it makes to holders of its debentures. If it cannot attract suitable clients, the company might well end up recording a fall in its net assets.

A customer who receives the finance company's approval might be expected to sign up either for a personal loan or as a party to a hire purchase/leasing agreement. In the former case, the customer is given a cheque drawn against the finance company's bank account. The finance company thus exchanges a claim on its bank for a claim on the client who has signed the loan contract. It hopes that the client will each month pay in a cheque for an agreed value. Part is intended to cover the interest on the amount of the loan that has been outstanding for the month in question; this will be an addition to its total assets and reserves. The remainder will repay part of the loan and merely change the composition of the finance company's assets, giving it bank deposits that it can lend to someone else.

In the case of a hire purchase or leasing contract, the finance company buys the item in question on behalf of the client, who is then entitled to use it for the term of the contract and may be in a position to claim tax relief on the rental payments (for example, in the case of a leased company car). However, as far as the analysis of the finance company's balance sheet is concerned, the monthly payments may be recorded in very much the same way as repayments of a personal loan. Each month the value of its balance sheet associated with the deal falls if the market value of the asset in question falls — wear and tear will normally ensure that this happens, unless prices of newly produced examples of the subject of the contract are rising sharply, or it suddenly acquires status as a collector's item. Despite this, the finance company's net assets, and its bank balance, will grow with each payment by the client so long as the depreciation write-down is less than the rental charge. A rise in the value of commodities that underlie particular contracts will leave the firm in the position of being able to record an increase in its assets and reserves by the value of the monthly repayment plus the increase in market value of the commodity.

What happens at the end of hire purchase and leasing contracts can take a variety of forms. In the simplest case, where it is agreed that the client can purchase the item in question for a nominal sum, all we really have is a situation where the last payment effectively sees that value of the item being written down to zero. One of the more complex cases would be where the last rental payment is accompanied by a substantial cash lump sum which takes the place of the item in the company's asset listing as the lessee becomes the item's owner. Whether or not the lump sum 'balloon' payment is seen as entailing a change in total reserves and assets would here depend upon whether the company has been doing a simple straight line historic cost-based depreciation of the item's value down to its agreed residual value or has been keeping a firm eye on what it would fetch if the client failed to meet payments and repossession had to occur.

At the end of each accounting period, the finance company's audit will reveal its change in reserves, which is the same as its net acquisition of financial assets for the period. If it has made neither accounting profits nor losses, then its NAFA will equal zero: it cannot pay out dividends to its shareholders without running down its net assets to a value below that of the end of the previous period, even if its total balance sheet has increased in size. Clearly, a financial intermediary that continues to expand its balance sheet without increasing its net assets it going to find it harder and harder to satisfy existing shareholders, let alone raise new equity and attract new liabilities. A financial intermediary that simultaneously experiences no growth in its net assets and suffers a reduction in its gross assets may look somewhat less vulnerable in the short term, but something is still going badly wrong if the balance sheet and reserve holdings of its rivals are growing steadily: its shareholders' funds would be better placed with the latter.

8.3 Intermediation Versus Direct Financing

Some questions appear to be in order now we have recognised that the NAFAs of solvent financial intermediaries must equal zero aside from changes in reserves resulting from profits or losses. Why are borrowers prepared to line the pockets of shareholders of financial institutions by paying to rent money from these bodies instead of borrowing directly from lenders and paying them a rate of interest somewhere between the loan and deposit rates set by intermediaries? In other words, why do borrowers not try to do without financial middlemen? Why do lenders not take similar initiatives and seek to undercut the middlemen and thereby lend directly? The obvious riposte to these queries begs a further question: 'in fact, some borrowers and lenders do avoid using intermediaries, but some don't, so how do we explain the structure of financing and changes in that structure?'

These questions are not merely of academic interest. Take first the area of consumer credit. We are not dealing purely with cases of direct financing that may be quantitatively somewhat insignificant: for example, where children find their parents keen to undercut interest charges of banks and finance companies by lending out money from their retirement savings, with the children paying the parents their opportunity cost return (for example, the interest their money would have earned had it continued to be kept in a building society). Rather, we need a way of understanding the explosion of direct financing that has taken place recently, as well as long-standing phenomena such as trade credit. Following the lead of Sears Roebuck in the US, retail stores such as Marks & Spencer and Debenhams in the UK, and Coles-Myer in Australia, nowadays try simultaneously to drum up business and the potential for interest earnings by supplying their customers with credit. Likewise, the big three US car companies each run their own finance companies, to lend their potential customers the money to buy their cars.

Such developments make it very tricky to define where direct financing stops and intermediation begins. It may well be the case that the consumer credit comes from financially distinct subsidiaries — such as Ford Credit — that do act as financial intermediaries to the extent that they raise funds externally, for example by issuing debentures. However, to the extent that the funds come from undistributed profits of the parent company, it is far less clear whether intermediation or direct financing is taking place — perhaps one should say that top managers with shareholdings are lending directly but external shareholders, and those employee-shareholders not involved in decisions about the allocation of corporate funds to consumer credit, are not, since the latter two groups are letting the former decide what to do with the retained profits.

On the side of corporate finance, we have to be concerned not merely with companies that may decide to obtain new equipment by using the funds from a fresh equity or debenture issue to purchase it, rather than by going to a bank to fix up a leasing scheme or to borrow the money to finance the purchase of the equipment. We should not forget the role of trade credit as a substitute for bank overdrafts, especially since sometimes this source of working capital may even provide the wherewithal for fixed investments: I well recall how, in the early 1980s, a tyre and exhaust specialist in the UK very rapidly built up a nationwide set of operations through its skill at turning over tyre stocks at a far faster rate than its suppliers required payment. More importantly, as was stressed in section 4.5 and as every MBA student knows, large manufacturing companies can channel the surpluses of their 'cash cow' divisions directly to their cash-hungry 'stars', 'question marks' and 'dogs', as well as frequently using their financial surpluses for purchasing each others' securities, even if they have no intention of making an outright takeover bid.

The phenomenon of direct financing — which the financial institutions see as *dis*intermediation — is becoming so widespread, particularly in respect of long term large-scale borrowing where marketable securities are displacing loans, that it is posing a major strategic challenge to even the largest banks, some of which are seeking increasingly to make their profits from broking activities rather than from intermediation (see Coggan, 1986, Ch. 1). The structural shifts between intermediated and direct finance are also of major importance for the monetary authorities, whose policies have hitherto concentrated on controlling the volume of aggregate demand via attempts to influence the size of financial intermediaries' (particularly banks') balance sheets: to put it bluntly, these developments are further nails in the coffin of policies that centre on monetary targeting (see further, Chapters 9 and 14 below).

There are five frequently proposed explanations of why people and companies are attracted to make use of financial intermediaries, despite the costs of doing so. The first I wish to consider is the claim that, by 'borrowing short and lending long', these institutions often *transform maturities* for people who wish to rent their money out for periods shorter than the time other people wish to be in debt.

Little thought is required to see that intermediation is not essential as a means for reconciling conflicting financial time horizons. So long as securities that represent long-term debt can be sold at short notice, borrowers may find it quite easy to sell them to people who wish to place funds on the market on a short term basis. In the late

1980s *securitisation* has broadened the market for loan paper beyond government stocks and corporate debentures and into the area of household credit. Mortgage securitisation involves parcelling together a body of individual mortgages as backing for a paper security, which yields a flow of income derived from the payments by mortgagors. These securities can be bought and sold, and hence passed from one short-term lender to another. Although traditional intermediaries are starting to take on some of the business of parcelling up and floating the securities and acting as collection/distribution agencies for repayments (even building societies could move in this direction and away from the business of deposit-taking), there is no reason in principle why such actitivites should not be undertaken by specialist broking firms with the kinds of skills one normally associates with merchant banks. In fact, as Hamilton (1986, p. 71) points out, mortgage securitisation has been encouraged for the past thirty years by the US government, which has given guarantees to bodies such as the Federal National Mortgage Association and the Student Loan Marketing Association, and it has grown to be a $500 billion market. The impetus towards securitisation has also come from banks, such as Bankers Trust, that have recently seen the securitisation of their loans as a way of getting out of most of their retail deposit taking activities once they have decided that their best chances of survival lie in corporate and investment banking (Hamilton, 1986, p. 102). There is no reason in principle why securitisation cannot be extended to cover personal loans for other consumer durables, with shorter lifespans than houses, or business leases on cars and computers.

Like debentures, mortgage-backed securities offering fixed interest rates can be aimed especially at institutional lenders — financial intermediaries such as pension funds who normally require steady earnings. (One would expect them to come to have a strong appeal to building societies as devices for dealing with occasional drains on their liquidity, for it is much easier to sell off previously purchased mortgage-backed securities than it is to try to recall particular mortgages prematurely.) For those who only wish to lend out their money on a short term basis, the purchase of such securities would be a somewhat hazardous exercise in times of fluctuating interest rates. However, it would seem perfectly possible to issue mortgage-backed securities involving indexed repayment obligations for the mortgagors: for example they could be related by some formula to the home loan rates set by intermediaries. A sudden rise in interest rates would then be less likely to entail a fall in the value of the securities.

As an alternative to the securitisation route, long-term borrowers could try to meet the requirements of lenders by arranging a succession of short term loan contracts. If the suppliers of funds found that they did not wish to access them at the end of the contract, then they could relend the money for another term. To the extent that previous lenders did require access to their funds, the borrower could make contracts with others who were newly entering the market, willing to part with access to their funds. The suggestion that *de facto* long term indebtedness can be arranged on the basis of, if need be, very short term loan arrangements should not seem at all far fetched. In practice, loan contracts *can* be made for very short durations, as in the case of the overnight money market (where, indeed, much of the business is between banks themselves), and short term loans are often 'rolled over' time and time again, as with many borrowings by Japanese businesses (see section 2.2) and less developed countries.

It might be objected that agents who borrowed in the latter way would have no guarantee of being able to refinance their debts when their existing loan arrangements expired, and that this would militate against them using such a method of finance. However, it should not be forgotten that financial institutions that do not match the maturities of their assets and liabilities face precisely the same problem. This was very apparent after the 1973-4 oil price increases: the OPEC countries were keen to place their surplus funds with banks, but initially they were only willing to do so on a rather short-term basis, in order to take advantage of the growing tendency towards exchange rate instability. Until the OPEC depositors began to take a longer term view, fears of sudden huge deposit withdrawals concentrated the bankers' minds wonderfully on the advantages of casting themselves in a loan broking role and encouraging disintermediation in the process of recycling OPEC funds to countries with increased balance of payments deficits.

A second rationale put forward for financial intermediaries is that they make it possible for small savers to lend to large spenders. However, pooling of financial resources can be achieved without intermediaries being involved: here, we can note the frequent cases of large users of funds, such as major corporations or sovereign borrowers, doing deals with smaller suppliers of funds — including banks themselves — grouped together as a consortium. It is also interesting that, at the more mundane level of housing finance, one finds 'small' borrowers, willing to pay the interest charges of intermediaries and yet having to put together a loan 'cocktail' from the coffers of several financial institutions because no single lender is prepared to put up the entire sum required: a bank or building society may limit the percentage of a house's valuation against which it is willing to put up a mortgage and suggest that the would-be buyer finances the balance in excess of her deposit by going to a credit union for a personal loan and going to appropriate agencies to check her eligibility for any low interest start-up loans provided by the government.

Thirdly, the rise of cash management trusts might be taken to suggest that financial intermediaries enable small depositors indirectly to take advantage of economies of scale in making deposits. Cash management trusts relend small deposits in large blocks on the wholesale money market and thereby earn higher rates of interest than their depositors could hope individually to achieve. However, this again begs the question of why such depositors do not get together and form some kind of cooperative or consortium to lend out their pooled funds directly. They could thereby avoid losing to the intermediary part of the return on wholesale lending. After all, the cooperative method has been used successfully by small independent grocers to gain greater buying power and thereby compete with multi-branch supermarket chains.

Fourthly, it may be suggested that financial intermediaries enable people to spread the risks associated with renting out their money. For those with funds who are worried about the risks of putting all their financial eggs in one basket, one possibility is to make small loans to a large number of borrowers: this is, of course, precisely what the typical financial firm does. For example, although an individual may be operating on a smaller scale than the managers of a unit trust, it is quite in order for her to buy small parcels of equities in many companies, for example, instead of subscribing to a broad-based unit trust and letting someone else hedge on her behalf. Although the individual may feel drawn to the unit trust because of doubts about her own expertise in playing the markets, she may also recognise that she can purchase expertise and then buy shares on her own account: it is not necessary to turn her money over to an intermediary. Moreover, it should not be forgotten that the existence of unit trusts, life assurance companies and deposit-taking institutions does not of itself necessarily eliminate all the worries that people might have about their abilities to hedge their bets in financial markets: there is still the risk that particular financial intermediaries may perform poorly, so it is no surprise to see people having claims on a variety of institutions (cf. sections 3.3 and 4.5).

Finally, let us consider the suggestion that financial intermediaries exist because of the difficulties that suppliers and users of funds may have in discovering each others' whereabouts. For example, until July 1988 a single branch intermediary called the 'Campus Credit Union Cooperative Society' operated at the university at which I work (following an uncontested takeover, the branch now functions as part of the somewhat larger Savings and Loans Credit Union — cf. section 8.6). If this body had not existed, members of the university who wanted to borrow money from their colleagues would obviously have found it very tiresome to ring round or go on door-knock expeditions to raise money directly. Such a problem would obviously have sent them elsewhere in search of their loans. However, if informational problems provided the rationale for the Campus Credit Union's existence, they did not mean it had to act as a financial intermediary. Membership could instead have involved access to an on-campus loan broking and payments collection service, with the cooperative's employees handling all the paperwork that might arise from lenders' maturity requirements and from any requests they made concerning the maximum proportion of their funds they wished to lend to any single individual with a particular credit rating. With such a service, it would not be necessary for lenders ever to come face to face with borrowers; indeed, so long as the cooperative's office kept charge of records of how particular loans had been syndicated, total anonymity could be preserved.

8.4 A Transaction Cost Perspective

The problem of finding a rationale for the existence of financial intermediaries is similar to that of trying to explain the contrasting strategies of firms in the non-financial sector that engage in vertical integration and other forms of diversification. In sections 4.4 and 4.5 I examined corporate diversification from the standpoint of the the recent literature of 'Transaction Cost Economics', making particular reference to the work of Coase (1937), Williamson (1975, 1985) and Kay (1982, 1984). This literature seems readily — or rather, particularly, given its overlaps with liquidity preference theory — applicable to firms in the financial sector. The relevance of Williamson's contributions in this context has been recognised by the political theorist Michael Moran in his (1986) book *The Politics of*

Banking (material from which is used in section 12.7 in relation to the regulation of financial systems), and in a paper by Williams (1986) intended for a readership of accountants. However, applications of transaction cost economics are conspicuous by their absence in the major surveys of literature on banking and the theory of the firm by Baltensperger (1980) and by the contributors to JMCB (1985). Nor, despite obvious commonalities, is it referred to in recent work by Diamond (1984) on the theory of intermediation.

As was noted in section 4.4, Coase argued in his seminal paper that the firm is a device for dealing with change without a need to rewrite contracts to cover the impact of changes on affected parties. The firm has a rationale only because there are costs associated with getting things done in the market. In the context of financial intermediation a Coasian perspective would run as follows. *Some kind of transaction cost will be incurred no matter which method is used for arranging flows of finance between lenders and borrowers.* An institution that internalises borrowing/lending activities within its own balance sheet does so in the hope of earning a margin by providing cheaper ways for lenders and borrowers to reconcile their divergent needs for finance and willingnesses to take risks. As far as depositors with banks, building societies, credit unions and so on are concerned, the key feature of the arrangement is that they are lending to the institution as a whole: trouble with any particular asset will have no impact whatever on the wealth of particular depositors provided that the intermediary can write it off against its reserves. Depositors only stand to lose if there are a large number of simultaneous losses due to widespread defaulting by borrowers and/or a collapse in security prices.

Compared with alternatives — such as simply holding on to notes and coin to avoid risks of lending, or hedging by lending small sums directly to a range of individuals or by holding a diversified portfolio of shares and government securities — deposits may be seen as offering great scope for achieving a satisfactory risk/return mix with minimal transaction costs. (It may be useful here to think back to the discussions in section 2.5 and note that a placement with a financial intermediary in preference to the purchase of equities and debentures takes a step further the advantages that the ownership of corporate securities has over the ownership of a specific physical asset which is rented out to a firm.) Depositors can access (or pay in) their funds via one simple withdrawal (or deposit) request. Moreover, they can do this without incurring significant fees. This is in sharp contrast to the situation that small savers often face if they want to put their funds into securities. There are obvious economies of scale in obtaining information about what to buy and when to sell, and in the brokerage costs associated with dealing in small parcels of shares. These are likely to ensure that the person with a small financial surplus may get a better net return from a time deposit in a bank or building society or by placing funds with one of the 'institutional' inter-mediaries that can benefit from economies of scale in playing the stock market.

An intermediary will need to ensure that borrowers can benefit from lower interest rates and/or loan set-up charges, for otherwise they will have no incentive not to use direct financing methods. Lower interest costs to borrowers may be possible in so far as lenders are prepared to accept that interest payments lower than those available on direct lending are the price they must pay for the service the intermediary provides in enabling them to meet their risk/return/ flexibility goals more easily than they might if they used other means of making their surplus funds available to others. Competition for funds amongst intermediaries will limit the price that lenders have to pay in this way. On the side of set-up costs for loans, the services offered by an intermediary may look attractive from the standpoint of a borrower who is not naturally in direct touch with potential sources of funds, or whose funding needs are not large enough to benefit from any economies of scale that exist in the loan broking business. Maturity transformation by intermediaries may give borrowers transaction costs lower than those that would be associated with frequent rollovers of short term securities. As deposits come and go, there is normally no need for the intermediary to consult borrowers at all, which is precisely as in cases where a loan is securitised and the ownership of some of the securities changes hands. However, compared with a securitised loan, a long-term loan from an intermediary is much more convenient should the borrower decide to pay off the debt more rapidly than had originally been planned.

Overdraft facilities provide a further example of a device offered by banks and, increasingly, even junior league intermediaries such as credit unions, which involves very low transaction costs. An initial agreement is made between the borrower and intermediary about how far the former's account may become overdrawn, but no formal contract is made concerning the time and actual extent of overdrawing and repayments (aside from banks typically specifying that they may demand full payment at any time, something they rarely do in practice). The borrower does not need subsequently to visit the intermediary to make arrangments for accelerated repayments or for increased indebtedness so long as the agreed ceiling provides adequate headroom. Credit cards offer much the same attractions, along with their means of payment capabilities.

It is not impossible for something akin to an overdraft facility to be arranged without the participation of an intermediary. The recent emergence of markets for debt options provides some food for thought in this connection (see Das, 1987, for a succinct guide). The debt instruments traded in practice are usually 90-day bank bills or bank bill futures, and those who buy them usually do so as a way of reducing their exposure to possible fluctuations in interest rates during the option period. In principle, however, options could pertain to potential debts of particular individuals and corporations.

One arrangement would involve the sale of loan options by would-be lenders to those who wanted guaranteed access to funds, at a guaranteed price, during the period before the option expired. If sellers of the options later had second thoughts about their willingness to provide funds if called upon to do so, they could get out of their commitments by buying similar options to borrow. It is easy to see scope for considerable transactions costs with this system, arising because of the costs of floating such securities. It would also be necessary to specify credit rating categories in the options and restrict exercise rights to those whose credit ratings were equal or superior to the specified category, for the writers of options would wish to prevent subsequent trade in them from leading to any increase in the riskiness of the loans they might be called upon to make.

In practice, the modern alternatives to overdrafts used by corporate borrowers are hybrids between options, bank loans and spot sales of commercial paper: NIFs and RUFs (respectively, note issuance facilities and revolving underwriting facilities) are offered by syndicates of merchant banks who contract to stand ready to issue and underwrite short- to medium-term securities for the client firms. The transaction cost advantages of NIFs and RUFs over the option system just described are obvious: the client is basically paying a fee for the option to have securities sold by an agent or syndicate of agents and then, until an actual need for funds arises, there is no need for the underwriters to enter the market at all.

8.5 Effects of Opportunism on the Choice Between Direct and Intermediated Financing

Williamson's (1975, 1985) extensions of Coase's work point to further complications and insights regarding the choice between direct and intermediated lending. As we saw in section 4.4, one of Williamson's main themes is that economic organisation may be affected by fears of 'opportunistic' behaviour — fears that decision-makers on one side of a transaction may guilefully exploit the ignorance of those on the other side. This is an idea which figured earlier, though not so prominently, in the behavioural theory of the firm proposed by Cyert and March (1963). Although the significance of their theory for monetary economics is more appropriately explored later on (see Chapter 13), a brief sketch of how they would see the relationship between a firm and its bankers is a useful prelude to an application of Williamson's work in this context.

Cyert and March portray firms as coalitions of agents who, so to speak, 'keep their cards close to their chests' as they make demands for a slice of the organisational output and promise to provide inputs. Such coalitions include suppliers of finance. Managers of a firm can never be sure quite how far they can push their luck with their bankers (nor with their shareholders, customers, workers or each other, for that matter), and bankers can never be sure quite how far they can push their luck with the managers before they will abandon projects involving loan finance or will turn to other sources of funds. In troubled times, managers may find their bankers surprisingly understanding, and bankers may be surprised at the restructuring the managers are willing to undertake to avoid foreclosure. In other words, under pressure coalition members start revealing more of their hands in order to avoid seeing the disintegration of the firm and the consequent need to incur the costs of trying to fix up new market transactions (such as new jobs for management, new corporate clients for the bank). The implication is that in the past both sides have been behaving with opportunism: management have been jeopardising their firm's balance sheet by permitting non-essential expenditures; the bankers have been giving the impression of being less willing to back the firm than they really were.

Implied in the Cyert and March analysis is the notion that the pressure of competition will affect the extent to which economic actors feel inclined to behave with opportunism. Williamson also makes use of this idea (with surprisingly little acknowledgement to his teachers, Cyert and March) but, as we saw in section 4.4, he sets it in a broader context by arguing that the incentive to use one's private knowledge in a guileful manner will vary according to the transactional environment in which one is acting. The possibility of opportunistic behaviour is guaranteed not to be an issue in a transaction only if the relationships between the parties to the deal can be specified fully and without cost in a contract that will subsequently be costless to enforce.

It is hard to imagine a market where scope for opportunistic behaviour arises more than in that for finance, even though the ready market for suitable premises, the scope for leasing computing equipment and the increasing ability of skilled personnel to extract their transfer earnings from their employers might all be taken to suggest it is a highly contestable one. Those who part with their money have great problems in the areas of information and property rights. For example, a lay-person may be unable to check the quality of financial advice given by a third party without investing in expertise herself or relying on the advice of a fourth party: how can she know if she has become sufficiently expert or that she is not being deceived by a fourth party? Guarantees may be offered in respect of flows of earnings or realisation values, but if the guarantor chooses not to deliver, it may be costly to go through the courts to obtain redress. It may be very difficult to distinguish sloth and incompetence from genuine bad luck in the event of non-guaranteed earnings being below expectations, and this could make it very unclear whether a change to another way of lending out one's money is in order. Let us explore these kinds of problems in some detail.

To begin, consider some of the worries a non-expert lender may have when initially shopping around for somewhere to place her funds. If she goes to an investment advisor, there is the risk that she will be offered biased recommendations. The advisor — who may be someone encountered in person or via the medium of an investors' magazine — may have personal holdings in particular securities and hence stand to benefit by encouraging the client to buy them too. (Editors of investors' magazines will similarly think twice about condemning the financial packages offered by those who provide them with major sources of advertising revenue.) If the advisor also fixes up the deal that the client has decided upon, it is possible that a commission fee will be forthcoming from the third party, who may well be a financial intermediary. Hence the advice offered may be shaped by the different sizes of commissions: for example, it may be that the advisor can earn more by encouraging the client to place her money with a particular unit trust or life assurance company, rather than by suggesting she purchases a particular portfolio of equities and bonds. Unless legislative safeguards are in operation, potential lenders to unit trusts and life assurance funds will not automatically be informed of the incentive structures with which advisors, brokers and dealers are working. The 1986 Financial Services Act in the UK has gone some way in the direction of providing such safeguards: it has ensured that since 29 April 1988 people seeking advice about life insurance packages are able to know whether they are dealing with Independent Financial Advisors or insurance company sales personnel.

If the lender is worried by the possibility that she will be given biased advice and by her own lack of expertise, she might consider avoiding the services of these agencies altogether, along with any attempt at direct financing, and instead focus her attention on intermediaries. But she could still go expensively wrong in trying to make up her own mind on the basis of the latters' past records and claims in their brochures. It might be better to pin unit trust and share listings to a noticeboard and choose on the basis of where darts happened to strike home after being tossed aimlessly in their direction — after all, if she throws in a truly random fashion and can adjust her portfolio quite frequently in the light of such exercises without incurring large brokerage fees, she can expect at least to beat the performance of the stock market index simply because the weights used in its compilation tend to be somewhat out of date.

Economic theory cannot predict on an a priori basis how the lender will eventually make up her mind, even if the size of her portfolio and her risk/return/flexibility preferences are known. We are dealing with a situation in which there is no obviously foolproof way of finding the preferred deal, so choices may vary greatly according to subjective perceptions. Practical investigations need to be made to discover the variety and relative frequency of use of beliefs actually used in portfolio choice. The hypothetical lender we have been considering *might* opt to go straight to an intermediary, because she believes that employees of intermediaries are be given strong incentives, such as bonus payments related to their firms' performances, to avoid making poor decisions about where to place their clients' funds. But she *might* choose that option on the basis of a multitude of other personal beliefs. Some lenders may feel that fund managers in intermediaries have much stronger longer term interests in making their money work well, because an 'advisor' may just receive a one-off kick-back for recommending a particular package. Compared with 'the institutions', brokers and advisors may seem more like potential fly-by-night operators if they have not been in the business for years and years. Other lenders, however, may see reasons to doubt such beliefs.

Those who see little need to regulate financial markets would probably wish to point out that advisors and brokers may think twice about letting their recommendations be biased by short-term considerations if these conflict with the possibility of building up the client's long-term goodwill and hence making money from repeat business and word-of-mouth recommendations. If the client discovers that she has been misled, then she may be able to do an opportunistic advisor a good deal of damage by spreading word to her friends, and this is something that an advisor, like a used car dealer, can point out to engender trust. As with motoring 'lemons', though, it may well be the case that this control mechanism works poorly: if would-be opportunists expect that most of their their customers would find it painful to confess expensive financial errors to their friends, then the risks associated with being an opportunistic advisor could seem worth taking. A further consideration favouring opportunism is that it is possible to lose clients even after giving 'genuine', 'independent' advice: if one cannot convince clients that their poor earnings are the result of events which a financial advisor could not reasonably have been expected to countenance as possibilities, then one may well end up being seen by them with suspicion. Given this, commission in the hand may look preferable to uncertain repeat business from current clients and from new clients that they might recommend.

Those who favour regulation of intermediaries would want to stress the scope for opportunistic behaviour on the part of employees of financial intermediaries. The history of banking is littered with examples of financial failures due to fraudulent activities. These have included cases of quite junior personnel engaging disastrously in unapproved speculation on their employers' accounts — as in the case of Lloyds Bank International (see Dow and Earl, 1982, pp. 156-7) — and doubtful top-level decisions to lend huge amounts to incestuously linked companies — as in the mid-1970s secondary banking crisis in Britain (see Reid, 1982). Such problems can even afflict small intermediaries that operate under the careful supervision of boards of trustees and which are subject to regular audits. As a member of the University of Tasmania's Campus Credit Union, I was myself shocked in mid-1987 to receive a letter recording the 'untimely death' of the Society's executive officer, but this was nothing compared with how I felt some days later when it became clear that this was a case of suicide and that, amongst other things, a good tenth of the Society's assets had allegedly been misappropriated. One was left wondering how many instances of financial fraud go totally undetected, despite the best efforts of auditors and supervisory bodies: the scope for massaging balance sheets to conceal doubtful loans is considerable; so, too, are the opportunities for pretending that bad debts are being written off when the truth of the matter is that funds are being siphoned away. The limitations of audits are made all too obvious by one survey discussed by Comer (1985), which found that more frauds were uncovered by information being proffered by vengeful mistresses than by auditors' revelations.

Depositors' and shareholders' interests may also be compromised by some of the entirely legal activities of managerial personnel in financial intermediaries. There is nothing illegal about the act of taking a chance and lending money to a very high risk client, even though the person authorising the loan stands to benefit from its seemingly beneficial short-term implications for the intermediary's balance sheet. In this connection, some comments in a paper on country risk analysis and the third world debt problem are worth noting:

Banks became overexposed sometimes because analysts made mistakes but mainly because the analysts' opinions were ignored. . . . The main reason for ignoring the analysts' view was that it was often incompatible with other goals of the bank, that is, the goals of marketing staff and senior management. Such goals might include keeping the bank in the top league of banks according to asset size or syndicated eurocredit or euroloan involvement, expanding the involvement of the bank in a market important to the banks strategically, the preservation of personal or inter-bank relationships and so on. . . . It was easy to rationalise the overriding of an analyst's negative view by the convenient argument that unlike companies which can be declared bankrupt, countries rarely disappear and a bank can usually expect to receive its money back eventually (Jackson, 1987, p. 333).

By the time bad loans surface as such, the senior management who authorised them may well be enjoying prosperous retirements or working for other institutions.

The mention of bad loans is a timely reminder that differences in possible opportunism on the part of advisors and managers employed by intermediaries are but one dimension of the problem faced by a lender. So let us now shift our focus to the task of guarding against defaults and disappointing yields from securities. In doing so, we should recognise the diverse origins of such problems. Some financial failures may be due to genuine bad luck, involving events which could not easily have been foreseen by the lender even if as much pertinent information as possible had been made available by the borrower. Others may arise because of guileful behaviour by borrowers, who at the time of seeking approval for funding deliberately conceal their true circumstances and/or their fears about what could go wrong with their plans. Yet others may be avoidable and nonetheless happen, because borrowers get into trouble during the course of their loans or indulge in questionable business and lenders do not discover what is going on until it is too late. For the remainder of this section, I will try to show why intermediaries may often be able to offer many lenders a better return than they could achieve by paying first for credit rating services and then incurring the costs of fixing up and monitoring a direct loan.

The superiority of intermediated loans does not arise purely because financial package deals enable a lender to engage in 'one stop shopping': *ex ante* and *ex post* credit rating and security purchasing services can, of course, be provided by a single agent, though an intermediary obviously has the edge in acting promptly in a crisis or in grasping opportunities for capital gains, since action can be immediate with no need to relay information and advice to clients and wait for their decisions. More importantly, one can see why intermediaries may also be able to cut the costs of appraisal, monitoring and obtaining redress from defaulting borrowers. Amongst intermediaries, banks have the most obviously advantageous position: in seeking some idea of likely behaviour of existing customers who are applying for new loans, they can look these clients' previous patterns of credits and debits (mindful, one would hope, of the possibility that previous patterns could have been created deliberately to lull them into a false sense of security!). As actual processors of payments after a loan has been made, banks also stand the biggest chance of being able to spot anything suspicious at an early date. These advantages will be diluted to the extent that bank debtors are borrowing from several institutions, but rival institutions obviously have some incentive to cooperate with each other in trying to keep clear overall pictures of their debtors' situations.

Access to credit-rating firms is restricted further for small lenders by a kind of 'public good' problem. A major worry for these agencies is that their hard-won information may be very easily resold by opportunistic clients, with the result that intelligence costs are not covered. The other side of the coin is that clients will be reluctant to pay the full costs of commissioning special studies if they believe the agency is likely to sell the findings to others. To avoid outright market failure, a rating agency may restrict circulation to a limited clientele of subscribers — preferably firms that have a competitive interest in not selling the information to other firms — who are each willing to pay a relatively fat fee. Only occasionally will such an agency deliberately release major ratings to a wider audience, and then mainly as a means of attracting further subscribers. The result of this is that agents with small amounts to lend are likely to be unable to obtain really detailed information about the circumstances of those to whom they might make direct loans. To get around this problem, they can place their money with an intermediary that does its own credit ratings but does not make its intelligence findings readily available (except to other intermediaries and rating agencies, for the reason outlined at the end of the previous paragraph), and/or which pays for the expensive services of credit rating agencies.

There is one other reason why intermediated lending could look attractive to those with surplus funds, even if they were not impressed with the case so far made. This concerns advantages that intermediaries often have over direct lenders in the matter of enforcing the terms of loan contracts, promoting high returns where precise levels are not specified in contracts and, if all else fails, mopping up after financial disappointment has occurred. The last of these affects the first two, since the greater a lender's ability to take action in the event of a default or deteriorating payments performance, the less likely it is that a borrower will knowingly embark upon actions which could give rise to financial difficulties.

A bankruptcy action against a firm may fail to recover much of the money it owes, but it will nonetheless involve some penalties for the firm's managers. Diamond (1984, p. 396) suggests that these include 'a manager's time spent in bankruptcy proceedings, costly "explaining" of poor results, search costs of a fired manager and (loosely) the manager's loss of "reputation" in bankruptcy'. If such penalties for giving one's creditors a bad deal were unlikely to be imposed, then borrowers could find opportunistic behaviour very tempting. A transaction cost perspective suggests that if lenders generally sought to hedge their bets by lending small amounts directly to a large number of borrowers, then attempts to obtain redress would be rare events and probably the only significant incentive against opportunism would be the difficulty one might have raising money a second time. The creditors in such a situation might well have rights according to the contracts in question, but the costs of enforcing them could well be prohibitive. To put it simply: they could find it difficult to get together to fight for their money. If their interests were also rather disparate, some might do badly even if they did try to come together, since the borrower might be able to manage a successful policy of 'divide and rule'. By contrast, if the loan had come from a single source or at least involved only a small consortium of lenders or was a relatively straightforward cocktail (for example, a house financed by a first mortgage from a building society plus a personal loan from a bank), then the borrower could face a much rougher time. Intermediaries thus provide means whereby lenders can seek to hedge their bets and at the same time concentrate the minds of the ultimate users of funds on the task of meeting their creditors' aspirations.

The argument just presented can be seen as an extension of one noted in section 4.5 and often made in the literature on takeovers and the theory of the firm when scope for a divorce of control between the owners and managers is being discussed. If a company is performing badly but the ownership of its shares is highly dispersed, then transactions costs may prevent dissatisfied shareholders from getting together to vote for a new board of directors. In the absence of a takeover bid from another company, the existing managers will thus remain in control.

The roots of these arguments concerning the superior control and enforcement capabilities of intermediaries compared with direct lenders are worth noting not merely because of their obvious relevance to attempts to understand how management of financial firms sometimes succeed in riding roughshod over interests of their shareholders (a particularly obvious possibility with bodies such as building societies where voting power is intrinsically highly dispersed because each depositor is a society member too). They may also help to ensure that in viewing intermediaries as conduits for loan finance we do not forget their often considerable equity interests. The growth of large shareholdings by 'the institutions' represents a potentially powerful threat to management teams who do not strive to meet shareholder aspirations. By ensuring that their own nominees attain places on company boards 'the institutions' can also enjoy monitoring advantages. When placing their money with these intermediaries, small lenders may therefore hope indirectly to get round the public choice and transaction cost problems they would otherwise face in trying to exert leverage over management. Such results are, however, by no means guaranteed. In the UK, for example, many of 'the institutions' used to take the view that they could not expect to be experts in the running of the diverse businesses in which they held equity; so, like small shareholders, they tended to sell out quietly if they were dissatisfied with yields (see Turner, 1969). Such a situation — nowadays rather less prevalent — contrasts strongly with the very active role played by bank representatives in the strategic management of German and Japanese enterprises.

If we continue to keep the literature on the modern business enterprise in our sights, it becomes apparent that some qualifications should be made to the arguments in the last three paragraphs: the rise of the large, multiproduct, multinational firm is something which threatens the supremacy of financial intermediaries as bodies able to enforce acceptable performances by management teams who have been given access to financial resouces. As was noted in section 4.5, such firms may organise themselves to function like miniature versions of the external market for capital. The work of Williamson (1970, 1971, 1975) leads one to expect that, compared with fund managers in the external capital market, the strategists in multidivisional firms would have superior capabilities in respect of auditing and the disposal of poorly performing staff and assets (though as I have elsewhere shown, the 'divide and rule' advantages of the profit-centres philosophy are by no means simple to achieve in practice: see Earl, 1984, pp. 162-72). Such firms may come close to matching many financial intermediaries in terms of the range of business risks with which they deal. Although they have no formal access to lender of last resort loans from the reserve bank, giant manufacturing firms are often politically too conspicuous to be ignored if they get into difficulties and cannot undertake major restructuring activities without enormous infusions of funds: hence, for example, the rescue of British Leyland and the Federal provision of loan guarantees to Chrysler.

For these reasons, the largest non-financial corporations may look more secure to many lenders than most banks do, so they can raise finance directly at lower rates than banks would need to charge to cover costs of attracting deposits. The sheer enormity of their financial activities enables them to spread very thinly the set-up costs associated with floating new loan stocks. Corporations with temporary financial surpluses can for the same reason cheerfully incur the costs of lending their funds directly, even for short periods (for example, by purchasing Eurobonds issued by other firms, and subsequently selling them when they need to increase their spending). It is no surprise that many, including IBM, Volvo, Xerox and BP, have developed their own in-house banking arms that function as profit centres in their own right.

It seems appropriate to end this section with a brief note on the possible significance of altruistic behaviour in financial systems. After all, it is difficult to ignore the fact that many financial intermediaries are formally cooperative societies that have grown up out of mutual self-help movements. The rules of cooperatives may specify non-financial directives which constrain their executive officers from acting as they would if working in a bank: as Williams (1986, p. 283) observes, 'In credit cooperatives altruistic motivation might be expected to be reflected in the valuation rules for withdrawal of claims, more casual bad debt policies, the incidence of higher credit risk policies, the incidence of low interest loans, and in the flexibility in loan repayments and default, etc.' However, this does not mean that such institutions will find themselves necessarily suffering from higher rates of default and hence be able to offer deposit rates of interest that will only appeal to those who are prepared to forego earnings in order to satisfy their altruistic inclinations (cf section 3.5). When workplace-based cooperatives typically receive loan repayments via direct salary deductions and may be able to secure loans against borrowers' superannuation, it becomes rather difficult for borrowers to default. Moreover, the fact that the victims of a bad debt will be the borrower's friends and colleagues, rather than a large, dispersed group of relatively anonymous bank depositors, may ensure that borrowers will feel much more compunction about putting themselves in a position where they might end up having to ask for their payments to be suspended; so, too, may the possibility of their friends and colleagues getting to know of their indiscretions. Financial cooperatives also benefit from being able to access the voluntary services of their members (for example, in a university credit union, the advice of economics and accountancy lecturers who serve on its board) and from the advantages that their more intimate knowledge of borrowers brings to the tasks of assessing credit risks and spotting emerging payments difficulties.

8.6 Strategic Aspects of Financial Intermediation

So far, I have taken it for granted that the market for loans is a dangerous place where diversification pays. But I have said nothing on the issue of how far an intermediary should diversify its portfolio, even though I have emphasised the fact that any lender needs skills in judging the behaviour of those with whom it deals. In trying to make sense of the evolution of firms in the financial services industry it is useful to recall the discussion in section 4.5 of Kay's (1982, 1984) 'synergy versus hedging' perspective on the relationship between transaction costs, diversification policies and changes in the characteristics of the environments in which firms operate.

If we think about financial markets from this perspective we would expect that economies can be obtained from specialising in related kinds of lending: either similar kinds of loans ('housing', or to a particular industry, for example), or loans to a select group of customers who need to borrow for a variety of purposes (such as a particular locality of borrowers). By initially investing in understanding a particular market in some detail, an intermediary can reach subsequent loan decisions at lower cost, and the same goes with knowing particular borrowers in a given market. However, that knowledge will never be complete, so sometimes mistakes will be made. In so far as the loans are related, the spill-over effects of such mistakes may be great. If the economic environment is highly turbulent, the risks to a financial intermediary of specialisation on either side of its balance sheet may be considerable.

Incentives for financial intermediaries to diversify their interests and regional coverage have been changed dramatically in the past decade or so: by deregulation — which has removed barriers between markets and changed the relative transaction costs of different ways of arranging borrowing and lending; by new technologies that have broken down barriers between international financial markets, reduced the costs of individual transactions and greatly increased financial firms' fixed capital requirements in terms of·computing facilities; and by the entrepreneurial initiatives of those who developed new financial 'products' to cater for the demand for protection against inflation and fluctuations in interest rates, commodity prices and exchange rates. Increasing regional disparities associated with changes in industrial structure also threaten to change the relative strengths of regionally localised and diversified firms: for example, as the UK became an economically divided nation under the rule of Margaret Thatcher, the Scottish banks and northern building societies could be excused for looking enviously at the prospects of their counterparts in the booming south of England.) It is clear from the recent books by Coggan (1986) and Hamilton (1986) that the recognition by financial firms that their environments are becoming more turbulent and their established roles no longer seem secure has led them to pursue a variety of offensive and defensive strategies. That it is by no means easy to decide upon appropriate strategies is something which is evidenced both by this variety and by the proliferation of 'how to' books on banking strategy, such as Aspinwall and Eisenbeis (1985), Donnelly *et al.* (1985), Gart (1985), Meiden (1984) and Nadler and Miller (1985). The remainder of this section considers some of the most popular strategies.

(1) Geographical Expansion

Sources of assets and liabilities may be expanded by moving into new territory: interstate, or internationally. Such policies may bring benefits of diversification as well as marketing synergy. For example, consider a building society based in an area where employment opportunities suddenly collapse due to a change in technology or fall in world commodity prices for its main output. It could find itself in trouble if the people started leaving the area or began to run down their financial assets: house prices (and hence the value of loan collateral) would get depressed and the unemployed might default on loans simultaneously with there being a drain on deposits. Such an institution could face difficulties in the form of a trading loss if it tried to reduce its deposit withdrawal risks by offering higher rates of interest on long-term deposits. By expanding the range of its branch network, it stands to be in areas of growth as well as of decline as the industrial structure changes. Moreover, when clients transfer geographically in search of better employment opportunities, they may well simply transfer their deposits between branches rather than go to the bother of starting up afresh with an unfamiliar intermediary whose standards of service might turn out to be inferior. They will be particularly likely to do this if other institutions want to be convinced of their track records as credit-worthy clients and worthwhile depositors and do not immediately offer to make mortgages available.

At the grander level of multinational banking, synergy themes are all the more conspicuous, for client corporations can be promised assistance when they embark on new trade ventures or set up subidiaries themselves in countries where their bankers already have operations. Glossy advertisements placed by multinational banks in the financial press almost invariably try to convey the message that there are advantages to be had from dealing with a bank that is as global in its perspectives as are its clients. It should not go unnoticed that a bank which lends to multinational corporate clients may also enjoy monitoring advantages by having a global branch network and dealing more directly with the subsidiaires that are using its money, rather than merely making loans via the clients' head officies or dealing with their subsidiaries from afar.

Synergy considerations in no way imply that such banks must necessarily own their overseas operations to present a uniform face to jet-setting executives of client companies and access a worldwide financial database. A bank could instead follow the kinds of strategy employed in the international hotel business (see Dunning and McQueen, 1982) or by McDonald's (see Love, 1986) and arrange franchising and agency deals with other deposit takers and lenders, for the use of its name, corporate image, buying power, information facilities and, if necessary, management expertise, without assuming its franchisees' business risks and without having to incur the costs of setting up operations for itself. The use of agents has, of course, been quite common when financial intermediaries have sought to expand their presence on a national basis: for example, building societies have often used real estate firms as deposit-taking agents, particularly in thinly populated areas where considerable spare capacity would exist in a specialist office; similarly, major credit cards such as Visa obtain global coverage through the participation of a remarkably diverse set of intermediaries, ranging from large banks to small credit unions.

Given the problems of coming to terms with different languages, legal and socio-economic systems, it may at first seem curious that banks so often seem to prefer to do things themselves in the international context. However, our earlier discussions concerning the effects of possible opportunism by agents on the choice between intermediated and direct lending seem ripe for extension to this context: it would be reasonable for parties on both sides of franchising and agency arrangements to hold fears about each other possibly behaving in an opportunistic manner. Just as high technology firms tend to operate as multinationals to prevent licensees from exploiting non-product-specific information in new contexts (see Galbraith and Kay, 1986; Kay, 1984), so domestic banks may be expected to be unwilling to provide, even for a fee, flows of information to overseas rivals who might be able to use it as a basis for invading their territories (cf. Yannopoulos, 1983, pp. 255-6). Likewise, just as poor service in one McDonald's restaurant can impact upon the sales of others, so network-wide goodwill losses may be suffered if a financial agent, working on behalf or under the corporate logo of a multibranch operator, disappoints customers by acting in its own local interests. To guard against such possibilities, exceedingly complex franchising and agency contracts could well be needed (possibly running into thousands of pages of regulations, given that the McDonald's franchising manual, for a far simpler product, runs into hundreds). The use of agents and franchise arrangements could also make it hard to provide guarantees of confidentiality as convincing as those that a unified banking operation can provide to its multinational customers.

Taken together, the risks of operating in unfamiliar territories, the problems associated with using the services of other firms and the additional costs of having to engage in competition for market share make it easy to see why geographical expansion has commonly been conducted via merger. That even the merger route has problems is well indicated by the heavy losses the British Midland bank suffered from its subsequently disposed of US subsidiary, Crocker National — though these should have hardly been surprising, given that Crocker had absorbed the failed United States Bank of San Diego shortly before being taken over by Midland. To judge from a study by Tschoegl (1982) of foreign bank entry into California and Japan, many banks must be aware of the hazards of such headlong plunges, for they have often made use of the scope for making gradual moves into foreign territories, though their choices of transactional framework have been somewhat constrained by host country regulations. It has been common for banks initially to confine themselves to the wholesale and corporate markets, first setting up an intelligence-gathering representative office that also solicits new business and liaises with host country operators who have borrowed from the head office. Somewhat greater commitment can come with the creation of a self-owned agency (as distinct from a subcontracted agent) to make loans and arrange overseas deposits for host-country clients, and it may then be quite a time before decisions are taken to open retailing branches to take local deposits or set up legally independent subsidiary companies.

(2) Market Penetration

Given the resource requirements and possible pitfalls of moves into strange territories, it should be no surprise that many financial firms have preferred to concentrate their efforts on encouraging higher usage rates of existing services, or winning new customers of their normal kind. The success of the building societies' attempts to build user-friendly images has been considerable, as has the use of advertisements in attempts to change attitudes towards indebtedness. The smaller intermediaries have largely ridden on the backs of larger ones as far as the latter possibility has been concerned, but they have tried to win market share by offering chequing facilities, bill-paying services, and longer opening hours. Sometimes those who make new deposits in credit unions are even rewarded with chances to win lottery prizes. The operating costs associated with such strategies may mean they turn out to be very expensive loss leader policies indeed if all they succeed in attracting are depositors who keep short term, small scale balances.

(3) New Market Strategies

Recent metamorphoses of financial intermediaries have included changes of focus within the world of finance — such as the acquisition of broking and merchant banking groups by major banks and insurance companies — and movements into other arenas — such as travel — where they can exploit their skills in the handling of information and acting as agents and offer their customers a bigger variety of products without having to open up new retail outlets. As with some cases of geographical expansion within a firm's normal range of focus, these moves have sometimes been quite traumatic. For example, American Express had internal problems during its attempts to build up a base in international capital markets by taking over Shearson Lehman and the Trade Development Bank of Switzerland. Such difficulties should be expected if the moves involve integrating businesses with entirely different organisational structures and corporate cultures, and even if a firm seeks to avoid them by growing internally, there may still be trouble due to insufficient knowledge of how to make goods loans in a new area. (For example, what would building society managers know about loan-making to small firms if they were suddenly allowed to do so by further deregulation?)

Following the creation of giant diversified and vertically integrated financial conglomerates, the potential for opportunistic behaviour in financial markets looms larger than ever before. The essential rationale for the old separation between stockbroking and jobbing activities in the British system had been that purchasers of shares could expect impartial advice from stockbrokers since, unlike jobbers, stockbrokers did not have to worry about disposing of depreciating shares held in their own portfolios. Stockbrokers would ask jobbers what their current prices for particular shares were without saying whether they were buying or selling for a client, so jobbers had an obvious incentive to quote a competitive price. Now it is much harder for people placing money on the British stock market to assess whether or not they are being cheated by their stockbrokers. As Coggan (1986, p. 40) observes, a similar problem arises when a company engaging in a takeover raid is seeking funds and advice in this connection from a bank 'which is also advising investors which shares to buy and is actively buying and selling shares itself', while 'groups with the financial muscle of a commercial bank to support them can manipulate share prices in their own interest if they have inside knowledge of a company's financial position'.

It is hard not to be cynical about the response of the new financial groups to public expressions of concern and calls for their regulation. They have each set up internal organisational partitions known as 'Chinese walls'. These are supposed to prevent abuses by barring flows of vital information between departments, but it is hard to believe such walls will not be overgrown by 'financial grapevine'. Indeed, if this does not happen, it is unlikely that many of the financial mergers between brokers, jobbers and bankers will deliver their expected synergistic payoffs.

The three themes of market penetration, entry into new markets and the scope of new forms of opportunistic behaviour also come together in the context of housing markets. In the UK, following deregulation of the market for housing finance, forward integration into estate agency businesses has been a popular means of increasing market penetration for banks, major building societies (such as the Halifax) and life assurance companies (such as Hambros and the Prudential). Would-be housebuyers calling on estate agents now find them giving the hard sell for mortgages and life assurance endowment policies as well as for houses. With these vertically integrated firms standing to make more money from housing finance than from selling houses for third parties, it is no wonder that buyers nowadays find themselves being offered a financing package even if they cannot pick a suitable house from the estate agent's listing: in this way, the financial firm that owns the estate agent may pre-empt the mortgage business from a rival chain that is actually able to find what the buyer wants. Of course, the ideal for the estate agent-owning financial intermediary is to be able to provide the house and the finance at the one stop, so that the buyer is less inclined to check out the financial deals that are available elsewhere. In the scramble to match each others' strategic advantages, the financial firms have made many owners of estate agencies rich overnight by purchasing their businesses at inflated prices that supposedly reflected the value of goodwill (for example, the Nationwide Anglia Building Society ended up with only £10 million in tangible assets after spending £120 million on 520 offices in 1987). Given the ease with which an experienced agent may set up shop again, it would not be surprising to find that some estate agents have succeeded in selling up more than once.

(4) Cooperation Between the Smaller Fry

To the extent that offensive strategies do not cause problems for firms that pursue them, one would expect those whose positions are thereby squeezed to seek out new problem-solving policies of their own. Obviously, the best form of defence might be attack, but this could be very dangerous for the small institution that lacks economies associated with large size, particularly those associated with the technological revolution in payments systems (see Lawrence and Shay, 1986, Ch. 2). The major banks may well see their common opportunistic interest can be served if they indulge in implicit collusion and each refuse to allow smaller institutions to hook up to their computer networks. To some extent, these difficulties are mitigated by the advantages of being able to avoid mistakes conspicuously made by pioneers with new technologies. Economies may also be achieved by consortium relationships (for example, a Union of Credit Unions or an Association of Savings and Loan Associations) that share or swap facilities such as computing systems and automated teller machines and yet, by stopping short of outright merger, enable the participants to continue to offer the kinds of personal service that have in the past given themselves a competitive edge against the big operators. Another possibility is to create a joint venture company to run a shared system. (Joint ventures have also been used to good effect by larger players: for example the creation of Chase-AMP Bank Ltd. enabled Chase Manhattan to enter the Australian retail banking market and the Australian Mutual Provident

Society to make use of synergy potential inherent in its reputation and infrastructure.) The main thing that would tend to get in the way of such cooperative arrangements would be inequalities of costs and benefits felt by the various parties. If negotiations of this kind failed, one would expect to see some smaller institutions concluding voluntary mergers — in which they hoped holistic considerations would prevail — and others attempting to find the least unsatisfactory large bank into whose balance sheet and organisational structure to become absorbed.

(5) Rationalisation

With the advent of a more competitive financial environment, some institutions have been driven to appraise carefully what their 'loss leader' policies are actually costing: even the major banks can be seen doing this as — in terms of the latest buzz-words — they 'unbundle' their charges for services on a 'user pays' basis. But it is by no means easy to decide which services to phase out in a business where one is providing a whole range of services to customers who use them in different degrees. Where banking staff are not permanently rushed off their feet, almost any small transaction can be argued to be making a contribution to overheads or long-run goodwill. An alternative perspective might suggest that ways should be considered to cut overheads by slimming down the organisational hierarchy, consolidating nearby branches, and so on. Branches that are poor performers are problematical as possible victims of a rationalisation purge: in so far as they are linked in their transactions with the 'successful' ones, their demise may undermine the whole system, just as a railway system may not be viable without 'loss-making' branch lines to act as feeder routes for their mainline activities. Here, though, institutions may be able to close branches with minimal losses by subcontracting business to agents in the areas from which they are retreating, or by replacing staffed branch operations with automated teller machines.

(6) Niche-Marketing

For some financial firms, a return to earlier policies of specialisation may seem to offer the best prospect for survival, particularly if resources are not available to copy offensive strategies of rivals. Market 'interstices' (as Penrose, 1959, calls them) may tend to be neglected by large intermediaries that recognise the managerial limits to infinite growth and can see profitable ways of using their resources in the 'big time' of, say, international banking. If this neglect and the interstices themselves seem likely to be a long-term phenomena, then, by specialising in a few of them, a small non-bank financial intermediary may be able to drive out those of its similarly-sized rivals that dilute their expertise by hedging and hoping for expansion in a larger number of markets.

8.7 Conclusion

The bottom line of this chapter's transaction cost perspective on the organisation of financial flows is both straightforward and highly non-deterministic, as befits this book's 'scenarios' philosophy: given the inherent ignorance, uncertainty and complexity in the business of lending, we are likely to observe wealth-holders, financial institutions and other borrowers experimenting in this area with a wide variety of strategies and with varying degrees of success. To conventional monetary economists, this may seem a terribly disappointing end result of such a lengthy discussion. At no point, however, have I promised to provide deterministic predictions about the way in which the financial system will evolve. Having objected in Chapter 2 to the focus of non-Post Keynesian monetary economics on a simplistic view of 'money', rather than on the broader notion of liquidity, my main intention in this chapter has been to help readers shed any tendencies they have towards an exclusive focus on 'banks' (or even banks plus non-bank financial intermediaries) as conduits for finance. As will be shown later chapers, such a focus may lead to misleading views of the scope for controlling aggregate demand via the traditional instruments of monetary policy. It may also divert attention from the scope for financial instability that may arise from the ways in which firms respond to pressures to take greater risks in order to meet their clients' aspirations.

9 The Growth of Monetary Aggregates

9.1 Introduction

Having explored reasons why some borrowers and lenders might prefer to arrange financing through intermediaries, we can move on to consider the determination of the overall volume of lending and borrowing in an economy and the origins of the various monetary aggregates upon which many policy-makers, particularly those with monetarist inclinations, focus their attention. The perspective that I will be employing is known as the 'portfolio theory' of the money supply, and is associated with the work of the Radcliffe Committee (1959), Tobin (1963), Goodhart (1975, 1984), Llewellyn *et al.* (1982) and Post Keynesians such as Minsky (1975), Moore (1979, 1983, 1988), Kaldor (1982), Rousseas (1985, 1986), Weintraub (1980) and some of the contributors to Jarsulic (ed.) (1985, Chs 1, 3 and 4). It gives a prominent role to the goals of the various participants in the financial process and to the significance of competitive struggles between them. As such, therefore, it involves practically all of the material so far considered in this book. To keep complexity within manageable bounds, however, I intend on most occasions to discuss only the general lending levels of rival financial intermediaries, and will therefore be assuming them already to have taken the strategic decisions about how they should apportion their resources amongst alternative and interlocking markets.

Given the age of some of the sources just cited, it may seem curious that the portfolio theory also goes by the name 'the New View'. Despite thirty years of development, it has not become part of the conventional wisdom of textbook monetary economics. There, the 'money multiplier' theory of the money supply continues to dominate, with at most a brief mention being given to the New View in the typical text (for example, less than two full pages in the strong selling and in many respects impressive work by Mayer *et al.*, 1984, pp. 188-90). The multiplier approach also seems to underpin much of monetarist doctrine. In the present context it seems appropriate to begin by devoting some attention to the 'Old View', and not merely because of its continuing high profile; it also bears some relation to the analysis in Chapter 8, because it gives the impression that there is something special about banks, something which has nothing to do with the transaction cost analysis that I put forward.

The arguments in Chapter 8 can be taken to imply that more lending may go on in an economy with active financial intermediaries than in an otherwise similar one that is devoid of such institutions: reduced transaction costs and risks of loss are likely to encourage people to part with their liquidity. Without needing to mention these dimensions, the multiplier analysis advances to a more radical conclusion: banks *create* money. Any increase in the volume of money deposited with banks is portrayed as giving rise to a *multiple* expansion of total bank deposits and lending, but it is suggested that the same does not hold to a significant extent for the non-bank financial intermediaries if they are considered as a group.

9.2 The Money Multiplier Theory of the Money Supply

To begin, let us focus on the banks. Reserve banks in most economies have a long tradition of laying down rules about the allowable compositions of banks' balance sheets. These rules usually involve some minimum ratio between the banks' holdings of 'reserve assets' and either their total assets or a particular class of their liabilities (such as deposits denominated in local currency). The reserve assets typically include, in specified ratios, deposits at the reserve bank and short-term (or nearly-mature long-term) securities of various kinds — often almost exclusively ones issued by the government. They should not be confused with the banks' 'reserves', considered in section 8.2, which are the difference between a bank's total assets and its liabilities. In the past, and very much with a view to the money multiplier analysis of monetary growth, these ratios were often justified by central bankers because of the part they could play in limiting monetary growth. But they happened conveniently also to provide a ready market for a good deal of government debt.

Nowadays a reserve bank will typically justify the imposition of such ratios on prudential grounds (for example, in the Australian context see RBA, 1985). Certainly, in the event of a run on deposits, such assets can easily be drawn upon or sold, and indeed in many countries reserve banks explicitly stand prepared to 'rediscount' eligible securities at an announced rate of interest if banks are short of cash and cannot get a better deal by selling them elsewhere. However, such a justification looks most peculiar: a bank which has been operating with the minimum allowed reserve assets cannot actually use these sources of liquidity to meet a cash drain without falling below the required level. From the standpoint of depositors, it is only if a bank is liquidated that liquid reserves held under such terms are preferable assets to unsecuritised loans or securities whose market prices have somewhat variable values.

Whatever the official reason put forward for their existence, the required reserve assets, plus any extra ones held by banks to deal with day to day liquidity fluctuations, are assigned great significance by the money multiplier theorist. Suppose banks are all in a state of 'portfolio balance': in other words, all their ratios are at the levels they need in order to comply with reserve bank regulations and meet their liquidity needs. Assume for the sake of convenience their ratio is ten per cent of their total assets, and that at least a fifth of this has to consist of deposits at the reserve bank. (If the reserve bank adopts the convention of paying a pretty poor return on its deposits, these will tend not to exceed two per cent of the total assets of any of the banks.) Now suppose the government engages in an additional $1000 of deficit-financed expenditure. The reserve bank accepts government securities and credits the government account with an equal amount. People fortunate enough to be on the receiving end of increases in government expenditure receive cheques drawn by the government against the reserve bank. To the extent that these people wish to deposit the cheques in banks rather that turn them into cash, the claims of the banks at the reserve bank will rise. The banks are now out of portfolio balance and they can think about increasing their lending.

Let us assume no one chooses to hold on to additional cash and that the banks thus receive $1000 by way of new deposits. According to the money multiplier theory, these constitute a licence to create new loans and deposits to the tune of $9000, with the end result of their initially receiving $1000 additional deposits being that both sides of their collective balance sheets expand by $10 000. Without breaching the rules of the game, they can collectively jump to this end result by crediting borrowers' accounts with $9000 and increasing their claims on borrowers by the same amount. The borrowers spend the money by writing out cheques and the recipients bank these cheques, thereby causing deposits to shift from account to account but not to leave the banks as a group unless there is a leakage back to the government as tax revenue or a leakage overseas. If we ignore these two leakages and presume the banks adhere to their minimum cash ratios, then the end result is that the growth in banks' assets consists of $200 deposits at the reserve bank, $800 holdings of liquid securities, and $9000 extra loans. Deposits have now increased by $10 000. We have a multiplier of ten.

This end result begs two obvious questions. First, we must examine how the individual banks expand their lending in such a way as to the produce overall growth in deposits. In simple probabilitistic terms, we would expect that, if an individual bank had a market share of ten per cent, it would only be likely to get back a tenth of any new deposits it created in the name of borrowers once the latter spent them to finance their purchases. If one bank in this position received an initial $100 in deposits as a result of the extra government expenditure, it could in principle increase its assets with new loans of $900 and increase its borrowers' accounts by the same value. But then it would lose around $810 in deposits, much to the delight of its rivals, amongst whom the departing deposits would be divided up. However, if the rivals had simultaneously increased their lending and deposits by $8100, after receiving an increase in deposits of $900, there would be no problem. As the loans were used, the rival banks would tend to receive around $7290 in deposits from those who had supplied goods and services that had been paid for by their extra loans. Along with $810 from the new deposits in their accounts arising from the expenditure of those who borrowed from the other bank, the change of ownership of $7290 of their own balances ensures they do not suffer a net cash drain. The other bank is in the same position: its rivals' outflow of $810 is added to the redeposited $90 arising from its own loans and equals the $900 of deposits that its borrowers have been credited with and have spent. Any short-term cash flow problems can be dealt with by borrowing on the interbank market.

Many textbook treatments of the money multiplier map out the route to such end results in a much more laborious manner than the one just presented. The individual bank is portrayed as acting in ignorance of the scope for credit creation that exists in the banking system, though perfectly aware of the limited risk that all deposits will suddenly be called for. In such an analysis, each bank only lends out deposits that it has already received, but then finds that its deposits increase yet further. Suppose we have ten identical banks and each bank has just received a deposit of $100 as a result of the government increasing its expenditure in the manner described before. Each bank lends $90 more to its customers and gives them cheques for the corresponding amounts. Each bank has, it thinks, temporarily increased its balance sheet by $90: its claims on its borrowers are up by $90, and it is now liable to the tune of $90 for the cheques it has drawn against itself. (Most expositions are so old-fashioned as to assume that bank loans are made in terms of notes and coin, but this is not essential for their analyses to work.) Those who sell to the borrowers receive payment and deposit their takings with their banks. If we assume that the sellers are evenly distributed across banks, then we can expect each bank to receive a new deposit of $90 even though it had been expecting a drain on its reserve assets of precisely this amount. Of the second round of deposits received by a particular bank — let us call it the JMK Bank — $9 will involve money being redeposited because the JMK Bank's own customers have spent their newly borrowed funds at firms that also keep deposits with the JMK Bank; the remaining $81 will come from the increased spending of those who have borrowed from other banks but have spent their funds at firms that are depositors with the JMK Bank. Each bank now has $190 more assets and liabilities than before the government undertook its extra expenditure. The next stage involves each bank in lending out $81 of its new deposit of $90, only to find that its deposits rise by $81. So the process continues, with ever decreasing increments of lending and depositing, until each bank has $900 more deposits and loan assets on top of the initial $100 of deposits it had received and which provided the basis for an expansion of reserve assets of $100. The end result is the same as in the first scenario.

The latter scenario fits in nicely with any desire we might have to portray banks as acting in a very cautious manner, for if an individual bank happens to be the only one to be increasing its lending and if it has a low redeposit ratio, its policy of only lending what it already has will not see it having to breach its operating ratio as its loans are used. For example, suppose a bank has received new deposits of $100 and has lent out $90 only to find that it has to meet $90 worth of claims by rival banks who have received its cheques. Its prudence means it can honour such claims by transferring $90 to its rival banks from its holdings at the reserve bank and still have $10 left over to maintain its ratio. However, although one might expect banks to act with some degree of caution, they might also be expected to have some knowledge of what would happen if they only lent out prior deposits. One might therefore expect them often to feel it safe to create credit at the stroke of a pen, as in the original scenario.

A second matter to consider is how the banks manage to dispose of low yielding excess deposits at the reserve bank and in their place acquire more attractive eligible liquid securities. One possible answer is that the reserve bank unloads $800 of eligible securities on to the market in order to prevent the banks' attempts to purchase $800 of eligible securities from raising the prices of these securities and depressing their effective interest yields. In other words, an *ex ante* increase of $1000 in government borrowing from the reserve bank is turned *ex post* into an increase of only $200. This answer is the one we will need if we are to keep the value of the money multiplier (the ratio of the eventual increase in deposits to the initial increase in deposits) down to the reciprocal of the reserve assets ratio (in this case, ten), in line with the orthodox view.

An alternative scenario would see the banks obtaining their liquid assets not from the reserve bank but from non-bank members of the private sector, such as large corporations and/or non-bank financial intermediaries that have been choosing to hold their financial reserves as short-term securities. If the banks purchase liquid assets from such institutions (or even from wealthy individuals who might also be holding them), the potential size of the multiplier is increased. The banks can pay for these assets by passing cheques drawn against themselves to those that are selling them and the sellers will deposit the cheques back with the banks. There will be no impact on the banks' holdings at the reserve bank, but banks' total deposits and assets will have risen by the value of the securities they have purchased. In other words, the banks have succeeded both in conjuring up further reserve assets and in creating deposits.

If banks' deposits at the reserve bank only have to equal two per cent of their total assets, and if there exist considerable non-bank holdings of securities that the banks can count as reserve assets, the maximum value of the money multiplier for the bank might be as high as fifty. Thus the initial increase in deposits of $1000 could produce the following end result: the assets of banks (and bank deposits) rise by $50 000, of which $1000 are extra deposits at the reserve bank, $4000 are eligible securities purchased from the non-bank private sector, and $45 000 are new loans. Such an outcome is not what one would normally find being considered in expositions of the money multiplier theory, but it is the kind of thing with which monetary authorities in the UK have sometimes found themselves having to contend on occasions when they have been seeking to control the growth in bank deposits by limiting the availability of new reserve assets. If, in practice, banks do not buy up pre-existing eligible securities from the non-bank private sector unless they have trouble in getting new ones from the public sector, the multiplier theory faces an empirical puzzle: the theory assumes that banks lend as much as they can, subject only to the constraint of meeting their reserve asset ratios, so why do the banks not try to corner the market for those securities that are listed as eligible reserve assets? As we shall soon see, portfolio theory has ready answers to this question.

9.3 Non-Bank Financial Intermediaries in the Money Multiplier Analysis

In looking at the determination of the overall volume of financial intermediaries' deposits and loans, we must be careful to distinguish between banks and non-bank financial intermediaries (NBFIs), such as building societies, credit unions, cash management trusts, finance companies and so on. As far as the general kinds of services they provide are concerned, there is little difference between banks and deposit-taking, loan-making NBFIs. They certainly differ in the ranges of customers with whom they deal and the degrees to which the compositions of their portfolios are regulated, but in the modern deregulated financial environment the clearest difference is that NBFIs bank with commercial banks and not the reserve bank. Should they run into liquidity troubles, NBFIs have no guaranteed access to lender of last resort loans. (In the past, this has been seen as the price they pay for enjoying far greater freedom from regulatory controls by the reserve bank over the composition of their balance sheets.) The practical importance of not having access to lender of last resort facilities may well be doubted by management of the largest NBFIs, particularly the giants amongst the building societies: the incidence of defaults on home loans is remarkably small, and the security of such assets should make short-term borrowing on the wholesale money market quite easy in the event of a drain on deposits; failing this, there may be the possibility of merging with a bank, something which the reserve bank might be expected to induce behind the scenes due to the wider ramifications for confidence of the failure of a major building society. In the eyes of their retail customers, NBFIs have become increasingly difficult to distinguish from banks. This is especially so on the liabilities side, where many NBFIs have sought to emulate banks by issuing their own chequebooks, giving their customers the opportunity to pay for things by drawing directly against their NBFI accounts instead of having to go along to NBFI branch offices to be issued with a cheque drawn on the NBFIs' own bank accounts.

Despite these growing similarities at the level of the individual institution, there is, according to the multiplier theory, a major difference between the two groups of institutions as far as credit creation is concerned. NBFIs are seen broadly as being able only to lend out fractions of deposits that have already been made with them, for the multiplier analysis assumes that, once loans are spent, redepositing to the NBFI sector is unlikely to be very significant. A typical scenario could be as follows. Suppose an NBFI is initially on the limit of, say, a 10 per cent ratio of reserve assets (let us assume, for simplicity, that these consist of bank deposits). A depositor comes along with a bank cheque for $1000 to make a deposit at the NBFI. The NBFI immediately banks this cheque: its deposits increase by $1000, and so do its reserve assets; total bank deposits have not changed, although their distribution will have done so if the depositor's bank is not the one with which the NBFI banks. Someone comes along to the NBFI and asks for a loan of $900 to buy a cheap used car. The request is granted and the NBFI gives the borrower a cheque for $900 which is then presented to and banked by the used car firm. After the NBFI's bank has honoured the cheque, it is left nicely in line with its target ratio: net, its reserve assets have increased by $100 and its loans have increased by $900. And there the story stops if the used car firm makes no new deposits whatever with any NBFIs as a consequence of selling the car. If one of the sales staff at the car yard receives an extra $50 in take-home pay as a result of selling the vehicle and has a marginal propensity to consume of, say, 0.9, then at most one might envisage a secondary deposit increase of $5, since the salesperson spends $45 of the increased income. We would thus be dealing with a very small multiplier indeed for the NBFI sector.

In the case just considered, the NBFI did not actually try to emulate a bank to the extent of issuing its own chequeing facilities and trying to create credit at the stroke of a pen. If it did attempt to do so, a money multiplier scenario would run as follows. Suppose an NBFI is initially operating at its target ratio (once again assume 10 per cent) of reserve assets. It then receives a deposit of $1000 and creates $9000 of additional loans by simply crediting borrowers with debts and matching deposits. The borrowers spend by writing out NBFI cheques. Recipients are very likely to want to put these into their bank accounts, not into the NBFI. To honour the cheques, the NBFI must run down its own bank deposits. Its liabilities and reserve assets must both go down by $9000. Clearly, it cannot honour the loan cheques without falling below its target ratio.

The case just considered is an extreme one, for it involves the NBFI initially in engineering the maximum expansion of its balance sheet that is possible without breaching its ratio. An NBFI following such a policy will rapidly find itself falling below its target ratio unless it has a redeposit ratio of 100 per cent. But it would run into trouble of this kind, albeit on a smaller scale, for *any* expansion in lending greater than $X(1 - r)$, where X is the initial growth in its deposits and r is its reserve ratio. Suppose as before that the NBFI's operating ratio is 10 per cent and it has received $1000 extra deposits, but that this time it only increases its balance sheet $901 further by expanding its claims on borrowers and the accounts of its borrowers. When the borrowers spend their $901 and the NBFI honours their cheques, its balance sheet will contract back to being only $1000 greater than prior to the start of the scenario. Of the net increase on the assets side, $901 will consist of loans, but now only $99 will remain as extra reserve assets, so it will be in breach of its ten per cent ratio if there is no redepositing and if it were operating on its ratio prior to the initial deposit being made. To make up the $1 shortfall in reserve assets, it will need to sell $1 of any non-reserve securities it holds or fail to make a replacement loan when next it receives a repayment of $1 (or, of course, any combination of these policies). Any other outcome would imply either an initial excess of reserve assets or an ongoing shortfall. Money multiplier theory thus concludes that, if there is negligible redepositing by recipients of expenditure paid for with NBFI cheques, NBFIs can only lend prior deposits and cannot create deposits.

Whatever the deficiencies that our imminent discussions of portfolio theory may raise about the conventional scenario, it does at least have the merit of forcing one to face the question of why NBFIs would want to issue their own chequebooks: given the low probability that an NBFI will be presented by its depositors with its own cheques, the clearing of such cheques automatically results in a loss of NBFI deposits in banks, just as would the clearing of an NBFI bank cheque drawn on its own account. However, although chequeing facilities increase the transaction costs of the NBFIs that provide them, they may serve a valuable deposit-attracting role by reducing the transactions costs and cash requirements of their depositors. Thereby such facilities may enable NBFIs to avoid competing for deposits by other means, such as offering longer opening hours, interstate branching, or deals that enable their depositors to access their money when away from home via other financial institutions who have agreed to act, for a fee, as agents.

9.4 A Marginalist View of Limits to Lending by Financial Intermediaries

Central to the New View of the process whereby growth rates of monetary aggregates are determined is the idea that the portfolio preferences of individuals, firms (both domestic and overseas) and the government limit the abilities of rival financial intermediaries to use competitive tactics to expand their liabilities and assets. At its most basic level this notion leads one to conclude that if people presently do not wish to increase their holdings of deposits and their indebtedness beyond particular levels, then there may be little that financial intermediaries can do about it without compromising their profit objectives. The easiest way to illustrate this basic point is to consider the portfolio decision of a person who has to deal with her latest monthly credit card statement from her bank, and who has bank deposits in excess of those she needs to meet both her expected cash expenditures prior to her next paycheque and her minimum repayment obligations to the bank. The 'spread' between her bank's loan and deposit rates, and the fact that she will have to pay tax on interest earnings, may lead her to repay more than the bank's minimum required sum (cf. section 7.2). Her deposits at the bank fall and so do the bank's loan assets. She has destroyed part of the money stock, just as, earlier in the month, she increased the money stock by using her credit card to buy things (since firms were credited with deposits when they presented her credit card vouchers to the bank, and the bank then credited itself with a claim against her). Had she been more willing to take extended credit, the money stock would have stayed at a higher level, and the bank would have found its credit card activities much more profitable. The ball is now in the bank's court.

If the bank wishes to maintain its growth in assets and liabilities, it will have to find more borrowers. One strategy that it might adopt is to make more credit cards available to less liquid members of society, who will normally use them for extended credit rather than mainly as debit cards. But this strategy may involve accepting greater commercial risks. Perhaps the bank should instead bid for some of the deposits and low risk customers of its rivals, or perhaps it should just acquiesce in the present situation. How can it decide what to do?

Despite ostensibly trying to take account of the role of financial intermediaries in the money supply process, the money multiplier analysis is totally unequipped to analyse this question, which is just one of many that can be used to indicate that the determination of interest rates and the volume of lending by financial intermediaries might have more than a little to do with the competitive conditions faced by such institutions. In the multiplier theory, the volume of lending that intermediaries can undertake appears to be totally unconstrained by the demand for credit but completely restricted by policies of the reserve bank that determine the supply of eligible reserve assets and lay down the rules of the game as far as balance sheet compositions are concerned. Financial institutions are depicted as ending up with supplies of reserve assets according to given depositing propensities of firms and consumers. The multiplier picture portrays banks and other financial intermediaries as operating in a mechanistic manner, without any regard to market considerations. Given that the modern world abounds with signs of competition amongst intermediaries for deposits and credit-worthy customers, the conventional portrayal looks a decidedly minimalist abstraction.

The multifaceted nature of bank portfolios on both the assets and the liabilities sides clearly makes it rather hazardous to try to depict financial intermediaries as if they are single product companies. (It may also be unwise to depict complex non-financial firms in this way.) But it may be useful to try to think about them from this standpoint as an approximation and brush aside complications such as the fact that borrowers may be charged different rates of interest depending on their risk categories and that interest received by depositors may be affected by the extent to which the intermediary is 'unbundling' its charges for withdrawals and cheques or is supposedly providing them 'for free'. What we have are firms that rent inputs (deposits of various kinds, as well as worker services and so on) and use them in the production of outputs (which we shall here think of purely as loans, disregarding the analysis from Chapter 8 about the subtleties of what intermediation actually involves). So we might think of them as having supply constraints which we could draw as marginal, average and total costs curves of the usual sort, and demand-for-loans constraints, which would imply marginal revenue curves. The 'prices' they charge are simply the interest rates on loans. The only really unusual feature of financial firms is that it is normally appropriate to treat their staff entirely as fixed factors (an exception would be life assurance firms whose sales personnel often receive substantial commissions for signing up new customers). If viewing things from the perspective of the standard marginalist theory of the firm, we might then conclude that the size of an intermediary's balance sheet will be determined by the point at which it is able to equate the marginal revenue from making a new loan (creating a new asset) with the marginal cost of obtaining a volume of additional deposits (new liabilities) of equal size.

Marginalist analysis would lead one to expect a downward sloping marginal revenue curve: lower rates of interest would need to be offered to attract new borrowers, and any existing borrowers not on fixed interest loans would end up paying less than before; also, marginal loans might be more risky, so expected net revenues could be reduced. By contrast, a marginalist would expect a rising marginal cost curve after some level of deposits. There are three reasons for this. First, growth in the size of the firm's balance sheet would represent a fall in its ratio of reserves (in the sense of net assets, as in Chapter 8) to liabilities. Higher deposit rates would become necessary to induce both existing and new depositors to shoulder the risks that this may imply. Secondly, as the firm expands the size of its balance sheet, it may find itself no longer able to suck funds away from its rivals without prompting them to retaliate. The cost of obtaining extra deposits will be further increased in so far as the higher interest rates have to be given to existing depositors who are not tied to fixed-rate deposits. A third source of rising marginal costs could apply in the case of a bank which is subject to reserve asset requirements. A bank that has been operating on its target reserve assets ratio will need additional reserve assets if it is to expand the size of its balance sheet by creating new loans. To obtain these assets the bank may find it necessary to increase its borrowing from the reserve bank, but the latter, like other depositors, may be prepared to expand its lending only at an increasing price. In practice, a reserve bank typically charges a constant interest rate for its funds but increases their non-pecuniary costs to borrowers as it makes more money available. For example, it may vary the duration of the loan in an increasingly inconvenient manner or impose more and more onerous auditing requirements and requests for justification: Moore (1988) calls the latter 'frown costs'.

This kind of analysis is employed extensively by Minsky (1975), who makes much of the fact that the positions of the curves depend greatly on prevailing feelings of confidence. Optimism may mean that a financial institution finds it easier to raise money at a given interest rate and is willing to lend more to particular classes of clients, even though such policies will increase its openness to bankruptcy by reducing its ratio of net assets to liabilities. The wisdom of portraying financial intermediaries in marginalist terms is limited, however, by the oligopolistic nature of the business in which such firms are competing: as far as borrowers and depositors are concerned, the typical financial intermediary may have a number of close substitutes. These may include not merely other intermediaries of the same class but also other classes of intermediaries and, increasingly, avenues for disintermediated financing. Fortunately, concepts used in Chapter 4 are readily adaptable to the present context, and they give a more realistic picture of interest rate and loan granting policies which is nonetheless perfectly consistent with the overall thrust of Minsky's work on confidence and financial instability. The analysis which follows is inspired both by the Post Keynesian work of Rousseas (1985; 1986, pp. 50-61) and the papers by Davies and Davies (1984) and Harper (1986) on the theory of contestable markets. Owing to the complex nature of the links between the balance sheets of banks and NBFIs (see section 9.7), it will help simplify the discussion in the next two sections if we confine our attention to substitutions between the assets and liabilities of a particular class of intermediary, such as 'banks'.

9.5 Liability Management

If a financial intermediary wishes to increase its lending, it can try to increase its deposit holdings by instituting policies aimed at attracting funds from the retail and/or wholesale money markets. Bank deposits may be relatively costlessly switched between rival institutions, especially given the latter's tendancy to congregate branchwise in particular city streets. Home banking using personal computers and telephone hook-ups with financial intermediaries may be expected to reduce switching costs still further. Hence, if one bank raises its deposit rates in order to expand its business, it may attract a very substantial increase in funds at the expense of its rivals, who will be driven to follow suit. But if a bank falls behind in its deposit rates, it will lose considerable volumes of deposits to its rivals. The latter have no necessary reason to cut their deposit rates individually and risk similar outflows. Deposit rate policy may therefore be an ineffective tool for making marginal adjustments of bank inputs and it is inappropriate to think of representing a bank's supply position in terms of upward sloping curves representing the demand for its liabilities and the marginal cost of expanding its liabilities. Rather, it is a price setter and quantity taker in the deposit market, but it must set deposit rates that are competitive with those offered by rival institutions (which may include overseas banks) on similar liabilities. A bank can seek to augment its customers' deposits by borrowing at a higher cost in the wholesale markets in which it is a price taker. Its retail deposit rates may therefore be thought of as being marked down by conventional amounts against wholesale rates. Arbitrage will ensure that wholesale rates are in turn closely pinned to the rate at which the reserve bank is prepared to supply funds to the banking system: banks will not wish to raise funds in the interbank market if these are to be had more cheaply at the reserve bank, whether by borrowing or by getting the reserve bank to rediscount wholesale assets that they had accumulated in previous periods when they had more deposits than retail loans.

In this 'horizontalist' situation (Moore, 1988), the price-setting bank can seek to cultivate depositor goodwill by innovative 'non-price' policies and by creating appealing new forms of liabilities. Even though successful financial innovations are likely to be copied by rivals, the first mover stands to keep a larger part of the market for so long as its rivals cannot come up with even more appealing competitive tactics: unless something still better is offered, those initially attracted by the first mover's will have no incentive to change their goodwill in favour of those of its rivals who are seeking to imitate its policies.

What has been said so far about the 'New View' may seem to have ignored earlier discussions about the ability of banks, if not other financial intermediaries, to create deposits. Certainly, banks may not be restricted to lending funds they have already borrowed. However, the fact that a bank can create deposits at the stroke of a pen when it makes an extra loan in no way guarantees that the deposits it creates will stay within its balance sheet, even if other insitutions are expanding their loans and deposits at a similar rate. Where additional credit creation is a possibility, a bank has to think about the probability it has generated of being able to avoid a negative cashflow once the new loan deposits are spent by borrowers. If a bank lets its rate of return slip behind what its rivals are offering, it reduces its probability of receiving replacement deposits as its new loans are used. Then it must either offer more competitive retail yields and borrow in the interbank market to balance its books until customers switch funds in its direction, or it must raise cash by disposing of some of its assets — which, for practical purposes, means selling securities or calling in overdrafts, as the bank is hardly likely to be able to insist on the premature repayment of loans with contractually specified maturities.

Once we recognise the scope financial intermediaries have for using liability management policies to affect their cashflows, it becomes harder to distinguish between banks and NBFIs in respect of their abilities to create credit at the stroke of a pen rather than being able only to lend deposits they have already received. NBFIs can emulate banks to the extent that they can offer further inducements for people to make new deposits with them to replace departing deposits recently created alongside new loans. An intermediary with a 10 per cent reserve ratio and a desire to expand lending by £900 has two descriptively different routes between which to choose. One way is to bid successfully for £1000 deposits and then lend £900 in the expectation of attracting no further deposits to offset the outflow occasioned by the spending of the loan. Another way is for the intermediary to bid initially for only £100, to create a £900 deposit in the borrower's name, and then to step up its competitive stance sufficiently far as to ensure that a further £900 arrives in deposits just as it becomes necessary to honour the borrower's spending cheque. At the end of the day, it is difficult to see what difference there is between the two routes: the important thing is that the extra lending has been arranged.

The only difference between these two NBFI scenarios and a credit creation example concerning a bank is that spending by the bank's new borrowers increases the deposit holdings of other banks *if* the bank does not bid to get replacement deposits. Its rival banks can expand their lending as it retreats to restore its ratio. The use of a bank loan does not result in a drain of deposits from domestic banks so long as the seller of the loan-financed goods and services neither turns the proceeds into cash nor deposits them overseas. By contrast, if a single NBFI attempts to create credit and suffers a deposit drain, there is no reason why other NBFIs' deposits will rise by an offsetting amount.

9.6 Asset Management

The lengths to which a financial intermediary will go in trying to acquire lender goodwill will depend on the extent to which it is prepared to risk reducing its ratio of net assets to liabilities, and on its ability to find assets which it believes offer acceptable probabilities of yielding enough to pay interest due on its liabilities and to leave a margin for profit. These two factors are obviously inter-related. In reality, and in contrast to the picture presented in money multiplier analysis, the supply of credit-worthy, credit-seeking customers is finite: as an advertisement for the Chemical Bank in *The Economist* (28 November 1987) observes, 'Bankers are the only salesmen who must drum up business and turn down would-be buyers — simultaneously'. If an intermediary has trouble finding suitable corporate and commercial borrowers, a variety of options are available: it can reduce its competitive effort in the area of liability management; it can place surplus funds in the wholesale market or increase its holdings of public sector securities; it can cut its loan charges for its normal kinds of clients, and risk retaliation from its rivals; or it can take on more risky clients.

The Appraisal of Loan Applications
Having succeeded in getting would-be borrowers to make their needs known, loan managers do not interview them one after another and then, on the basis of the latter's different risk characteristics, choose the optimal group to whom funds will be provided. Competitive pressures force them to offer speedy replies to would-be borrowers, and this means they will have to judge them in satisficing terms (cf. Winter, 1964): a behavioural theorist would expect them to develop routines for deciding whether or not to commit their banks' scarce lending capacities to the would-be borrowers they interview today, given that those they see tomorrow may be better credit risks.

The use of a satisficing scoring system seems widespread in the case of the market for personal loans. A useful discussion of such procedures is provided, complete with a sample scoring questionnaire, in work on Australian credit unions by Crapp and Skully (1985, pp. 83-5; 193). They note how credit decisions are based on the following factors (p. 83):

> Stability of residence (buying, renting, boarding);
> Stability and position of employment;
> Dependants;
> Credit rating obtained from a commercial credit reference bureau;
> Stability of character;
> Security offered;
> Ability to repay whilst still maintaining an accustomed lifestyle (often expressed as a debt ratio where all monthly outgoings as a proportion of net weekly pay after tax should not exceed a designated percentage);
> Purpose of loan;
> Current assets and current outstanding liabilities.

Several possible answer categories are allowed in each case, and points are assigned to them: for example, Where do you live? With relatives? (two points) In a rented house or flat? (four points) In your own house or flat? (eight points). Ruthlessly applied, these kinds of scoring systems deprive loan applicants of finance if their totals fall below a particular target. They can also produce some decisions that are very worrying in these times of rising personal bankruptcies (in 1987, credit card companies in the US absorbed $3.8 billion in delinquent debt).

If I have already been granted access to four credit cards, but have so far not used them much, I am, other things equal, more likely to get a personal loan than someone who only has two credit cards, despite the fact that the latter person is less able to run amok with a credit-card-financed consumption binge and then find the monthly repayments overwhelming. Indeed, an Australian consumer affairs television programme (*The Investigators*, 21 May 1987) showed how, in an actual finance company scoring system, emphasis on an unchanged source of income and residence produced the bizarre result that a long-term unemployed person would pass a loan test that a graduate army officer would fail! There is clearly something lacking in credit-appraisal systems that result in cases such as that reported by Sheehan (1988) concerning a 23 year-old Houston secretary who had 150 cards to her name even though she had never earned more than $22 000 a year. She ended up bankrupt to the tune of over $400 000, owing between $700 and $7500 on each card. Many of her credit card accounts were opened purely as a means of obtaining cash advances to service her debts on her older credit cards. In the US at least, the incentive to try to live so wildly beyond one's means is strong: most bankrupts end up paying back very little, for under the Bankruptcy Code a bankrupt person is allowed to keep her home, two cars, clothes, tools of trade, heirlooms, pension and retirement.

Given the possibility that some applicants for personal and housing loans might act in an opportunistic manner and lie about their circumstances, one might expect financial intermediaries to make assiduous use of external credit references when processing loan applications. Here, too, investigative journalism has uncovered disturbing evidence. The BBC's *Panorama* team (18 July 1988) interviewed people who, despite being unemployed, had obtained huge mortgages by making fraudulent declarations of their status. Failure to service these mortgages would simply see the houses being sold on the rapidly rising market with the opportunists making off with the capital gains and using them as deposits against yet bigger mortgages, fraudulently obtained from different institutions. Interviews with heads of major building societies revealed that they had largely given up checking with banks on the credit records of intending borrowers. The building societies had some bitter experiences of the costs of caution: on finding that one of its creditworthy customers was seeking a mortgage with a building society, a bank was prone to contact the person in question and beat the building society to a mortgage offer.

The message that increasingly competitive conditions in financial markets may be a mixed blessing for the more honest members of society was further enhanced when the same programme revealed that financial institutions had refused to cooperate to establish a national register of mortgaged properties. (This was to have used the Post Office's computer list of all UK addresses, with a simple system of starred and unstarred addresses.) The financial institutions claimed to be concerned about protecting the confidentiality of their relationships with their clients. However, in the absence of any means of identifying mortgaged properties, crime syndicates had started to raise multiple mortgages on individual properties. They could do this because the housing boom had caused delays of six months or more at the under-staffed and under-computerised Land Registry. Crooked solicitors who were syndicate members would claim that the title deeds could not yet be handed over to the institution issuing the mortgage but, rather than risk losing mortgage business, the latter rushed to make the funds available in the interim. Given the rate at which the market was rising, a loan thus raised could then be used to finance deposits on other properties which could be resold at a profit before the lending institution ever had the title deeds in its custody and without the borrower ever actually having been the official owner of the property in question. Safely repaid within six months, the loan would be judged as a profitable deal by the unwitting lending institution, but it would not have been without its social cost (see section 2.7).

At the grander level of corporate and country risk analysis there may be somewhat less pressure for speedy responses, but here the greater complexity of these cases puts those who perform credit rating operations (be it the intermediaries themselves, or agencies acting on their behalf) under some pressure to develop scoring systems. As McWilliams (1977, p. 111) observes after reviewing a number of credit scoring techniques for commercial loans, 'Everyone making credit analyses finds a set of favourite ratios'. Sometimes, these ratios are combined with the aid of weights derived from multiple regression analyses of past cases. A useful review and critique of systems used in country risk analysis has been provided by Bird (1986).

Competition and the Cost of Borrowing
In so far as it is legitimate to assume that a stable demand for loan finance exists, anyone who sought to estimate it would be very likely to find that observed points on it came within its inelastic range: in other words, if interest rates were raised, few existing borrowers would be induced to pay off their loans at a faster rate and few new borrowers would be deterred from accepting loans, so the overall revenues of lenders would rise. This much we would expect from the discussions of household and corporate behaviour in Chapters 3 and 4, and it seems amply evidenced by recent experiences in many countries where 'tight money' policies have been pursued and unusually high real interest rates have been produced. That borrowers are not normally asked to pay the sorts of rates which they would be prepared to pay is to be explained by the fact that individual lenders do not enjoy demand functions that are scaled-down versions of what might be found, for a given state of expections, at the level of the market. Each intermediary has to recognise that loans by rival intermediaries may be close substitutes for its own products. Hence banks and NBFIs will usually avoid letting their loan charges rise above those of rivals, and only an institution engaged in a strategy of building up its market share by aggressive price leadership will persistently seek

to undercut the interest rates that other institutions need in order to achieve satisfactory rates of profit. In other words, financial institutions are price setters and quantity takers in loan markets: their average and marginal revenue curves are horizontal, and how far along them they get will depend upon the general level of demand for loan finance and on the success of their non-price methods of competing for market share. Increases in interest rates will thus normally reflect increases in the cost of obtaining liabilities, rather than attempts to push up profits at the expense of borrowers.

In working out their asset management tactics, financial intermediaries have to worry not merely about rivals in the form of current suppliers of similar loan packages, but also about potential suppliers, who may include direct lenders (if necessary, in conjunction with loan brokers, investment banks and so on) as well as other intermediaries. Incumbent lenders of a particular kind will tend to match each others' pricing policies, but not necessarily those of other classes of lenders whose normal clienteles are somewhat different. For example, the cost of financing a new consumer durable may be, say, 18-20 per cent through a bank, but 22-24 per cent through a finance company. The higher charges of the latter will reflect the higher outlays these institutions have to incur to raise liabilities, owing to perceptions that they are more risky — due to their typical customers being those to whom the banks are unwilling to lend (one would expect the differential to be even higher if the finance companies were making personal loans available rather than doing hire purchase deals, for then the costs of dealing with those who could not meet their payments would be even higher, involving legal action rather than repossession) — or because they do not accept liabilities as liquid as those accepted by banks.

Figure 9.1 is an attempt to encapsulate in diagrammatic terms this application of Post Keynesian oligopoly theory to the business of banking. OR is the weighted average of returns that the bank earns on its reserve assets of various kinds, which amount in total to OA. This rate of interest is portrayed as being somewhat less than OD, the deposit rate offered by the bank to its retail customers, though whether and/or how far this would be the case in practice would depend on the proportion of reserve assets that had to take the form of cash deposits at the reserve bank on which a meagre rate of interest was paid. The bank has succeeded in obtaining OB deposits. OL is the rate of interest it is charging on its loans, and at this rate there is a demand for loans of AC from customers whom it judges to be satisfactory credit risks. The bank's present ratio of reserve assets to total assets is thus OA/OC. OW is the rate at which the bank can obtain funds on the wholesale market, either from other private sector institutions or from the reserve bank. Although funds obtained from the latter may involve increasing 'frown costs' at the margin, the supply price of wholesale funds is constant in pecuniary terms. Since the bank represented in Figure 9.1 has been more successful at finding borrowers than retail depositors, it must borrow funds to the value BC in the wholesale/interbank market. But the reverse might be true for other banks and the latter would be lending their surpluses out at wholesale rates. Clearly, the size of the bank's balance sheet is indeterminate unless we refer to the success of its policies of non-price competition. Outlays associated with these policies are, however, in the nature of fixed costs, which the institution will be hoping to recover, along with its target profits, from its 'spread', its gross mark-up between its deposit and lending rates, which is DL on Figure 9.1.

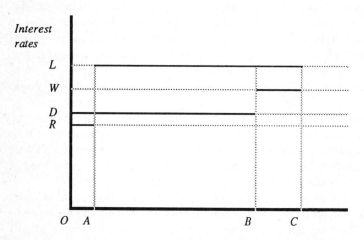

Figure 9.1 *Borrowing and Lending by a Banking Firm*

The spreads that banks and other financial intermediaries can safely try to earn will be limited by the opportunity costs of their rivals. To the extent that rivals' normal lines of business are enjoying boom conditions, it will be more costly for them to use their limited resources in trying to capture new markets. Hence existing institutions might be able to command bigger margins without attracting entry. (But we should be aware of a possible qualification to this statement. Aside from depositor and borrower goodwill, skilled loan managers are the chief constraint on succesful expansion in the world of finance, and it may take a long while for new ones to be properly trained. We might therefore expect competitive bidding for existing skilled loan officers to raise their relative pay and thereby help stop bank profit margins from increasing in boom times.) The spread charged by financial intermediaries may also be expected to increase when pessimism grows regarding default risks on previously contracted loans, for if such pessimism is justified the banks would find themselves otherwise having to run down their net assets. Although their profit margins may vary with the ups and downs of the business cycle, along with hindsight shifts in the perception of the wisdom of loans such as those to developing countries, intermediaries will be limited in their average margins by the ease of entry for rivals. In general, we would expect them to be operating with profit margins far lower than they could make on a short run basis if they sought to 'exploit' their existing clients to the full.

The spreads that banks and other financial intermediaries will need in order to earn satisfactory profits will be affected by the extent to which their funds are tied up in relatively low yielding assets that serve their liquidity needs and the reserve asset requirements they have to meet. Liquidity needs arise for a number of reasons:

(1) Outflows of deposits may start to exceed inflows.
(2) Customers with credit cards, 'lines of credit' and overdraft arrangements with the intermediary may expand their borrowing in the direction of their previously agreed credit limits. (Unlike an overdraft, a line of credit is a contractual agreement about a supply of funds and if the lending institution is short of liquidity it cannot insist on repayment or stop further borrowing up to the specified limit. However, goodwill considerations will normally mean that overdraft arrangements are treated in practice as if they are formal lines of credit.)
(3) Existing, valued customers who do not have unused overdraft or credit card limits may be disgruntled if they need to borrow more and find their wishes are not accommodated.
(4) If new customers come along asking to borrow, an inability to satisfy their demands this time round may mean they turn elsewhere and stay elsewhere so long as other banks can satisfy them.

Although the business of banking presents perhaps the classic instance of long-term relationships between firms and their customers, banks do not need to maintain, with a view to the preservation and growth of their goodwill, the amounts of excess capacity that one might expect to encounter in other lines of activity. For example, during the period 1960-85, Australian trading banks typically only exceeded their LGS (liquid and government securities) requirements by around 3 per cent of their total assets. Even this looks large compared with the situation in the US where, according to Mayer *et al.* (1984, p. 185) the excess reserve assets of banks in the period 1981-82 'accounted for less than one per cent of total reserves and in only one month of this period did they equal as much as 1.1 per cent of total reserves'. The US figure may partly reflect the fact that overdrafts are very much a British/European idea and are not common in the US, where, as Hamilton (1986, p. 115) points out, corporate borrowers instead have to make more use of commercial note issues. Working against this possibility, however, is the fact that the average adult in the US, who owes $3500 on her credit cards, is only using about half of her extended credit capacity (see Moore, 1988). Given the scope for herd-like behaviour among consumers to lead to a simultaneous increase in credit utilisation rates, the smallness of excess reserves is at first sight quite remarkable.

There are several reasons why banks can operate with such narrow margins of slack. The first is that, unlike manufacturing firms, for example, they do not have to wait to acquire and install new fixed capital if they lack spare capacity and find themselves suddenly snowed under with customers. Secondly, they can usually count on being able to purchase additional reserve assets by obtaining additional funds on the interbank market or as a last resort (if there are 'frown costs' attached) from the reserve bank. Failing this, banks can substitute between kinds of lending, making room for extra non-securitised loans by selling securities that are not eligible to count as reserve assets, though prudential considerations will clearly deter them from pushing this policy to extremes. Despite these advantages, banks may sometimes find themselves having trouble meeting all the requests from customers whom they would normally regard as eligible for loans. On these occasions, long-run considerations may make them prefer to ration credit according to some system of priorities, rather than making life difficult for their existing borrowers by raising their interest rates in an effort to clear the market.

Central bankers are well aware that reserve asset requirements raise the yields that commercial banks will need to earn on their loans if they are to achieve a satisfactory overall return. To the extent that would-be borrowers are deterred by higher interest charges on bank loans (either in general, or because they can substitute to other sources of funds), the reserve bank may be able to use increases in reserve asset requirements and/or reduced yields on reserve assets as means for deterring banks from expanding their lending and engaging in liability management. A very well-known example of such a policy is the supplementary special deposits scheme of the Bank of England, often otherwise known as 'the corset'. Banks that increased their interest-bearing eligible liabilities at a rate faster than that prescribed faced a tax in the form of increasing marginal requirements to place non-interest-earning deposits with the Bank of England.

With the growth of enthusiasm for policies of 'freeing up the market', reserve assets ratios and devices like the corset are falling out of favour amongst central bankers as means for limiting the growth of bank lending. There has been a growing belief that these instruments have been at best somewhat ineffective as means of bringing expenditure under control and have at worst produced inefficient distortions in the workings of financial markets. In some countries, they have been pretty well totally abandoned. The most extreme case is perhaps New Zealand, whose Reserve Bank on 11 February 1985 abolished all compulsory investment requirements on the country's major groups of financial institutions (see RBNZ, 1985). The UK had already gone nearly as far as this, for the 10 per cent reserve assets ratio was abolished in August 1981 (after being reduced from 12.5 per cent in January of that year) and all that remained, aside from a stipulation that 6 per cent of eligible assets must be held as secured call money, was a requirement that banks hold 0.5 per cent of their eligible assets as non-interest bearing deposits with the Bank of England, as a means of financing the Bank's operations (the ratio was cut to 0.45 per cent in 1986). Increasingly, therefore, a greater reliance has been placed upon the use of open market operations to affect the opportunity cost of funds and hence the structure of portfolios. In essence, the idea is that if yields on bonds are pushed up as a result of the reserve bank of the country in question unloading bonds on to the market, it will cost banks and other financial intermediaries more to persuade people to accept their liabilities; hence they will need to charge their borrowers more and the unwillingness of borrowers to pay more should, so it is hoped, result in a slowdown in the growth of expenditure.

9.7 Interactions Between the Balance Sheets of Banks and NBFIs

Many students taking courses in money and banking try to argue that 'an increase in deposits at NBFIs necessarily entails a reduction in bank deposits, since deposits are being transferred from one instution to another'. In terms of the money multiplier analysis presented in section 9.3, students who make this sort of claim are mistaken, for in that analysis changes in the sizes of NBFI balance sheets had no effect on the volume of bank lending. When a person with a bank account was attracted to make a deposit with an NBFI via a cheque in-payment, the fact that NBFIs also have bank accounts ensured that the bank deposit simply changed ownership, either within an individual bank's deposits records or between those of a pair of banks. If the NBFI then increased its lending, keeping part of the new deposit in its reserves in its bank, and writing out a cheque for the borrower to pass on to whoever is selling her something, part of the deposit changed hands yet again, possibly moving between banks, but remaining within bank balance sheets all the time, unless someone turned it into cash or there was a leakage to the government or overseas sectors.

From the standpoint of portfolio theory, the students' argument may in *some* circumstances have a lot to commend it, even though it is clearly incorrect as a statement of the immediate impact of new NBFI deposits on bank deposits. NBFIs certainly can, as a group, bid for deposits by various means without reducing total bank deposits. But this fact must not distract us from their subsequent need to get extra borrowers from somewhere. The students' argument would be ultimately wrong in a situation where would-be borrowers were coming away away empty handed from bank managers owing to the latters' unwillingness or inability to extend them credit. If such people do not have access to disintermediated loans as a substitute for bank finance, their willingness to incur any slightly higher costs entailed in obtaining funds from credit unions, finance companies and building societies would encourage such institutions to engage in more active liability management policies. This is precisely what has happened in the past when the growth of bank lending has been restricted because the banks (a) have agreed to requests for voluntary restraint; (b) have been prevented by legal restrictions and goodwill considerations from raising interest rates and thereby putting pressure on the reserve bank to engage in open market operations and supply them with reserve assets; or (c) have been subject to rules such as those entailed in 'the corset'. By way of illustration, the experience of the Bank of England in using the corset to do battle with bulging expenditure is worth noting in some detail.

As a means of monetary management, the corset was limited in its effectiveness owing to the ability of banks to increase their lending by expanding their non-eligible liabilities, such as certificates of deposit and non-sterling eurodollar liabilities, and by the ability of borrowers to raise money by direct financing or from NBFIs who saw the weak bidding of the banks for retail deposits as a signal to expand their own activities (Llewellyn *et al.*, 1982, give due attention to the growth in disintermediation as well as the growth in NBFI lending; see also Hotson, 1982). During the period in which the corset was in operation, a monetary aggregate based on bank liabilities (such as *M3*) could thus be exhibiting slow growth, whilst a broader definition (such as *M6*) was expanding rapidly along with nominal expenditure. Attempts to control *M3*, in the belief that there was a predictable link between *M3* growth and growth in aggregate demand, thus provided a neat example of the workings of Goodhart's law, 'that any observed statistical regularity will tend to collapse once pressure is placed upon it for control purposes' (Goodhart, 1984, p. 96). Had the corset been extended to cover the activities of NBFIs whose liabilities were included in broader definitions of money, which came to seem better related than *M3* to expenditure levels, then Goodhart's law would have led one to expect bigger increases in remaining uncontrolled areas. When it was abandoned in June 1980, there was a sudden upward lurch of Sterling *M3* as banks adopted more aggressive policies of liability management; broad money could continue to grow pretty much as before, but the share of it accounted for by NBFI liabilities would be falling, even if they experienced no absolute reduction.

In situations where bankers do not find their hands tied by the monetary authorities, it may well be the case that NBFIs can only expand their lending if they 'steal' customers from banks by demanding a lower rate of loan interest. Their success in doing this depends on the responses of the banks. The latter can judge that they have got their interest rates wrong and lower them to try to restore their share of the loan market, or they can simply contract the sizes of their balance sheets by cutting the volume of new loans they make to replace those that are being repaid (or they can implement a combination of both policies). If $X has been repaid, banks could, if they wished, simply write themselves $X new loans and deposits. But if replacement borrowers can only be won through lower loan rates or by taking on greater risks, banks might prefer simply to let their deposits go down by $X. What we could have, then, is that an NBFI makes a new loan of $X to customers who otherwise would have borrowed $X from banks, and the banks contract their balance sheets by $X compared with what they would have been. An increase in NBFI deposits and loans is thus reflected in a reduction in bank deposits and loans: here, the students' conclusion seems to hold, despite being founded on a rather naive premise.

It is probably appropriate to see the rival scenarios as interrelated in practice. If NBFIs successfully expand the sizes of the balance sheets without adversely affecting those of the banks, the monetary authorities may become alarmed at the overall growth of spending/ borrowing and pursue a tighter monetary policy, causing the banks to reduce the rates at which they expand their deposit growth (for further variations on this theme, see Llewellyn, 1979, pp. 23-4).

9.8 The Role of the Reserve Bank

Like a commercial bank or an NBFI, a reserve bank has to decide, in the light of prevailing conditions in financial markets, how fast it wishes its liabilities to grow. Just as a reserve bank may be more concerned about the growth of some classes of liabilities of commercial banks than others — for example, deposits in domestic currency rather than eurocurrency deposits — so, too, it may think it more important and/or feasible to manage the growth of particular liabilities of its own. For practical purposes, a reserve bank will not normally seek directly to control the volume of notes and coin in circulation with the public. If banks found that they could not run down their own deposits at their reserve bank to obtain cash to meet customers' demands for deposit withdrawals, one would either expect there to be a major panic about the solvency of banks, or a rapid change in methods of payment in favour of cheques, credit cards and electronic funds transfer systems. It would be foolish for a reserve bank to promote panic and futile for it to try to discourage spending by such means. Consequently, as far as a reserve bank is concerned, its operating focus will only be on the the volume of bankers' balances that it holds, and the levels of vault cash held by banks: like Goodhart (1984, p. 203), I will assume that if a reserve bank says it is trying to control the 'monetary base', then it means it is trying to keep within chosen bounds the rate at which the sum total of these two classes of liabilities is growing.

Over time, the liability management policies of individual banks can be expected to change the relationship between the monetary base as just defined and the total supply of high-powered money. For example, the introduction of interest-earning cheque accounts will encourage people to make less use of currency as a means of payment and hence typically have less cash in their wallets. The monetary base could thus rise without there necessarily being any rise in the liabilities of the reserve bank. Otherwise, though, the policies of an individual bank will only tend to affect the monetary base of an economy with a floating exchange rate in so far as they provoke a response from the reserve bank. If a commercial bank wishes to increase (reduce) its holdings at the reserve bank, it can sell (bid for) securities and accept cheques as payment for them (pay for them with cheques drawn against itself). If the buyers (sellers) of securities are its own depositors, then the total size of its balance sheet will fall (grow), without its deposits at the reserve bank changing (cf. the end of section 9.2). If the buyers (sellers) are depositors at other banks, then the latter banks' holdings at the reserve bank will fall (rise). Only if the buyer (seller) happens to be the reserve bank will bankers' balances at the reserve bank rise (fall) when securities are sold (purchased). If an individual bank tries to increase (dispose of some of) its reserve bank holdings by raising (lowering) its deposit rates, it will cause a contraction (promote growth) in its rivals' balance sheets and in their deposits with the reserve bank.

Evidently, if the reserve bank does not expand its liabilities by buying bonds at a time when banks are trying to raise funds, then security prices will fall and deposit rates will rise. The fall in security prices will be limited by the terms on which the reserve bank is prepared to provide banks with lender of last resort facilities either by directly lending to them or by purchasing assets from them. The reserve bank appears therefore to be in a position to 'rule the roost' in the money markets over which it watches: the relative competitive strengths of rival intermediaries and direct borrowers will determine relative rates of interest and market spreads but the average rate of interest observed at a particular point has an upper limit determined by the price of obtaining funds from the reserve bank. Though the reserve bank can limit the extent to which wholesale rates can rise, it is, like the banks to whom it lends, a quantity taker in its lending activities. How much banks wish to borrow from it will depend on how much their own clients wish to borrow, given the rates of interest that the banks are asking.

By way of illustration, suppose the reserve bank has recently raised its own lending rate. Banks with money owing to the reserve bank will find their profits squeezed. Interest rates will be marked up generally. If the rise in interest rates induces members of the domestic non-bank private sector to try to reduce their net indebtedness by paying off pre-existing bank loans, they will initially succeed only in reducing their deposits by an *equal* amount. The banks' ratio of reserve assets to total assets rises. However, if the government does not reduce its NAFA, the current account of the balance of payments will move towards a (bigger) surplus, equal in size to the desired increase in the non-bank private sector NAFA. If the reserve bank wishes to stop upward pressure on the exchange rate, it will build up foreign currency reserves in exchange for claims on itself in terms of domestic currency. When exporters deposit their earnings in the domestic banking system, the banks will be able to reduce their net borrowing from (their liabilities to) the reserve bank by this amount; the banks' ratio of reserve assets to total assets thus remains at the increased level it reached when the loans were repaid, but the banks' customers will now have succeeded in increasing their deposits relative to their borrowing. Alternatively, the banks may increase their demand for government debt, but the result is essentially the same since less of the government's borrowing will now have to be financed by expanding the monetary base: bank liabilities will grow less than they would otherwise have done, by an amount equal to the reduction in net indebtedness of the domestic non-bank private sector.

By reversing the signs in this example, one can see how the banks as a group could come to increase their net borrowing from the reserve bank: in so far as the government did not increase its NAFA in response the reduction in the domestic non-bank private sector's NAFA and foreign-owned deposits in domestic banks did not rise, newly created deposits would leak overseas as the additional loans were spent. Gross borrowing by the banks might need to rise somewhat further, for the banks might run into their target cash/total assets ratios as they expanded the scale of their balance sheets.

If the reserve bank were not operating in the market, average rates of interest would be determined by financial intermediaries' borrowing rates plus their spreads, and borrowing rates would depend entirely on the confidence and transactions cost positions of those potential depositors who could choose to lend their money directly or simply hold it as cash rather than place it with an intermediary. In other words, the average level of interest rates would be purely a 'bootstraps' phenomenon, constrained by the subjective marginal yield to holding cash, just as in Keynes' (1936, Ch. 17) analysis. The presence of the reserve bank enables financial intermediaries to engage in their asset and liability management policies in an orderly manner so long as the price of last resort funds is not expected to be 'varied capriciously' (Goodhart, 1987a, p. 501).

If the reserve bank were purely interested in the rate of growth of the monetary base, it would have to be prepared to abandon its lender of last resort role and stand aside in the face of interest rate fluctuations produced by changing demands for liquidity and finance and changes in the competitive strengths of other suppliers of funds. Unless banks were so cautious as to operate with considerable excess reserves, any sudden widespread demand for liquidity — even for things as innocuous as seasonal tax payments and Christmas spending — could potentially lead to pressures for a very violent multiple contraction in bank lending, to which banks would not unnaturally react by aggressive liability management policies if they thought the problem were just a short-term one. Matters would hardly be much better for portfolio managers if the reserve bank did not totally back out of its lender of last resort role but let it be known that it was only prepared to make funds available via open market operations when it saw fit.

It is not hard to see why most reserve banks would regard a policy of strict monetary base control as a practical non-starter, even though it would make it very easy for them to account for their actions. During the three year experiment of the US Federal Reserve in monetary base control, from October 1979 to September 1982, there was a four-fold increase in the volatility of short-term interest rates, along with greater instability in long-term interest rates and in the exchange rate, even though rediscounting facilities were not made totally unavailable (Goodhart, 1987a, p. 501). One might have expected that short-term reductions in bank lending would come to be neatly offset, at a small cost in terms of increased interest rates, by short-term increases in direct lending by non-financial corporations with cash surpluses. But the US financial system was not able to smooth out these fluctuations, even towards the end of the period.

Less formalised attempts to pursue a 'tight money' policy over a sustained period will also tend to present central bankers with dilemmas that cause them to allow a more rapid growth in the monetary base than they might ideally like to see. For example, rises in interest rates may lead to attempts by overseas residents and firms to increase their deposits in the country in question. This would put upward pressure on the country's exchange rate and thereby make matters difficult for local producers of traded goods and services; the crowding out of such producers might be very difficult to reverse. Increases in interest rates will also concern the reserve bank in its role as the manager of the public sector deficit, and because defaults by people and institutions unable to cope with unexpectedly high interest rates may threaten the stability of the financial system. In practice, therefore, reserve banks normally make clear the terms on which they are prepared to make funds available, and only change their terms gradually. They then supply, on these terms, whatever cash the system requires. Hence the growth of even those monetary aggregates (such as *M1* and *M3*) that one might expect to be most directly under reserve bank control normally depends on the demand for finance, not on some predetermined growth in the monetary base times the relevant multiplier coefficients.

9.9 Conclusion

The message of the New View of money creation is that the growth rates of monetary aggregates are endogenous phenomena, heavily dependent on the willingness of borrowers and lenders to substitute between alternative financial intermediaries. Precisely what happens to the various monetary aggregates depends very much on the competitive strategies of rival financial intermediaries, which money supply definition the monetary authorities are trying to affect, and on the confidence of would-be lenders and borowers. In this chapter, the role of confidence in the money supply process has been somewhat downplayed; it will receive due attention in Chapter 10 where I explore further the concept of money supply endogeneity. The broad compass of the view of endogeneity implied by the portfolio approach needs to be emphasised before we proceed to these discussions, for proponents of the Old View are sometimes also to be found claiming that they are including money supply endogeneity in their models (for example, see Challen and Hagger, 1981, Ch. 8): it must be understood that the Old View only treats monetary growth as endogenous in the sense that, consequent on an initial injection of base money and response by the banking system, equilibrating feedbacks from the balance of payments and flows of tax revenue to the government will affect the net growth in base money and bank deposits. The money multiplier analysis otherwise treats credit creation in a deterministic manner, as a phenomenon that is controlled exogenously by the reserve bank: propensities to divide deposits between banks and NBFIs are taken as given and neither interest rates on deposits and loans, nor confidence, enter multiplier scenarios at all; if the reserve bank chooses to allow a particular growth in the monetary base, total lending by banks is restricted to a multiple of this, set by their reserve ratios, and total lending by NBFIs is limited by their reserve ratios and the propensity of deposit owners to divide their holdings between bank and NBFI deposits.

Given the ubiquitous nature of signs that financial institutions are engaged in competition, there would be strong grounds, in terms of portfolio theory, for doubting the usefulness of the Old View even if reserve banks did not behave in the manner assumed in multiplier models. One wonders whether the multiplier analysis would continue to dominate economists' thinking were it not for its 'rabbit out of a hat' aspect: it offers a simple way of giving the impression that economists can see features of the economic system which would not strike lay observers as obvious phenomena. The portfolio approach is much more subtle but turns out to be more thought-provoking in respect of policy issues in the modern monetary environment.

10 Income Multipliers and the Money Supply Process

10.1 Introduction

This chapter is an attempt to examine the determination of aggregate demand and employment in the light of all that has been so far said about portfolio choice and the workings of modern financial systems. After discussing and criticising money multiplier theories in the previous chapter, it is appropriate to turn our attention to the income multiplier that was so central to Keynes' view of the economic system. The relationships between monetary growth and the processes of income generation run both ways: credit creation by banks may lead to a multiple expansion of spending, as well as to further repercussions on the supply of finance, depending on what people and governments decide to do with the incomes they receive. Given the long menus of possibilities that arise for decision-makers in modern financial systems, and the scope for changes through time in attitudes towards rival possibilities, readers should not be surprised to see that I make no attempt to investigate the relationships in a deterministic manner.

Much of the inspiration for the chapter comes from a recently published attempt by Victoria Chick (1985) to promote 'process analysis' — in other words, thinking in terms of possible sequences of events — as an alternative to the conventional strategy of using the notion of equilibrium for avoiding the difficulties of facing up to the existence of historical time. Process analysis has a long tradition of popularity in Scandinavia, but it has been slow to achieve popularity amongst Post Keynesians, let alone orthodox macroeconomists. In a sense, the methodology could be said to involve the use of intricate story-telling exercises and relatively simple numerical examples for coping with the passage of time, rather than the construction of full-blown macreconomic models using difference equations and complex lag structures, for which simulations could be run over a very long time scale. Those readers who are used to working with such models may wonder why I have not chosen to do likewise, given that complexity forces anyone using process analysis to leave things open ended after exploring only three or four time periods. The reason is simple. While I certainly prefer such macroeconomic models to those that are built around the notion of equilibrium, their greater capacity to follow possibilities further into the future is achieved with the aid of more complex technical apparatus which rely on a presumption that their coefficients are stable. If this stability is in doubt, so, too, seems to be the wisdom of setting up a technically complicated system.

10.2 Initial Sources of Finance and the Possibility of Crowding Out

A change in the flow of production of goods and services in an economy may be induced, in principle, by an increase in the net demand coming from consumers, firms, government or from overseas. For present purposes, let us focus on an increase in investment expenditure by firms. The first question we must address is how this is financed, for the financing methods used by firms can affect the rate of spending in the economy. Finance might come from the following sources:

(a) bank deposits previously accumulated by the firms, which otherwise would not have been used to purchase anything else;

(b) NBFI deposits previously accumulated by the firms, which otherwise would not have been used to purchase anything else;

(c) bank and NBFI deposits previously accumulated by the firms, which otherwise would have been used to pay for other things (such as better worker remuneration, bigger shareholder dividends, newly-issued debentures of other companies, or pre-existing securities);

(d) the sale of new securities, which are paid for from bank deposits;

(e) the sale of new securities, which are paid for from NBFI deposits;

(f) the sale of new securities, which are purchased by overseas buyers;

(g) the sale of securities (such as equity holdings in other firms and public sector notes and bonds) previously accumulated by the firms themselves, which are paid for from bank deposits;

(h) as for (g), except that purchasers pay by running down their NBFI deposits;
(i) as for (g), except that they are purchased by overseas buyers;
(j) loans from domestic banks and NBFIs;
(k) loans from overseas banks.

Only in case (a) is it obvious that firms can pay for their investment goods without in any way crowding out expenditure which would otherwise be taking place at the same time.

In each of the cases where firms sell securities to raise their finance, there is the possibility that the purchasers would otherwise be purchasing goods and services or securities being sold by other bodies seeking to raise money to undertake expenditure. The latter would then need to offer a more attractive deal to persuade other suppliers of funds to come forward, and this could lead to less expenditure being undertaken. However, if the securities are purchased from bank deposits that otherwise would not have been used to purchase anything, then other forms of expenditure will not be displaced. In case (c), those who would have received money from the firms are deprived of it at the expense of those who provide the investment goods, so the expenditure of the former is likely to be reduced unless they are able/willing to raise money from other sources or run down their liquidity.

In each of the cases where securities are bought with NBFI deposits, lending by NBFIs will fall unless the NBFIs find it viable to bid for replacement deposits or have excess reserve assets which they are willing to use up. If the firms themselves raise money from NBFIs they will be displacing other borrowers unless the NBFIs can raise additional deposits on terms which permit insignificant changes in lending rates. If the firms borrow from domestic banks, they might do so directly at the expense of other would-be borrowers, who would then be forced to consider somewhat more expensive sources of finance — in which case some expenditure projects may be abandoned — unless the banks try to expand the sizes of their balance sheets. In the past, before the development of liability management policies, the former scenario would have been the more likely of the two: by the end of the Second World War, banks' portfolios had become top heavy with government securities, so when private sector demands for finance increased, the banks commonly responded by unloading some of these securities on to the market. More recently, one might expect to see the latter possibility arising: where banks' reserve assets are defined only in relation to their short-term deposit liabilities, banks can build up their holdings of liabilities that fall outside the definition, for example by offering attractive rates on certificates of deposit (CDs). With the composition of their liabilities thus reweighted, they can then create additional loans along with replacement short-term liabilities (see Goodhart, 1984, pp. 150-3). There could still be some displacement in this case — both to the extent that other expenditure was deterred as a result of any general rise in bank borrowing charges, and in so far as holders of CDs would otherwise have placed their funds with NBFIs or lent them out directly.

Expenditure displacements may be averted if the reserve bank enters the market and buys back government securities as their yields start to rise. If the reserve bank is seeking to maintain stable interest rates and if the banks tend not to operate with substantial excess reserves, these open market operations will only involve the purchase of government securities to a fraction of the value that the firms are seeking to raise by their own sales of securities. With the aid of the new reserve assets arising from the deposits of those who sold securities to the reserve bank, the banks can create multiple extra deposits in the course of increasing their lending by an amount equal to the displacement that otherwise would have occurred.

When funds are raised on world markets, one would expect their elasticity of supply to be such that direct crowding out of other domestic borrowers who were seeking to raise funds on international capital markets would not be an issue. A much more serious area for concern is the possibility that the capital inflow may lead to an appreciation in the exchange rate and make business more difficult for domestic exporters or those competing with imports: if the exchange rate is floating without any reserve bank intervention, funds borrowed in terms of overseas currencies could only be imported by persuading holders of domestic currency to turn more of it into overseas currencies than they otherwise would have done. If the currency parity is at least partly managed by the reserve bank, the capital inflow could involve a smaller appreciation of the exchange rate and instead an accumulation of additional foreign exchange reserves by the reserve bank. Whether or not this would entail an increase in the monetary base would depend on whether the reserve bank sought successfully to engage in a policy of sterilisation. Such a policy could clearly involve displacement of other expenditures unless those who purchased government securities would otherwise simply have kept their money as bank deposits. It is perhaps worth adding at this point that such displacements of expenditure may also be achieved even where capital inflows are nothing to do with increased expenditure on newly produced goods and services: scope for something of this kind loomed large in Australia in 1987 when Robert Holmes a Court sought to finance a takeover bid for Australia's largest company, BHP, via an enormous loan from the Standard Chartered Bank in London, but fortunately for the rest of the economy (and probably for Mr Holmes a Court, given the subsequent battering that his company took from the collapse of share prices later in the year) the project was abandoned when Elders-IXL entered the fray as a rival bidder.

If displacements of expenditure of the kinds discussed above actually occur, they will cause the value of the multiplier to fall somewhat short of the value that one would infer from the various marginal propensities. However, given the scope for substitution in modern financial systems it is difficult to imagine that contraints on the supply of finance could be so great as to give the multiplier a zero or negative value in situations where the reserve bank is not tending to accommodate increases in the willingness to spend by pursuing a policy of using open market operations to keep interest rates stable.

In general it seems reasonable to say that, if the financial community does not (does) expect interest rates to rise significantly when expenditure increases, then they will not (will) do so: if interest rates are not expected to rise, any tendency for security prices to fall will lead speculators to purchase them in the expectation of a capital gain, by running down their lower-yielding liquid assets, and vice versa. When taken together, liquidity preference theory and the portfolio analysis of the money supply process imply that if an increase in expenditure reflects or causes a general increase in confidence, interest rates can even fall as the volume of financing increases. Reserve bank intervention is not required to achieve this; all that is necessary is for those with bank deposits to become willing to use them to purchase securities or NBFI liabilities that they would hitherto have thought too risky. By contrast, when the economic mood swings in the opposite direction, we can have a slowdown in overall lending, despite a faster rate of growth of *M3*, as those with surplus funds remove their deposits from the riskier kinds of NBFIs in search of the greater security of banks and/or reduce their volumes of direct lending. In such cases, an accelerated growth in bank lending would arise not because expenditure is increasing at a faster rate but because the banks find it less costly to keep borrowers away from

NBFIs and from avenues for direct financing. The implications of this downside scenario, which Minsky (1975, 1982, 1986) has been at pains to highlight, will be explored at length in the next two chapters.

In the numerical example in the next section, I will assume, for simplicity, that the increase in investment is financed in a way which avoids *any* crowding out. This is *not* to say that I would wish to downplay its importance in all contexts — indeed, it might be said that it is one of the major concerns of the last chapter of this book — though the portfolio perspective on the money supply process does lead me to doubt that *financial* crowding out is as significant as some orthodox economists would have us believe.

10.3 A Numerical Illustration of the Income Multiplier

Before we consider how a process of macroeconomic expansion may proceed once an initial spurt of expenditure has been undertaken, a few words of revision may be in order concerning macroeconomic identities. In states of equilibrium, it is easy to see that flows of saving and investment are definitionally equal if there is no government deficit or surplus and no balance of payments deficit or surplus. An income recipient's saving flow is what is left over after expenditure on consumption, which in a layperson's terminology is the increase in that income recipient's total 'savings'. Investment is that part of expenditure which goes on fixed capital and increased stockholding, rather than on consumption. Aggregate income and expenditure flows are equal, therefore saving equals investment. Not only this, but the equalities hold for both planned and realised flows of saving and investment. Were this not the case, the system would not be in equilibrium. If the government and/or overseas sectors are not in balance, then the equilibrium condition requires that leakages from the circular flow of income (saving, tax payments and imports) equal injections (investment, government expenditure and exports). Once we move into an analysis of historical processes these identities still hold as far as recorded outcomes are concerned, but expectations and outcomes may differ: an expansion may thus involve unplanned disinvestments (as stocks fall unexpectedly low), unplanned savings and windfall flows of tax revenue for the government.

Any process description of the Keynesian income multiplier is by its nature complex and potentially confusing. Ideally, one would like to capture the different ways in which different decision-makers may respond to disturbances in their income flows, but here I propose to keep things manageable by assuming a uniform set of marginal propensities, which can be thought of as proxies for a set of weighted averages of marginal propensities: I will suppose that everyone faces a marginal rate of income tax of 25 per cent and has a marginal propensity of 0.8 to spend from net income; I will also assume that the rate of indirect tax is 10 per cent and that the marginal propensity to purchase imports is 0.25, with imports being free of any tariff imposition and subject only to the normal rate of indirect tax. Although an end result for the value of the multiplier is computed — which would nearly enough be reached after about nine rounds of expenditure — this is included mainly to show how macroeconomic accounting identities hold for an infinity of expenditure rounds as well as for individual time periods, and I hope readers will not forget that the various propensities may well change long before all the repercussions of an initial disturbance have been fully felt.

Consider what happens when firms undertake an extra $1 million expenditure on building and equipping new factories. The government receives $100 000 of the total expenditure as indirect taxes. Income payments are thus $900 000, but since only three quarters of the expenditure is aimed at domestically produced goods, domestic pre-tax incomes have increased by $675 000. Post-tax incomes are increased only by three quarters of this, that is, $506 250. Now, suppose the financial year ends at this point. This means that any multiplier effects of the increase in investment will have to wait till next year. Taking stock of the impact of the investment so far, we find that injections and leakages are equal, even though the economy is in no way presumed to be in equilibrium. The injection is simply $1 million, namely the investment. Leakages are $100 000 indirect taxes, $225 000 imports, $168 750 income taxes and $506 250 saving, which sum to $1 million. Only the saving figure should give pause for thought: four-fifths of this is unplanned, forced saving which has only occurred because the recipients of net incomes have not yet had time to spend them.

The repercussions of the additional investment expenditure can now be followed into the next year. There will be an initial burst of consumption demand of $405 000 (that is, $506 250 times 0.8) from the first-round income recipients. The government receives $40 500 in indirect taxes and since a quarter of the expenditure is aimed at imports, pre-tax domestic incomes of only $273 375 are received (in other words, $[405 000 - 40 500] times 0.75). Post-tax incomes are $205 031.25, and income tax revenue is $68 343.75. Round three begins with the second-round income recipients spending $164 025, of which the government receives $16 402.50 as indirect taxes. Pre-tax domestic incomes only rise by $110 716.87, owing to the purchases of imports. Post-tax incomes of round-three recipients are $83 037.65, for the government takes $27 679.22. If we stop and take stock of things at this point, the second year's picture is as follows. Consumption expenditure is $569 025, but domestic post-tax incomes are only $288 068.90 (in other words, $205 031.25 + $83 037.65). We have dissaving of $280 956.10. Indirect tax revenue is $56 902.50, and income tax receipts are $96 022.97, so total government revenue from these year two events is $152 925.47. Imports involve a leakage from the economy of $128 030.63 (that is, $0.25[405 000 - 40 500] + $0.25[164 025 - 16 402.50]). If the figures for dissaving, for government revenue and for imports are summed together, we get zero, exactly as we should, given that we have not recorded any additional investment expenditure, increases in government outlays or exports.

A clear implication of the four marginal propensities here assumed is that the marginal propensity to respend factor incomes on domestic goods is 0.405. By using the standard formula of $m = 1/(1 - c)$, where m is the multiplier and c the marginal propensity to spend, we can discover that the end result of the multiplier process is that the $1 million increase in investment causes an additional $680 672.20 increase in consumer expenditure at market prices. When the multiplier process has finished working itself through the economy, the indirect tax revenue of the government will be $168 067.22 greater than it would have been in the absence of the increase in investment expenditure; $100 000 of this comes from the investment expenditure itself and the remaining $68 072.22 comes as a result of increased consumer expenditure. Total imports will be $378 151.22 higher: $225 000 will be due to the investment activity; $153 151.22 will be due to increased consumer expenditure. Gross incomes at factor cost will be up by $1 134 453.70, of which $675 000 will have been been earned in the capital goods sector and $459 453.70 in the consumption goods sector, and hence revenue from income tax, charged at a marginal rate of 25 per cent, will be $283 613.40 higher than it would otherwise have been. From the increased domestic disposable income of $850 840.20, the additional consumption worth

$680 672.16 at market prices will have been generated, but the leakages to indrect taxes and on imports will have ensured that this only amounts to $459 453.70 of income at factor cost. Additional savings to the value of $170 168.04 will have been accumulated. The end result is that the original injection of $1 million is equal, subject to rounding at the second decimal place, to the grand total of the sums of all the subsequent leakages: that is, $168 067.22 + $378 151.22 + $283 613.40 + $170 168.04.

The example just considered has one major difference with equilibrium treatments of the multiplier in conventional 'income/ expenditure' expositions of 'Keynesian' macroeconomics: it focuses on the repercussions of a particular, one-off injection of expenditure — which in this case happened to be private sector investment, but could just as well have been an increase in government expenditure, an increase in exports (or a reduction in the propensity to import), or a reduction in the propensity to save — whereas orthodox expositions treat the injection of expenditure as something which is repeated in each period, so that the economy settles down at a particular equilibrium level of income. An income/expenditure treatment using the figures we employed would thus see the flow of investment rising by $1 million at market prices, with a rise in disposable income flows of $850 840.20, and so on.

Whichever kind of expenditure injection is being considered, the economic analyst must be prepared to face up to the problem that precisely how long it would take for the bulk of the expenditure repercussions to be felt is something which cannot be pronounced upon on an a priori basis. The same is true for their employment impacts, which will depend on the availability of stocks (see Chapter 13) and the extent to which demand expansions are judged merely to be temporary. A modern econometrician would no doubt hope to infer the lag structures of a detailed macroeconometric model from past data series, but the predictive value of estimated coefficients could go seriously astray given the large number of potentially variable factors that in practice impinge on the multiplier process. I would like to echo the behavioural-sounding tone of Ackley (1951, p. 368):

Not only does income change only by a process that takes time, but to determine the speed and extent of that process involves an analysis of business practices, attitudes, responses; of technical conditions of production and supply; of consumer behaviour, income distribution, lay-off and hiring procedures; of indirect impacts on government budgets through tax collections, transfer payments, social security contributions;

of indirect impacts on the money market; indeed of every aspect of the economic process. To understand them we need a vast fund of institutional knowledge about the business system, and, perhaps even more important, an understanding of the psychological frames of reference of business firms and individuals, which determine the way in which and the speed with which they respond to changes in objective facts.

It is to these kinds of issues that I will now turn my attention.

10.4 The Transactions Demand for Money

If people and firms increase their rates of spending, they may tend to hold on average a greater value of liquid assets. For example, consumers whose incomes have risen will be tending to walk around with more money in their wallets than in the past and shops that are doing more business will tend to operate with a bigger 'float' of money in their tills. Manufacturers, similarly, may find they need larger holdings of bank deposits to meet bills for inputs while they are waiting for payments from customers to come through, for their access to trade credit may be less than the trade credit that competitive conditions force them to provide. The equilibrium perspective of mainstream expositions of Keynesian economics tends to conflate such increases in the 'transactions demand for money' with increases in the need for loan finance that may be necessary to push the economy to a faster pace of activity and which we discussed in section 10.2. While both these kinds of demand can be met by a reduction in speculative holdings of liquidity, the conflation causes enormous confusion for students: it is easy to forget that transactions demands for money affect the system only so long as the money is being held prior to spending, whereas a demand for loans is a demand for an asset to pass on to someone else in an act of spending.

From the blinkered standpoint of a money multiplier analysis of the money supply it is difficult to avoid the orthodox conclusion that a rise in the transactions demand for money will push up interest rates, or its implication that the size of the multiplier may be rather less than than one might expect purely from looking at the various marginal propensities. If the monetary base is given, the leakage of cash into wallets and tills produces a multiple reduction in the amount of lending that banks can undertake, so one would expect banks to have to put up their interest rates to equate the demand for loans with their ability to supply them.

If cash as such does not leak out of bank deposits, one would expect that a rise in the rate of expenditure would involve at least a greater preference for more liquid kinds of bank deposits. For example, suppose firms pay for increases in their investment expenditure by presenting their banks with mature certificates of deposit and tranferring the money to the suppliers of investment goods, who then use much of it to meet factor payments. Workers in the investment goods industry may be avid users of cheques and 'electronic funds tranfer at point of sale' (EFTPOS) systems, but while they are deciding what to buy they will be keeping higher call balances in their banks than before. Once these deposits are spent, the recipients likewise may tend to keep some of them on call. Hence the rise in activity will have been associated with a change in the maturity structure of bank liabilities and the banks might therefore be expected to become less willing to make long-term loans. Furthermore, if certificates of deposit fall outside the list of bank liabilities against which reserve asset requirements are defined, such a change in the composition of bank deposits could mean that banks started to fall short of their target operating ratios and were then faced with a choice between raising their returns on certificates of deposit or cutting their lending — either way, one would expect interest rates to drift upwards.

From the standpoint of the portfolio theory of the money supply, it is natural to argue that the extent to which increases in the transactions demand for money drive up interest rates will depend upon how far the reserve bank is pursuing a policy of stable interest rates, and on how willing agents are to switch their portfolios between different kinds of financial assets in response to small changes in relative yields. In other words, the points made in the penultimate paragraph of section 10.2 apply once again. Increases in confidence and financial innovations may even allow a fall in interest rates to occur while the transactions demand for money is rising.

10.5 Taxation Windfalls and Aggregate Demand

Government tax revenues in our numerical example are increased by the expansion in investment activity and, subsequently, in consumption. The question therefore arises as to how the government might respond to such a windfall. Additional revenue flowing in at the end of one period provides a means of paying for public sector expenditure in the next period, but this by no means guarantees that the government will increase its expenditure or cut taxes and thereby start off a secondary multiplier effect whose size will not be constrained by initial financial crowding out. Nowadays, the popularity of 'cutting the deficit' as a political goal makes such a reaction to windfall tax revenues unlikely unless the public sector deficit has already been reduced to a level that the government judges to be satisfactory (the tax-cutting March 1988 Budget of the UK Chancellor of the Exchequer, Mr Nigel Lawson, is an example of the latter kind). It would be less surprising, therefore, if increases in tax revenue led either to a reduction in sales of government securities — in which case there may subsequently be some 'crowding in' of private sector expenditure — or to a reduction in borrowing from the reserve bank and hence to a reduction in the rate of growth of bank lending. How far interest rates would tend to rise in the latter case would depend not merely upon the willingness of banks to bid for deposits, but also upon which were the favoured resting places for the rising volume of private sector saving and on the size of this flow relative to the increased flow of tax revenue.

In so far as difficulties in obtaining deposits at the reserve bank prevent banks from expanding their lending — in other words, in so far as one can take seriously the money multiplier analysis of monetary growth — a reduction in government borrowing from the reserve bank could result in bank lending falling, by a multiple of this amount, below the figure that might otherwise have been recorded. In the absence of any rise in relative rates of interest for NBFI deposits or on direct loans, only a fractional non-bank offset to such a reduction in the growth of bank lending could be expected. In a case like our numerical example, where savings increase more slowly than tax revenue, such an offset would indeed be small if relative yields did not change for one would only expect a fraction of the new savings to go automatically into NBFI deposits and direct lending. If one takes the money multiplier idea seriously, then the possibility of some kind of second-round crowding out seems to arise when the growth rate of the monetary base falls as a direct consequence of increased tax revenues that arise from an expansion of expenditure. A careful exploration of this worrying possibility produces the surprising result that, given the assumptions employed in our numerical example, crowding out on even-numbered expenditure rounds is more than offset by 'crowding in' on odd-numbered expenditure rounds.

Suppose the money multiplier has a value of ten and recall that in our numerical example the first round impact of a $1 million increase in investment on tax revenue is $268 750 ($100 000 indirect taxes plus $168 750 income tax). If, in the second period, the reserve bank cuts the rate of growth of the monetary base by this amount and the world works as in the money multiplier analysis, then bank lending will be $2 418 750 less than it otherwise would have been (that is, nine times $269 750). But this is by no means the end of the story. If there is no substitution in favour of financing by loans from NBFIs and by sales of securities, and no increases in financing via reductions of liquidity, then expenditure of this amount will fail to take place. This will eat into the government's tax revenue, for had this sum been spent, $241 875 more would have been received as indirect taxes and, given our assumed 0.25 marginal propensities to import and pay income tax, $408 164.05 more income tax revenue would have been received, making a total of $650 039.05. To find the government's net loss of revenue in the second round, we must subtract from this figure the revenues it receives from consumer expenditure in this period that is a consequence of the original injection of investment expenditure; these revenues are $40 500 indirect tax and $68 343.75 income tax. The end of the second round thus leaves the government down by $541 195.30.

If in round three the government then increased its borrowing from the reserve bank by the amount of its extra shortfall at the end of round two, and if the banks responded as in the money multiplier analysis, then, with a money multiplier of ten, bank lending would expand by $4 870 757.70. If there were no substitutions away from other forms of finance, expenditure would increase by this amount, which would bring in an additional $487 075.77 indirect tax, along with $821 940.35 extra in income tax. The working through of the original multiplier process also generates $16 402.50 indirect tax revenue and $27 267.22 in income tax in the third round. Therefore, compared to the revenue position it would have been in had the injection of investment expenditure not taken place in period one, the government goes into the fourth round with a borrowing requirement of $1 352 685.80 less than it would otherwise have had. The net effect of the second and third rounds on the sizes of the monetary base and on bank lending are that they are, respectively, $272 445.30 and $2 452 007.70 higher than they would have been had the injection of investment expenditure not occurred in round one. But if we carry on assuming that the government uses any tax windfall at the end of one period to reduce its borrowing from the reserve bank at the start of the next period, then there will be a quite dramatic contraction of bank lending in period four, along with a fall in tax revenue. In other words, non-convergent cyclical behaviour seems to be implied by our assumptions of a particular set of stable marginal propensities, a given money multiplier value, and a government that consistently tries to pursue a policy of 'sound finance'. The combination of a process view of the income multiplier with a money multiplier view of monetary growth opens up scope for instability that one would not tend to consider from the standpoints of conventional *IS-LM*-style equilibrium models or macroeconomic models that incorporate complex lag structures but fail to build in links between public sector borrowing and monetary expansion.

In practice, of course, the desire of the reserve bank to avoid gyrating interest rates would mean that windfall tax receipts at the end of one expenditure period are not matched on a one-for-one basis with reductions in borrowing by the government from the reserve bank at the start of the next period. Interest rate increases caused by a decline in the rate of growth of bank lending will prompt the reserve bank to make open market purchases of government stock, or (and this amounts to the same thing) to finance less of the public sector deficit by sales of securities during the expenditure round in question. The portfolio analysis of monetary growth in any case suggests that the need for such interventions will be reduced in so far as the implications of money multiplier analysis are overturned by substitution between bank loans and other sources of finance; by the ability and willingness of banks to borrow additional reserve assets from the reserve bank; and by the willingness of banks to engage in policies aimed at building up liabilities that fall outside the lists of liabilities against which their reserve asset requirements are stipulated.

Neoclassical economists might prefer to add something of a rational expectations and permanent income perspective to allow such oscillations to be avoided even in the absence of the kinds of factors mentioned in the previous paragraph. They would suggest that the public would soon come to realise what was going on and would make their consumption behaviour dependent on the trend that their incomes seemed to be tracing out, rather than on their current incomes.

10.6 Savings Modes and Aggregate Demand

The numerical example totally ignored the question of how people choose to hold their extra savings. The demand impacts of alternative savings modes warrant attention whether or not there has been the kind of spurt in the pace of activity portrayed in section 10.3; for even in a stagnant economy some private sector saving will normally be going on. In fact, the possibility that choices of savings modes may have a major role in determining whether or not an economy *is* in a state of stagnation was one of Keynes' central concerns. He recognised that people who choose not to spend all of their incomes in the period in which they receive them need not automatically make their surplus funds available to others to allow the latter to spend in excess of their incomes. In choosing not to spend their current receipts, people may choose to lend their surpluses in a variety of ways or they may choose to exert liquidity preference and simply hoard them. As we explore this theme, I hope it will not be forgotten that changes in the supply of finance can also arise if those who are not accumulating financial assets change their liquidity preference and reshuffle their portfolios: just as increases in saving do not automatically increase the supply of finance, so the supply of finance can be increased without a change in the rate of saving. I will focus on household saving, but the same arguments apply for corporate saving.

In Keynes' time, markets for personal savings were relatively poorly developed and most workers received their wages as cash. This made it easy for the economic theorist to draw the dividing line between lending and hoarding. If workers spent part of their incomes and then put the rest in a bank, they would be lending out their new savings. If they spent part of their income and then hid the rest in piggy banks or under mattresses, or wherever, they would be hoarding their new savings. Now that many people receive the wages in the form of direct inpayments by their employers into the bank accounts, the distinction between lending and hoarding is much less clearcut. Suppose some workers have run down their bank balances to zero by the time payday comes. Their pay goes into their bank accounts and during the course of the ensuing month they spend some of this money. Their bank balances thus decline once again, while the firms from whom they make purchases enjoy increased bank balances. At the end of the month, the consumers have some money left over in their bank accounts; this sum of money is their saving for the month in question. If they just leave the residual money where it is, they are giving no signal to producers as to what they will eventually do with it, nor are their actions obviously increasing the ability of others to spend. If they had spent the money, they would have changed the composition, but not the level, of bank deposits: they would have less in the bank, and shopkeepers, say, would have more. As it is, they may be receiving interest on their bank deposits, but their willingness to lend out their savings does not seem to promote an increase in spending by others to offset their own failure to spend. This result, in a modern credit money context, is akin to a 1930s scenario where hoarding of commodity money occurs.

In the modern context, our hypothetical savers can still hoard in the strict 1930s sense of the word: they can decide to withdraw their residual balances at the end of the month and simply keep them at home, safe from bank failure risks but at some cost in terms of foregone interest and risk of loss due to burglary. In this case, though, matters are made far worse. Bank deposits have fallen, and so too have bank reserve assets. It may well be that bank lending therefore falls, by a multiple of the deposit withdrawal (though probably with some of the disappointed borrowers succeeding in persuading NBFIs to expand their lending), or that replacement reserve assets are obtained at a price the banks are only willing to incur because they can charge extra for their loans, albeit at the cost of deterring some potential borrowers. This would mean that these workers' acts of saving have not merely withdrawn from the flow of expenditure the sum which they themselves did not spend; they have also reduced expenditure by the amount of the lending cutback that their choices of saving modes have produced.

Aggregate demand might be in a much more buoyant state if the savers chose to transfer their residual funds to NBFIs. Although, as far as the savers are concerned, the advantages of doing so may be somewhat minor, such acts open up the possibility of an increase in a broad definition of money, and in overall lending. As we saw in Chapter 9, the act of making a deposit with an NBFI may have no immediate impact on bank deposits, for money is simply transferred from the saver's bank account to the bank account of the NBFI. How far total lending then increases depends on the extent to which the NBFI poaches good borrowers from the banks or from other NBFIs and thereby causes the latter institutions to cut back somewhat on their growth of lending. For example, if banks tend not to operate in the market for housing finance — as was the case in Britain until the late 1970s — a growth in building society deposits may lead to an expansion of expenditure on housing by people who would not otherwise have borrowed money. By contrast, a rise in credit union deposits might mean that fewer credit union members go to banks or finance companies to obtain funds to buy new consumer durables.

A further possibility is that savers engage in direct lending, by buying securities. The impact of this mode of saving on aggregate demand is by no means as straightforward as one might initially expect. The savers may simply purchase existing securities that someone else is selling. If the seller merely keeps the money as a bank deposit, the new flow of saving only promotes expenditure on newly produced goods and services in so far as it helps keep security prices somewhat higher than they might otherwise have been: for example, the willingness of firms to invest may be a function of stock market prices. If the seller uses the money to purchase other securities, we have much the same problem: the buck has been passed to whoever sold the other securities, although we might expect security prices to be somewhat higher overall. However, the seller of securities might actually spend the proceeds on consumption or investment expenditure; if so, the new flow of saving, coming into the security market, has helped ensure that crowding out does not occur. Similar arguments would apply if savers decided to 'invest' their money in existing physical assets such as real estate and antiques.

Where savings are directed into the purchase of new securities, the impact on aggregate demand depends very much on what these securities are. For example, the easier central government finds it to fund its deficit by selling securities, the less it may wish to borrow from the reserve bank. Hence saving that takes the form of purchasing central government securities may promote a smaller growth in bank deposits than would occur if another savings mode were chosen (note the similarities between this possibility and the case discussed in the previous section, where windfall tax revenues are allowed to affect the rate of growth of bank lending). By contrast, where increases in saving are directed at corporate and local government securities, the supply of funds available for other uses will expand, though we should not ignore the possibility that this may cause funds initally to start heading in the direction of higher-yielding existing assets rather than towards the purchase of current flows of output: for example, a bank that is deterred from buying local government securities might purchase shares rather than lending more to corporate and individual clients.

A modern-day perspective on savings and the supply of finance should not ignore scope for placing funds overseas. As stock exchanges around the world become more and more integrated, the possibility grows that small savers may take a global view of their opportunities; indeed, my experience is that already some Australian economics students seem to think nothing of speculating with US stocks and shares. Even if small savers in the main do not start behaving in this manner on their own accounts, it is likely that a good part of their savings may still end up purchasing overseas assets, having been channelled that way by life assurance companies and superannuation funds. In all of these cases, the analysis is the reverse of that for the case investment funding via overseas borrowing, discussed towards the end of section 10.2: a lower exchange rate is what we would expect to result, but with no reduction in bank deposits if the exchange rate is being freely floated. Activity in the tradeable goods sectors is thus 'crowded in'. Obvious examples of this happening in the 1980s are the flows of funds from Japanese savers into assets such as US government stock or Australian real estate. These flows helped to counteract the tendency of the yen to appreciate due to both the high Japanese propensity to save and the competitiveness of Japanese goods on world markets.

Since the numerical example makes no mention of a backwash of export demand coming from countries that supplied the increased imports, it would be quite in order to suggest I am making the implicit assumption that there is an offsetting inflow of foreign capital to make the overseas account balance. Increases in imports due to a rise in domestic activity may lead therefore to an expansion in the supply of finance available to domestic residents, additional to any rise due to the increased flow of domestic savings. However, the impact of a capital inflow on money supply growth and aggregate demand may depend on which assets the overseas savers are buying. Here, the real-world case of the Japanese capital outflow is once again instructive. If Australians buy Japanese consumer durables and the Japanese savers buy Australian real estate, employment is only created directly in Australia if new real estate is purchased. Otherwise, all that happens is that property prices may rise somewhat and the bank deposits of sellers of existing real estate rise by an amount equal to that by which deposits of purchasers of consumer durables fall. However, if American consumers buy Japanese consumer durables and the Japanese savers buy US government securities, the growth rates of the US monetary base and bank lending could be reduced — though by how far would depend upon the extent to which the Federal Reserve were prepared to permit gyrations in interest rates (note the similarities of this case with the discussions in the previous section).

10.7 Saving in the Longer Run

Amongst mainstream thinkers, there still seems to be a quite widespread adherence to the pre-Keynesian notion that the ability of households to accumulate wealth is determined by their willingness to save, and that interest payments or other earnings on assets are rewards for postponing consumption — for 'waiting', as some Classical economists put it — rather than rewards for parting with liquidity and security. From this view have followed policy prescriptions aimed at providing incentives to increase saving, such as the introduction of a consumption tax and an offsetting reduction in income tax rates. Post Keynesians are normally alarmed by such proposals, for they see them as signs of ignorance of the 'paradox of thrift' — Keynes' idea that attempts to increase total saving are self-defeating. It is interesting to explore the conventional wisdom in the light of the numerical example from section 10.3, for this example seems superficially to support the mainstream view.

If the income recipients in the numerical example had been keener to save, the sum of the increases in imports and tax revenue, plus the flow of saving, would still have equalled the initial injection of investment expenditure. However, the flow of savings would have been a greater fraction of total leakages and the increase in imports and in tax revenue would have been smaller. For example, suppose the marginal propensity to consume had only been 0.6 in the numerical example. Consumer expenditure from first-round disposable income of $506 250 would then have been $303 750, rather than $405 000, in the second round. Using this 0.3038 marginal propensity to respend on domestic goods, we may recalculate the cumulative effects of an injection of $1 million investment expenditure. We have a total increase in expenditure of $1 436 256.70 at market prices and hence an increase in direct tax revenue of only $143 636.57, compared with $168 067.22 in our original example with a 0.8 marginal propensity to consume. Imports rise by only $323 159.77, rather than $378 151.22, and income tax revenue by $242 369.81 instead of $283 613.40. With the 0.6 marginal propensity to consume, the induced accumulation of additional private domestic savings is $290 843.77 rather than $170 168.04.

This perspective certainly highlights limitations in conventional expositions of the paradox of thrift, that assume there are no leakages of expenditure to tax revenue and imports. With private domestic saving as the only macroeconomic leakage, a rise in the propensity to save that is not offset by an injection of expenditure on investment, by the government or on exports, cannot increase total saving. The share of saving in national income is only able to increase because the flow of income falls. Once imports and taxation are introduced, total private domestic saving can increase at the expense of saving by the overseas sector and the government. But this should not distract us from the fact that income flows are still reduced. Thus while the paradox of thrift no longer seems to hold as far as domestic private savers are concerned, attempts to increase saving are nonetheless unfortunate in so far as they tend to reduce aggregate demand below the full employment level. Moreover, it appears that policies which seek to change the tax mix in order to promote the accumulation of personal wealth could run into trouble owing both to the reductions in the flow of tax revenues, and to increasing calls upon the government for unemployment benefit and allowances for low earners. From the Post Keynesian standpoint, then, it still appears that policies to encourage a higher rate of saving may need to be supplemented by fiscal and/or monetary expansion to prevent them from leading to unemployment.

Such a conclusion may trouble mainstream economists who have never quite grasped the central messages of Keynes' work. The following comments by Pearce (1976, pp. 25-6) indicate how Classical ideas still survive (see also Heathfield and Pearce, 1982):

But the truth is that the act of saving does not ordinarily hold up the circular flow of money at all. If I choose to save more, I buy a bond with my savings, an act which is only possible if someone sells a bond. The money I have saved is immediately available to the seller of the bond to buy goods. There is no failure of demand. A failure of demand occurs only if someone chooses *not* to pass the money on but to hold a larger stock of money than usual. This will cause unemployment. But such unemployment must be transient. No part of the stock of money is destroyed. Failing some fundamental change in institutional conventions the very sum hoarded will eventually be released and demand restored. If, at the moment of each transient failure of demand, governments rush to create and put into circulation new money in accordance with the

Keynesian prescription, inflation will occur as soon as the temporary hold up in the flow of the old money ceases.

Like Chick (1984), I find Pearce's perspective on Keynesian ideas ultimately misplaced, but nonetheless highly thought-provoking.

An obvious Keynesian response is to suggest that the tools of monetary policy could be used to remove the 'new money' once it was no longer needed. But given the difficulties of engaging successfully in policies of fine-tuning it would be unwise to ignore what seems to be Pearce's real point: namely, since that savings are generally built up with the intention of spending them later on, the economic system may possess more scope for self-stabilisation than Keynesians normally admit. This case against intervention is at its most potent where a decline in consumer demand (or in investment demand by firms) reflects a postponement of discretionary purchases due to a lack of confidence or to 'sticker shock' following substantial price increases. Funds that are presently resting in some financial 'backwater' may suddenly return as a flood of aggregate demand once confidence is restored or the costs of repairing ageing consumer durables (or business equipment) become more frightening than the costs of buying replacements. If such floods tend to be too much for the monetary authorities to mop up without raising interest rates so sharply as to disrupt the plans of those with prior financial commitments, it becomes less easy to recommend policies aimed at smoothing out expenditure troughs by encouraging people and firms to take on financial commitments.

The case against intervention looks much weaker if the bulk of consumer saving is undertaken for lifecycle reasons. If a downturn in aggregate demand reflects a long-term shift in patterns of saving resulting from demographic changes, we really do have a case for a Keynesian intervention on the ground that 'in the long run we're all dead'. Pearce might be expected to argue against this by saying that retirement-oriented saving is increasingly contractual in nature, so an increase in such saving will tend to lead to increased lending by NBFIs and purchases of financial assets by 'the institutions'. However, we must once again be aware of the possibility that increased NBFI lending may be at the expense of bank lending and that such additional funds as do become available may mainly end up inflating the prices of existing physical and financial assets rather than contributing directly to an increase in employment. The implication seems to be that policy-makers must somehow devise ways to distinguish genuinely transient increases in personal and corporate savings rates from those of a longer term nature.

Unfortunately, if firms react to reduced sales of investment and consumer goods by cutting back (further) on their investment spending, longer-term depressions may sometimes emerge from supposedly 'transitory' withdrawals of demand. Even if an increase in the propensity to save initially produces an easing of the terms on which finance is available, firms may react to their reduced sales by cutting back on their investment spending. In this case there would be further reductions not merely in income and employment, but also in aggregate savings — in so far as these depend on income from employment and profits (both dividends and, in the case of corporate saving, retentions); in government tax revenues — and in the growth of the stock of physical and human capital. In so far as the foregone savings would not merely have been left as bank deposits had they materialised, and to the extent that the government reacts to its fiscal shortfall by selling bonds to those who would otherwise have lent to the private sector, this could subsequently reduce the supply of finance available to private sector borrowers. Thus, even if an increase in savings propensities initially increases private domestic savings, an economy may ultimately suffer from a financial squeeze. Worse still, once the time comes for an increase in spending, firms may be unable to cope with the demand owing to their lack of investment. The result may be inflation, brought about by rising prices for raw materials and skilled workers and by a collapse in the exchange rate as imports are sucked in (see also Chapter 13, and Kahn and Posner, 1977). If, in the interim, expansionary policies were used to prevent a collapse in investment, there would be less risk of inflation when demand recovered.

10.8 The Employment Effects of Investment

The comments just made point to the dual role of investment in macroeconomic systems: while being undertaken it adds to aggregate demand, but once undertaken it affects aggregate supply conditions. Harrod (1939) and Domar (1946) are generally credited as being the first economists to face up to the possible problems that might arise from this. Their work prompted a considerable literature on macroeconomic aspects of economic growth and much debate about the ability of economies to generate self-sustaining growth pathways that involve full employment (Kregel, 1973, and Jones, 1975, are among the most useful introductions to the field). In this section, I wish to do no more than raise some of the complications presented by a growing capital stock for the orderly functioning of a macroeconomic system. Those interested in pursuing these issues further must be warned that much of the literature in the area is highly mechanistic in its perspective and plays down the dependence of investment on business sentiment. Moreover, the typical steady-state growth model is very highly aggregated and does not consider the ability of innovation and structural change in particular sectors to disturb aggregate expenditure flows. The best attempt simultaneously to model growth and structural change in formal terms is probably that of Pasinetti (1981), while the evolutionary works of Foster (1987, 1989) provide fresh perspectives in this area.

In the macroeconomic approach to growth economics, the central issue is that if aggregate demand does not expand in line with the economy's enhanced capacity to produce, the result may be that older vintages of equipment with higher operating costs are scrapped instead of there being an expansion of output. If so, further investment may be discouraged. On the other hand, if firms happen to expand their investment by enough to make it seem that capacity expansion undertaken in the previous period was justified, then the potential for the problem to surface in the next period will have been created: next period, capacity will be greater still, so there will need to be an even greater demand for investment goods if the excess capacity is not to appear. If the reserve bank is not pursuing a policy of interest rate stabilisation, there is scope for the supply of finance to pose a barrier to the neccessary growth in total spending, though this may be overcome to the extent that financial innovations and more optimistic economic sentiments lead to more direct lending, greater NBFI activity and growth in bank assets and liabilities that are not covered by reserve asset regulations. However, it must be noted that even if investment happens to expand at such a rate as to ensure that aggregate demand grows at the same rate as aggregate capacity — thereby ensuring that expectations in this area are not disappointed — the economy could be experiencing growing unemployment due to the supply of labour growing more rapidly than the demand for personnel to use the new equipment.

Now, of course, investment may not merely be aimed at expanding the capacity of the economy, it may also be undertaken with a view to economising on labour inputs. In the latter case, one implication would be that when the new equipment comes on stream — say, in round two — firms may be expecting the sorts of revenues they were receiving prior to making the investment, but they will be paying out less in wages to workers. This brings a new layer of complexity to the multiplier story, for these reductions in wage payments will tend to drag consumption expenditure down at the same time as the spending of income flows associated with the spurt of investment spending is pushing up consumption demand. However, whether or not this reduces the size of the multiplier will depend upon the pricing and savings policies of the firms undertaking the investment.

It is somewhat unlikely, even in the absence of indirect taxes, that a firm would lower the unit price of its products by a dollar for every dollar it saved on its per-unit labour costs. If it did so, it would only be amortising its investment from the profit margins it received on any additional sales that were generated by the lower price. But suppose for a moment that this actually happens and that there is no automatic indexation of income tax allowances to the general price level. In this case, a person who would have bought the product even if its price had not been reduced by, say, $10 finds herself in effect $10 better off. However, a worker whose gross income is reduced by $10 may feel only $7.50 worse off if her marginal tax rate is 25 per cent. If both people have the same marginal propensity to consume — say 0.8 — aggregate demand will rise when the labour saving technology comes on stream: the buyer spends $8 more elsewhere if she does not increase her consumption of the good in question, whereas the worker involved in its production only reduces her expenditure by $6.

Matters would be rather different if the firm cut by $10 the labour costs of making a unit of its product but only reduced the price per unit by $7. An effective rise in disposable income of $7 would then lead to an increase in spending elsewhere of $5.60, so, despite the price reduction, aggregate demand would fall by $0.40 for each $10 saving in labour costs unless investment spending increased. This problem would be compounded if the marginal propensity to consume were a decreasing function of income — for example 0.8 on the downside but only 0.7 on the upside.

An extreme version of the second scenario would be one in which firms undertake labour-saving investments with a view to amortising them by charging exactly the same prices as before and earning higher gross profit margins. If prices do not fall, employed workers will receive no increases in real income, so in the absence of an increase in investment demand there is nothing to counteract the fall in spending by technologically-unemployed workers. The shorter the payback periods of labour-saving investments, the greater will be their depressing effects on aggregate spending immediately after they come onstream. Of course, shorter payback periods may also be expected to entail firms planning more rapidly to reappear in the market with demand for investment goods which they expect to finance from profits retained during the payback period of their initial investments. Unfortunately, since the attempts to earn higher gross profit margins involve an increase in the corporate propensity to save, firms are likely to be disappointed by how long it takes to recoup their investment spending. If they are to avoid disappointment, they must increase their investment spending by an amount equal to the cutback in spending by the workers they displace with machinery; in other words, given a particular fractional marginal propensity to consume on the part of the workers who lose their jobs, the corporate sector must spend the same fraction of its expected increase in profits in the periods in which these profits are expected to materialise, otherwise the profits will fail to eventuate. Bridging finance will be necessary to pay for this if the firms have initially run down their liquidity in order to pay for the labour-saving equipment.

Should such an expansion of investment spending not occur owing to a lack of confidence or because of an inability on the part of firms to raise the necessary funds, things may at first nonetheless appear to be going fine in the consumption goods sector. This is because the reduction in expenditure coming from technologically-unemployed workers may be offset by demand from the successive respending of portions of the spurt in income in the investment goods sector. But the latter demand will soon wither away and the income multiplier effect of the labour-saving investment will turn negative. This will do little to encourage firms to carry on with their higher rate of investment, let alone increase it.

The statements in the previous four paragraphs ignore some additional complicating factors. If the unemployed are cutting their expenditure by only a fraction of their loss in income, they must be financing their remaining expenditure by running down their net assets or from unemployment benefits. We should therefore recognise that there could be effects on the supply of finance — for example, NBFI deposits may be run down, with possible effects on the volume of loan-financed expenditure — and on the pattern of government spending or the public sector deficit, and we should note, moreover, that these sources of funding may only be available for a limited period of time. If the introduction of labour-saving technology led to job sharing rather than increases in full-time unemployment, cuts in expenditure by less than reductions in income might be met by smaller rates of saving, rather than by dissaving, in which case the volume of NBFI deposits and of direct lending might continue to grow, but at a slower rate.

Similar arguments could be set out for investments in new products that caused unemployment in other firms by rendering their existing products obsolete. In both cases, the rise in domestic unemployment will be limited, at the cost of higher unemployment overseas, in so far as lower prices for domestically produced goods increase the economy's international competitiveness and net exports rise.

10.9 Conclusion

The dominant paradigm in macroeconomics uses the device of equilibrium to avoid confronting the complications caused by emerging patterns of events in historical time. Instead of there being a past in which things have happened, a present moment in which choices are made, and a future in which things might happen, economic affairs in equilibrium models are treated as if they 'are happening' (cf. Shackle, 1982, p. 437) by repeating themselves in a never-ending roll-over process. In this chapter I have sought to depart from such a way of looking at things, beginning by stressing that an act of expenditure requires a prior source of finance. It was shown how this can come from the sale of previously accumulated physical or financial assets by those undertaking the expenditure, or it can come from the creation of new financial assets as loans are provided by those willing to increase their financial liabilities. If the monetary authorities are not acting so as to encourage growth in bank lending, the growth in the supply of finance needed for a continuing growth in the scale of economic activity will have to come from a reduction in liquidity preference — possibly encouraged via financial innovation — such that there is an increase in NBFI deposits and direct lending. If domestic residents are unwilling to accumulate such financial assets, the economy will either have to suffer a reduced rate of expenditure growth or its borrowers will have to be more willing and able to raise funds overseas. The latter event will enlarge the economy's balance of payments deficit by pushing up the exchange rate.

It is certainly true that an act of spending puts those on its receiving end in a position to pay off an identical value of previously contracted debts and thereby to liberate funds from which the same amount of spending may once again may be undertaken. However, once an expenditure process has been started, there is no guarantee that it will simply roll over with a steady (or steadily expanding) flow of payments and a constant (or steadily expanding) total stock of financial assets. Much will depend upon whether or not flows of expenditure, and their repercussions, promote the mere realisation of expectations, or outcomes that exceed or fall short of such values. On the one hand, increases in confidence may lead to an increase in the desire to borrow and in the willingness to lend, so the flow of income may speed up on the basis of a net increase in the supply of financial assets. On the other hand, if lending and/or borrowing looks too risky, the stock of financial assets may contract and with it the flow of income: those who receive income flows may choose simply to accumulate financial assets in the forms in which they have been paid, rather than spending their incomes or lending them out to those who wish to borrow to maintain their spending rates.

11 Unemployment and Inflation

11.1 Introduction

The analysis of income multiplier processes in Chapter 10 focused on financial aspects almost totally to the exclusion of any investigations of the effects of changes in expenditure levels on rates of unemployment and inflation. This chapter attempts to redress the situation by undertaking an exploration of the contrasting views of Post Keynesian and mainstream economists on these topics. It is appropriate to consider unemployment and inflation together since much of the literature on unemployment presumes that an expansion of output necessarily entails a rise in prices. The question is then raised as to the likely responses of unemployed and currently employed individuals to changes in money wages relative to the cost of living.

Post Keynesian views of what these responses are likely to be are generally similar to those of Keynes, who saw them as implying that a lasting shift of nominal aggregate demand to a higher level could produce a sustained increase in the level of employment and real aggregate demand at the cost of a *one-off* increase in the price level. Hence, when unemployment looks unacceptably high, policies aimed at expanding expenditure may play a useful role in its reduction. As far as modern Post Keynesians are concerned, an *ongoing* process of inflation may often reflect the ways in which the underlying institutional structure of the economy affects the process of wage bargaining, rather than any chronic excess of aggregate demand. Therefore, to control inflation, it may be neccessary to devise new institutional structures, among which may be long-term prices and/or incomes policies.

The mainstream view, by contrast, is that any increase in employment arising from an increase in the level of nominal aggregate demand will be temporary, for sooner or later prices will rise by such an amount as to ensure that real aggregate demand falls back to the level it was at prior to the increase in nominal spending. Hence policy-makers would be unwise to attempt to deal with unemployment by measures aimed at increasing aggregate demand. Since mainstream economists see ongoing processes of inflation as symptomatic of chronic excess demand, they view prices and incomes policies as failing to deal with the underlying causes of inflation and hence able only temporarily to hold it down by bottling up demand which sooner or later must escape and manifest itself in higher prices.

Although such divergent conclusions arise from different perspectives on the likely responses of members of the workforce to changes in real wages, Keynes and mainstream economists actually share the initial assumption that the price level will rise to some extent when output expands. Modern Post Keynesians, however, feel somewhat uneasy about accepting this premise, given that empirical studies of the cost functions run counter to the mainstream view that firms are typically operating under conditions of rising marginal costs. Keynes (1936, p. 10) not only accepted the general idea that firms suffer from diminishing returns as they expand production, but details of his (1936, pp. 42, 299-300) thinking overlap with more modern work which argues that short-run marginal costs may rise because newly hired workers tend to be less productive than more experienced ones already employed in a particular kind of job slot, and/or because the extra production may involve bringing older vintages of machines back into use. Therefore, if firms expand employment, they must be expecting to sell larger quantities of output at higher prices. In so far as Post Keynesians are prepared to accept the idea that the price level and output rates might be related, they see the connection arising via the possibility that horizontal or downward sloping cost curves of firms could be moved bodily upwards by increases in raw materials prices when output in general expands; for without such increases in prices, marginal sources of primary products might not be exploited. Nonetheless, it appears quite possible that upward pressures on prices due to rising input costs could be more than offset by falling average fixed costs as output expanded.

For most of this chapter I shall set such worries aside and presume that diminishing returns do indeed provide a source of cost-based price increases when output is expanding. This involves playing down one aspect of the Post Keynesian critique of modern views of unemployment — views which at heart are little different from those with which Keynes had to contend over half a century ago. But it must be stressed that if I had assumed, on the basis of empirical findings and the logic of the Post Keynesian analysis of the firm, that firms did not run into diminishing marginal returns, the numerical example developed later in this chapter would be far less complicated and the critique of orthodoxy all the more powerful.

11.2 Perspectives on the Nature of Unemployment

Once the rising supply curve assumption is accepted, the entire debate on inflation and unemployment seems to pivot on the fact that neither Keynes nor Post Keynesians accept 'the underlying assumption of the classical theory that we are *always* in a condition where a reduction in the real rewards of factors of production will lead to a curtailment of their supply' (Keynes, 1936, p. 304, emphasis in original). The reason they take this view is that they recognise the possibility that, at the most recently negotiated set of money wage rates, the aggregate demand for labour may be less than its aggregate supply. In such a situation, individuals may find themselves unable to obtain new jobs or keep their present ones and firms may not find it necessary to offer higher wages to attract more people into employment.

If the aggregate supply of labour at the current set of wage rates exceeds the aggregate demand for labour, it may only be in markets where structural bottlenecks are present that firms will find it necessary to offer higher wages to attract more workers. Otherwise, firms should have little trouble expanding output when they perceive an improvement in sales prospects, even if the pay they offer seems unlikely both to bring real wages up to the level thought to have been reached at the start of the previous wage settlement and to match the probable rise in the cost of living before the next wage round. The Keynesian view does not preclude the possibility that offers with such unsatisfactory implications for existing workforces could get voted down by employees: they each might feel that their chances of a suitable deal were high enough, and the danger that they might lose their jobs and be unable immediately to find an alternative way of achieving satisfactory earnings was low enough, to make it seem better to fight for an improved offer rather than accept a deal which they see as inadequate. If some firms did give in to such demands but were then forced to cut the number of workers that they employed, output could still be increased and unemployment reduced if other firms sought successfully to gain market share by taking on some of the presently unemployed who were eager to work even if pay increases were thought less likely than unemployment benefits to match the rate of inflation.

Keynes would have characterised the situation just described as one involving involuntary unemployment (see Keynes, 1936, p. 15). The term 'involuntary' is something which mainstream economists find problematic, for it suggests a form of unemployment is not something to be explained in terms of the labour supply decisions of workers. Keynes certainly seems to have intended his readers to come to recognise that often at least part of observed unemployment should be seen in precisely this way, as something which workers could not overcome by offering to work for less, and which involves a failure of market forces and missed opportunities for the achievement of higher levels of consumption. Over fifty years later, the mainstream view is pretty much the same as that which Keynes sought to challenge: it is widely held that unemployment arises and persists either because workers seek excessively high money wages in their attempts to obtain their desired standards of living, or because they have an insufficiently strong incentive to work. In other words, it is seen as the result of choice, not as a symptom of market failure.

Clearly, one can tell a 'logic of choice' story pertaining to those who have only just lost their jobs after gambling unsuccessfully that they would not be on their employers' redundancy lists. For example, such workers may have taken the view that if they had accepted money wages cuts (or a slower rate of increase of pay, or poorer non-pecuniary terms), their standing would have fallen relative to that of others in the economy who have similar skills and have obtained better deals. Since the labour market is in a constant state of disequilibrium due to workers retiring and so on, they are likely to have recognised that there will exist vacancies for jobs similar to their own at the original wage rate. On such a basis they may have allowed their unions to call the bluff of their employers and will not yet have had time to find alternative jobs that meet their requirements. These newly-fired workers can presently be said to be voluntarily unemployed, even if they would later have lost their jobs anyway, had they accepted lower pay increases. But what of those who have been out of work for some time and who suffer from no obvious physical disability? Should we attach derogatory labels such as 'social security scroungers' and 'dole bludgers' to all of these, or are they really out of work because they cannot find employment no matter how hard they try?

No doubt some unemployed people who claim unemployment benefits really have no intention of working so long as life on the dole compares as well as it does with the wages they expect they could earn. This is not to say that all such people necessarily have an aversion to work or find dole payments adequate to support their lifestyle requirements. For example, it could that a strong disincentive to work arises because of the way the taxation and social security system works to produce an effective marginal tax rate of more than 100 per cent: this can arise if the wages these people can earn are both dispiritingly low and yet high enough to ensure that they lose their entitlements to social security allowances once they start receiving income. In other cases, the problem may be that once a person has paid for child-minding and travel to work she would be worse off than if she stayed on the dole, harsh though that lifestyle may be. By cutting unemployment benefits and social security payments, it might be possible to push these people into employment. But a more civilised approach, which recognised the linkages between unemployment and poverty, could be framed around measures including a negative income tax/social dividend scheme, and/or increases in the provision of charge-free creche facilities and in spending on worker training programmes to enhance prospects for attaining a decent wage.

It is less easy to convince a Post Keynesian that those who have been out of work for quite a time since losing reasonably well-paying jobs are not involuntarily unemployed. Growing evidence from empirical work by social psychologists (for example, Warr, 1983) suggests that many people find long-term unemployment a profoundly depressing experience because it makes them feel they are not in control of their lives. Such findings do not give the impression that those who have been out of work for a long time believe their situations result from the choices they have made about where to position themselves in the labour market. Nonetheless, as far as mainstream economists are concerned, such people are to be seen as remaining unemployed owing to their failure to apply for positions that offer less than they were earning at the time they lost their jobs. The following comment by the Right Honourable Sir Keith Joseph, MP, (on BBC Radio 4, 29 June 1980) reflects this view neatly: 'I do want to emphasise that just as people can price themselves out of jobs, they can price themselves into jobs.... It is in the interest of the people out of work to offer a contribution to employers even at a slightly lower unit labour cost figure.'

If workers took heed of such advice and were prepared to move somewhat down market with their job applications, employers seeking to hire labour at particular advertised wages rates would be pleasantly surprised by the volume and quality of applications they receive for jobs. Employers might take this to imply that they had misjudged the position of the labour supply function and that, next time they hired people or renegotiated wages, they could be less generous in their offers. (It should not be forgotten that the supply curve of labour only defines minimum wages that need to be paid to attract a particular number of workers. Wages actually may exceed the corresponding point on the supply curve in an out of equilbrium situation where individual firms are not sure of the overall state of the market and have to make experimental offers.) In the future, therefore, the supply curves of firms would be lower than they otherwise would have been. According to the mainstream view, this would enable firms to increase their output and employment, lowering prices as they did so, and the lower prices would make even more of the unemployed willing to apply for less remunerative jobs, causing the process to be repeated until labour market equilibrium is attained.

The mainstream analysis thus essentially treats unemployment as the result of mistaken expectations whenever it is not associated with structural imbalances such as skill mismatches caused by changes in technology. Those who are presently out of work, and representatives of those in employment who are bargaining for wages, are failing to take account of what would happen to the price level if they moderated their remuneration demands. If a cut in money wages (or a cut in their rate of increase) had been seen as involving at least some reduction in the price level (or in its rate of increase), more workers would have been prepared to accept it; but so long as the price level (or the rate of inflation) was expected to fall by less than wages (or their rate of increase), employers would have been prepared to hire more workers. From this standpoint, cuts in unemployment benefits provide an obvious way to encourage people to start applying for jobs at lower money wage rates. Such a policy should change the relative merits of searching part-time, whilst employed in a lesser post, for a job that provides one's target wage, compared with searching full-time for an appropriate job whilst receiving only unemployment benefits (see Phelps, ed., 1970, for a seminal collection of articles in which mainstream economists explore the relationship between job-search and wage inflexibility).

Orthodox thinkers, such as Friedman (1968), argue it is a mistake for governments to believe they can deal with unemployment more effectively by reflationary policies rather than by the politically more troublesome policies of cutting unemployment benefits or of simply waiting for expectations to adjust. They envisage the following scenario. Increases in sales may certainly induce firms to hire more workers, but since the supply curves of firms are upward-sloping, any excess demand will only be partly eliminated by increased output; part will be mopped up by the higher prices that firms will be setting to cover the costs of supplying their marginal units of output. The rise in prices entails an unexpected reduction in real wages to which workers respond by revising downwards their offers to supply labour. This shift in the labour supply function raises the supply functions of firms, so they cut back their output and raise prices further. Eventually, the output and employment in the economy will settle down just as it was before the increase in the aggregate demand. However, all nominal values will have increased in the same proportion. In order to keep output and employment always at the enlarged short-run level, the growth nominal demand, and incease in the price level, would have to proceed at an ever-increasing rate. This would have to run ahead of workers' expectations (and these expectations would, it is argued, tend rationally to anticipate such an acceleration and thereby thwart the success of such a policy). Pushed to the limit, such a policy would result in a complete collapse of confidence in the currency; it is best not embarked upon in the first place.

A Post Keynesian will not rush to accept this theoretical and policy analysis, for it begs some major questions, not least of which is the validity of the assumption of a rising supply schedule. First, although it is true that unemployment often co-exists with a flow of job vacancies, it is by no means obvious that people may not be choosing to remain unemployed as a more efficient basis for job search, instead of accepting pay cuts or low grade jobs while looking for something better. Many workers will be aware that employers are suspicious of people who do not already have jobs (Goodhart, 1975, p. 197). Furthermore, one may get to hear about more good job prospects from within other firms — both internal jobs and from talking with other people at work — than one would hear from the relative social isolation of unemployment. 'Highly qualified' people may experience great difficulty in pricing themselves into 'down-market' jobs, since employers would not wish to train them and then find them leaving for better paid jobs more suited to their particular qualifications.

Secondly, in presuming that resistance to reductions in money wages or their rate of increase comes from workers who are failing correctly to anticipate the rate of inflation, the orthodox analysis ignores the possibility that firms may be wary of such reductions because their existing workers might lower their productivity or leave. They would not wish to lose these workers and replace them (at some hiring cost) with others from the ranks of job searchers because these would not have the productivity capacity that comes with experience: it could look far more profitable to maintain wages (or the rate of wage increase) and make quantity adjustments in employment and output (for example, on a last-in/first-out basis) when demand falls (see Earl and Glaister, 1979, and Malcolmson, 1981).

Thirdly, if all sectors of the labour market were strongly unionised and unions generally were in a militant mood, it would be difficult to see how workers displaced by militant action in one sector could price themselves back into employment if they lowered their horizons and tried to get jobs in other sectors.

Fourthly, even if firms face rising supply schedules, reflationary policies need not threaten real wages, for they can involve indirect taxes and subsidies to stop prices rising as more workers are hired, or income tax cuts that enable purchasing power to be maintained even if prices do rise somewhat.

Lastly, there is the issue with which Keynes was preoccupied and which arises because reductions in wages affect the purchasing power of workers: how can one be sure that if workers did accept less attractive terms their jobs would not be shortlived owing to the aggregate demand function falling at least as much as the aggregate supply function? This question is explored at length in the next three sections.

11.3 Wage Flexibility as a Cure for Structural Unemployment

There is a tendency for persisting problems of unemployment to be associated with structural change: workers shed by firms in dying industries often end up chronically without work rather than employed in 'sunrise' industries or in job slots voluntarily vacated by workers moving from mature industries into growth areas. To the extent that, for reasons of external economies of scale, firms in sunrise industries find it profitable to locate in geographical concentrations that are distant from the locations of 'sunset' industries, structural adjustment may be accompanied by geographical movements of workers. If housing costs in more prosperous areas are considerably higher than those in areas experiencing decline, workers left unemployed by industrial decline may be reluctant to move, even if they do not feel bound to their present localities by family and social ties, unless very substantial pay differentials are provided. Life on the dole may be pretty bad, but life in a new job that cannot pay for a roof over one's head may be even worse: hence, one might say, the current economic divide in the UK between the prosperous south, enjoying the fruits of the microelectronics revolution, and the stagnant north, witnessing the demise of its once thriving heavy industries.

Such a perspective leads one to ask whether workers made redundant from declining industries could have preserved their former jobs — either in the long run, or merely until superior opportunities came up for them in other sectors — by agreeing to cuts in wages. A reduction in wage payments to workers in one sector clearly will not be without its implications for the revenue streams of firms in the economy. Hence, to argue that structural unemployment is not involuntary in nature, we must consider whether the acceptance of wage reductions by workers in a declining industry can remove their employers' losses without simply passing the problem to other firms. By employing an analysis somewhat reminiscent of the discussions in section 3.8, concerning 'back-to-back wealth effects', and in section 10.8, concerning the impact of investments in labour-saving equipment on aggregate demand, I think it is possible to show that only in a limited set of circumstances is it correct to say that structural unemployment is basically due to institutional rigidities.

The main points can be made if we consider the simple case of a structural change arising from a change in tastes. Suppose that, say, demand for cars has gone up and demand for furniture has gone down. In the short run it will be difficult profitably to shift furniture workers into car production. Yet, as Keynes himself noted in 1932, if costs were sufficiently flexible in this kind of situation, then

Relative prices would change sufficiently *to force expenditure along the old channels* pending the gradual redistribution of the forces of production in accordance with a new long-period equilibrium. Thus there would be no need for unemployment even during severe transitions (reprinted in Keynes, 1979, p. 51, emphasis in the original).

Keynes' 1932 scenario of structural adjustment proceeds as a paragon of economic orthodoxy, making no hint towards his subsequently-developed analysis of effective demand. Nonetheless it can be recast as follows in terms of the theory towards which he was struggling. A fall in furniture workers' wages will permit a cut in furniture prices. Furniture workers will have less to spend but the real incomes of other members of the economy will rise. It is conceivable that these two opposing changes will cancel out. If they do, and if the contraction in investment in furniture production is no greater than the expansion of demand for investment in the car industry, then wage reductions seem capable of preventing structural unemployment.

However, a problem of aggregate demand clearly arises if expenditure reductions by still-employed furniture workers are not matched by expenditure increases arising from increased real incomes of workers and firms in other sectors; if, for some reason, the axiom of gross substitutability fails to hold and a change in relative prices cannot produce the necessary switch in purchasing patterns; or if the furniture sector has a larger incremental ratio of expenditure on equipment to changes in value of output than does the vehicles sector. In such circumstances, our conclusions about the efficacy of wage flexibility as a means for dealing with structural unemployment must be the same as those concerning the ability of wage flexibility to deal with unemployment that is tending to arise because of reductions in aggregate demand in general. But before we move on to explore the more general case, it is appropriate to note that when wage cuts do not materialise in industries facing structural decline, the resulting unemployment may ensure that what starts out as a structural problem ends up looking rather like a problem of a general deficiency in aggregate demand which happens to be impacting rather heavily upon a particular sector. Here my discussion is inspired by Casson's (1983) interesting re-examination of the differing interpretations of inter-war unemployment provided by Keynes and 'Classical' economists such as Pigou and Cannon.

In the absence of a cut in money wages in an industry facing a decline in demand, the higher level of demand in newly-favoured industries can be maintained until workers in the declining industry are made redundant, so long as there is no reduction in aggregate investment expenditure. If this is the case, then, until redundancies occur, there will be a flow of funds away from firms in the declining sector into the hands of firms in the growth sector that are raking in higher profits by charging higher prices. If the latter firms allow waiting lists to grow, the would-be consumers of their products will be the ones to pile up funds. However, firms in the declining industry will not tolerate this state of affairs indefinitely and, once they start shedding labour, the consequent reduction in expenditure by their former employees will depress demand in other sectors.

How far demand will fall will depend upon the redundant workers' marginal propensities to consume and the extent to which the government is adhering to a particular target for its deficit. If the structurally unemployed have a marginal propensity to consume that is close to one and if the government does not allow falling tax receipts and rising dole payments to blow out its deficit, then although there may be notional excess demands for goods in the other sectors — in other words, demands that would become apparent if the unemployed actually had jobs and incomes — actual signals of excess demand for the products of such sectors (and, sooner or later, for workers to produce them) will largely disappear. Total investment may fall if the smallness of the demand excess leads to an expansion of investment demand in the growth sectors that is smaller than the decrease in investment demand coming from the declining sectors. If so, the vestigial excess demand may totally disappear.

Although there may be no symptoms of excess demand for goods and services when wage inflexibility in declining sectors leads to structural unemployment, it would be unwise to jump to the conclusion that the authorities should attempt to increase employment by implementing conventional 'across-the-board' policies of reflation. Such policies would only help reduce unemployment of workers in the declining sectors if they could make products of these sectors look more attractive by generating longer waiting lists and higher prices elsewhere. Further price increases could arise if workers — some of whom have already displayed their willingness to risk finding themselves on redundancy lists in order to avoid reductions in their living standards — reacted to this by insisting on offsetting pay increases. (The wage-price spiral would be less likely to begin to operate if the earlier resistance to money wage reductions reflected a concern with relative wages and if workers were prepared to tolerate a reduction in living standards so long as everyone else had to do so.)

Now, of course, it may well be necessary for some actual excess demand to appear in order to signal to firms that they should be investing more heavily in the sectors in which substantial notional excess demand exists. But to the extent that policy-makers wish to avoid adding to inflationary pressures in such situations, they would do well to note that, in 1937, when one worker in seven in Britain was without a job, Keynes himself had written to *The Times* to argue against policies involving a general expansion of aggregate demand, and in favour of *ad hoc* measures to reduce unemployment. (Keynes' letters, on 'How to avoid a Slump', are reprinted in Hutchison, 1977; see also Killingsworth, 1969.) To allow an orderly rundown in declining sectors without causing a rise in the price level, the authorities need temporarily to implement structurally based policies, such as deficit-financed subsidies to firms in declining sectors or to purchasers of their products. It needs hardly to be added that the introduction of such policies could lead to trouble for the economy in the longer run if, in the face of pressure from interest groups opposed to change in the declining sectors, the authorities failed to phase out assistance progessively as capacity came on stream in growth sectors.

11.4 Can the Involuntarily Unemployed Price Themselves into Jobs?

In Chapter 19 of his (1936) *General Theory of Employment, Interest and Money*, Keynes sought to show that if unemployment were due to a lack of aggregate demand, attempts to tackle it via money wage reductions could be futile and might even make matters worse. Keynes' analysis of these possibilities centres upon changes in income distribution that such policies entail, and on the consequences of workers and firms having only fractional marginal propensities to spend on consumption or investment. His arguments are basically simple but, as a student studying his book, I always wished he had provided a numerical example to show how they work for, in prose alone, they never seemed fully convincing. In this section, I offer such an example; some of my choices of numbers loosely reflect the fact that it was originally worked out in the early 1980s when unemployment in the UK stood at 'only' two million. Like Keynes, I shall assume the economy is closed, recognising that it *may* be quite easy for wage cuts in an open economy to succeed in increasing domestic employment at the cost of exporting it elsewhere.

In Keynes' analysis, the volume of employment offered depends on firms' expectations about demand over the relevant planning period, on their existing corporate resources (which will shape input/output possibilities) and on the input prices, including labour prices, that they can negotiate. If these expectations are, in the event, realised, costs (including required profits) and revenues will be equal and, if nothing happens to change expectations, the economy will display no tendency to change. If we argue that all current inputs are of labour (so there are no natural resource inputs to be consumed/rented), the numbers can be kept quite simple. Workers lend money to the government and corporate sectors from their previous holdings of funds and from savings they make during the course of the year, but we will ignore interest earnings and payments to keep things simple. We begin by assuming that, in period t=0, the pattern of factor payments and revenues is as follows:

(i)   Twenty five million workers are each paid at the annual rate of £10 000, while expected corporate profits are £20 billion, so expected factor payments in total are £270 billion, there being no other kinds of factor incomes. Given their profit expectations and their willingness, together, to pay out £250 billion in wages, firms must be expecting at least £270 billion total revenue.

(ii)   Firms' expectations are realised since total demand is made up as follows (assume there is no government expenditure other than dole payments and no taxation, for dole payments are financed by the sale of savings bonds):
  (a) Each employed worker spends £8000, so demand from workers is £200 billion.
  (b) Two million unemployed workers each spend their entire dole payments of £4000 each, so demand from the unemployed is £8 billion.
  (c) Aggregate investment expenditure by firms is £62 billion; initially all of this is financed by borrowing, but at the end of the year profits are used to retire £20 billion of outstanding loans.

Hence aggregate demand (a + b + c) is £270 billion. Given its realised profits of £20 billion, the corporate sector records a NAFA of -£42 billion but it is also recorded as saving £20 billion since none of its

255

income has been spent on consumption. Saving by workers — their NAFAs of £50 billion — equals the sum of the increase in corporate indebtedness and dole payments (£42 billion + £8 billion). The NAFA of the unemployed is zero, but that of the government sector is -£8 billion.

Now suppose that, at the start of period t=1, tripartite talks aimed at eliminating unemployment are held between the trade unions, employers and the government and that agreement is reached concerning a 25 per cent cut in both money wages and dole payments. If the cut in money wages causes no workers to withdraw from the labour market, then the employers will be able to hire two million more workers. For simplicity let us assume that this is what happens, though it might be the case that some of the hitherto-employed workers would now prefer to quit their jobs to go on the dole and/or start searching for better opportunities, and some of those already claiming dole payments might prefer to continue to do so while trying to avoid accepting what they regard as unsatisfactory employment offers: if the firms had only succeeded in increasing their net hiring by, say, one and a half million workers in period t=1, at least half a million workers could have been said to be voluntarily unemployed, even if this many were claiming dole payments.

If 27 million workers are hired in period t=1, the wage bill for the economy will be £10 000 times 0.75 times 27 million = £202.5 billion. To work out expected total revenue and profits we need to know what is going to happen to the price level and the volume of output. Employment has gone up by 8 per cent, so let us suppose that output is expected to expand by slightly less, owing to diminishing marginal productivity. (Things are much simpler if wages and prices both fall by the same amount, for the consumption of people already in employment will not change in real terms.) Let us assume output is expected to rise by 7 per cent. Now, if the corporate sector operates in keeping with conventional competitive assumptions, prices will equal marginal costs of production. Given our assumptions about the extent of diminishing marginal productivity we can therefore say that, other things equal, the 7 per cent expansion in output would only be permitted by firms if they expected to be able to charge prices that were 114.29 per cent (that is, eight-sevenths) of their previous level and sell all of the output. However, the reduction in money wages has lowered the aggregate supply curve by a quarter, so the intended price level in period t=1 is only 85.71 per cent of the t=0 level (that is, 114.29 times 0.75). If we ignore the index number problems of adding up different kinds of outputs and assume that $Q_{t0} = 1$ billion units, then $Q_{t1} = 1.07$ billion units. The average price per item for period $t=0$ is simply total revenue (£270 billion) divided by the number of units sold (1 billion), which is £270. The average intended price per item for period $t=1$ is therefore £231.43 and total expected revenue is £247.63 billion (that is, £231.43 times 1.07 billion units). Expected profits are the difference between this figure and total wage payments (£202.5 billion), in other words, £45.13 billion.

With $t=1$ prices only 85.71 per cent of those in $t=0$ and money wages only 75 per cent of those in $t=0$, real wages are reduced to 87.5 per cent of their $t=0$ values. (This is obtained by noting that the new price index would increase $t=0$ real wages to 116.67 per cent of their $t=0$ values — that is, the reciprocal of 85.71 — but only 75 per cent of these real wages are going to be paid.)

The next problem is to work out consumption demand. Keynes portrayed consumption as a function of real income, implying that workers arrive at the shops, see what prices are and then decide how much to spend. Here we have 25 million workers who have suffered a fall in real incomes and two million, formerly on the dole, who have enjoyed an increase. Let us assume that if, in period $t=0$, the two million unemployed actually had jobs, and had the same pay (that is, £10 000 each, £6000 more than the dole) as those who were actually employed, their consumption would have been £8000 too, rather than £4000. Their marginal propensities to consume thus seem to be £4000/£6000 = 0.67. Let us assume that this marginal propensity to consume holds for everybody, regardless of the direction or magnitude of their real income changes — in other words, we are assuming a simple linear consumption function with a slope of 0.67.

To maintain their $t=0$ consumption levels with $t=1$ prices, those who were already in employment need to spend £8000 times 0.8571 = £6856.80. But their real wages are dropping to 87.5 per cent of their $t=0$ values, so we must expect them to cut their real expenditure. If prices had stayed at $t=0$ levels and real wages had dropped to 87.5 per cent of $t=0$ levels, workers already in employment would have cut their spending by £0.67(10 000 - 8750) = £833.33. They each would only have spent £(8000 - 833.33) = £7166.67. To find their spending at $t=1$ prices, we deflate this figure by 85.71 per cent, and arrive at a $t=1$ expenditure per worker of £6142.55. Aggregate spending by this group of workers is thus £6142.55 times 25 million = £153.56 billion.

Unemployment and Inflation

Given they have the same consumption functions, the hitherto-unemployed each must also spend £6142.55. Some readers may prefer to see the logic behind this spelt out from the standpoint of these workers. It runs as follows. If the unemployed were still on the dole, but faced t=1 prices, their real consumption could be unchanged even if dole payments were only £3428.40 each, rather than £4000. But in t=1, their potential consumption, like that of the already-employed, is £7500 each, which, with t=1 prices, is 218.76 per cent of their real dole incomes in t=0. They will each spend two-thirds of this 118.76 per cent increase in real income, plus £3428.40 — that is, 0.67(£7500 - £3428.40) + £3428.40 = £6142.80. (Note: rounding errors are the only thing that stop the expenditure per capita by this group from coming out exactly the same as that of the already employed.) Aggregate spending by hitherto-unemployed workers is thus £6142.80 times 2 million = £12.29 billion.

Aggregate demand from the 27 million workers amounts to £165.85 billion, which is £81.78 less than expected aggregate demand. Whether or not firms are to be disappointed thus depends on how much they decide to spend on investment: the more they spend, the closer they get to realising their expectations. But there is no guarantee that they will spend £81.78 billion on investment. Here, I will consider three particularly interesting scenarios.

The first involves no real increase in investment expenditure by firms. In this case the demand for investment goods will amount to £62 billion times 0.8571 = £53.14 billion and there is a shortfall in demand of £81.78 billion - £53.14 billion = £28.64 billion. There will thus be unplanned investment in stocks valued at £28.64 billion. Part of the problem here is that there is no longer any government expenditure, but if the government kept its net spending the same in real terms, by, say, giving subsidies to firms to the tune of £6.86 billion (that is, 85.71 per cent of the £8 billion of dole payments it no longer has to pay), the firms would still be £21.78 billion down. Either way, as far as the firms are concerned, the experiment in cutting wages and producing more has been an expensive mistake.

Secondly we might consider a scenario in which the corporate sector has a 0.67 propensity to spend increases in its *expected* real income on capital investment: this case is of special interest because it produces a result that is not dependent on differences in propensities to save on the part of workers and firms. To calculate the corporate sector's increase in expected real profits we must scale t=0 profits (£20 billion) down by the t=1 price deflator and subtract the

258

resulting figure (£17.14 billion) from expected profits (£45.13 billion) to give £25.99 billion. Given the assumed 0.67 marginal propensity to spend, total investment demand will be £17.32 billion higher than in our first scenario: there is still a gap between expected and realised demand, even if the government maintains its real level of expenditure at t=0 levels.

Thirdly it is natural to consider the case in which the corporate sector boldly spends all of its expected real profits on investment and continues to increase its real borrowing at the same rate as in period t=0. In t=0 borrowing expanded by £42 billion, so in this case investment demand in t=1 would be (£42 billion times 0.8571) + £45.13 billion = £81.12 billion, which is clearly very close to the expectation-realising figure of £81.78 billion. If the government kept up its real spending as before, albeit on something other than dole payments, then the economy would actually experience an inflationary gap of excess demand in this third case. This is a much happier scenario than the other two, but it is by no means an inevitable one. In general we would be wise to recognise that the fall in the price level has increased the real value of corporate debt, so firms may find their gearing targets making them hold back from increasing their real investment; they may also be inclined to adopt the attitude that 'a bird in the hand is worth two in the bush' and be reluctant to increase their investment spending by running down their liquidity positions on the expectation of soon being able to repay their increased debts from higher profits. Furthermore, it must be stressed that the almost negligible demand shortfall in this third scenario is very much a result of the particular coefficients and values with which we are working in this example: in general a tendency to spend all expected increases in profits on additional investment demand will not be sufficient to guarantee the absence of a shortfall of aggregate demand.

A non-negligible shortfall in demand of the kind experienced in the first and second scenarios would encourage employers to cut back output and employment towards period t=0 levels. If they did so while also marking prices down to 75 per cent of period t=0 values then the shortfall would vanish if nothing happened to change real invesment demand, the propensity to consume, and the real value of dole payments. Although the employers may each have felt, at the start of period t=1, that since reductions in wage costs would lower their supply curves, they would be able to produce more, offer it at a lower price and not lose out in the process, they were making two mistakes.

One was that they were overlooking the need for themselves to plough back into investment demand their expected profit gains before they actually realised them. The other was that they were failing to pay sufficient attention to the ways in which real wage changes affect real consumption expenditure. They should have taken account of the possibility that the changes in real expenditure by themselves, the already-employed and the hitherto-unemployed could imply realised revenues less than the level of 'effective demand' (expected revenue) assumed in their employment decisions — in other words, a deflationary gap, opened up by real expenditure rising less than real output. Depending upon the division of the population into groups with different savings propensities and changes of circumstances, an experiment in cutting wages could run into trouble even if the immediate reaction of some of the hitherto-unemployed to their improved fortunes was run up overdrafts or make use of their credit cards, thereby exhibiting marginal propensities to consume greater than unity. (It needs hardly be to added that if such consumers *did* initially spend enough to fill in a potential deflationary gap, it would soon open up with a vengeance once they slowed down their pace of spending in order to repay their debts.)

According to Keynes' analysis, money wage cuts are only guaranteed to 'solve' the problem of unemployment that has arisen due to a deficiency of aggregate demand in situations in which the marignal propensity to spend in the economy in question is equal to unity. Just as he would have expected, no gap between effective demand and realised sales occurs in our example if we set the marginal propensity to consume at unity instead of 0.67 *and* if net government expenditure in real terms is kept constant. The latter requirement is all-too-easily forgotten — partly because the dole is commonly called a 'transfer payment' rather than part of government expenditure, since it does not involve the government in making a direct claim on output; and partly because Keynes' own discussion (1936, pp. 261-2) does not highlight the issue of how workers subsist when unemployed. If the marginal propensity to spend is unity, the already-employed workers will each cut their expenditure by the same amount as their fall in real incomes — that is, by £1071.38 (in other words, £0.8571[10 000 - 8750]) rather than by £714.25 — and they will therefore spend £5785.42, rather than £6142.55. By contrast, the hitherto-unemployed workers will each spend £7500 rather than £6430.19. Consumption demand is therefore (£5785.42 times 25 million) + (£7500 times 2 million) = £159.64 billion and this, plus £81.13 billion investment demand and £6.86 billion government expenditure, gives the expected figure for aggregate demand of £247.63 billion.

11.5 Indirect Impacts of Wage Reductions on the Demand for Labour

If the direct route of wage reductions to sustainable increases in the level of employment does not work, it is not in order immediately to jump to the conclusion that wage reductions cannot deal with unemployment that is due to a lack of aggregate demand. It is possible that various indirect mechanisms might come into play and fill the gap in demand that may exist at the new levels of output and prices. Keynes looked around for such mechanisms and devoted careful consideration to a number of possibilities, but he was not optimistic that they could be relied upon. The most obvious route is via the effects of lower domestic prices on the balance of payments, but this also suffers from the obvious problem that overseas countries may retaliate with their own wage cuts or that their governments may be unable/willing to accumulate both public sector and balance of payments deficits and hence be reluctant to engage in expansionary policies to prop up their levels of domestic demand.

If falling wages were followed by falling prices, a variety of interest rate and wealth effects on expenditure could also arise, along with effects on the real level of investment arising from changes in confidence. Keynes (1936, p. 263) suggested that if wage cuts are followed by price cuts and a falling nominal rate of aggregate expenditure, the transactions demand for money is reduced, even if real transactions are not, so some people will have spare cash balances. They might use these to buy financial assets. Interest rates may thus fall as asset sellers accept the 'spare' balances in payment (these then become 'speculative balances', if they are held in preference to other assets). If the fall in nominal interest rates is a fall also in real interest rates, this may encourage higher spending by consumers and firms, that would help close the deflationary gap.

Such spending could be augmented by a kind of 'one-sided wealth effect' which, following Leijonhufvud (1968), has become known as 'Keynes' windfall effect'. The idea behind it is that a fall in the rate of interest raises the value of marketable securities such as long-dated government bonds without changing the nominal repayment obligations of the agency that issued them. The owners of such securities may then increase their expenditure. (It is perhaps not entirely legitimate to call it a one-sided effect, since interest payments may have fallen on bank deposits and loans: savers will possibly feel unexpectedly worse off, since their savings are not going to accumulate so rapidly for a given rate of depositing, while borrowers will feel better off.) For example, a company may not have had sufficient assets for it to be willing to risk losing them on a particular investment project, and so had used them to purchase government securities, pending the accumulation of greater reserves of liquidity. With the fall in interest rates, such a company receives a windfall gain and could then feel itself able to commit itself to the project. Investment would thus be inversely related to interest rates but this would not be because borrowing costs had changed.

Keynes feared that the interest rate effects of wage cuts could be held up by falls in the rate of interest being limited by expectations that interest rates would rise again before long, causing bond-holders to suffer capital losses. Delays in interest rate reductions which saw unemployment emerging could lead to a reduction in confidence and thereby necessitate an even bigger fall in interest rates. Keynes' comments in this area were mostly made from the standpoint of a very simple 'bonds versus cash' model, but he did observe briefly that 'If the quantity of money is itself a function of the wage- and price-level, there is indeed nothing to hope in this direction' (1936, p. 266). He would not therefore have been very optimistic had he examined these interest rate effects in the context of modern financial systems where the money stock is an endogenous phenomenon.

While the price level is falling, some debts will naturally be repaid, so banks will have an ability to make new loans. Since prices are lower, the original nominal value of loans will buy more goods. If interest rate reductions bring forward credit-worthy customers, more goods may thus get purchased. However, it it is possible that too few potential new borrowers may appear (and be judged as sound) for such interest rate reductions to seem profitable. Banks may prefer simply to allow deposits to fall as loans are repaid, so instead of there being an expansion in real lending as the price level falls, *M3* may decline. Even if banks do lower their interest rates, we should not overlook the effects that this will have on the behaviour of NBFIs (who may also find their real lending power increasing). Customers who get loans from banks may otherwise have got them from NBFIs. The

262

NBFIs, rather than banks, may have trouble finding replacement, profitable, credit-worthy borrowers. They may prefer to lower their deposit rates rather than hold on to costly excess reserve assets. If their deposit rates fall relative to those of the banks, people will switch deposits to banks, reducing the money supply according to a broad definition such as *M6*.

Mainstream economists have given the 'real balance effect' or 'Pigou effect' the central role in their discusisons of indirect routes by which an economy could attain full employment equilibrium if only wage flexibility could be instituted: as the price level falls, the value of money balances increases, so those whose wealth includes money balances will find themselves unexpectedly better off; if they increase their expenditure they will cause the gap in real demand at the full employment level of output to close, and if it is closed completely, there will be no excess supply of labour and no downward pressure on wages so the money wage rate and price level will then stabilise.

A vital part of this scenario is the idea that the real balance effect is a one-sided wealth effect because cash balances are not liabilities of the general public but of the government. If cash in my pocket goes up in value, the real value of outstanding government debt has gone up at the Reserve Bank, but this will not deter the government from spending. However, the smaller the ratio of cash balances to deposits (what Gurley and Shaw, 1960, would call the ratio of 'outside money' to 'inside money'), and the greater tendency of people to speculate in favour of further price falls, the more the price level will have to fall if the real balance effect is to exert any leverage. Once we recognise that cheque payments, the use of credit and debit cards, direct debiting and the spread of electronic funds transfer at point of sale (EFTPOS) systems have ensured a modern economy is, for all practical purposes, an 'inside money economy', it seems far from obvious that the real balance effect is something we can rely upon, in conjunction with flexible money wages, to ensure full employment.

The larger the fall in the price level, the greater is the danger that destabilising double-sided wealth effects will arise. Owners of inside money balances will do very well, so long as they are keeping them with solvent financial intermediaries, but debtors whose income flows are falling in nominal terms will feel severely squeezed even if their income flows are moving in line with the general price level. Attempts to sell assets to repay increasingly burdensome loans may yield disappointing proceeds, and debtors may go bankrupt, destroying creditors' wealth. Debtors and creditors may then both cut back their expenditure on currently produced goods and services. In a multilayered financial system, such defaults could easily snowball. A falling wage rate could be associated with a more rapidly falling volume of financial assets and liabilities, and movements away from, not towards, a stable position of full employment. This theme will be explored in more depth in Chapter 12. If substantial falls in prices are likely to produce bankruptcy problems, there seems to be much to be said for Keynes' recommendation that, if unemployment arises because of insufficient aggregate demand, official measures to increase expenditure directly, at the existing level of money wages, are preferable to measures aimed at producing downward wage flexibility.

Given the simplicity of monetary sectors in mainstream models and the desire of mainstream economists to stress that consumption demand is driven by wealth rather than short-run flows of income, it is perhaps hardly surprising that much mainstream analysis has been built around this type of wealth effect — questionable though it seems from the standpoint of modern Post Keynesian analysis. What is surprising, as Graaff (1987, p. 877) has recently pointed out, is that although the real balance effect is most famously associated with Pigou's (1941) critique of the Keynes' work, it had been discussed by D.H. Robertson, the Cambridge contemporary of Pigou and Keynes, as early as 1926, with Robertson (1926, p. 50) attributing the idea to Keynes himself. This irony requires us to inquire why the *General Theory* seems to contain nothing that most economists find themselves able to construe as a discussion of real balance effects. Clues to the solution of this puzzle may be found by examining passages in which Keynes (1936, p. 231) expressed serious doubts about applying the principle of substitution in the case of money. Keynes argued that:

The second *differentia* of money is that it has an elasticity of substitution equal, or nearly equal, to zero; which means that as the exchange value of money rises there is no tendency to substitute some other factor for it.... This follows from the peculiarity of money that its utility is derived solely from its exchange value, so that the two rise and fall *pari passu*, with the result that as the exchange value of money rises there is no motive or tendency, as in the case of rent-factors, to substitute some other factor for it.

What he seems to be saying is that whereas, for example, a fall in the price of land will make people switch out of high-rise buildings in favour of more land-extensive accommodation, a fall in the price level will not lead people to move out of money and into goods, since the value of money — and hence its utility-providing capabilities — will have improved. For all my enthusiasm for theories of choice that do not rely on the principle of substitution, I must confess to having always found this claim by Keynes a very curious one unless one considers it in the broader context of his views on speculation and liquidity preference and adds a movement trader perspective: if money prices are expected to fall it pays to hold on to money, as it will be possible to exchange it for more goods in the future. If this is what Keynes meant, it would make it it easy to see why he did not trouble to write about real balance effects. The difficulty may be due to Keynes using 'exchange-value' to describe the role of money: it is an unusual phrase, which could refer either to what are commonly called money's 'store of wealth' role or to its 'medium of exchange' services. Keynes' famous (1937b) article most assuredly centres on money's role as a store of wealth, with little reference to its role as a facilitator of transactions.

11.6 Aggregate Demand and Inflation

From the standpoint of mainstream economics, inflation is only seen as the result of excess demand, even if firms say they are putting up their prices due to increases in their input costs. Monetarists, who typically assume crowding out is complete, would normally characterise inflation as arising from 'Too much money chasing too few goods', but to the extent that crowding out is incomplete, a bond-financed fiscal deficit could also be the underlying cause of excess demand. Trade union militancy has no long-run impact on the rate of inflation in this analysis. If unions succeed in pushing up wages and prices in some sectors, people who pay more for the outputs of these sectors will have less to spend elsewhere so there will be a tendency for firms in the other sectors to reduce their demand for labour, driving down pay rates amongst non-unionised workers. The ranks of these workers will also tend to have been swollen by people priced out of jobs in the union-dominated sectors. By a similar argument, it can be claimed that there was nothing inherently inflationary in either the OPEC energy price increases in the 1970s or government-induced increases in prices, associated with attempts to reduce the public sector borrowing requirement. (There was a period in the UK in the early 1980s when almost every price rise one encountered seemed to be of the Thatcher government's making: mortgage interest, rates, gas and electricity prices, petrol prices, increases in indirect taxes. Yet, all the while, the government claimed that continued inflation in the general price level was due not to this but to pre-Thatcher policies of monetary expansion.)

If inflation has been proceeding apace for some time without unemployment emerging, expectations of a continued rise in the price level and growth in nominal demand may have been built up. Unforeshadowed attempts by the government to bring it to a halt by cutting back its real expenditure or the rate of growth of lending are therefore likely to produce unpleasant surprises in the economy. Disappointments are also likely when politicians cause surprise by living up to what have been hitherto seen as doubtful promises to deliver such measures. Firms will have to deal with the fact that they have agreed to wage increases on the expectation of sales revenues that now will not materialise. Some may succeed in finding ways of improving their productivity and emerge, in Margaret Thatcher's terminology, 'leaner and fitter'. Because of their greater competitiveness, these firms may not need to make any workers reduandant, but they will be increasing the difficulties faced by their rivals. The latter will either have to cut their workforces or negotiate less generous terms with their workers. If workers could see that if they had their money wages cut back to previous levels this would hold the price level back likewise, rather than reducing their real wages, it might be possible to stop inflation in its tracks, with expectations turning out to be self-fulfilling. But things are unlikely to be construed in this manner unless all workers adjust their pay at the same time and firms likewise cut their prices back to the level prevailing at the start of the period. Hence the more likely immediate result of the removal of excessive aggregate demand is that unemployment will emerge. Instead of being able to shift their cost curves downwards by the same amount as their demand curves, firms would be moving leftwards along their existing cost curves; so to the extent that supply curves were upward sloping, those who remained in employment would be pleasantly surprised to find themselves enjoying rising living standards.

If unemployment does arise in this way, and if the attempt to remove only an 'inflationary gap' of excessive aggregate demand does not produce adverse effects on confidence and hence a reduction in investment spending and consumption demand, then, sooner or later, once price expectations are revised downwards, there will be greater competition for advertised jobs, followed by reductions in rates of increases in wage offers and in nominal wage demands. Eventually, cost curves will be lowered by the same amount as the original lowering of demand curves. The typical worker who chooses to remain unemployed in the interim will find that her period of 'full-time job search' fails to have its expected payoff. Although she will eventually reattain her former level of real income, she will, in the interim, have been foregoing income, while those who are not retrenched will have been enjoying temporarily enhanced real earnings. In this scenario, search will not typically result in higher real living standards than could have been obtained if there had been a general acceptance of wage cuts at the onset of the slowdown in growth of nominal demand.

If wages happen to start drifting up again for any reason, this analysis predicts that the process will rapidly be put into check by the emergence of unemployment as reductions in the real supply of money lead to reduced demand via increasing real interest rates and negative real balance effects. In other words, the inflation-free equilibrium is seen as a stable one, so long as the government does not come along and start injecting excess demand all over again.

Post Keynesians do not presume that inflation is necessarily due to excessive aggregate demand and is a self-stabilising phenomenon in the absence of fiscal and/or monetary accommodation. By inverting all of the arguments in the previous two sections one can see that, just as money wage cuts may not make higher levels of employment viable, so money wage increases brought about by aggressive wage claims need not make prevailing levels of employment (at full employment or below) unviable. Upward money wage flexibility may just allow a wage/price spiral: the outlays of firms rise, but so too do their revenues so long as they do not change their hiring policies. The financial sector may accommodate the extra nominal demand for money and loans without a rise in real interest rates, and the predominance of inside money, along with the incentive to 'buy now, before prices rise', is likely to swamp any real balance effects. The biggest threat to jobs comes from the loss of sales to rival firms overseas that have been enjoying lower increases in wages but, nowadays, this may be largely removed by a downward float of the exchange rate. In so far as inflationary wage increases actually pose a threat to employment and real income growth they do so via indirect routes. For example, they may emerge from strikes that damage customer goodwill by holding up production flows and breaking the continuity necessary to generate excellent build quality, while rampant inflation may lead to the diversion of entreprenerial skills into speculative activities and send demand in favour of non-reproducible assets.

The Post Keynesian view that incomes policies may have a role to play in the control of inflation follows from this inversion of the analysis of the failure of wage cuts as a device for promoting higher levels of employment. Only when there is an inflationary gap of excess aggregate demand (such as the wartime situation discussed by Keynes, 1940) are demand-reducing measures allowed a role by Post Keynesians; for without them, attempts to check inflation via prices and incomes policies could prove unworkable — in the face of excess demand there would be strong profit incentives for firms to reclassify their products and job slots so as to be able to put up their prices and bid for more labour, and if firms were public-spirited enough to resist them black markets would be likely to emerge. Otherwise, Post Keynesians see such measures as only able to reduce inflation to the extent that unemployment is an effective device for frightening workers into being less aggressive with their pay claims.

If workers do not automatically price themselves out of jobs by pushing for, and winning, inflationary pay increases, the analysis of the general price level is indeterminate unless we close it by introducing a theory of how money wages are determined. Here, I wish to commend the work of Tylecote (1981), whose analysis of inflation integrates the behavioural theory of the firm, normal cost theories of pricing and case study material from a variety of insitutional contexts. Tylecote argues that if changes in the level of unemployment are to affect the rate of inflation via their effects on money wages and hence on production costs, they must do so by changing the bargaining stances adopted by unions and management. One's toughness at the bargaining table depends on one's assessment of the costs of resisting making a climb-down, and on one's assessment of the costs of climbing down — in other words, on the balance of resistance costs versus concession costs. These costs will vary with the state of the economy and its institutional structure. Unfortunately, space limitations leave me room only to explore the first of these factors and prevent me from exploring Tylecote's penetrating analysis of the role of institutional factors — such as union structures and patterns of corporate ownership — in determining differences in inflation rates between economies.

As far as workers are concerned, the costs of resisting employers' offers will seem to be increased in a time of depressed demand if they believe there is a greater risk that firms will not react to higher wages by seeing whether they can pass them on successfully in higher prices, but by making retrenchments (either by cutting output or looking for ways of reducing input requirements). But if they expect that the rate of inflation is going to slow down, their concession costs will fall, since not getting a big pay rise will not be so much of a blow to living standards. However, working against these forces making for a softer bargaining stance in times of depressed economic activity are reduced resistance costs: if taxes have been increased as part of an austerity budget, and/or if opportunities for overtime work have been reduced, a strike involves less of a loss of purchasing power for the workers than would be the case when the economy is working flat out.

By contrast, the resistance costs of firms are likely to have been reduced by an unexpected fall in sales, for if they find themselves with surplus stocks they are in a position to allow a strike to take place without having to jeopardise the goodwill of their customers by being unable to make deliveries. Many firms may see their concession costs as having risen if they are worried about a possible breakdown of oligopolistic discipline in their markets due to the downturn in activity having increased the risk that their weaker rivals will engage in desperate price reductions to overcome a cash crisis: if such a price war does materialise, it would be unfortunate, to say the least, to have recently given one's employees a substantial pay increase. Such considerations may be expected to lead firms to adopt tougher bargaining stances when activity is declining and this, coupled with unions' moves in a softer direction, would reduce the rate of money wage increases.

Tylecote argues that, as a slump persists, it is possible that wages will eventually start to increase at a faster rate. This scenario would arise if shortages of skilled workers appear, owing to cutbacks in training programmes, and because firms will eventually get rid of their surplus stocks and once again be in a position where strikes could prove disastrous for their customer goodwill. In such a situation, success by skilled workers in obtaining wage increases will not merely make firms rethink their training programmes; if relative pay matters a lot to workers — and the growing literature in psychological economics supports decisions by Post Keynesian economists to assume it does: see Baxter (1988) — it may also make other workers rethink their bargaining stances in the light of squeezed differentials.

The message of all this seems to be that that wage inflation is a result of the recent history of output and employment (plus expectations about inflation and real demand, and any other institutional and political changes that affect bargaining stances) rather than its main driving force. To try to stop inflation by cutting aggregate demand seems grossly inefficient, not merely in terms of lost current output but also because of the potentially inflationary problems such policies can create for the future if they lead to reductions in investments in human and physical capital and hence to structural bottlenecks. Historical experience does not make Tylecote optimistic about the long-run scope for using prices and incomes policies as devices for the control of cost-based inflation, and he thus favours institutional changes to affect bargaining power.

While accepting that conventional kinds of incomes policies can easily disintegrate due to loopholes and consequent scope for evasion, I feel that some of the innovative and as-yet-untried prices or incomes policies outlined by leading Post Keynesians may warrant serious attention. Weintraub's (1978) TIP proposal involves a tax on firms whose price increases exceed a specified rate (see also Seidman, 1978 and the more recent work of Foster, 1987, Ch. 12); this is broadly similar to measures advocated by the Liberal party in Britain through the 1970s. Still more ingenious are MAP and WIP plans of Lerner and Colander (1979, 1980) and Lerner (1978) which involve, respectively, the issuing of limited supplies of tradeable price- and wage-increase permits, possession of which would be a legal prerequisite for firms intending to increase their prices or rates of remuneration. Briefly, the idea is that required holdings would be tied to turnover and firms intending to make above-average increases in prices or wages would have purchase permits from those who were making below-average increases; the gains to be had from selling permits would provide a strong incentive for employers to take a tough stance and aim for below-average wage increases, while the willingness of unions to make aggressive bids for higher pay would be dampened by their knowledge that the cost of purchasing permits to legitimise inflationary pay increases could force firms to make cuts in employment levels.

11.7 Conclusion

There is no guarantee that the problems of unemployment and inflation would tend to be self-correcting if markets worked in the idealised manner assumed in much of mainstream economics. The central thrust of conventional macroeconomic wisdom seems to be that people who would like to be working at a particular real wage end up (temporarily) not working because their mistaken expectations of inflation lead them to hold out for money wages that actually entail real wages in excess of their minimum requirements. While Post Keynesians would agree that changes in money wage demands may affect the rate of inflation, they do not in general agree that it is in the power of workers to alter their real wages via the money wage demands they make. When there is unemployment, reductions in (the rate of growth of) money wages may fail to result in reductions in (the rate of growth of) real wages. If firms do hire extra workers and produce more when money wages are cut, the price level may fall even more than the money wage level, since workers hired at the margin will not necessarily spend all their marginal income and the excess of output will have to be sold off at a knock-down price. The increase in employment would not be sustainable and falling prices could promote disruptive wealth effects. 'Sticky' money wages are a prerequisite for macroeconomic and monetary stability.

12 Financial Instability and Prudential Control

12.1 Introduction

It was easy for Post Keynesians to feel somewhat smug on Black Monday (19 October 1987), when sharemarkets crashed and jokes about former yuppies began to proliferate. They were in a good position to say 'we told you so', for it has long been a central theme in the research programme of Post Keynesian monetary economics that the speculative dimension of portfolio choice makes financial systems inherently prone to instability (see Cramp, 1970; Dow and Earl, 1982, Chs 11 and 12; Miller and Lonie, 1978, Minsky, 1975, 1982, 1986). Most would trace their mode of thinking back to the writings of Keynes (1936, Ch. 12), who emphasised the parallels between gambling casinos and markets for financial assets and noted that 'When the capital development of a country becomes a by-product of the activities of a casino, the job is likely to be ill-done' (p. 159). But one should not overlook the fact that pre-Keynesian monetary history is littered with examples of major financial booms that went bust and led to bouts of regulation (for a readable set of case studies, see Kindleberger, 1978). Such events not unnaturally captured the attention of the economists of the day, and many of their ideas have a modern-day relevance: in this respect, it is particularly hard not to be impressed by the writings of Walter Bagehot (1873) in his book *Lombard Street*. This chapter explores the forces that underlie episodes of financial instability, with the aid of ideas from behavioural economics that have not hitherto been used in the Post Keynesian literature and in the light of modern case study material. The view that financial markets are in need of careful regulation by government agencies is then examined.

12.2 The Changing Propensity to Speculate

The exchange value of an asset can rise as a result of a favourable change in beliefs about the appropriate price for it, which arises because of a change in information in the economic system. Should everyone agree about the significance of the new information, no market transactions are necessary for such a revaluation. It is more often the case, however, that when a particular kind of asset rises in value trade does take place: money tries to pour in at a rate which swamps the supply of assets offered by people who have created new assets or have decided to sell out in favour of another market. In the latter situation, the population of speculators must be increasing or existing speculators must be staking more of their wealth in the rising market.

Both kinds of changes in the propensity to speculate give Post Keynesians cause for concern. If new speculators start playing the markets, they may lack experience and hence fall prey to opportunists or be prone to panic unduly when a bull market ends and uncharted waters are entered. If existing speculators are increasing their commitments, they may be more likely to go bankrupt if the market falls sharply, or may at least be more likely to curtail their expenditure on current output in the event of a capital loss, rather than merely saying to themselves 'you win some, you lose some'. In the events leading up to Black Monday, both kinds of changes in the propensity to speculate were very much in evidence. By definition, yuppies were young, too young to have experienced and too busy to read about the bear markets of even the mid-1970s, let alone the Great Crash, and greed was now good, rather than reprehensible. The seasoned players, whom one might have expected to know better, had let their debt/ equity ratios rise substantially as they pursued takeover raids in the hope that they could later unload their shares at prices which would more than cover the interest charges and capital repayment obligations to which they were committing themselves.

Prior to the 1987 crash, it would have been appropriate to describe the mood of speculators with a favourite term of Minsky (1975, 1982, 1986), namely, 'euphoric'. After a number of 'psychologically significant' market thresholds had been crossed, speculators had begun to believe that 'the sky's the limit' as far as how much money they might make. The possibility that they might get left behind in a bear run did not loom large on their minds. Satisficing theory makes it easy to see why such attitudes may develop. When the performance of an individual's (or an economy's) activities rises beyond its normal reference point, into another league, it is no longer clear what the new, reasonable target level for attainment might be or what prudential measures are now necessary. If it is difficult to see potential barriers to one's success in unfamiliar territory, it will be easy to end up seeing one's capabilities and prospects through rose tinted spectacles.

I found this particularly apparent when reading some of the business history literature during research for my (1984) book *The Corporate Imagination* — as a detached onlooker, I could easily anticipate corporate crises even though the managers themselves had been oblivious to the problems they were storing up for their firms. In a euphoric mood, managers take on new activities at a faster rate than they can create management teams to deal with them (see Penrose, 1959, on managerial limits to firm sizes in the short run) and then their firms suffer dreadful indigestion problems (for some examples, see Earl, 1984, pp. 69-72). They tend to take chances with debenture finance which may be cheaper than paying dividends but, unlike equities, carries fixed requirements to pay interest. They may embark on long-term investment projects without having assured themselves of the availability of funds for further instalments. They venture into unfamiliar territories believing they 'can do anything'. Individuals make analogous errors in durables purchases and commitments: the most obvious examples are the pop stars and owners of rising small businesses who unexpectedly find themselves in bankruptcy courts after failing to think ahead about the tax implications of their new income levels.

Existing tendencies towards euphoria in a rising market may be reinforced if decision-makers set their aspirations in the light of what people they see as similar to themselves seem to be able to achieve. Prior to Black Monday, the following kind of logic may have been quite commonly employed by those jumping on the speculation bandwagon: 'People around me are playing the markets, and I will be left behind in the status race if I do not follow suit. The fact that members of my reference group are bragging about how their conspicuous consumption has been financed by successful speculation suggests that I ought to be able to speculate successfully too: they are no smarter than I am and no more able to obtain inside information, so if they can do it, despite little prior experience, why shouldn't I be able to do at least as well?' Those who acted on this sort of belief helped to push up prices still further.

Despite the lessons from history, the behaviour of speculators prior to Black Monday seems to have been horribly akin to that of skaters on an ice-covered pond: the more skaters there were on the ice, the more that would-be skaters seemed inclined to infer that it was safe to join in, even though one could also infer that the greater number of skaters meant the ice was more likely to crack. Such behaviour is easy to comprehend from the standpoint of cognitive dissonance theory, as Kaish (1986) has ably demonstrated. Dissonance theory argues that people do not tolerate inconsistent cognitions, and seek to remove inconsistencies with as little bother as possible. In the case of the skating allegory, Kaish (1986, p. 36) notes that, as the ice gets more crowded, someone who is already skating could (a) dismiss warnings about the possible dangers of staying on the ice, (b) keep telling herself how cold it has been recently, and therefore how thick the ice could be, or (c) get off the ice and warn others to do likewise. Unless overcrowding is already causing a problem, option (c) involves the most bother and is therefore the one least likely to be adopted. These cognitive and social forces making for an increase in speculative activity were augmented by financial deregulation and technological changes which opened up opportunities that previously did not exist.

It seems likely that the speculative mania of the mid-1980s was superimposed on an earlier and more lasting increase in the propensity to speculate that came about because portfolio managers had encountered problems in using their hitherto-favoured strategies for meeting their aspirations. Such problems could have arisen either because attainments had fallen (or were expected to fall) or because events were seen by such managers as implying a need to raise their aspirations. Consider the following recent observation by Carew (1985, p. 135), concerning changes that have taken place in the nature of portfolio management over the past thirty years:

Gone are the days when portfolio management meant buying parcels of securities from time to time and sitting on them till they mature. No-one can afford such a passive approach; the objective now is to buy to trade, taking a view on the direction of interest rates, maximising opportunities to arbitrage between different markets (locally and overseas), between different securities and different maturities, buying in and selling out when rates and timing look right.

Carew's comments were made with respect to the financial markets of Australia, but I have no doubt that they would be applicable to other nations with well-developed financial markets. Post Keynesians may find them rather puzzling, given that fifty years ago Keynes was arguing that 'the professional speculator is *forced* to concern himself with the anticipation of impending changes, in the news or in the atmosphere, of the kind by which experience shows the mass psychology of the market is most influenced' (1936, p. 155, italics added). Carew's comments give the impression that it is only recently that something has happened to warrant the stereotyping of financial market participants in Keynes' terms. By implication, she is suggesting that thirty years ago Australian portfolio managers did not have to adopt the role of an active speculator. (It might also be tempting to argue that speculation on price movements was not even possible until recently in the Australian case, as before 1983-5 the money markets were heavily regulated. This seems a doubtful rationalisation given that there was ample scope for speculation with equities.) The following satisficing perspective, coupled with the recognition that there existed a ready supply of assets (for example, five year local government bonds) with maturity dates that came within the planning horizons of portfolio managers, makes the passive 1950s situation readily explicable.

Keynes' portrayal of the workings of financial markets was obviously coloured by his own philosophy for making money in them — very much that of the active speculator — but to a behaviouralist it seems to neglect the costs of behaving as he did or of delegating the task to a professional, for example, by buying into a unit trust. Satisficing theory notes that it may well be the case that many individuals feel able to achieve entirely adequate (according to their own criteria) returns on their wealth without placing it in the hands of someone else and even without taking an active interest in possible movements in financial markets. If they never sell assets prior to maturity they may incur opportunity losses, but they avoid some of the costs of speculation: not only do they avoid brokers' fees and the risks of judging price movements incorrectly; they also avoid building their lives around worrying about the state of the market.

Even if some people do decide to place their wealth with life assurance companies and unit trusts rather than personally managing their portfolios, there is no guarantee that the professional managers will be always particularly active and speculate as Keynes himself did. The reason for this is that, to stay in business in a particular risk area of the financial markets, fund managers merely need to offer relatively competitive rates of return; they do not have to maximise returns. (As we saw in section 9.5, the rate of return which they feel they must offer is likely to be determined by their conjectures of what they must at least offer to keep would-be entrants out of their part of the financial market.) If fund managers generally are able to meet customers' aspirations without taking greater capital risks through speculation, an individual fund manager may be under no pressure to behave differently. In the absence of pressure from suppliers of funds to generate a better yield, pressure for professional portfolio managers to engage in more active policies is unlikely to be felt unless a particular institution is able consistently to generate above-average returns without being seen by the public as engaging in much more risky activities. To seek to improve the yield of one's fund by engaging in more risk-taking when there is no pressure from customers or a market leader to do so could seriously misfire if one ends up getting labelled as a higher-risk operation. Things may be rather different following financial deregulation: easier entry increases the pressure on incumbent fund managers to seek higher returns as a means of preserving their market positions.

Deregulation is by no means the only event in the past two decades which is likely to have driven wealth-holders and their agents in the direction of strategies involving more active speculation. A passive portfolio strategy might work very well in times of low inflation: interest rates may be barely positive in real terms but could suffice to enable passive wealth-holders to meet their targets for the real value of their future consumption potential, given the rate at which they find it acceptable to add to their wealth via current saving. However, if inflation suddenly accelerates, as it did in the late 1960s, the passive approach may begin to seem unsatisfactory. In this situation, satisficing theory predicts that the negative real rates of return will prompt search for alternative ways of keeping the value of their wealth intact. The solution to the problem may be seen as lying in a more active approach, whereby capital gains are used as a substitute for inadequate interest earnings. Interestingly enough, such a change of strategy may help perpetuate the negative real interest return that prompts its initial use. For example, consider a middle-aged couple who have been cautiously (and, some would say, foolishly) building up retirement funds in a deposit account at a bank. If they switch their wealth to a unit trust, then they do not reduce the supply of bank deposits in general and do not add to pressures forcing banks to raise their deposit rates.

Behavioural theory recognises that people may continue to engage in active portfolio management even after the initial motivating force has evaporated. Consider again the scenario in which accelerating inflation prompted active speculation. If the inflation rate comes down, continuation of an active policy may lead to the attainment of returns that are in excess of the wealth-holders' targets. In this situation one possibility is that aspirations could rise into line with attainments. If so, a resurgence of inflation could lead to a search for even higher yields from speculation. If ways of achieving them were discovered, there would be no need for wealth-owners grudgingly to lower their sights. In this case, some kind of ratchet effect would be in operation, somewhat akin to that in Duesenberry's analysis of savings behaviour. Alternatively, the slowdown of inflation might lead to a reduction in the extent of active speculation, and a retreat to somewhat less risky modes of portfolio management. This would seem likely in situations where the wealth-owner's aspirations were hierarchically ordered (as is assumed in the 'behavioural lexicographic' model of choice) and where she had been able to continue to meet her financial yield goal only at the cost of compromising a lower order goal — for example, her tolerable number of sleepless nights spent worrying about her exposure to financial risks!

12.3 The Prediction of Turning Points

The kinds of speculation alluded to in the previous section are of the 'movement trading' variety, rather than the 'classical' mode envisaged by orthodox economists who have in mind specialists confined to a particular market in which they smooth away temporary supply and demand mismatches by accumulating or running down buffer stocks. For movement traders, success depends not on a detailed knowledge of the underlying ('real') supply and demand conditions, but on the ability to predict the behaviour of other traders. Behaviour by movement traders as a group tends to be self-fulfilling: for example, a belief that gold is about to displace property as the best hedge against inflation will, if acted upon, result in a collapse of the price of property and spiralling gold prices. The actions of those who hesitate, or who find it difficult to believe the market is going to move very far, will dampen price movements, but if very many traders believe the market is going to move further a very sharp price movement may be necessary to balance orders to buy and sell.

If one fails to guess that the market is about to move, the next best thing is to be one of the first to act once prices have started moving. Speed is of the essence if one is to avoid undue opportunity losses, and the advent of programmed trading, using the superhuman speed of computers, should therefore not seem surprising. But the pace of the action in speculative markets can hardly be said to be conducive to carefully considered choices. This should not worry us too much as regards those who sell when markets are falling, since their flight is usually a non-commital one, out of specific kinds of assets and into cash. Of greater concern are the decisions of those who commit themselves to assets at speed in order to avoid the possible costs of holding back: for example, a person may feel that if she procrastinates about the choice of a house on a rapidly rising market, she may find properties shooting out of her budget range; a hasty decision, though, may leave her with a house that is unexpectedly expensive to maintain, or perhaps in an area that fails to enjoy the greatest appreciation in value. Those who take hasty decisions are much more likely to fall prey to dubious investment schemes.

An ability to predict turning points is a requirement not only if one wishes to be a highly successful speculator but also if one is a Post Keynesian economist seeking to avoid accusations that one is a nihilist, able only to say that instability can occur in asset markets but not when it is likely to occur. Although I have discussed some of the factors that may lead to an increasing propensity to speculate, I have no intention of trying here to list all the factors that have hitherto been claimed to have been the triggers of major downturns. These have varied enormously. The resignation of a single director of London and County Securities in 1973 was sufficient to occasion suspicions about this secondary bank's operations and, in less than two weeks, its failure, which in turn led to a flight of deposits from similar banks (see Moran, 1986, pp. 76-7). Economists are still arguing about the causes of the Crash of 1987. The Brady Commission (Brady, 1988, p. v) concluded that

The precipitous market decline of mid-October was "triggered" by specific events: an unexpectedly high merchandise trade deficit which pushed interest rates to new high levels, and proposed tax legislation which led to the collapse of the stocks of a number of takeover candidates. This initial decline ignited mechanical price-insensitive selling by a number of institutions employing portfolio insurance strategies and a small number of mutual fund groups reacting to redemptions. The selling by these investors, and the prospect of further selling by them, encouraged a number of aggressive trading-oriented insitutions to sell in anticipation of further market declines. These institutions included, in addition to hedge funds, a small number of pension and endowment funds, money management firms, and investment banking houses. This selling, in turn, stimulated further reactive selling by portfolio insurers and mutual funds.

This view is questioned by Shiller (1988), who interviewed nearly 900 investors immediately after the crash. Only four of his respondents actually mentioned the 'proposed tax changes' story as a significant factor. Instead, the most common theme among the investors reflected the cover page of the October 1987 issue of *The Atlantic*, which was already on the newstands when the crash happened. It argued that the US was about to wake up to 'the morning after' effects of the biggest borrowing and spending binge in its history. About a third of the individual investors and half of the insitutional investers that Shiller interviewed reported that a few days before the crash they had been talking or thinking about the events of 1929. Shiller's own interpretation of his findings was that people had begun to realise the situation was not sustainable and had been left wondering 'Is this "it"' by the big price declines in the preceding week. After the weekend they reacted by assuming 'it' was happening.

Since future changes in the financial tide may be triggered by factors that no one has yet imagined, policymakers could do well to equip themselves with means for making assessments of how market participants are likely to construe the significance of changes in the economic news. To this end, a foray in to the 'artificial intelligence' arm of the behavioural research programme may be necessary. Information gathered on the systems of rules by which participants in financial markets tend to organise their ideas could probably be turned into sets of computer programmes, one programme for each stereotypical financial decision-maker. It might then be possible to run interactive simulations involving these representations of groups with different decision methodologies, with market outcomes being dependent not merely upon the decision rules ascribed to particular participants but also on the size and initial composition of their portfolios. The significance of a succession of particular exogenous shocks could thereby be investigated, in addition to whether or not the system behaved explosively or achieved convergence following a single initial shock. It should not be impossible to model which kinds of changes in the 'state of the news' may be likely to turn particular kinds of speculators from 'bulls' into 'bears', or vice versa. That this would be a valuable exercise is clear from the way that the rapidly unfolding events of Black Monday and its aftermath were associated with great differences of opinion about how far expectations should be revised downwards in particular markets, with some people switching between markets sooner than others and in different directions, and some people not switching at all. (Except for greater complexity of the programmes entailed, there is an obvious and ironical sense in which the sort of simulation work I am proposing is akin to a laboratory version of the most extreme form of programmed selling alleged to have occurred in the Crash of 1987, which involved no human traders, merely computers talking to each other around the world.)

12.4 The Aftermath of Euphoria

Euphoria is a troublesome phenomeon because it tends to spread like a disease across important sections of the economy, rather than being confined at any moment to individual decision-making units. For example, consider the conspicuous consumption that so characterised the world of the yuppies in the mid 1980s. Such purchases are means by which people make statements about the new financial leagues they have entered. Since status goods by their nature are not things whose supply it is easy to expand, their prices will tend to rise as euphoria takes hold, and this will promote a speculative demand for them. Early movers will make capital gains and feel they can take even bigger risks, while followers may mortgage themselves up to the hilt in the belief that prices will continue to rise and in the fear that if they do not buy there and then they will never be able to enter the market. The failure of events to turn out as expected may bring euphoric decision-makers down to earth with a bump. If they have purchased financial assets on borrowed money with a view to capital gains rather than because of their potential to yield streams of income, the failure of prices to rise as far as had been hoped may leave them with major cashflow problems. Interest on the loan will have to be met, but the yield from the assets may be insufficient to cover this. Matters are doubly worse if instead of rising in value, asset prices have unexpectedly fallen, for then the borrower may be unable even to recover the value of the principal by selling the asset.

The forced sale of the Rolls Royce and mansion owned by one bankrupt pop star is something markets will normally absorb with ease. But when overcommitments are bunched together, the end of a speculative boom may see many people finding themselves simultaneously having to pay for their speculative excesses. This will cause markets to be flooded with secondhand assets at a time when confidence needed to purchase new ones is ebbing away: for example, in New Zealand — where the plunge in share prices after Black Monday was particularly severe — the prices of new Mercedes Benz cars were discounted by a quarter as dealers struggled to shift stock and house prices in Auckland, the country's financial centre, fell on average by around 10 per cent in the six months immediately after the crash.

If borrowers cannot meet their loan obligations from other income sources or by selling other assets, those who supplied them with funds may find themselves in a similar predicament. The latter, in turn, have made a mistake in extending a loan to the former and may also be forced to default, and so on, depending on the number of layers in the financial nexus. Here, again, events in New Zealand are instructive. Early in 1989, it was announced that the state-owned Bank of New Zealand had set aside $NZ480 million to cover bad debts (its loss for the year to March 1989 eventually turned out to be $NZ649). Many of these arose from the failure of property companies that had borrowed from it before October 1987 during the boom in commercial construction. This boom had been associated with financial deregulation and the massive growth in share ownership by a general public that sought to emulate the successes of the likes of Sir Ron Brierley, Bruce Judge and Allan Hawkins, whose share trading moves seemed to be taking Australia and the rest of the world by storm. As the nation's bank, the BNZ had felt itself almost obliged to support these aggressive 'entrepreneurs' who seemed in the eyes of the general public to be showing the country the key to economic success (see *Australian Financial Review*, 9 March, 1989, p. 13). With no experience of a major property and sharemarket downturn, the bank paid little attention to the debt servicing capacity of its borrowers and lent heavily on the perceived value of property and equity investments. The expected failure of many of BNZ clients did not merely deal a severe blow to BNZ's own reserve position. Next in the chain of disappointments came the government, which lost expected revenue because, in these circumstances, it had no alternative but to shelve its plans to privatise the bank.

Chain reactions due to falsified expectations can clearly occur where both sides of a balance sheet have the same maturity horizons. They may be all the more dramatic where suppliers of funds (such as bank depositors) are lending short to an intermediary who is lending long to some agency (such as a property company) whose position is rumoured to be precarious. A loss of confidence on the part of the depositors may result in mass withdrawals. The intermediary will then need to find cash in a hurry. It may seek to do this (a) by borrowing from the intermediaries with whom its former depositors have now placed their funds; (b) by borrowing from the reserve bank, as the lender of last resort; or (c) by calling for overdraft repayments and refusing to rollover maturing loans. If the first two options are not available, and the third is tried, a forced sale of the property company's assets may trigger a general collapse of property prices, affecting other property companies and other financial intermediaries. Some banks may simply fail altogether with the depositors' wealth, and the money supply, shrinking in the process. This scenario might come into actuality even if, had the rumours been true about the property company, the bank would have been able to write off the bad debt against its capital reserves so long as there had not been a panic by its depositors.

To the extent that financial intermediaries recognise that their images of soundness are inter-related, one would expect them to club together to ensure that individual defaults do not occur. For example, a run on deposits started at the University of Tasmania's Campus Credit Union in August 1987, as rumours about opportunistic behaviour began to circulate following the suicide of the Society's executive officer. But the run was rapidly brought under control by the announcement that other credit unions were going to provide assistance while the Society's affairs were being restructured. However, such behaviour can by no means be relied upon to prevent insitutions from collapsing. For example, although the run on the Continental Illinois Bank and Trust Company in 1984 eventually did see a group of 28 banks providing it with a $5.5 billion line of credit, the original reaction of banks had been to downgrade its rating on the interbank market or even to refuse it credit altogether. Their subsequent adoption of a much more charitable attitude coincided with a promise of unlimited access to funds from the discount window of the Federal Reserve Board.

Whatever their willingness, the ability of other insitutions to act as financial Good Samaritans may be limited because there is no guarantee that a flight of funds away from one kind of financial asset and into another will not reduce the total suply of available funds. For example, a flight from NBFI deposits into bank deposits does nothing directly to increase the supply of bank deposits from which banks might provide distress loans to NBFIs. Similarly, although those who sell shares and 'go liquid' may increase their bank deposits, those to whom they sell their shares might pay by running down their deposits with banks and/or NBFIs. Companies thereby deterred from making new equity issues as a way of raising finance might thus find intermediated finance no more easily available than before security prices tumbled. Given this, it seems rather difficult at first sight to make sense of claims made in some countries by financial journalists and politicians in late 1987/early 1988 to the effect that accelerations in *M3* growth were due to money being taken out of the stockmarket and placed in bank deposits. Matters look less puzzling, and rather more promising in respect of option (a) in the previous paragraph, once we recall the portfolio apprach to monetary growth, discussed in Chapter 9.

Portfolio theory points to a variety of routes by which a collapse of share prices or loss of confidence in NBFIs *might* lead to an expansion of *M3*. For example, suppose that marked-down shares were seen as bargain buys by those who would otherwise have chosen to run down their indebtedness to banks. Then, even if the banks only made the volume of new lending that they would in any case have done, their total balance sheets would have been larger by an amount equal to the value at which the shares changed hands, plus any additional reserve assets the banks had to acquire to avoid breaching their target ratios. A sudden collapse in confidence may also lead to a net increase in the demand for and supply of finance if banks are willing to extend their lending to firms that have had unexpectedly to pile up stocks as a result of would-be buyers postponing purchases, some of which would have been made from previously accumulated bank deposits. Additional reserve assets would be easy to come by if a collapse of share prices was making it more difficult to finance the public sector deficit, for then one would expect the reserve bank to be buying bonds on the open market. Such a reduced demand for public sector securities could be due to fears about possible rises in interest rates, but it might arise for other reasons: for example, those who step into the market to buy up what they see as bargain-priced equities might otherwise have purchased government bonds with their surplus funds.

In fact, the growth in monetary aggregates in the months following Black Monday was due largely to monetary authorities around the world having no desire to see a re-run of the aftermath of the 1929 Great Crash. Therefore they deliberately added to the liquidity of their economies. They were so successful in preventing a collapse of confidence outside the world of fast money that, within nine months, the focus of debate had shifted in many countries to the possibility of 'overheating' in manufacturing and construction industries and moves were afoot to raise the price of credit.

12.5 A Case Study of Financial Instability: The Sydney Property Market

There are many case studies that provide excellent practical illustrations of Post Keynesian hypotheses on financial instability. From the 1970s, one could choose the UK secondary banking crisis (see Reid, 1982), or the collapse of the Franklin National Bank of New York (see Spero, 1980). Obvious candidates from the mid-1980s would be Continental Illinois — whose troubles, which led to what was then the biggest rescue operation in American banking history, were mentioned briefly in the previous section and are touched on again in section 12.6 below — and the Johnson Matthey Bankers (JMB) scandal in London — which led to JMB being taken over by the Bank of England to prevent spillover problems in the gold bullion market and threats to even the Midland Bank (then suffering from the strain of its misguided acquisition of Crocker National in California) (see the epilogue to Moran, 1986). Even while this book was being written, new cases surfaced. Most noteworthy in the US were events in Texas, including the enormous losses of the Texas thrift industry, whose net worth moved from $1.6 billion at the end of 1986 to minus $10.1 billion in March 1988 (see *Economist*, 28 May 1988), and the $4 billion rescue of the First RepublicBank of Dallas, whose crisis stemmed from the weak Texan economy — where difficulties in the oil business had caused property prices to plummet — and developing country debts. Meanwhile, in the middle of 1988, the British government found itself in hot water as a result of the collapse of the Barlow Clowes investment company, whose licence had been renewed by the Department of Trade and Industry just days before DTI inspectors launched an investigation into its affairs. Parochial readers in Britain and America may therefore feel justified in accusing me of parochialism for my decision to choose an Australian case study, namely the Sydney property market in the 1970s.

My interest in events in this market was in fact fostered several months before I set foot in Australia, when I happened to see the thriller movie *Heatwave*, much of the plot of which is alleged to be a thinly disguised version of the more shadowy side of the actual business of property development in Sydney. In fact, as is clear from the excellent account provided by Daly (1982), this is anything but a singularly Australian case: events in Sydney were strongly bound up with financial problems overseas. Not only did the Crown Agents fiasco (one element in the the British secondary banking crisis) originate in large degree in unfortunate investments in Sydney, but the American giant Citicorp also suffered losses in 1977 as a result of previously having lent $A450 million to Australian property speculators, $A66.1 million of which had to be written off as bad debts. And these were by no means the only losers from Britain and America. The Japanese and even the Russians were also involved. A Post Keynesian assessment of the role of the Reserve Bank of Australia in this episode has since been provided by Stanford and Beale (1987), while a further perspective, somewhat less critical of market participants, is to be found in Clarke and Dean (1987). Here I can do no more than highlight some of the main themes from these sources.

From 1968 to 1974, Sydney experienced an unprecedented property boom that greatly expanded the city's fringe, its supply of industrial and retailing space, and reshaped the central business district. Shock waves from the crash that followed reverberated up to 1980. It is estimated that investors and firms lost between $A1.5 billion and $A2.0 billion in the building industry in the 1970s. The origins of the boom are particularly complex, but seem to include:

(a) The minerals boom of the late 1960s led to a dramatic improvement in the balance of payments, but Prime Minister McMahon ignored advice to revalue. This led to a speculative inflow of $A1.5-$A2.0 billion in 1972 and much of it went into the purchase of property shares and sites. However, the minerals boom had a wider significance in that it had brought Australia to the attention of international investors looking for an outlet for spare funds.

(b) The emergence of the eurodollar market in the late 1960s provided a financial environment far more flexible than the regulated world of domestic Australian banking and big Australian mining companies flocked to borrow in it. Such interests encouraged foreign banks to set up in Sydney, bringing with them easier access to foreign funds and a great demand for office space. Such inflows of funds seem to have offset by nearly half the attempts of the Reserve

Bank of Australia to restrain monetary growth from 1968 to 1972.

(c) After 1968, Australia's inflation rate increased like that of the rest of the world and the Government tried to increase interest rates. Meanwhile a flood of eurodollars were pushing down European rates. This attracted British property developers, who were already well meshed with the London money market, to seek out higher returns in Australia.

(d) The New South Wales State Planning Authority in 1968 released the *Sydney Region Outline Plan*, which set out growth corridors that would be released for development to deal with population growth over the next thirty years. This led to a scramble to gain the best sites well in advance of their release dates, something that would not have happened had there been uncertainty about where development was going to be allowed. The planners were so swamped with applications that processing delays occurred; land prices thus rose before development releases were approved, so there was an even bigger incentive to get in the queue. Developers confidently presumed they could use such rises in demand to pay off debts incurred to install roads, sewerage and so on, in respect of which much higher standards were being required.

Once underway, the boom was considerably fuelled by the following factors:

(e) Crowd behaviour was promoted by the use of auctions rather than fixed-price land sales.

(f) There was a widespread belief that great knowledge was not required to participate in the property market. (The phrase 'as safe as houses' may have a lot to answer for.) People with less and less expertise and less wealth joined in. First estate agents and solicitors started to speculate; rich amateurs such as doctors and dentists followed; then people from all walks of life.

(g) The participation of the ignorant was greatly facilitated by the growth of finance companies' involvements in property. Initially, the finance companies were cautious, using money from banks or solicitors' trust funds to finance second mortgages. But gradually they started taking more chances, lending finance to builders and taking a stake in the acquisition and development of property. The belief grew that, since land prices were going to be higher in future, it was hardly necessary to worry about the credit-worthiness of the borrowers so long as one had the security of the mortgage over the land. Increasingly, they gathered funds by issuing debentures and unsecured notes, which were purchased by small savers and insurance companies

(10 per cent from retired people, 25 per cent from housewives). Building societies were doing very well in the period 1968-73, partly aided by restrictions on bank interest rates, but finance companies did even better as receivers of deposits.

(h) Finance companies also boomed as a result of Australian regulations which prevented foreign banks from competing on a par with domestic ones. The foreign banks saw major finance company shareholdings as a way of getting a presence along with quasi-banking business. The credibility of finance companies was also enhanced by the fact that they were in many cases supported by major local banks, via shareholdings and loans, or by insurance institutions or major companies. (For example, when the Royal Bank of Scotland sold its interests in Associated Securities Limited, they were bought by Ansett Transport Industries.) Some property firms were actually major shareholders in finance companies (as was the case with the Hooker Corporation and Network Finance).

(i) Finance companies/developers (drawing the line became increasingly difficult) repeatedly revalued their properties and borrowed more on the security of these past 'successes'. As Daly observes, 'A dangerous circularity ensued. The value of property was determined in an overheated market in which the competitors were largely primed by funds from the finance companies; and the security of those funds rested on the soundness of the property market' (1982, p. 74).

As the participating companies became ever-more highly geared, and a glut of property began to appear on the horizon, companies continued to raise funds via various risky and questionable means:

(j) Short-term funds were taken on in the hope of quick sales, but these meant that when the market crashed, rollover problems would be acute — especially as interest rates moved up.

(k) Accounting practices enabled them to report fake profits. Two weeks before the Mainline Corporation crashed (the ANZ bank was appointed receiver, having underwritten $A10 million of its business), its profits were reported as being 2.1 per cent, 25.7 per cent or 51.8 per cent ahead of its previous six months, depending on how one looked at them. Interest obligations were commonly capitalised into the value of property assets on the presumption that when projects were completed they could be sold at a price which would cover them. When land was actually sold, it was rather vague as to when a 'profit' on it could be incorporated as such. Sometimes, an 'accrual basis' would be used, taking 'profits' into account the moment a binding contract was signed; at other times, a 'cash-emergence' basis would be used, recording profits only as payments were made. By changing practices at appropriate times and selling land in incestuous deals, rosy profit pictures could be created as balance sheets became ever more flimsy.

There is considerable evidence that risky portfolios were made all the more dangerous by the exceedingly rapid growth rates of many of the developers. Mainline Corporation is one example: after beginning in 1961 by building a seventeen storey Double Bay home unit block, it moved on to build the $A10 million Goldfields building in 1965, then the AMP centre, IAC building, Bank of NSW building and AJC centre. In 1972-3, it was involved in many major developments in Sydney, hotels in Newcastle, Port Macquarie and Canberra, seven projects in both Melbourne and South Australia, a new town beside the Northern Territory Nabalco aluminium works, and developments in New Zealand, Fiji and the US.

With such goings on, minor delays in completion and sale of developments (for example, due to bad weather or strikes) could be disastrous for fragile balance sheets. When collapses came, other companies were called into question, not merely because of the hierarchical nature of financing but also because of the proliferation of joint ventures. The major buffer force was the ability of large banks at the end of the chain to absorb losses. For example, Federal opposition led to the abandonment of a major redevelopment plan at Woolloomooloo. Amongst the many losers was the Moscow Norodny Bank, owed $A20 million by the failed Regional Landholdings.

Some of the biggest crashes took four or more years to break. Major finance companies held on to property assets after the crash of 1974, hoping for a recovery in prices as demand growth caught up with supply. Through 1975-7, the Reserve Bank of Australia bought bank-approved bills of finance companies, but then stopped on finding they were being used as rollover finance for medium-term property debts. After something of a shake out, the market recovered a little in 1978 with a rise in demand and inflows from the Far East money markets. But in 1979 Associated Securities Limited and the Finance Corporation of Australia crashed with losses of $A220m. FCA's major creditor, the Bank of Adelaide, had to be absorbed by ANZ at the request of the Reserve Bank. The Reserve Bank's insistence that ANZ should take over the Bank of Adelaide was a highly *ad hoc* measure: it was of somewhat doubtful legality since the Reserve Bank did not follow prescribed procedures and the intervention had the effect of protecting both shareholders of the Bank of Adelaide and holders of unsecured notes and debentures of the FCA, despite the Bank's protective role extending only to bank depositors. However, Stanford and Beale (1987, p. 496) argue that it is difficult to imagine any intervention that could have protected Bank of Adelaide depositors without also protecting the bank's shareholders, while if the Reserve Bank had delayed action by following all the formal procedures, or if the Bank of Adelaide had been allowed to collapse, it is likely that a more widespread collapse of confidence would have ensued and that the wealth of depositors in other banks would thereby have been threatened.

If finance companies such as ASL had been able to obtain lender of last resort facilities from banks that were prepared to take a longer term view of the strength of their assets, they would have been far less vulnerable to the cash flow problems that resulted, in the event, from the shortening of their borrowing maturities and the consequent maturity mismatch. As Clarke and Dean (1987. p. 452) point out, by 1981, increases in property prices had begun to justify the rosy expectations that only a few years before had proved financially disastrous.

12.6 The Case for Regulating Financial Markets

A common reaction of those who have suffered losses in a major financial crash is to cry out 'this sort of thing should not be allowed to happen'. The Crash of 1987 was followed by suggestions that there should be limits on the amounts by which typical share values could change in a single day's trading or that reserve banks should extend their stabilisation activities to equity markets. Earlier disasters led in many cases to reappraisals of existing company and banking laws and to restrictive new laws (for example, in the 1720s, the bursting of the so-called South Sea Bubble was followed by tough controls on the formation of joint stock companies), which loosened up once the financial system seemed to have evolved on to a new level of sophistication. In section 2.7 I considered some of the social costs associated with 'paper-shuffling' speculation even if it does not result in a major financial collapse; in this section, attention is given to possible rationales for measures aimed at preventing financial instability and the failure of financial insitutions.

Most of the literature on the need for prudential regulation of financial activities is concerned with measures to safeguard the value of financial wealth of lenders, and ignores the fact (noted by Goodhart, 1987b) that bank crises also affect borrowers, who may find it unexpectedly difficult to obtain new funds or rollovers for existing loans, particularly since such crises tend to happen at precisely the times when borrowers face adverse conditions. This literature appears to be built around the normative view that people should not *have* to behave as speculators; for without making this presumption, it is difficult to present any case for measures aimed at guaranteeing the value of wealth by preventing financial failures. One might try to take a different normative starting point and assert that everyone has a right to work and that financial instability is incompatible with jobs being continuously available to all those who wish to work. (For the wealthy, a temporary loss of employment opportunities is akin to a loss due to unwise speculative choices, in that it reduces consumption opportunities. However, for those who lack financial wealth, the absence of a current source of income is a disaster.) But even this rationale for prudential safeguards looks somewhat flimsy in an economy in which subsistence needs of the unemployed are met from government dole payments.

If we do not presume that people should not have to take financial risks, it is difficult to see why bank deposits should be seen as any more worthy of protection than equity values. This is particularly so now that non-bank mutual investment funds are starting to offer bank-like payments services: this means that unit trust certificates, for example, may serve like banknotes in the role of means of payment. As Goodhart (1987b) implies, bank deposits are coming to look particularly distinctive as 'money' only in terms of their ability to serve as a store of wealth: deposits are redeemable at a fixed nominal value so long as the institution that issued them remains solvent, whereas money placed in equities or unit trust certificates can only be recouped by selling them for whatever value happens presently to be accorded them by the market. So long as a deposit-taker is solvent, the only threat to the value of deposits is inflation. However, whereas the value of a unit trust's liabilities moves in line with the market prices of its assets, a deposit-taker can find itself insolvent if the value of its assets collapses or there is a run on its deposits. Those who place their money with deposit-takers thus suffer risks of loss but receive no prospect of a capital gain unless a fall in the price level is expected. Without the security provided by deposit insurance schemes and lender of last resort guarantees from the reserve bank, bank depositors might not even have the compensation of interest payments for shouldering this risk and thereby helping to line the pockets of bank shareholders (interest-bearing current accounts are very much the product of recent moves towards financial deregulation).

Individuals who do not wish to engage in risk-taking activities are not obliged to buy shares or assume business risks associated with direct enterprise. Yet, if they opt out of such activities and wish neither to commit themselves to holding their wealth in illiquid physical assets nor to risk losing their savings to housebreakers, they are practically obliged to make deposits in financial institutions. (Given the risk of opportunistic claims, it is hardly surprising that insurance companies do not normally provide household contents policies which give cover against the loss of cash.) Salary payment systems increasingly force ordinary individuals to hold bank accounts and thereby to risk losing their pay if bank failure occurs on payday, before they can convert it into cash. If nominal values of deposits are not guaranteed against the failure of the deposit-taking institutions, those who wish to avoid speculative behaviour would have to incur the costs of hedging against the risks of financial failure by spreading deposits among many accounts. Moreover, the interlinked nature of financial institutions could mean that hedging turned out to be ineffective, for if one major institution failed, many others might follow.

If we accept the idea that wealth-holders should not be forced to speculate, we should recognise that it does not necessarily imply that there should be prudential controls on all deposit-taking institutions. Nor does it imply that government intervention is necessary. All that risk-averse wealth-holders need to have is some kind of 'safe haven' for their assets, and while this could comprise a government-guaranteed bank for current accounts and easily redeemed, inflation-indexed government savings bonds, we need to ask whether the market mechanism would fail to provide a similar haven at lower cost if the government did not step in to fill the gap.

If wealth-owners were keen to avoid speculation and were not so unsophisticated as to be ignorant of the risks of making deposits, then, in the absence of government intervention, a variety of entrepreneurial initiatives might attempt to cater for their requirements. One would expect that independent sources of advice, such as *Consumer Reports*, *Which?* magazine and *Choice*, could win subscribers by investigating the soundness of rival deposit-taking institutions. Groups of financial intermediaries, like travel agents, would have incentives to set up accreditation and regulatory bodies to inspire customer confidence and reduce the risks of opportunistic behaviour. Opportunities for individuals to insure their deposits would also be likely to spring up, and be taken up.

But the case for leaving such things to the market is questionable. If people have little recent experience of financial failures or if they construe as similar financial environoments that differ in their riskiness, they may well decline to seek careful advice about the soundness of the institutions with which they decide to place their money: for example, I doubt that British readers migrating to the US or Australia would guess from their previous experience with cooperative forms of savings institutions just how unsafe it could be to place with a savings and loan association or credit union the funds that they had previously kept in a small building society in the UK. There are also grounds for doubting the efficacy of self-regulated financial markets, notwithstanding the enthusiasm of the UK Department of Trade and Industry to delegate its regulatory authority to the privately-run Securities and Investments Board (SIB) (Hamilton, 1986, p. 145). This policy, which contrasts with the continuing view in the US that the Securities and Exchange Commission should be a public body, is not worrying merely because of the fact that the Lloyds insurance scandals took place in a self-regulated market that had hitherto been greatly respected. Disturbing, too, is the obvious scope for conflicts of interest within a body such as the SIB, staffed by former City employees. While 'poachers turned gamekeepers' may have a better ability than public servants to find out what has been going on, they are also in a position to exploit that information for personal gain and, as Coggan (1986) has pointed out, will probably find it difficult to face up to a need to discipline their friends and former colleagues.

Just as small savers, like big speculators, may need to be protected from their own short memories and judgmental rules and from the opportunism of others (all of which are problems associated with bounded rationality), they also require shelter from the risk of outright failure in the market for deposit insurance. Whereas fire insurance companies can usually be confident that fire damage can be contained in a limited area, interlinked balance sheets and the tendency for confidence to be a social phenomenon make it far less likely that financial failures will not be bunched together. Private insurers would need to incur the costs of hedging their own bets amongst banks, and to reinsure on a wider, international market, in order the reduce the risk of their funds failing. In the event of a worldwide crash even reinsurance might not be effective, unless some international government-backed body, such as the IMF, stepped in to keep the system liquid. Given this, society might be better off with a system of government controls and guarantees.

12.7 Complexity, Opportunism and the Regulation of Financial Institutions

In a complex and turbulent financial environment it is very easy for policy interventions in one area to have unexpected repercussions elsewhere. The following two examples illustrate how the effects of myopic banking legislation may be ameliorated or exacerbated by innovative strategies on the part of the players who fall under its jurisdiction. Prior to the deregulation of money markets in Australia, deposit interest rates had been controlled in the belief the interest rate competition would increase the riskiness of bank portfolios and thereby raise the probability of bank failure. However, this made it very difficult for banks to survive problem periods, given that the Reserve Bank of Australia took a very strict view of its role as lender of *last* resort (in contrast, one might say, to the recent stance of the Bank of England, which Chick, 1984, has described as 'ever more accommodating, to the point of acting as Lender of First Resort'). It was therefore fortunate that the regulators had left one loophole in their regulations: when the Bank of New South Wales found itself suffering a drain of deposits in 1974 it successfully attracted deposits by offering unprecedented rates of return on certificates of deposit, which were then the only uncontrolled type of deposit available (Swan, 1983, p. 185).

Although an innovative push into the wholesale money market enabled the Bank of New South Wales to get round a liquidity squeeze, it was precisely such a move that led to disaster for Continental Illinois (the discussion here draws on Hamilton, 1986, pp. 212-14). Fearing that the growth of larger banks in the US could bring enhanced market power and hence threaten consumer welfare, many state governments tried to prevent increasing concentration in the banking industry by prohibiting or restricting branch banking. Faced with such limitations on its ability to expand its deposit base by increasing the number of its retail branches, Continental Illinois sought to grow on the basis of large deposits and successfully acquired billions of dollars from corporations, institutions and other banks. In 1984, when rumours of trouble with its assets led to a flight from Continental by these large depositors, the bank found itself unable to find replacement funds on the interbank market. This was despite the fact that, unlike the Penn Square Bank which failed after a run two years before, Continental's loans were not in such a bad way as to imply negative reserves. The run on Continental was especially rapid because of the electronic nature of the wholesale markets: it could not be slowed by the build-up of queues. Had Continental's deposits come mainly from smaller clients, there would have been far less need to panic, for since 1933 the government, through the Federal Deposit Insurance Corporation, has guaranteed deposits of up to $100 000. When the FDIC was set up, such a limitation would have seemed sensible, for the wholesale market was much less developed, but the politicians had not thought ahead to the ways in which the system might evolve in response to their well-intended legislation.

Moran's (1986) study of the politics of banking in the UK not only illustrates the complexity/surprise theme admirably, it also leaves one with the depressing feeling that players in modern financial systems are simply too smart to be subject to effective control. Along with the cases just considerd, there are, at the entirely legitimate end of the spectrum, the kinds of innovative policies that underpin Goodhart's law (mentioned in section 9.7; for a finely detailed account, see Podolski, 1986) and make monetary targeting a somewhat futile exercise. The other extreme, downright opportunism, is something which is becoming much harder to ignore as the business of banking moves rapidly from the honourable, goodwill-driven world of 'gentlemanly' dealings to the hotly contested greed-driven world portrayed in the movie *Wall Street*. Moran uses the case of Johnson Matthey Bankers (JMB) to show that opportunistic behaviour may arise in even the most reputable of insitutions if the authorities do not keep a close watch on their actions.

The 1979 Banking Act divided financial intermediaries in the UK into two classes for purposes of prudential control: 'recognised banks' and 'licensed deposit-takers' (LDTs). This may seem a sensible thing to have done by way of providing a limited number of safe havens for those who wished to avoid speculating with their wealth. To apply identical controls to all deposit-takers in an attempt to equalise risks would certainly help protect the really unsophisticated depositor who could not discriminate between types of institution, but it would also greatly narrow the present spectrum of risk/return possibilities. (Even amongst insitutions allowed to call themselves banks, with the low risk connotation this term carries, identical controls would unnecessarily reduce the return on capital enjoyed by the strongest banks, if the controls were geared to guaranteeing the safety of the weakest.) However, the Act looks far less sensible once one recognises that the LDTs were actually to be subject to much more onerous ongoing supervision, while banks, having qualified for their elite status, would be left pretty much to their own devices.

This might have worked satisfactorily had the Bank of England only accorded the status of bank to the big, well established firms. But it did not: by 1984, when the JMB scandal broke, there were 290 recognised banks and 308 LDTs. JMB had been recognised as a bank in 1980, when its main concern was with bullion dealing, and at that time its commercial lending only amounted to £34 million. Left to its own devices, JMB exposed itself to huge loans to doubtful borrowers and by 1984 its lending had grown almost ten-fold, to £309 million. Of this, £245 million turned out to be irrecoverable. Given that JMB's bad debts completely exhausted its reserves it is not surprising that the Bank of England was unable to find a bank that was willing to stage a rescue/takeover operation.

The JMB affair indicates how dangerous it can be to try to supervise the business of banking on the basis of a simple dual league philosophy, such as that embodied in the 1979 UK Banking Act, which labelled as similar insitutions that were very different in their ranges of interests, past records and prospects. Ideally, one might prefer to devise tailormade requirements for each intermediary, concerning the compositions of its loans and reserves. This may be asking too much, however, since the vulnerability of a deposit-taker depends on a complex mix of, amongst other things, asset quality, management competence, the maturity structure of assets and liabilities, and the extent of fixed interest commitments in respect of assets and liabilities. Even the structure of a bank's branch network matters, because the geographical distance of a bank's management from its borrowers can make a difference to the latters' performance. The task of the supervisory body is rendered particularly difficult by the fact that transnational banking firms typically operate in a multitude of countries that take very different views on the division between reserves and liabilities and which follow different accounting principles. Furthermore, if one is worried about the adequacy of a deposit taker's attempts at diversification, one needs to consider not merely the quantity of loans to individual customers, but also how specialised these loans are in respect of their industry/location/size distribution amongst customers. From one standpoint, a specialist loan-making institution may look like it has dangerously many eggs in too few baskets, yet its expertise may be such that it is able to make good loans in the narrow area. As a non-specialist, a reserve bank may be poorly suited to make such judgments. (In the US, industry norms are used to judge outliers, but outliers may not inherently be prone to failure.) All too often banks run into trouble not because of a failure to judge high risk loans as such and charge high interest rates or diversify accordingly. Rather they succumb as a result of unanticipated events (for example, major macroeconomic downturns, such as the one led by the OPEC oil price hike in 1973), or, especially with smaller institutions, insider abuses and fraud.

For these reasons, capital adequacy requirements seem likely to be costly to work out as well as highly arbitrary. Moreover, they would not even safeguard depositors against a bank run if access to lender of last resort loans were made contingent upon the tolerable risk position being met. A bank that had been deemed unsatisfactory at the time of its inspection and which could not rapidly reshuffle its asset/liability structure would have to raise new capital — which might be far from easy in the circumstances. A commitment by the reserve bank to support a bank that met its requirements would distort risk/return possibilities since that commitment would appear as a safeguard to all of its depositors regardless of the nature of their deposits.

To economise on the costs associated with investigation-based capital adequacy schemes, governments are likely to find it tempting to seek to protect depositors with a requirement that a 'bank' must insure its customers' deposits against failure on its part. Here, too, the policy-maker's task is by no means straightforward.

Deposit insurance schemes, like other types of insurance, need to be designed with an eye to possibility that the fund may be inadequate if many claims are made simultaneously, and to the dangers of 'moral hazard' (if complete cover is provided and negligence is hard to prove, then agents may take less trouble to prevent the occurrence of the event that has been insured against). Hogan and Sharpe (1987, p. 396), for example, have advocated a limited, variable premium insurance scheme, which would involve banks in paying higher premiums (which would affect the returns they could offer to depositors) if they had higher risks. If the insurance were limited to, say, demand deposits, banks would still have an incentive to take care; their depositors could choose to be tempted into making other kinds of deposits with higher returns and higher risks, but they would have a safe haven (inflation aside) in which to store their wealth in liquid form. However, like capital adequacy requirements, such a policy runs up against the question of how the riskiness of individual bank portfolios can be properly judged.

In US, banks have to insure their deposits *and* meet capital adequacy requirements: the authorities see the latter as a device to protect the insurance fund, rather than to protect deposits directly. Although deposit insurance premiums in the US are simply fixed as a proportion of deposits, it is hoped that banks are discouraged from engaging in excessive risk-taking by the $100 000 limit on the insured value of accounts in the same name with a single bank: the idea is that wealthy individuals, who might be expected to enjoy economies of scale in search and/or transactions costs, may switch to other banks if they judge their present bank to be behaving too recklessly. (Flannery, 1986, provides a useful discussion of the effects that fixed-rate FDIC insurance would have on banks' risk-taking incentives in the absence of capital adequacy requirements and limited coverage.) Premiums have been kept very low because the FDIC has only occasionally fallen prey to opportunistic behaviour involving the concealment of losses and has usually been able to avoid any payouts by ordering that failing institutions are wound up just before their reserves are exhausted. In so far as it seems likely that the FDIC can continue to operate in this manner, the case for risk-related premiums seems much weaker, for the risk of loss to the FDIC is low, regardless of the riskiness of individual institutions (see Horvitz, 1986, p. 274).

The case of Continental Illinois points to limitations in deposit insurance schemes which concentrate on protecting retail depositors in an age when wholesale banking has come to account for an increasingly large proportion of deposits: had that crisis not been brought under control, it could have spread to other insitutions that had (or were simply rumoured to have) lost large deposits and the ability of the FDIC to protect even retail depositors could have been called into question. In the UK, likewise, a re-run of the mid-1970s secondary banking crisis would have very rapidly exhausted the Deposit Protection Fund that was mandated by the 1979 Banking Act: the levy on banks was designed to raise a mere five to six million pounds annually, and only secured 75 per cent of the first £10 000 of a deposit. (Bank depositors are now covered for 75 per cent of their first £20 000, while the building societies' compensation scheme now protects 90 per cent of a depositor's savings up to a maximum of £20 000.) A much better deal is provided by the new Investors' Compensation Scheme, which came into operation on 27 August 1988 to offer protection against the collapse of investment management and advisory firms. It covers a maximum single loss per person of £50 000 in any one firm, with a maximum payment on such a loss of £48 000 (on claims up to £30 000, full insurance is provided, but only 90 per cent cover is given on the next £20 000). But the overall compensation provided in any one year has been restricted to £100 million by the Securities and Investments Board and does not cover funds placed overseas. This would be little help in the event of a repeat of the Barlow Clowes scandal, which broke shortly before the new arrangements came into force: the vast bulk of Barlow Clowes losses were incurred by the firm's Gibraltar-based offshoot, whose fund appeared to have a shortfall of £108 million; however, the domestic and offshore operations were very closely linked and many investors had been led by advisors to believe that the firm's licence covered its offshore operations (see *Observer* 31 July 1988, p. 57).

Before we proceed to a conclusion to this chapter, some further words are in order, under the present heading, about the psychology of financial instability. It seems reasonable to argue that just as cognitive dissonance and creative accounting may lead to the build-up of doubtful portfolios, so they may help keep the system from behaving in a disorderly manner, provided that room is left for subjectivity. Goodhart (1987b, p. 87) has recently observed that:

Central Bankers have been, at most, lukewarm about allowing a market to develop in large syndicated loans to sovereign countries, whose ability to service and repay on schedule was in doubt, because the concrete exhibition of the fall in the value of such loans could impair the banks' recorded value and potentially cause failures. An economist might ask who was being fooled. Yet on a number of occasions financial institutions have been effectively insolvent, but, so long as everyone steadfastly averted their gaze, a way through and back to solvency was achieved.

Goodhart's essentially psychological view of how crises may sometimes be avoided makes the growing trend towards the securitisation of loans look somewhat alarming. It should make one hesitate about jumping to the conclusion that cases such as those of Continental Illinois, Penn Square and JMB imply that financial intermediaries should be forced to provide more information about the 'true' values of their assets (although part of the problem in the case of JMB was that the Bank of England for a long time failed to take any action even when faced with information that should have been a cause for concern); for it would be if difficult to make such a policy reveal anything 'objective' unless banks were forced to securitise the larger part of their loan portfolios.

The scope for continuing the debate about the real scale of difficulties arising from doubtful sovereign loans is further enhanced by the lack of consensus about the appropriate level of reserves that banks should have: for example, shortly after Moody's, the American credit rating agency, stripped J.P. Morgan of its AAA rating because the bank had let its provision against third-world loans fall below 30 per cent, the *Economist* (27 February 1988) urged international bankers and ratings agencies to be more cautious about jumping to unfavourable conclusions and reported that a study of the Bank of America had found that the latter bank's reserves could be measured in 18 different ways.

In the case of the Sydney property market, prospects for repayment can be seen, with the benefit of hindsight, to have been more immediate than with many doubtful sovereign loans. Had property companies been able to persuade potential suppliers of replacement funds to turn a blind eye to the objective fact of sliding property values, they might have been able to emulate the Third World's success in rescheduling its debts and obtaining rollover credits: if suppliers of funds could have been persuaded to wait a few more years, immediate difficulties in matching interest obligations with interest and rental earnings on their assets would not have proved ruinous. Since that episode, financiers appear to have become more adept at turning a blind eye to doubtful loans, and to the possible implications of doing so. As Chick (1984, p. 248) observes, 'One can, if one is not afraid to look, see [in the tendency toward vague and elastic repayment times] that a basic presumption of capitalism is being undermined: the presumption that debt is to be repaid at a definite time and that default carries consequences.'

12.8 Conclusion

It is far easier to explain how financial crises happen than it is to dream up foolproof ways of preventing them or stopping them from getting out of control. The more onerous the monetary authorities make their systems of prudential control, the bigger is the incentive for shrewd and possibly opportunistic financial managers to evade them by dreaming up strategies which fall outside their regulatory spans. One might ideally like to see the occasional financial failure and consequent disgrace of incompetent or devious management being allowed as a means to concentrate the minds of players in financial markets. In practice, however, the scope for a single bankrupt financial institution to exit from the market without spreading shockwaves into other firms is limited, owing to the interconnectedness of corporate balance sheets and images of soundness. Given that prudential schemes involving capital adequacy requirements are unlikely to succeed totally in eliminating major financial failures, and given that the provision of deposit insurance to cover people against a really major financial calamity is about as feasible as the provision of fire insurance to cover the effects of a nuclear war, it is essential to have a lender of last resort that stands at all times ready and willing to pump funds into the system if lenders start to lose their nerve and/or their money. If decision-makers with wealth to lose recognise the disruptive effects of a flight into cash and yet try to adhere to the maxim 'Don't panic, but if you must, panic first', a reserve bank acting in the role of lender of last resort would be unwise to be too circumspect about the quality of the assets it should buy when dealing with a liquidity crisis.

13 Bottlenecks, Slack and Macroeconomic Dynamics

13.1 Introduction

Despite their inclination to make a case for leaving financial markets to their own devices, most mainstream economists would freely acknowledge that financial systems alternate between periods of orderly behaviour and turbulent activity. They would depict orderly episodes in terms of models of states of dynamic equilibrium, while periods of dramatic upheaval would be portrayed as resulting from major disturbances which changed the parameters of the system and necessitated a period of experimentation by agents until they uncovered a new set of rational expectations. The orthodox methodology might yield quite acceptable predictions for epochs when the system was not in a state of upheaval, but its prospects for modelling disorderly epochs do not look good; nor does the conventional methodology — in so far as it treats parameter-upsetting disturbances as random events, not to be rationally expected from current knowledge of the system's neoclassical mechanics — offer much to anyone wishing to anticipate when regime changes could be prone to arise and shift the economy from one set of supply and demand functions to another. Because of these limitations, I set out in this book to analyse the behaviour of today's rapidly changing financial systems from an altogether different perspective. The notion that financial systems should be seen in terms of conventional supply and demand functions grinding out equilibrium solutions was abandoned very early in this book (section 1.2); optimality was jettisoned a little later (section 3.1). Since then, my focus has been on processes of muddling through, that may or may not produce overall coherence and outcomes that individual decision-makers judge to be satisfactory.

These processes have been studied from the standpoint of two literatures which can be portrayed as embodying strongly polarised visions of what Coddington (1982) called the 'texture' of economic systems. On the one hand, I have drawn much inspiration from the behavioural school (particularly Simon, 1959; Cyert and March, 1963; Kornai, 1971; Nelson and Winter, 1982), whose members emphasise that decision-making is costly and therefore often delegated to routine devices. The use of routines gives the system a good deal of inertia and opens up great scope for heavily channelised behaviour of a reasonably predictable nature (Heiner, 1983). On the other hand, I have also made extensive use of the work of Post Keynesian thinkers (especially Minsky, 1975, and Shackle, 1974) who, like Marxian scholars, stress the scope for the orderly workings of the economic system to be upset by revolutionary discontinuities — economic kaleidics, as Shackle calls them — and processes of cumulative causation that magnify disturbances. This recapitulatory penultimate chapter weaves together many of the underlying themes from earlier discussions, in an exploration of forces that affect transitions between routinised evolutions and kaleidic revolutions (or vice versa).

13.2 Inertia, Linkages and Decomposability

A training in neoclassical economics encourages one to think of economic systems as if they undergo marginal adjustments in response to steadily changing circumstances. Behavioural theory, by contrast, postulates the existence of economic 'inert areas' and suggests that decision-makers may only change their behaviour once they have crossed particular 'response thresholds' (see especially Kornai, 1971; Leibenstein, 1976). For example, if attainments are falling from a level that has been in excess of a person's aspiration levels, she will only start to search for ways of improving things if she expects the deterioration to continue so far as to produce outcomes that she would label as unsatisfactory. It may take a long time for her to face up to the possibility that she is dealing with a trend rather than a temporary disturbance. She can let things slip meanwhile because she started with a surplus. When she eventually does respond, possibly following a particularly vivid signal of the way things are heading, her actions may change dramatically, rather as if she had suddenly woken up or undergone a religious conversion. Such a perspective implies that in trying to understand and anticipate the dynamic performance of an economy we should investigate the presence of any kinds of slack that may serve as a buffer between changing circumstances and actions.

While slack may enable decision-makers in a changing environment to carry on going down previously chosen pathways, bottlenecks of various kinds may hold up their progress. One way of explaining such phenomena is in terms of the physical inflexibility and immobility of human and physical capital when supply shortages are encountered. However, in so far as there are no institutional impediments to changes in relative prices, a case may be made for saying that bottlenecks ultimately are due to price incentives being completely dominated by quality/non-price considerations (as in the 'characteristic filtering'/'lexicographic' theory of choice discussed in Chapter 3): were it not for breaks in substitution chains, losses in output and the generation of unemployment and inflation could be avoided in a structurally imbalanced system via a set of relative price adjustments that would temporarily divert demands elsewhere, whether between sectors or between time periods (cf. section 11.3 and the end of section 11.5).

Slack and bottlenecks are by no means unrelated phenomena. Those who have had their plans thwarted by supply-side bottlenecks are likely to react sooner or later by taking measures to give themselves more room for manoeuvre on subsequent occasions. The result, to put it simply, is a speculative hoarding of resources by some decision-makers, which may cause supply-side problems for others. This is a variation on the central theme of Hazeldine's (1984) superbly argued book on policies for achieving full employment without generating inflation. His work implicitly echoes the earlier claim by Cyert and March (1963) that decision-makers devote a great deal of attention to achieving a 'negotiated environment' to prevent their attainments from being affected by the erratic workings of the market. The trouble is that if some decison-makers succeed in increasing their own spans of control by tying-up resources with the aid of mergers, regulatory programmes and so on, then the rest of the economic system has access to fewer resources than before. Thus, as Hazeldine (1984, p. 3) observes, there is a paradox:

Each successful attempt by a firm or interest group to control or 'plan' its own immediate environment reduces 'plannability' for everyone else. The net effect of each agent acting in their own best interest is a system in which they are all worse off. Such is the process whereby the stock of elasticity in the economy has been depleted to crisis levels.

If an economic system is short of slack and/or prone to suffer from bottlenecks, the scope for chain reactions in the event of disturbances may be considerable. This will be only too obvious to anyone who has arranged a complex travel itinerary which leaves little time between connections. If unexpected weather conditions cause a delay at one airport, it may be impossible to catch later flights on the itinerary and if the airlines do not have spare seating, it may be impossible to change flights slightly so as to arrive only a few hours late. This may mean that the original intention of the journey cannot be fulfilled. The traveller who cannot afford such a disappointment and is aware of what Hart (1948, pp. 198-202) called the 'principle of linkage of risks' will take steps to ensure she is not given a taut itinerary and will take her credit cards with her in case everything goes wrong and she needs to make expensive outlays to salvage the situation.

If a system comprises a set of self-contained modules, then it may be possible for one module to be suffering from grave problems whilst the rest of the system remains unaffected. In other words, the resilience of a system is a function of its 'decomposability' (Simon, 1969). This idea is very easily grasped in the context of the spread of disease: for example, AIDS would have been a far less terrifying problem for most people in the developed world had members of the gay community not tended to be internationally mobile, highly promiscuous and, in some cases, bisexual. In the economic context, any shock which affects the demand or supply of a commodity that is 'basic' in Sraffa's (1960) sense will be particularly significant for the overall system: we speak of the Oil Crisis of 1973 as a crisis not merely because it was associated with an increase in the world propensity to save as income was transferred to oil producing nations, but also because the fourfold rise in the cost of oil affected the cost of producing practically every other commodity, directly or indirectly.

The severity of any episode of financial failure will depend on patterns of linkages between individual balance sheets and on the diversity of asset holdings. For example, the 1929 Wall Street Crash was associated with particularly severe wealth effects and unemployment in the US because ordinary individuals had put their savings into speculative ventures and lost them, and many banks also failed. By contrast, in the mid 1970s the secondary banking crisis in the UK destroyed many speculative fortunes and financial inter-mediaries (even despite lender of last resort action by the Bank of England and 'lifeboat' loans by major banks), yet it did not have much direct effect on employment. The collapsing 'speculative' sector had borrowed from the major banks, but these banks also had major interests in the 'productive' sector so none of them failed. Furthermore, since much of the speculation was a separate whirlpool of exchange amongst assets not easily reproduced, the destruction of wealth did not have much direct impact on the demand for newly produced goods and employment.

Since then, new technologies, deregulation, the spread of multinational banking corporations and round-the-clock trading have made world financial markets all the more indecomposable. In so far as companies have taken the view that it is easier to make money by trading shareholdings than by developing new products, the dividing line between the speculative and productive sectors will also have become more difficult to draw. That the immediate aftermath of the Crash of 1987 was not much more severe outside of the financial sector must therefore appear something of a mystery unless we keep the other sources of resilience in mind and do not focus simply on the structure of the system. However, the decomposability theme may still provide many clues as to how the shockwaves were absorbed. For example, while the crash temporarily disrupted the market for new prestige vehicles, matters would have been far worse for producers, importers and dealers if their typical customers had actually conformed to the yuppie stereotype portrayed by the popular press: in fact, surveys of purchasers of Porsche cars in 1986 and 1987 undertaken by the British importers revealed that only 5 per cent of their customers for new Porsches were stockbrokers and the average age of buyers was 39. There was still much business to be done in other market segments and the failure of prices of used vehicles to collapse (see section 2.3) meant that new ones could still be sold on their appeal as an investment.

In the next three sections I discuss a variety of potential bottlenecks and sources of slack that may affect the dynamic performance of macroeconomic systems. During these sections readers should keep in mind a picture of an economy which can be sucked forward in some areas but whose progression will be dependent on restraining forces: for example, the wearing out of durable physical assets in households and firms may tighten up the system and get a multiplier process going even in the absence of fiscal and monetary intervention, but only if appropriate slack exists elsewhere. Whether actual or merely anticipated, bottlenecks may lead to unemployment of a 'demand deficiency' kind arising due to a failure of workers to be hired, or the failure of expenditure to take place due to unavailability of goods right now (postponed demand). However, as Hirschman (1958) and Moss (1981; 1984, Ch. 8) have argued, bottlenecks of some kinds can provide a decisive stimulus to investment activities — so long as they are not held up by bottlenecks of other kinds. Even in a deep depression bottlenecks internal to firms may lead to problem-solving innovations whose implementation will place pressure on their rivals to follow suit. Of course, an upswing thus generated may be shortlived if the bunching of investments leads to a rapid exhaustion of slack in the system.

13.3 Cognitive Factors

Post Keynesians have been keen to stress the potentially upsetting role of changes in 'the state of the news'. However, whether or not a piece of economic news will lead decision-makers to wish to reorganise their affairs will depend on the sytems of thought they use for forming expectations (see sections 3.2 and 3.8). If a person thinks about life with the aid of a set of rules that separate it out into many subsystems, she will find it easy to absorb a piece of bad news by changing a single expectational subsystem and adjusting a few of her actions accordingly: she has what the psychologist Kelly (1955) called a highly 'permeable' way of looking at the world. By contrast, people whose views of life are much more indecomposable may find the same piece of bad news threatens them on very many fronts. Some may find it easy to preserve their key beliefs by constructing many new expectations and changing their behaviour accordingly. However, others may initially find that the only way they can maintain their core constructs is by distorting both their behaviour and their more peripheral mental notions in a grotesquely Procrustean manner (cf. also the discussions of cognitive dissonance in sections 12.2 and 12.7).

A Procrustean response to information that some would take as implying the need to change course is more likely in contexts where change is difficult to undertake because it would involve the disposal of illiquid assets and a long period during which the decison-maker, who may have been accustomed to regarding herself as an expert, would be trying to rebuild her expertise (see further Earl, 1986, pp. 154-70). We should not be surprised to see managers of undiversified enterprises finding it hard to summon up the courage to change course as market conditions move against them and instead allowing their balance sheets to suffer a progressive deterioration. Nor should cases in which people go to great lengths to conceal from their families the fact that they have lost their jobs seem particularly bizarre: denial is the first stage of a grieving process. Luddite-like behaviour of workers faced with technological changes may also be framed in these terms: they are not just fighting against threats to their incomes but also against threats to their images of themselves. (So, too, can the failure of orthodox economists to switch paradigm in the face of suggestions from behaviouralists that the world does not conform with predictions of theories that assume optimisation: it is much easier to massage the figures and argue about the evidence than it is to become acquainted with the literature of behavioural economics.) By contrast, a 'paper-shuffling' movement trader is not tied to her holdings of financial assets on the basis of years of accumulated knowhow and she can sell her holdings far more easily than an entrepreneur can dispose of fixed capital: so long as she has not made her entire financial future contingent on a fall in the price of her assets not occurring, she can readily accept the rumour that a crash is about to happen and hence may be expected to sell out rapidly.

In so far as actions are matched to the shapes of expectations, we should expect that those who think in terms of ranges of possibilities will be able to carry on down their existing pathways in the face of changes in their environments, for they will have built slack into their plans at the physical and financial levels. Hicks (1980a, p. 85) used this idea as a way of defending the use of equilibrium notions in economics, and on some occasions it might not be at all Procrustean of neoclassical economists to follow his lead. However, until the scenarios philosophy becomes widely used by decision-makers, many choices are likely to be made without due attention being paid to the 'principle of linkage of risks' so there is a case for believing Weintraub (1982, p. 452) was right to stress that

Unfortunately, small errors can have major consequences, whether "a miss is a good as a mile" or "for the want of a nail" all was lost. A little inaccuracy can in many contexts make a prodigious difference, as any golfer watching a put slide by the hole would attest. A pianist who strikes adjacent keys can assault the ears. Corporate profits often depend on narrow margins and right guesses on sales volume.

Even in the absence of pessimistic attitudes and fragile plans, cognitive factors may still play an important role in determining whether or not an expansion is sustainable. It may be brought to a halt by three kinds of cognitive bottlenecks. Hicks' (1974) himself made much of the possibility that shortages of particular kinds of skilled workers may hold up investment programmes. The obvious policy remedy to counter this bottleneck is for the government to invest in job training programmes in shortage areas. An early reflationary response to an economic downturn will also help to ensure that firms do not cut back on their worker training programmes and unemployment does not lead to an erosion in the motivation and capabilities of workers. Governments should also be careful not to enhance bottlenecks by competing for the scarce workers. In the case of the US, it is difficult to believe that private sector high technology activity is not being crowded out by the enermous scale of expenditur? on military activities such as the Strategic Defense Initiative: half of research and development activity in the US is tied up in the area of defence. An improvement in the US balance of trade position may therefore have a reduction in military spending as one of its prerequisites.

Policies which help remove this kind of bottleneck may have beneficial effects on the rate of inflation in so far as competition for such workers would otherwise lead to a rise in their relative wages and cause other groups to push for higher pay increase to restore their relative positions. However, in economies in which concerns about relativities have a high priority in wage bargaining processes, governments might do well to try to implement the incomes policy proposals of Wood (1978), who argues, in essence, that wage bargains throughout the economy should be settled in relative terms before agreement is reached on the average rate of increase in money wages.

A second cognitive barrier to continuous macroeconomic expansion is a kind of mental indigestion: growth in the recent past often needs to be consolidated before another burst of new activity seems worthwhile. If one reads the business history literature it is quite common to see a firm's growth path reach the kind of temporary plateau discussed by Penrose (1959) and Chandler (1962). This is often associated with the recognition that the firm's activities, and its costs, are getting somewhat out of control because the organisational structure has not been changed in line with the change in the scale of the firm's activities. Households, likewise, may feel the need to restore their composure after a spell of rapid change (see Toffler, 1970). This barrier will be most pronounced if there has been a general tendency towards rapid expansion. It will be less important if the failure of one group to use its discretionary purchasing power is offset by the reappearance of another group that has, so to speak, got its breath back, and is keen to start investing in new activities — particularly if members of the former group do not merely let their surplus financial resources lie idle in bank deposits against which loans have already been made.

The third cognitive bottleneck is rather bound up with the second: booms may slacken off due to the temporary failure of decision-makers to decide in which direction to expand next. Such a creativity block was discussed by Shackle (1938, p. 101) for the case of firms which find themselves lost in new and strange circumstances, but we can think of it in even broader terms, to include both failures of problem- solving skills on technical developments, and the ending of corporate research programmes which have been so successful that no further potential innovations remain to be pursued.

Bounded rationality can also give an economic system a good deal of supply-side elasticity. To some extent this comes from the partial conquering of cognitive limitations. For example, learning effects of both Penrosian (improved management teamwork) and learning-by-doing ('practice makes perfect') kinds can augment the effective capacity of a given set of physical resources. Here we could also include the discovery of 'X-inefficiency' (see Leibenstein, 1976) during problem-solving activities, and technical progress in a much broader sense. This source of plasticity of costs arises somewhat paradoxically from a lack of cognitive slack: problem-solving innovations would not occur if people simply lowered their sights when they failed to meet their aspirations, and one can only say that something is wrong if one has spelt out rather precisely what one intends to regard as a satisfactory outcome (see Williams and Scott, 1965). Among the obvious incentives to search for methods of reducing input requirements are rising input costs and an appreciating exchange rate which increases the pressure of overseas competition. Depending on their scale, cognitive victories may enable firms to suffer defeats at the wage bargaining table without needing to raise their prices.

Ignorance is central to the concept of organisational slack proposed by Cyert and March (1963) (see also section 8.5). As the attainments of a firm improve, the aspirations of members of the corporate coalition are likely to follow them with something of a lag. If workers and shareholders fail to realise that they could extract more from the management team and do not immediately demand higher pay/benefits and dividends, then management may be able to put more funds aside for further investment in capacity. It may also be the case that managers in good times unwittingly let other parties have a better deal than the minimum they would accept before leaving the coalition: shareholders may be prepared to accept smaller dividends, consumers may accept higher prices and workers may accept a worsening of their pay and conditions. If so, then a firm which faces a tighter environment and cannot innovate itself out of trouble may nonetheless survive, rather than becoming the origin of a destabilising set of financial disappointments and the dissipation of a boom. (However, we should be careful to note that if there is already a general problem of deficient aggregate demand, an individual firm which takes up slack in this way may simply make things tighter for other firms — see sections 11.3 and 11.4.)

Finally, it might be said that bounded rationality plays a key role in the Friedman (1968) and Phelps (1970) analysis of unemployment, in which an expansion of aggregate demand can temporarily lead to an increase in output and employment. Changes in relative prices act as a kind of noise in amongst signals that imply an increase in the general price level and for a time may lead people to make more factor services available than they would if properly informed.

13.4 Financial Factors

Financial linkages between system elements are the driving force of Keynesian income multiplier processes: no individual decision-maker can reshuffle her portfolio without affecting the portfolio of someone else, for each item bought is an item sold by someone else, and each item not bought forces an increase in an inventory held by someone else. Since it is common for people to lose their jobs outright rather than to be put on short-time working when demand falls, one might want to call the idea of a fractional downside marginal propensity to consume into question. But the fractional marginal propensity to consume plays a vital shock-absorbing role: if the marginal propensity to consume had a value of unity, we would be in a nightmare world in which income levels explode (implode) without limit in the event of a slight increase (decrease) in investment spending (see Leijonhufvud, 1973, for an example of such thinking). Fortunately, three forms of financial buffering to a greater or lesser extent normally enable those who have lost their incomes to carry on spending. These buffers are: dole payments from the government; assistance via extended family networks (with employed relatives cutting back on their savings in order to provide assistance); and prior accumulations of liquid assets, including unused borrowing entitlements.

So long as such buffers exist and people are not afraid to make use of them, the multiplier effects of a reduction in expenditure somewhere in the economy may be very restricted: as Leijonhufvud (1969, pp. 42-4) observes, 'The multiplier is an illiquidity phenomenon', and an economic system becomes prone to great disasters 'only when it has first been squeezed dry of liquidity'. From Leijonhufvud's perspective, Friedman's permanent income hypothesis is a key element in the monetarist critique of Keynesian thinking: if a consumer chooses her rate of consumption expenditure on the basis of a long-run view of her wealth position, she just adjusts her liquidity position when her income falls. Although Friedman's view of the multiplier seems quite plausible for people who are used to having erratic employment, it looks less likely to apply where people have no expectation that they might find themselves deprived of their income flows. In the latter case, unemployment would be a major shock and one might expect them to be puzzled about its likely duration and/or to be short of substantial reserves of 'money for a rainy day'. They would be likely to find it hard to liquidate their human capital by borrowing against their future income and would normally prefer to cut back on their expenditure rather than raise cash by hurriedly selling their physical assets at whatever price these would realise.

Debates about the importance of financial crowding out can also be cast very easily in terms of the bottlenecks/slack perspective: Keynes himself seemed to have precisely this imagery in mind when he commented that 'The investment market can become congested due to a shortage of cash' (1937a, p. 669). The inert areas concept might also be applied, instead of conventional elasticity notions, in respect of debates about the power of monetary policy to engender expansions: just as 'you can lead a horse to water but you can't make it drink' and 'you can't push with a string', so the reserve bank may be able to expand the monetary base without succeeding in making other decision-makers overcome their liquidity preference. This is particularly likely if would-be lenders are using a rule of thumb approach to credit allocation, based on prudential ratios, and would-be borrowers who have approached their maximum ratio are refused further credit rather than being asked to pay a risk premium for further borrowing (or if would-be borrowers themselves are making their decisions about whether or not to apply for a loan on the basis of similar rules of thumb). On the other hand, from the standpoint of the portfolio theory of the growth of monetary aggregates, unlike that of the multiplier model explicitly or implicitly employed in monetarist analysis, the reserve bank may find its attempts to rein expenditure in are thwarted by an expansion of lending by NBFIs; by intermediaries disposing of excess reserve assets; by increases in financial disintermediation; and by accumulations from the past that permit self-financing of activities.

Finally, we should note that expanding economies may run into a foreign exchange bottleneck as imports are sucked in before increases in investment activity bear fruit in the form of higher net exports. This may send speculators into a panic or lead to onerous borrowing terms being required by overseas lenders. Countries whose expansions are held back by the unwillingness of other nations to respend or lend out their export earnings can seek to overcome this bottleneck with the aid of structurally-oriented macroeconomic policies if bodies such as the IMF are reluctant to increase international liquidity. Investment in import substitution schemes, for example, could be used to release foreign exchange to pay for goods that could not so easily be produced at home but which were needed in greater quantities as output increased. (Note: I am not suggesting that import substitution policies are devices to reduce total imports and export unemployment elsewhere; they are devices to shift the propensity to import.) In the absence of such policies and of adequate means for supporting the exchange rate, such an expansion is likely to grind to a halt unless workers are prepared to live with cuts in living standards brought about by a drop in the exchange rate.

13.5 Physical Factors

In trying to deal with unacceptable levels of unemployment with the aid of expansionary fiscal and monetary policies, governments have often overlooked the fact that an income multiplier process cannot begin to work unless there are stocks of machines and raw materials, as well as spare workers (Hicks, 1974). It is all too easy to assume that macroeconomic expansions and contractions are symmetrical: a downturn in demand may result in some equipment being run more slowly than usual, or for fewer hours each week, with older machinery being 'mothballed' pending a recovery in orders; such slack can be used up when demand expands. However, the longer a recession is allowed to persist, the more likely it is that a recovery will run into physical bottlenecks, owing to firms having scrapped their older machines and cut back as far as possible on their working capital. Stagnant demand conditions may also do little to encourage minerals exploration and investment in plantations. To the extent that firms are individually failing to create capacity because they fear that they will collectively create excessive capacity, governments would do well to consider taking a more lenient line with respect to horizontal corporate mergers and information agreements between firms (see Richardson, 1960). Whatever its origins, a shortage of physical capacity at the time of an expansion of demand is likely to exacerbate any shortage of foreign exchange reserves.

The increasing popularity of the Japanese 'just in time' manufacturing philosophy in place of the Anglo-Saxon 'just in case' method of deciding upon inventory levels must also be noted under this heading. An entire production system may be disrupted if an upstream supplier fails to deliver due to, say, a strike or a major breakdown, or a downstream customer suddenly cannot use normal volumes of inputs and refuses to accumulate stocks. In Japan, the desire to avoid industrial confrontations and the willingness to sit round a table to sort problems out before they get out of hand has provided a kind of mental slack which has helped firms to operate with only a few hours' worth of stocks. The viability of such a system in Australia, the UK or the US is more questionable, given the greater tendency towards confrontation and, particularly in the US, the tendency to use litigation as a substitute for the cooperative renegotiation of problematic contracts (see Morita, 1987).

It would, of course, be unwise to assert that an economy does not typically operate with at least some spare physical capacity; indeed, in section 4.2 it was argued that many firms plan to operate with some spare capacity so that they can satisfy new customers without losing goodwill by letting its established customers down. Firms may also be able to increase the potential output of a given set of inputs by doing things in groups in so far as this enables them to avoid duplication of indivisible items of capital or information, or to enjoy beneficial spill-overs between system components — in other words, they may achieve 'synergy' (see sections 4.5 and 8.6).

13.6 Conclusion

The evolutionary pathway carved out by a complex economic system results from the interaction of diverse and often opposing pressures and tensions, whose influences are shaped by the underlying structure of the system. Practising macroeconomists should therefore focus their attention less on aggregates and more on structural indicators that suggest how taut or fragile parts of the economic system are becoming and whether it or not it needs re-engineering to prevent it from becoming stuck in a low-performance channel or running along a high-performance one that is unsustainable. In doing so, they should recognise that any attempt to introduce slack into models of economic systems naturally tends to bring indeterminacy, for it involves replacing binding constraints with discretionary ones. It may well be possible to quantify many sources of slack and see them being used up, but some are inherently subjective and leave one only able to work with broad guesses about how fragile the system is becoming. However, from the scenario planning standpoint, there is nothing particularly laudable about being precise in one's predictions but wrong by a wide margin.

Work on the decomposability of modern economic systems may prove more appealing to those who do not take easily to the subjectivist philosophy. Over fifteen years ago, before Minsky's work on financial instability was widely known, Roe (1973) recognised the potential for disaggregated analyses of flows of funds to reveal newly emerging financial structures and deteriorating sectoral balance sheets. More recently, behavioural economists such as Kay (1982) have recognised that the vulnerability of large corporations to shocks can be assessed by exploring the extent to which their portfolios of activities make heavy use of linkages between markets, production methods and technologies: company reports make it easy even for undergraduates to draw rough and ready but nonetheless revealing 'synergy maps' of corporate diversification patterns. In the future, as computer databases of market census information become more highly developed, the decomposability of macroeconomic systems is going to be increasingly easy to investigate with a view to discovering whether their structures tend to make shocks dissipate or multiply.

The ideas canvassed in this chapter seem to point to a more insightful way of contrasting monetarist and Keynesian views than that found in conventional textbook treatments which discuss their differences in terms of diametrically opposed views on the relative slopes of *IS* and *LM* curves. Instead, we may contrast these perspectives in terms of their assumptions about the presence and distribution of slack in economic systems, though as we do so we should not forget that they also differ in their core beliefs about the efficacy of market mechanisms to deliver signals that facilitate coordination. The monetarist vision of the system sees both the financial and 'real' sectors in mechanistic terms, in effect as if they are fully employed, by appealing to the money multiplier view of the money supply and a Walrasian analysis of the labour market. But it is is by no means a completely taut system, for it is one in which there is a good deal of resilience in expectations because people take a long-run view of their prospects and make their plans on the expectation that in some periods they will fare unusually well whilst in others things may go rather badly. By contrast, the Keynesian view centres on the slack in the financial system implied by the portfolio analysis of the money supply, and on the slack associated with the presence of involuntary unemployment, where real returns stay above workers' transfer earnings. But it portrays expectations as exceedingly fragile constructs and consumption as highly constrained by current wealth positions.

Proponents on either side should follow Minsky and recognise that whether or not the system actually approximates to their vision may depend very much upon its recent history. A period of turbulence is likely to encourage decision-makers to build slack into their expectations and portfolios; this will enable the system to cope more easily with surprises and hence will promote its orderly evolution. But since slack has costs as well as benefits, a period of steady progress is likely to lead decision-makers to organise their activities with less slack: for example, personal consumption will become more a function of current income, because current incomes will be seen as permanent. In doing so, they will be increasing the fragility of the system. Neoclassical economists might want to argue that this tightening up of the system would not happen, because people will learn from experience. Behavioural economics suggests otherwise: bounded rationality makes it difficult for decision-makers to keep in mind both immediate events and the broader sweep of history.

14 Monetary Policy in a Deregulated Environment

14.1 Introduction

The task of constructing monetary policy in the 1990s is complicated by the remarkable changes that took place in the previous two decades both in technology and in the rules of the game in financial systems around the world. Advances in communications systems, in conjunction with the easing of foreign exchange controls, helped to foster the integration of financial markets on a global basis. These innovations reduced the costs of monitoring yield opportunities and switching between assets, and in doing so opened up scope for greater market volatility: huge volumes of funds could now switch between economies in response to tiny changes in relative yields. Having found that financial innovators were almost invariably able to circumvent rules aimed at limiting the growth of expenditure, the monetary authorities in many nations began to conclude that the main result of their policies had been the distortion of incentives. To improve efficiency, therefore, they set about abandoning controls over interest rates, deposit terms, quantitative limits on lending growth, entry into particular market segments, restrictions on portfolio compositions and so on, and they sought instead to ensure that vigorous competition prevailed: for example, where foreign bank entry had once been discouraged it was now seen as a means of undermining tendencies of local banks to engage in collusive behaviour (see Llewellyn, 1985, Coggan, 1986, Hamilton, 1986, Mohl, 1988).

It should be evident from earlier chapters that a Post Keynesian approach to monetary economics does not lead one to enthuse about the kind of financial system that has emerged. There has been a dramatic increase in the number of speculative contracts, and consequently in the scope for the system to behave in an unstable manner when financial gamblers make catastrophic errors of judgement. A wave of mergers in the financial services industry has concentrated operations in the hands of fewer firms, producing conglomerates that in some cases may be more able to threaten the public interest by acting in an opportunistic manner, and that in other cases may have achieved diversity at the cost of increased vulnerability due to top management not appreciating the demands of their new lines of business. Exchange rate instability has made enterprise calculation increasingly difficult. Real interest rates have soared to previously unheard of levels. Dramatic increases in real estate prices have divided the populations of some countries into those who enjoy the freedom that results from their having bought property in time to realise substantial capital gains in areas where housing costs exploded, and those who find themselves condemned to remain in rented accommodation or confined to owning homes in peripheral regions. And of course, in the midst of all this, there was the Crash of 1987.

It should therefore come as no surprise that some of the policies preferred by Post Keynesian monetary economists go strongly against the grain of recent thinking. These include:

(1)   the adoption of techniques of indicative planning akin to those favoured in France, which involve subjecting financial intermediaries to quantitative guidelines to force them to direct their lending towards investment expenditure and away from speculative activities and the financing of luxury imports (cf. Eatwell, 1982, pp. 77-8);

(2)   a return to a system of managed exchange rates and foreign exchange controls, to make investment decisions easier to take and to reduce the risk that foreign currency speculation may lead to financial failures;

(3)   the use of high rates of capital gains taxation and transactions taxes (such as stamp duties) to discourage financial speculation in general;

(4)   a much more careful assessment of the social implications of mergers between financial institutions.

In the prevailing climate, however, it is difficult to envisage a major retreat from the philosophy of leaving matters of finance to the free workings of market forces. The most that governments now seem willing to impose are prudential controls on financial intermediaries, along with other regulations to protect people who lend their out money and who might fall prey to opportunistic and incompetent financial advisors and fund managers or who might otherwise fall victim to misleading portrayals of the costs of borrowing.

Such considerations suggest that it is appropriate to focus the attention of this chapter on two main policy questions:

(1) What, if anything, can the monetary authorities achieve with the limited tools that remain at their disposal?

(2) Can one conceive of novel regulatory policies that would seek to make greater use of financial markets in the attempts to restrain growth in aggregate expenditure and which therefore might have some chance of appealing to the financial community?

14.2 The Transmission Mechanisms of Monetary Policy

Monetary policy aims to change expenditure (and, in an open economy, to affect capital inflows from the rest of the world) by bringing about substitutions between assets in decision-makers' portfolios. In the past, quantitative controls over lending were often used to bring about changes in behaviour. For example, attempts at demand management in the UK in the 1950s made extensive use of regulations concerning the minimum percentage deposit and maximium repayment periods permissible in hire purchase deals (see Dow, 1964, pp. 253, 275-82). Big impacts upon consumer spending could be produced without it being necessary to make major changes in interest rates. In a modern deregulated environment, the monetary authorities have to rely upon substitutions induced by changes in the cost of finance and returns to holding financial assets. Open market operations and/or changes in the price of last resort funds from the reserve bank become the key method of influencing spending without changing fiscal policy.

If most participants in the market believe neither that interest rates ought to be changing nor that the authorities are seriously intent on changing them, then it is conceivable that the reserve bank will find it very difficult to bring about such a change as an inducement for people to substitute between physical and financial assets. In such a situation rises in bond prices are expected to be reversed, producing capital losses for bond holders, and vice versa. A small rise in bond prices offered by the reserve bank in an attempt to lower rates of interest may therefore result in a mass exodus from bonds into close substitutes, thereby making the bond price increase difficult to sustain. In the reverse situation, offers of bonds at slightly reduced prices may be met with much eagerness to buy on the part of the private sector, making an interest rate increase difficult to engender. With such a willingness to make substitutions between financial assets, any contraction in the monetary base and in bank lending would swiftly be overcome by growth in the balance sheets of NBFIs and in the volume of securitised lending. The public would, overall, simply be exchanging loans of one kind to the government (monetary base claims on the Reserve Bank) for another (government bonds), while changing the channels through which they lend to private sector borrowers.

Fortunately, such situations seem unlikely to be common. Uncertainty about the economic environment means that expectations are very flimsy constructs (Keynes, 1937b), and since portfolios are held on the expectations of changes in assets price stability itself can be a cause of nervous reappraisals. Hence the authorities are in a strong position to lead opinion — at least, so long as they stay within a range that the market regards as reasonable. As Dow (1987, p. 23) observes,

Lacking a clear objective basis for forming an opinion, the market is eager to clutch at pointers; and the actions of the authorities, or their apparent intentions, provide one of the few clear pointers to catch at. This does not mean that the authorities' power is unlimited. They have a similar power to influence exchange rates; and, as with exchange rates, their power depends entirely on carrying the market with them. Were they to seek to push market rates to a level too high, or too low, to be sustainable, their power would evaporate — as Dr Dalton found.

(Dow's reference to Dalton is noteworthy, for as Chancellor of the Exchequer in the 1945 Labour Government in the UK, Dalton was an early practical exponent of Keynes' view that interest rates are a psychological phenomenon and can be changed without changing monetary aggregates so long as the authorities engage in appropriate forms of psychological warfare. But he could not persuade the British public to buy his undated 2.5 per cent stock, despite his best attempts at 'conditioning' the market to accept the idea of cheap money: see Dow, 1964, pp. 225-7.)

Success in moving interest rates is, however, no guarantee of success in changing the pace of expenditure. At this juncture the arguments in sections 3.7 and 4.6 should be recalled, for they led to the conclusion that changes in interest rates are likely to have significant effects on expenditure only if particular circumstances prevail and if the authorities indicate that the interest rates they are generating are going to last for a considerable period. It was also stressed that the effects of interest rate increases may be confined mainly to areas, such as markets for exports and import substitutes, where one would prefer not to see a reduction in activity.

It is doubtful that modest interest rate changes induced by the reserve bank will be very effective in restraining expenditure unless the authorities make a careful attempt to affect the psychology of the markets. If a mood of pessimism is gripping the economy, there is no guarantee that the reserve bank will find success if it attempts to push up expenditure by making open market purchases of bonds. This is not to deny that such measures may increase the deposits of banks at the reserve bank, leaving them in a position to lend more. Nor is it to deny that the reduction in bond yields brought about by the reserve bank's activities may impose a general downward pressure on loan and deposit rates. However, if confidence is depressed, banks may have trouble drumming up additional business from those who have good credit ratings unless they poach such borrowers from NBFIs or the market for commercial paper. If NBFIs cannot find alternative customers who can meet their own credit rating criteria, they will be driven to dispose of excess funds by lowering their deposit rates further relative to those offered by banks. There will be a switch of deposits out of their accounts with the banks, to the bank accounts of their former depositors: interest rates may fall and $M0$ and $M3$ may rise, but $M6$ may be stagnant, and so too the rate of expenditure. These effects could all be reversed for the case of an attempt to reduce expenditure via moderate increases in interest rates when feelings of confidence are strong.

Difficulties in getting much of an impact from small changes in the rate of interest should not be taken to imply that the answer is to apply bigger doses rather than to contrive ways of changing attitudes. A major increase in interest rates could cause a big fall in asset values and a fierce speculative collapse instead of an intended moderate reduction in the growth of expenditure. Thresholds that separate 'small' and 'large' shifts in interest rates may be difficult to identify experimentally and may, in any case, be far from stable themselves.

Summing up, we can say that breaks in the chain of substitution between different kinds of assets can both help and hinder the attempts of reserve banks to influence the pace of expenditure: a great willingness to substitute between financial assets makes it hard to influence the growth of total lending, whereas it is difficult to affect spending if people are unwilling to substitute between financial and physical assets. These breaks will be promoted by the use of decision rules that clash with the principle of substitution (see sections 3.4 and 3.5) and by anything that threatens asset liquidity (see sections 2.3 to 2.5). The Post Keynesian emphasis on confidence as something which stands between the cost of finance and shifts into or out of physical assets may ultimately be reduced to a concern with the transaction costs and/or capital losses that may be entailed in attempts to switch back from physical goods into money. It should also be noted that suppliers and demanders of finance may also experience transactions costs in switching between accounts or refunding loans, while many financial contracts are for fixed terms and not readily marketable. Financial intermediaries have preferred clienteles in whom they can trust, and trust is not built up overnight, while customer attitudes may also make for a reluctance to change market habitats as interest rates change or queues for loans emerge. This may limit the speed with which growth in NBFI balance sheets and a switch to securitised lending may be expected to offset reductions in the rate of growth of bank lending.

Breaks in the chain of substitution depend on monetary policies that have been adopted in previous periods, for these will influence expectations about liquidity. For example, if the authorities have conventionally kept interest rate movements within a narrow margin, risks of capital losses on long-dated government bonds may be seen by the market as minimal. Such bonds are therefore more likely to be treated as very close substitutes for bank deposits and it will be easy to conduct open market operations or to float government debt without producing sharp changes in the rate of interest. But if such an interest rate 'norm' does not exist, open market operations may result in volatile shifts in interest rates instead, with significant wealth effects on expenditure.

14.3 Monetary Targets

The freeing up of competitive processes in financial systems in the late 1970s and early 1980s coincided with the heyday of monetarism, and a shift away from a focus on interest rate policy. Monetary policy became concerned with ensuring that the growth rates of particular monetary aggregates did not exceed the targets that had been set for them. The wisdom of building monetary policy around targets for the growth of such aggregates is something that our earlier discussions of portfolio choice would lead us to question, for decisions to borrow and lend are made on the basis of expected relative yields. But rates of growth of monetary aggregates can be relevant to portfolio choices in so far as they affect these yields. For example, decision-makers might believe that changes in monetary growth can affect the rate of inflation and thereby produce changes in nominal interest rates. To affect portfolio choices and hence the rate of interest and the volume of expenditure, such a belief need not be empirically well founded, merely widely held.

To explain how mainstream thinkers tried to justify the setting of monetary targets, we need to examine the relationship $MV = PT$, in which M is the monetary aggregate under consideration, P is the average price per transaction, T is the number of transactions, and V is the 'velocity of circulation' for that particular monetary aggregate. Usually one is referring to an income velocity of circulation, where PT means the value of nominal final expenditure on new goods and services in the period in question. Exchanges of existing assets and trade between firms in terms of semi-finished products are neglected. If a firm takes over its input suppliers and produces and sells exactly as before, PT may not change and neither will V. Yet there may actually be a decline in the number of market transactions involving money, since no money now changes hands when inputs are delivered; there is merely a book-keeping record inside the firm.

The equality between MV and PT must always hold by definition, but monetarists preferred to see the relationship as an equation, to be read from left to right. They also asserted that empirical studies had shown the velocity of circulation to be stable, implying a stable relationship between money income flows and the desire to hold a stock of money as an asset. Faith in the stability of the demand for money led them to the recommendation that the authorities should seek to expand the money supply at a steady rate in line with the steady growth in the transactions demand for money that occurs as economic growth increases income and wealth; attempts to fine-tune the economy by changing the quantity of money or by fiscal policy are unnecessary. Friedman (1968) argued that, if the authorities react to a rise in unemployment by promoting a faster rate of monetary growth they will prevent the economy from returning automatically to equilibrium at the nominal income level implied by the original MV configuration. With V assumed constant except in the very short run, an increase in M requires that P and/or T must rise to restore the stock/flow equilibrium. If T is constrained by an absence of slack on the supply side, then an equilibrium can only be achieved through a rise in the price level.

But there are other ways of looking at the causal underpinnings of the $MV = PT$ identity and at studies which appear to imply a stable velocity of circulation. Because they are not locked into the outdated imagery which appears to make monetarists think of 'money' basically as if it is currency (cf. Bootle, 1984), Post Keynesians use their analysis of the money supply process to suggest that it makes better sense to see causation in the reverse way: growth in expenditure determines growth in monetary aggregates. On this view, attempts to fix the growth of the money supply may result in instability in the velocity of circulation. Such stability as is observed may simply reflect the willingness of the reserve bank to set its roost-ruling rate of interest and lend as much as is required by the financial system at this rate. With rates of interest thereby pinned down, the financial system creates as much finance as is required by those who wish to borrow and who match up with the selection criteria employed by lenders.

In deciding how the quantity equation should be interpreted, monetarists appeared to pay little attention to the details of how the working of modern financial systems might affect the relationship between monetary growth and nominal income. Nor did they take seriously the possibility that shifts in velocity might arise as a result of changes in confidence or financial innovations and changes in banking regulations. All too often, injections of money were treated simply as if they were forced upon the economy by the reserve bank dropping banknotes from a helicopter, and then spent by a public that demanded bank deposits only for transactions purposes and was unwilling to accumulate them as a store of wealth.

The basis of the justification for viewing monetary expansions as the cause of expenditure rather than as caused by decisions to spend was the assertion that rises in expenditure follow growth in monetary aggregates with a lag of around two years. The reasons for the alleged lag were not spelt out in detail. Certainly, bank deposits might rise as companies unloaded bonds on to the market to pay for increases in their investment spending, because the reserve bank might step in as a buyer to prevent these bond sales from pushing up interest rates. But it would make little sense for such firms to ready themselves financially a long while before undertaking their spending. Such considerations would make it difficult to explain the existence of a two year lag except by seeing monetary growth as a consequnce of a fiscal expansion that had not been financed purely by sales of bonds. In fact, as Kaldor (1980, 1982) has shown, links between public sector borrowing and monetary growth are unreliable and the existence of the two year lag is either a myth or (in the much discussed case of the UK between 1971 and 1978) a temporary statistical quirk caused by changes in banking rules.

Instead of looking at the facts in the carefully critical manner of Kaldor, monetarists were much more inclined to devote their attention to debates about which would be the most appropriate aggregate to target. For example, monetary base control was favour by Friedman, who attempted to argue his case before the House of Commons Treasury and Civil Service Committee with the aid of an analogy (Friedman, 1980, p 58). He likened the role of the monetary base in determining aggregate expenditure to the role of steel as an input in the production of cars. Restrictions in the supply of steel would make things very difficult for car manufacturers, and Friedman, arguing from the standpoint of the money multiplier theory, asserted that base money is a similarly crucial input in the production of loans by banks.

This was really a surprising kind of argument to come from such a famous proponent of the adaptability of private enterprise to changes in market conditions. Normally, one would have expected Friedman to highlight the power of substitution rather than treating production as involving fixed coefficients. Hence, attempts to control car production by restricting the supply of steel would be expected soon to lead to product innovations — such as greater use of plastic, glass and ceramic components — and changes in the mix of products in the direction of compact cars. Limited output of steel would not be an insurmountable barrier to car production so long as there was a willingness of car buyers to pay a bit more for rather different cars and so long as car producers had some design flexibility. The steel shortage in the domestic market might also be overcome via a resort to steel imports.

Elementary price theory also leads one to recognise that the smaller the fraction of the total price of a commodity accounted for by a particular input, the larger must be the increase in the input's price to deter firms from trying to use it. In the case of the production of bank deposits in the UK at the time Friedman was making his case, less than five pence was required as a cash reserve against each pound of deposits. Hence, the cost of obtaining reserve assets would have to rise very sharply indeed to raise the average cost of banking to a significant degree: as Miller (1981, pp. 74-5) pointed out, 'If only 1/20th of a £ deposit goes into cash, then a rise in interest rates of 10 percentage points would be necessary to widen the spread between deposit rates and loan rates by half a point!' To impose very high cash reserve requirements on banks would make it easier to meet a monetary base target without pushing up interest rates, but this would make it more difficult for domestic banks to compete on even terms with NBFIs and foreign banks; it would therefore run counter to the philosophy of deregulation.

The error involved in using the steel/cars analogy is compounded by the fact that the business of banking is far more adaptable than the manufacturing industry when faced with input shortages or regulations about what it can produce. It is not tied to highly specific items of capital equipment and has a history of being able to keep several steps ahead of the authorities' attempts to control its rate of output (cf. sections 9.7 and 9.8 and Podolski, 1986). Anyone who wishes to discuss policies of monetary control with the aid of an analogy might do better to follow Dow (1964, p. 328) and liken them to attempts to conduct a war by bombing major traffic intersections: for a time there will certainly be disruption, but pretty soon the traffic will discover other routes to its preferred destinations.

During the 1980s many reserve bankers preferred to concentrate on targeting broader aggregates than base money: for example, the US moved on to *M1* after abandoning its policy of monetary base control in 1982, while *M3* was the main focus in Australia and the UK. By 1987, each of these countries had adandoned monetary targeting. It had proved difficult to meet targets most of the time, given that the authorities usually were reluctant to allow interest rates to rise without limit. Moreover, there had been a growing recognition that even when open market operations and increases in the price of reserve bank loans were used ruthlessly enough to ensure that the targets were met, control over expenditure could be thwarted by changes in the behaviour of money supply velocities.

For example, the wisdom of trying to hold *M3* growth down to a particular rate looked questionable when deregulation was leading banks to bid more aggressively for loans that might have been either securitised or provided by NBFIs, for *M3* growth could largely reflect a change in the banks' share of deposits, rather than growth in overall lending. It made still less sense when mergers between banks and building societies were taking place, for these produced overnight leaps in the size of *M3*. Such events would hardly be expected to change the scale of expenditure, even if they caused the *M3* total to depart from its target range; no wonder, then, that falls in the velocity of circulation of *M3* were being observed.

Nor could a reserve bank really feel much of a sense of achievement if it succeeded in keeping deposit growth under control but failed to control lending because banks and NBFIs used their freedom to borrow foreign currencies or offshore sources of domestic currency as a means of funding a greater volume of loans. In Australia, for example, the attempts of the Reserve Bank to use monetary targeting to prevent excessive growth in imports were partly overturned because 'in the space of a year, banks moved from a position of balance in their foreign currency liabilities and assets to a position of net foreign currency liabilities of around $A4000 million', while 'from June 1984 to May 1987, non-banks' borrowings from non-residents rose from $A2.0 billion to $A11.8 billion; merchant banks accounted for over three-quarters of this growth and finance companies most of the remainder' (Mohl, 1988, p. 54). In these circumstances, the Reserve Bank decided that it might be better to abandon monetary targets in favour of a more complex 'checklist' of indicators.

14.4 Effects of Interest Rate Deregulation

Among the controls that were jettisoned in some countries in the course of financial deregulation were ceilings on the interest rates that financial intermediaries could pay their depositors or charge their borrowers. These might have included the stipulation that interest could not be paid on current account balances, or upper limits that had been set on mortgages. The motivation behind this aspect of deregulation had been to promote efficiency by allowing greater competition in money markets. For example, banks would be able to compete directly with each other and with NBFIs through their interest rates rather than by offering a higher implicit return in the form of 'free services'. If this led to the demise of smaller NBFIs, then the community might benefit from lower costs of financial services as greater economies of scale were achieved, and through the beneficial effects of the freeing up of prime real estate sites formerly occupied by those NBFIs which failed to compete successfully.

The importance of interest rate deregulation varied enormously: in the UK, for example, it was not an issue, but in Australia many such controls were removed and some local economists argued that this was actually the most important aspect of deregulation (see Davis and Lewis, 1983; Swan, 1983). For Davis and Lewis, the key issue was that the efficiency advantages appeared likely to entail a significant cost: the new environment was going to be a place in which interest rates would on average be higher and much more volatile than before.

The kind of scenario that Davis and Lewis had in mind is very similar to one considered in the UK by Cramp (1962, 1971), long before policymakers had become preoccupied with monetary targets. If financial intermediaries are free to choose their interest rates they may be able to counteract attempts of the reserve bank to use open market sales of bonds to restrict the growth of lending and deposits. As higher yields attract people to buy government debt that the reserve bank is selling, banks will find themselves losing deposits and may retaliate by offering higher deposit rates. In so far as their liabilities are seen as close substitutes for increasingly lucrative bank deposits or government bonds, NBFIs may be expected to raise their rates to avoid a drain of deposits. The same may be expected of local authorities and corporate borrowers in the market for commercial paper. The reserve bank will then have to offer an even higher yield on the stock that it is selling, but in doing so it may provoke further retaliation.

Interest rates will continue to spiral upwards until either the authorities give up trying to limit monetary growth or banks and NBFIs find that their borrowers are no longer prepared to pay the rates they were asking, or public sector borrowers decide to reduce their expenditure levels. Before this happens, the demand for finance might actually increase despite the rising interest rates, owing to companies needing to borrow more to carry on with investment plans (or finance stock holding) because a greater part of their cash flows are going on interest payments. Something along these lines seemed to be happening during attempts at monetary targeting in the UK in the early 1980s, and in this case the need of firms for funds was increased by an upward pressure on the exchange rate caused by capital inflows which made life difficult for domestic producers of internationally tradeable commodities.

Much the same kind of scenario applies if banks are obliged to meet significant reserve asset ratios and the reserve bank raises its discount rate in an attempt to deter banks from borrowing from it to pay for additional reserve assets. Banks may then seek to attract deposits instead of making use of expensive reserve bank funds.

However, higher deposit rates at banks cannot actually increase the banks' balances at the reserve bank unless people can economise on cash or capital inflows arrive from overseas and the reserve bank accumulates foreign currency reserves rather than letting the exchange rate rise. In the absence of these two conditions, the only way that members of the domestic non-bank private sector can increase their bank deposits is by disposing of their holdings of financial assets. Collectively they cannot succeed in doing this. If they sell them to the banks, displacing new loans to the private sector, the rise in deposit rates will actually increase the number of would-be private sector borrowers in the queue for loans.

In both cases the spiralling problem arises because portfolio choices depend on relative rather than absolute returns to holding assets of various kinds. If deposit rate ceilings exist, banks cannot retaliate against a loss of deposits by raising interest rates, and hence they do not provoke retaliation from NBFIs or from those who are trying to sell new securities. An interest rate ceiling on bank deposit rates provides an anchor for the price of finance in the system as a whole, since the loan rates that banks can charge are limited by the prices of loans from other sources, whether from the market for commercial paper or from NBFIs, which are in turn limited by the interest rates that sellers of securities and NBFIs have to pay to attract depositors away from banks. Interest rate ceilings thus permit the reserve bank to engage in open market sales of bonds and contain the growth of the monetary base without pushing up interest rates in general to a significant degree. But, of course, success in containing the growth of the monetary base or bank deposits is no guarantee of success in containing the growth of nominal expenditure.

When the control of bank deposit rates is abandoned the risk of bankruptcies rises and with it the need for the authorities to stand ready to make lender of last resort loans. The freedom to set deposit rates certainly gives financial institutions the chance to stave off a run by making an aggressive bid for funds (as in the case of the Bank of New South Wales, mentioned in section 12.7). However, those who have borrowed on terms that are subject to change may find themselves unable to meet sharply rising debt servicing costs. Some will be able to pass these costs on to others, as in the case of banks that raise their loan charges to their corporate borrowers who in turn put up their output prices with little loss of business. But others may find themselves having to dispose of assets on a falling market.

An obvious long-term response of financial intermediaries to increasing feelings of vulnerability associated with interest rate variability is for them to move away from the business of intermediation and reorient themselves more and more as providers of information and arrangers of transactions. This would imply much greater securitisation of debt, and a tendency toward increases in the velocity of circulation for monetary aggregates based on bank deposits, in contrast to the falls observed in the 1980s.

14.5 A Case for the Wider Use of Prudential Controls

Volatile interest rates in the market for new loans would not present so much of a problem to borrowers if they could raise money at a fixed price. If interest rates on new loans fell, they could refund their loans, albeit not without incurring some transaction costs. If interest rates rose, they would not suddenly find themselves faced with higher outgoings. But if financial deregulation spells greater interest rate volatility, we should be unwise to predict a return to the kinds of fixed interest loans that have existed in decades past, for such loans have to appeal to lenders as well as borrowers. For example, intermediaries will be living dangerously if they lend at fixed rates but take deposits at variable rates. If lenders believe there is a likelihood that interest rates on new loans will rise in the near future, they will be reluctant to make fixed interest loans of a long duration. Borrowers who need ongoing access to funds will face the choice between the risk of having to roll over short-term fixed interest loans at higher rates of interest and the risk of higher interest charges on long-term loans. At best, they might seek to insure themselves via the market for debt options, but this may seem unsatisfactory for transaction cost reasons or because the market does not extend far enough into the future to cover them against a prolonged credit squeeze.

Problems with the market for debt options ought to lead borrowers to operate with a bigger margin of financial slack if financial deregulation increases the likelihood of interest rate volatility. (This likelihood may be compounded to the extent that labour market and exchange rate deregulation open up greater scope for greater macroeconomic instability and higher rates of inflation.) However, in a world of bounded rationality, it seems unwise to presume that decision-makers will automatically raise their precautionary demands for assets when the rules of the financial game are changed. In fact, in so far as deregulation leads to more aggressive competition in the loan market, it may well lead them to move in the opposite direction.

Nowhere is this more obvious than in the housing market. If mortgage rates are not regulated, anyone who borrows on such as scale as to leave herself with hardly any discretionary expenditure will be in a very vulnerable position until inflation of her money wages has reduced her monthly mortgage repayments as a proportion of her outgoings. A sharp rise in interest rates may leave such a person unable to meet the combined costs of servicing her interest charges and her basic living expenses. An attempt to sell up and move back into the rental market may also prove financially disastrous, not merely because of the transactions costs that it will be necessary to incur but also because the property market may have gone into decline. By disposing of the property at a forced sale price the person may avoid bankruptcy at the cost of losing much of what she had put down as a deposit at the time of purchase.

In the late 1980s such gloomy possibilities should have led people to reduce the ratio between their monthly incomes and their outgoings on mortgages and personal loans. But instead, they found banks and building societies clamouring to lend them money and relaxing their rules to increase the amount lent. Where once a couple might have found they could borrow, say, a maximum of 2.5 times the prime earner's gross salary, and no more than 80 per cent of the valuation of the property, they might now find themselves able to borrow, say 3.5 times their joint salaries and up to 95 per cent of the valuation of the property. Had housing prices not exploded, the new rules would have made it much easier for first-time buyers to get a foothold as owner-occupiers. But, of course, the new conventions practically guaranteed that the real estate market would explode, particularly in areas favoured by young professional couples who were not starting families. As it exploded many first-time buyers felt under increasing pressure to borrow right up to the limit in order to get on the property merry-go-round as soon as possible, rather than fight a losing battle to build up a substantial deposit.

The market for corporate loans may similarly be expected to produce dangerous outcomes if competition between financial institutions hots up as a result of deregulation. Here, too, deregulation appears to go hand in hand with rising gearing ratios. On the one hand, intermediaries may have throw caution to the wind to keep borrowers away from competitors; on the other hand, if they do not do so, they may fail to earn enough on loans to keep themselves able to offer competitive terms on deposits. To the extent that they would rather stay clear of uncertain new ventures, banks may seek to expand their loan portfolios by encouraging corporate mergers or may seek to generate earnings with less risk to themselves by acting as underwriters of 'junk bonds'.

An extension of prudential controls from financial intermediaries to individual and corporate borrowers seems an obvious policy response to reduce the incidence of disruptive bankruptcies and forced sales of assets. So long as borrowers are restricted in terms of how much money they can raise rather than in terms of whom they can raise it from, such a policy is perfectly compatible with measures aimed at promoting competition between rival suppliers of finance. In the case of the housing market, it might also be employed as a means of removing what appears to be a social obsession with property prices. As incomes rose, the government could progressively tighten the regulations limiting how much people were able to borrow against property, thereby compressing the purchasing power of the average housing loan. Over a long period, it might even be able to use this policy gently to produce a fall in house prices in real terms without disrupting the market for existing houses or the building of new homes: this would be made possible by a reduction in the percentage value of housing that was accounted for by land, the demand price for land being a derived demand rather than constrained by production costs. Even though one would still expect houses in some areas to be more expensive than in other localities, such measures would reduce the proportion of portfolios accounted for by real estate. Hence they would be a powerful means toward reversing some of the inequalities that recent property booms have helped to create.

14.6 Licences to Borrow

My enthusiasm for imposing limits on the kinds of portfolios that participants in financial markets are allowed to have should not be taken to imply that I advocate a return to using increases in reserve asset requirements of financial intermediaries as a means for restraining the growth of expenditure. Such policies will either produce precisely the kinds of interest rate increases that one is seeking to avoid — for lenders will ration customers by raising the cost of borrowing if additional reserve assets become expensive to obtain — or they will be undermined by the activities of shrewd financial innovators who engineer a further expansion of securitised lending. However, I do believe it worthwhile to take a fresh look at the idea that expenditure may be held down if particular assets are made available in a limited supply while borrowers are required to keep a ratio of these assets to their total loans or assets. In its traditional form the idea has been applied only to financial intermediaries as, for example, in monetary base control. In this section I will attempt to show how governments might instead seek to control expenditure growth by using a novel system of marketable licences to borrow which applies not just to intermediaries but to the ultimate spenders of borrowed funds. The system is built round the same sort of philosophy as the inflation control proposals of Lerner (1978) and Lerner and Colander (1979, 1980) that were mentioned in section 11.6. In keeping with the endogenous money philosophy of this book, it aims to restrain lending by rationing on the demand side rather than the supply side.

Suppose the government legislates that all taxpaying units have to provide details of their net indebtedness at the end of each financial year. This information could easily be collected by asking only a few extra questions on tax return forms. Suppose further that the government establishes itself as the sole issuer of a financial instrument called a Credit Permit (CP). To prevent forgeries from appearing, CPs are manufactured using the same techniques employed in the production of banknotes. These CPs are denominated in units of the national currency and are offered for sale by tender. Those who buy CPs are allowed to take physical possession of them, or they may deposit them for safekeeping with their banks, accountants, lawyers or even at their local taxation offices. Owners of CPs are free to sell them on the open market whenever they want. The government also enacts legislation requiring that each individual or corporate tax-paying unit has to declare, and be able to prove that, at the end of the financial year, it possessed CPs whose face value was no less than its net indebtedness on that date. One way of making it very easy for such proof to be available would be for all CP transactions to be recorded on a central computer. Those who failed to be in possession of the appropriate number of CPs would be fined at a rate in excess of the market price of CPs at the close of trade on the last day of the financial year. This would give an incentive for debtors to end the financial year holding the stipulated amount of CPs.

In the year in which the CP scheme is introduced the government will have to make available CPs to the total value of the indebtedness of the domestic private sector at the end of the previous financial year, plus the the amount by which it is prepared to allow loan-financed expenditure by this sector to increase during the current year. In subsequent years, it will only be supplying CPs up to the value of its ceiling figure for the increased indebtedness of the domestic private sector.

Suppose the scheme has been running for some time and that this year the government wishes to limit the growth in the indebtedness of the domestic private sector to $10 billion. It creates only $10 billion worth of CPs and puts them up for tender, either all at the start of the year, or in tranches, at intervals, possibly with a view to seasonal borrowing tendencies. Bids are ranked and the CPs then go to the highest bidders. The issue is underwritten by the reserve bank in the sense that, if total demands amount to less than the issued volume of CPs, then the reserve bank will purchase the remainder for a nominal sum. Any revenue raised by the government from the sale of CPs may be returned to the market by reductions in either taxation or bond sales, or by increased government expenditure.

If members of the private sector collectively wish to increase their overall borrowing by more than $10 billion in this year they will not be able to do so, at least not without breaking the law. The greater their desire to spend, the higher will be the price of CPs in the open market. One would expect this market for CPs to develop in such as way as to enable people to make purchases of them in banks and other financial insitutions, or even in large stores. One would also expect that if CP prices are high and are not expected to fall before the end of the financial year, some borrowers may abandon their spending plans. If CP prices are high and rising there is an incentive for those with outstanding debts from previous years to cut their current expenditure and repay their loans more rapidly: this will leave them in a position to sell some of their CPs when they think the market has peaked. When they sell them, they will make room for others to increase their indebtedness.

There would be no inherent need for individuals to submit tenders for CPs each time they were made available, which might be well in advance of them having firmed up their spending plans. Rather, one would expect financial institutions to make speculative purchases of CPs, which they would then hold in stock to sell at a profit later on. An obvious time for consumers and firms to make their CP purchases would be when undertaking major increases in their indebtedness. This would not merely permit them to engage in one-stop shopping if stocks of CPs were held by financial intermediaries; it would also enable them to guard against ending the tax year with insufficient holdings of CPs. However, it would not be necessary for borrowers to try to safeguard their positions in this way, at the risk of losing out owing to a subsequent fall in the price of CPs. Rather, they could insure themselves by trading in the CP-futures and CP-options markets that would no doubt rapidly appear.

Since the focus of the CPs system is on net changes in an indivdual's indebtedness between the start and finish of the financial year, it obviously requires some forward planning and knowledge of the rates at which monthly repayments erode the value of their outstanding debt. However, in this age of programmable calculators and miniature electronic substitutes for filofaxes, I do not think this complexity needs to give cause for concern. I would also expect that, as part of the process of non-price competition, financial institutions would start making 'CP-planning' services available for a modest fee to those who feared that they would make errors if left to their own devices. It is in any case probably desirable for consumer credit legislation to be amended to require that those who provide loans must also provide details of the amounts that will be outstanding at each month up to the end of the loan as scheduled repayments are made. Borrowers should also be given the right to demand printouts of the implications of any unscheduled repayments on their repayment profiles. With modern computers there is simply no excuse for banks and other institutions not to provide this information, though they might well be reluctant to concentrate their clients' minds on the slowness with which some loans are acutally repaid!

Under the CP system, the focus of reserve bank policies becomes CP prices, not the rate of interest. It can set the rate at which it lends to the banking sector at whatever level is felt to be desirable on distributional grounds, and then leave it at this level until there is a change of government policy in this area. As in present systems, the cost of funds from the reserve bank will provide an anchor for other rates of interest, but a lowering of this rate will not lead to an increase in domestic debt-financed expenditure unless the supply of CPs is increased. Rather, a fall in the rate of interest on loans and deposits would be offset by a rise in the price of CPs if the desire of people to get into or out of debt were a function of the rate of interest.

Once the CP system is in operation growth in private sector debt can be restrained at the margin without disrupting the plans of intramarginal borrowers. If the authorities see that spending is growing more rapidly than they would like, the supply of new CPs can be curtailed and the reserve bank may even enter the market to make purchases of CPs. A squeeze on lending thus involves a rise in CP prices, not a rise in the rate of interest. Not only will debtors such as people with mortgages not find themselves suddenly having to find larger monthly sums to service higher interest charges, but they will actually enjoy a capital gain due to the rise in the value of their CP holdings.

Unlike systems of monetary control built around reserve asset controls, the CP system is comprehensive in its coverage: it affects all borrowing, whether it involves funds raised from domestic banks, building societies, finance companies, through the sale of securities and the provision of trade credit and intra-family transfers, or raised on money markets overseas. It could also be readily adapted as part of an attempt at indicative planning: all the government has to do is subdivide CPs into particular kinds of categories — for example, investment CPs, real estate CPs and CPs for the residual category of debt-financed consumption expenditure.

14.7 A Consideration of Some Objections to the Credit Permits System

The appeal of the CP system to politicians and reserve bankers is likely to be moderated by a number of practical difficulties. Logically, the first problem to consider is the question of how such a scheme might be made part of an electoral manifesto without raising fears among existing borrowers about the cost of obtaining CPs. Those who had recently borrowed might fear that the first CP year could be one in which there was a strong demand for credit so that, even if interest rates fell, the cost of buying CPs would be as painful as a sharp rise in interest rates would have been. One way round this problem would be for the CP system to be announced at least one year, and preferably two years, before it came into operation. The government would start selling CPs during this period, giving borrowers two or three years to accumulate CPs before they had to meet their first CP obligations. The information about net indebtedness could be collected on tax forms in the last year or two before the first CP year begins, enabling borrowers to familiarise themselves with the system and enabling improved planning of the initial issues of CPs. During these years of transition, it should be possible for the reserve bank to engineer a reduction in interest rates without causing a blowout of aggregate demand, for people would be starting to build expectations of the cost of CPs into their assessments of the cost of borrowing.

Secondly, politicians may expect to face objections to a CP scheme from those who expect to be net lenders. With conventional monetary policies, lenders may benefit when higher interest rates are used to deter expenditure, whereas under the CP system the gain goes to holders of CPs. The obvious argument for politicians to raise to counter such resistance to the use of CPs is to point out that the system should reduce the scope for financial instability due to bankruptcies by borrowers, and hence lending will be a far safer business.

Thirdly, it may be objected that controls over the volume of lending could fail to restrict the volume of expenditure because those with financial surpluses, or who otherwise would have been undertaking saving, can increase their spending without having to equip themselves with CPs. In other words, a CP approach to monetary management is vulnerable, like more conventional policies, to being undermined by shifts in confidence that produce shifts in the velocity of circulation. There is an obvious, but radical, way of attempting to tackle this problem: instead of trying to restrict demand by restricting the supply of licences to borrow, the government should build the system around Spending Permits (SPs). At the end of the financial year, taxpaying units would have to declare their spending for the year, detailing their sources and uses of funds, and be in possession of the appropriate number of SPs. As in the CP system one would expect spot, futures and options markets for the permits to develop. If this method of demand management were used, it would seem natural to consider replacing income taxation with an expenditure tax, such as that suggested by Kaldor (1955) and the Meade Committee (Meade, 1978).

The SP system would be somewhat more complex to administer because one would be trying to control final consumption and investment demand, not total turnover in the economy. When assessing companies, one would not wish to cover their expenditure on factors of production and inputs purchased from other firms, but only on their spending on investment goods. When assessing inidividuals, the authorities would have to choose how to incorporate durable items that had been paid for from borrowed funds. The least complicated method for dealing with loan-financed durables might be to exclude the initial act of spending and then count all subsequent repayments in the periods in which they occurred, rather than to make the assessement in terms of the initial sum spent followed by the interest component of each subsequent repayment. However, the latter method would be more directly linked to the current demand for goods and services that the SP scheme sought to restrain.

Fourthly, it may be argued that a CP scheme (or an SP scheme) may be no more effective than conventional approaches to monetary policy for promoting expenditure in times of depressed confidence. Critics might suggest that, however effective a permits system might be as a device for restraining expenditure, a reduction of permit prices in times of pessimism can only serve to make borrowing and spending easier; it cannot force additional demand from people whose decisions are being overwhelmed by non-price considerations. As they say, 'you can't push on a string'. But the permits approach does have one potentially significant advantage in this respect: it may help to foster confidence by reducing the risk that repayments obligations could be forced up by rising interest rates.

Fifthly, I would expect Post Keynesian economists to be rather surprised to see me suggest that one should introduce yet another financial instrument which would be traded not just on a spot basis but also through futures and options markets. A question obviously arises as to how for we could rely on the accumulation and sale of buffer holdings in these markets to sort out mismatches between the timing of permit sales by the government and decisions to get into debt and/or undertake major increases in spending. The possibility that speculation in CP or SP markets could be of the movement trading rather than the classical variety needs to be taken seriously, along with the possibility that options writers and futures traders might go bankrupt if their guesses about permit prices turned out horribly wrong.

Those who had neither insured themselves nor purchased permits at the time they took out major loans (or increased their rate of expenditure in an SP system) could be ruined by an unexpectedly sharp increase in permit prices that did not reverse before the end of the tax year. Those who had sought to insure themselves via the futures and options markets might get into difficulties if parties on the other side of the contracts defaulted. However, the reserve bank could try to smooth out changes in prices of permits by making open market purchases and sales of them. The danger of speculative errors would be much reduced if it established a clear trend and avoided sharp changes of policy. Surveys of patterns of spending and financing could be conducted during the year to discover whether a potential excess demand for permits was building up and, if it were, the reserve bank could make open market purchases or cut back on the rate at which it increased the supply of permits. In doing so, it would push up permit prices earlier in the year, thereby giving a signal that borrowing and/or spending should slow down, and later in the year it could step up sales to bring the permit supply back up to the planned end-year size.

Sixthly, the issue of how a CP system works in an open economy setting obviously has to be addressed. Like its SP counterpart and conventional approaches to fiscal and monetary policy, a CP system can only help indirectly to restrain expenditure on imports. Opening the economy does not legally entitle domestic borrowers to avoid acquiring CPs, but neither does it oblige foreign residents to purchase CPs if they borrow in the domestic money market. If non-residents have not accumulated speculative holdings of CPs, a domestic resident who raises funds overseas can only obtain additional CPs by bidding them away from other domestic residents. If they are not selling off speculative holdings of CPs, the domestic residents must be ones who are running down their own indebtedness. As the latter repay their loans, domestic lenders (who may or may not be intermediaries) will need to attract new borrowers. But there can be no extra borrowing if the government does not increase the supply of CPs at a faster rate. Consequently domestic lenders will fail to make replacement loans unless they find it viable to bid borrowers away from overseas sources of finance. Either they will ration customers at the existing rate of interest by being more fussy about credit rating scores or, under competitive pressure, they will reduce their interest rates. In the latter case, attempts to take advantage of cheaper finance will be thwarted by rises in CP prices.

Unless foreign exchange controls are introduced it will be difficult for an open economy to set its interest rates on distributional grounds and simply confine the focus of its monetary policy on the supply of CPs. This is because an exchange rate depreciation can occur when the capital account worsens as a result of finance flowing overseas in search of higher interest yields; it need not be caused by domestic macroeconomic overheating or declining relative competitiveness. In such a situation, the reserve bank might see no need to improve the country's current account any further by using a contraction in the supply of CPs to reduce domestic living standards. Rather, it might seem to make more sense — particularly given the sensitivity of international capital flows to small differences in risk-adjusted yields — to raise interest rates in line with world movements and thereby stop the capital outflow. Clearly, such measures would reduce somewhat the benefits that intramarginal borrowers derived from the CP system; speculators holding CPs would also suffer a loss.

Finally, we must come back to the question of opportunism, perhaps the biggest problem of all for the CP system, as for conventional policies built around reserve asset requirements. Restrictions in the supply of CPs could fail to control borrowing if taxpaying units under-reported their indebtedness. To avoid this difficulty it would be necessary to create a comprehensive computer database covering outstanding financial securities and loans from financial intermediaries. Though informal loans such as trade credit would be difficult to include in such a data base, their under-reporting would not be a major cause for concern: companies that were lending to their customers would have an incentive to report how much they were owed, so firms that were users of trade credit would be living dangerously if they failed to declare the value of their unpaid bills outstanding at the end of the financial year. But even this resort to Big Brother tactics could founder if loans were fixed up offshore and if debtor companies took over those with financial surpluses.

Such possibilities rather imply that the CP system might be best restricted to the personal sector, where the likely evasion of CP requirements would be limited mainly to loans between parents and their children and avoidance would be minimal unless individuals started to acquire a taste for overseas loans. Even here, though, matters are not so simple as they first seem, since the restricted application of the CP system would provide a powerful incentive for individuals to set themselves up in business as self-employed contractors, consultants and so on.

Opportunism would present a similar problem for the operation of an SP system, particularly one combined with an expenditure tax. Although the trend towards electronic methods of payment opens up scope for a Big Brother approach to the monitoring of each individual's spending behaviour, one would expect the introduction of an SP system to lead the 'black economy' to account for a larger proportion of transactions, and for people to engage more in social barter and 'do it yourself' activities.

14.8 Conclusion

The inherently speculative nature of portfolio choice implies that expenditure is unlikely to be a stable function of either interest rates or a particular money supply definition. Even if expenditure has in the past been observed to be related to a particular monetary aggregate, it cannot be concluded that a change in the size of this aggregate will cause a particular change in expenditure, for such observations may reflect previously passive responses of the authorities to changes in the desire to spend. Hence success in manipulating either of these policy variables is not guaranteed to have a predictable effect on aggregate demand. As it becomes harder to distinguish between banks and NBFIs, as computer databases reduce the costs of organising loans through securitisation, and as unit trust certificates and other securities become more easily encashable (if always at an uncertain nominal value), conventional policies will become increasingly unable to exert much leverage on the volume of expenditure unless they involve severe and potentially destabilising increases in interest rates.

Such considerations might be taken to imply that governments should not merely bury the idea of monetary targeting. They should also give up trying to control expenditure by manipulating interest rates unless they can master the art of buttressing small changes in the price of money with carefully contrived announcements to affect the mood of financial markets, consumers and firms. Instead, they should pursue a completely passive approach to monetary policy, allowing the supply of finance to grow in line with the demand for it. If they were reluctant to introduce some kind of CP or SP system, fiscal policy would then be left as the main vehicle for influencing aggregate demand. Here, too, the authorities would do well to take account of how private sector expenditure plans might be affected by the presentation of their policies, and not just by their content.

Unfortunately, fiscal policy may also be too dangerous to use on its own as a tool for reducing the pressure of demand in an economy that is overheating. Ideally, one would like to avoid situations in which the authorities suddenly slammed on the macroeconomic brakes. But the reluctance of governments to be seen to be increasing taxes or cutting expenditure is likely to make them seek to avoid doing so until things are already getting out of hand. For those who have left themselves little room for cutting back on discretionary expenditure, the news of an increase in rates of tax on incomes or goods and services, and/or the introduction of charges for publicly provided services may be just as painful as a rise in the rate of interest. The case imposing prudential requirements on individuals and firms thus appears to hold even if interest rates are not the main weapon for containing the growth of aggregate expenditure. Variations in individuals' prudential ratios, such as minimum deposit requirements and maximum ratios of indebtedness to income, could also be used to affect the scale of credit-financed expenditure.

The proposed CP and SP systems are clearly not without their own imperfections. However, many of these are problems that they share with conventional monetary policies whose impacts are felt by all borrowers rather than being confined to those who would like to increase their rates of expenditure. Given the potential advantages of using credit or spending permits to restrain aggregate demand and the fact that only the basic idea has been presented in this chapter, I hope that serious attention will given to the task of designing in detail a workable permits-based scheme which will be both easy for ordinary decision-makers to comprehend and difficult for opportunists to undermine.

Bibliography

(Note: numbers in brackets at the end of each entry refer to the pages in the text on which the work in question is cited.)

Ackley, G. (1951) 'The Multiplier Time Period: Money, Inventories, and Flexibility', *American Economic Review*, **41**, June, pp. 350-68 (224).

Adams, F.G. (1964) 'Consumer Attitudes, Buying Plans and Purchases of Durable Goods: A Principal Component Time Series Approach', *Review of Economics and Statistics*, **46**, pp. 347-55 (54).

Anderson, W.T., Cox, E.P. and Berenson, C. (1976) 'Bank Selection Decisions and Market Segmentation', *Journal of Marketing*, **40**, January, pp. 40-5 (43).

Ando, A. and Modigliani, F. (1963) 'The "Life Cycle" Hypothesis of Saving: Aggregate Implications and Tests', *American Economic Review*, **53**, March, pp. 55-84 (54)

Andrews, P.W.S. (1949) *Manufacturing Business*, London, Macmillan (65).

Andrews, P.W.S. (1964) *On Competition in Economic Theory*, London, Macmillan (65).

Andrews, P.W.S. and Brunner, E. (1951) *Capital Development in Steel*, Oxford, Basil Blackwell (88).

Andrews, P.W.S. and Brunner, E. (1975) *Studies in Pricing*, London, Macmillan (65, 72).

Ansoff, H.I. (1968) *Corporate Strategy*, Harmondsworth, Penguin Books (80).

Arestis, P. (1985) 'Is There any Crowding Out of Private Expenditures by Fiscal Actions?' in Arestis, P. and Skouras, T. (eds) (1985) *Post Keynesian Economic Theory*, Brighton, Wheatsheaf (107).

Argy, V. (1981) *The Postwar International Money Crisis — An Analysis*, London, George Allen & Unwin (134).

Aspinwall, R.C. and Eisenbeis, R.A. (1985) *Handbook for Banking Strategy*, New York, Wiley (176).

Bacon, R. and Eltis, W.A. (1978) *Britain's Economic Problem: Too Few Producers* (2nd edn), London, Macmillan (101).

Bagehot, W. (1873) *Lombard Street: A Description of the Money Market*, reprinted 1917, London, John Murray (272).

Baltensperger, E. (1980) 'Alternative Approaches to the Banking Firm', *Journal of Monetary Economics*, **6**, January, pp. 1-38 (162).

Barro, R.J. (1974) 'Are Government Bonds Net Wealth?' *Journal of Political Economy*, **82**, November, pp. 1095-117 (108).

Baumol, W.J., Panzar, J.C. and Willig, R.D. (1982) *Contestable Markets and the Theory of Industrial Structure*, San Diego, Harcourt Brace Jovanovich (67-8).

Bausor, R. (1982) 'Time and Economic Analysis', *Journal of Post Keynesian Economics*, **5**, Winter, pp. 163-79 (8).

Bausor, R. (1984) 'Towards a Historically Dynamic Economics: Examples and Illustrations', *Journal of Post Keynesian Economics*, **6**, Spring, pp. 360-76 (8).

Baxter, J.L. (1988) *Social and Psychological Foundations of Economic Analysis*, Hemel Hempstead, Wheatsheaf (269).

Bird, G. (1986) 'New Approaches to Country Risk', *Lloyds Bank Review*, No. 162, October, pp. 1-16 (202).

Bird, P.J.W.N. (1981) 'An Investigation of the Role of Speculation in the 1972-5 Commodity Price Boom', Unpublished Ph.D. Dissertation, University of Cambridge (33).

Black, F. (1970) 'Banking and Interest Rates in a World Without Money', *Journal of Bank Research*, Autumn, pp. 9-20 (31).

Blatt, J. (1979) 'The Utility of Being Hanged on the Gallows', *Journal of Post Keynesian Economics*, **2**, Winter, pp. 231-9 (58).

Boland, L. A. (1986) *Methodology for a New Microeconomics*, Boston, MA, Allen and Unwin (37-8, 41).

Bootle, R. (1984) 'Origins of the Monetarist Fallacy: The Legacy of Gold', *Lloyds Bank Review*, No. 153, July, pp. 16-37 (324).

Brady, N.F. (1988) *Report of the Residential Task Force on Market Mechanisms*, Washington, US Government Printing Office (279).

Brooks, M.A. (1988) 'Toward a Behavioral Analysis of Public Economics', in Earl, P.E. (ed.) (1988) *Psychological Economics: Development, Tensions, Prospects*, Boston, Kluwer (84).

Buchanan, J.M., Burton, J. and Wagner, R.E. (1978) *The Consequences of Mr Keynes*, London, Institute of Economic Affairs, Hobart Paper 78 (100).

Buchanan, J.M. and Wagner, R.E. (1977) *Democracy in Deficit*, New

York, Academic Press (100, 106).

Carew, E. (1985) *Fast Money 2: The Money Market in Australia*, Sydney, Allen and Unwin (275).

Casson, M.C. (1981) *Unemployment: A Disequilibrium Approach*, Oxford, Martin Robertson (22).

Casson, M.C. (1983) *Unemployment: A Historical Perspective*, Oxford, Basil Blackwell (252).

Challen, D.W. and Hagger, A.J. (1981) *Unemployment and Inflation*, Melbourne, Longman Cheshire (214).

Chandler, A.D. (1962) *Strategy and Structure: Chapters in the History of the American Industrial Enterprise*, Cambridge, MA, MIT Press (309).

Chick, V. (1982) 'A Comment on "*IS-LM*: An Explanation"', *Journal of Post Keynesian Economics*, 4, Spring, pp. 439-44 (4).

Chick, V. (1983) *Macroeconomics After Keynes*, Deddington, Philip Allen Publishers (x, 8).

Chick, V. (1984) 'Monetary Increases and their Consequences: Streams, Backwaters and Floods', in Ingham, A. and Ulph, A. (eds) (1984) *Demand, Equilibrium and Trade: Essays in Honour of Professor I.F. Pearce*, London, Macmillan (275, 294, 300).

Chick, V. (1985) 'Keynesians, Monetarists and Keynes: The End of the Debate — or a Beginning?', in Arestis, P. and Skouras, T. (eds) (1985) *Post Keynesian Economic Theory*, Brighton, Wheatsheaf (216).

Clarke, F.L. and Dean, G.W. (1987) 'Uncoordinated Financial Strategies: The Case of ASL', in Juttner and Valentine (eds) (1987) *The Economics and Management of Financial Institutions*, Melbourne, Longman Cheshire, pp. 437-50 (286, 290).

Clower, R.W. (1965) 'The Keynesian Counter-Revolution: A Theoretical Appraisal', in Hahn, F.H. and Brechling, F.R. (eds) (1965) *The Theory of Interest Rates*, London, Macmillan (10).

Clower, R.W. (1967) 'A Reconsideration of the Microfoundations of Monetary Theory', *Western Economic Journal*, 6, December, pp. 1-9 (10).

Coase, R.H. (1937) 'The Nature of the Firm', *Economica*, 4 (New Series), November, pp. 386-405 (76, 161).

Coddington, A. (1983) *Keynesian Economics: The Search for First Principles*, London, Allen and Unwin (36, 62, 302).

Coggan, P. (1986) *The Money Machine: How the City Works*, Harmondsworth, Penguin Books (157, 176, 180, 293, 317).

Cohen, S.C. and Zysman, J. (1986) 'Countertrade, Offsets, Barter and Buybacks', *California Management Review*, **28**, Winter, pp. 41-56 (29).

Comer, M.J. (1985) *Corporate Fraud*, (2nd edn), London, McGraw-Hill (169).

Cramp, A.B. (1962) 'Financial Intermediaries and Monetary Policy', *Economica*, **29**, May, pp. 143-51 (328).

Cramp, A.B. (1970) 'Does Money Matter?' *Lloyds Bank Review*, No. 98, October, pp. 23-57 (272).

Cramp, A.B. (1971) *Monetary Management*, London, George Allen & Unwin (328).

Crapp, H. and Skully, M. T. (1985) *Credit Unions for Australians*, Sydney, Allen and Unwin (48, 199-200).

Cripps, F., Godley, W. and Fetherston, M. (1974) 'Public Expenditure and the Management of the Economy', Memorandum G21 presented to the Expenditure Committee, 17 June 1974, reprinted in the *Ninth Report from the Expenditure Committee*, London, HMSO, HC 328 (145).

Cripps, F., Godley, W. and Fetherson, M. (1976) 'What is Left of "New Cambridge"?' *Cambridge Economic Policy Review*, No. 2, March, pp. 46-9 (145).

Cuthbertson, K. (1979) *Macroeconomic Policy: The New Cambridge, Keynesian and Monetarist Controversies*, London, Macmillan (145).

Cuthbertson, K. (1985) *The Supply and Demand for Money*, Oxford, Basil Blackwell (1-2).

Cyert, R.M. and March, J.G. (1963) *A Behavioral Theory of the Firm*, Englewood Cliffs, NJ, Prentice-Hall 96, 165, 303-4, 310).

Dale, R.S. (1988) 'Financial Regulation After the Crash', *The Royal Bank of Scotland Review*, No. 158, June, pp. 3-17 (19).

Daly, M. (1982) *Sydney Boom, Sydney Bust, Sydney*, Allen & Unwin (286, 288)

Das, S. (1987) 'Options on Debt Instruments for Australian Banks and Other Financial Intermediaries', in Juttner, D.J. and Valentine, T. (eds) (1987) *The Economics and Management of Financial Institutions*, Melbourne, Longman Cheshire, pp. 107-23 (164).

Davidson, P. (1978a) *Money and the Real World* (2nd edn), London, Macmillan (8).

Davidson, P. (1978b) 'Why Money Matters: Lessons from a Half-Century of Monetary Theory', *Journal of Post Keynesian*

Economics, **1**, Fall, pp. 46-70 (8).

Davies, G. and Davies, J. E. (1984) 'The Revolution in Monopoly Theory', *Lloyds Bank Review*, No. 153, July, pp. 38-52 (196).

Davies, J.E. and Lee, F.S. (1988) 'A Post Keynesian Appraisal of the Contestability Criterion', *Journal of Post Keynesian Economics*, **11**, Fall, pp. 3-24 (67).

Davis, K. and Lewis, M.K. (1983) 'Monetary Tactics and Monetary Targets', *Economic Papers*, **2**, Special Edition, April, pp. 82-100 (328).

Debreu, G. (1959) *Theory of Value*, Cowles Commission Monograph, New York, Wiley (9).

Diamond, D.W. (1984) 'Financial Intermediation and Delegated Monitoring', *Review of Economic Studies*, **51**, pp. 393-414 (162, 171).

Dinkel, R. (1981) 'Political Business Cycles in Germany and the United States: Some Theoretical and Empirical Considerations', in Hibbs, D.A., Jr, and Fassbender, H. (eds) (1981) *Contemporary Political Economy*, Amsterdam, North-Holland (99).

Domar, E.D. (1946) 'Capital Expansion, Rate of Growth and Employment', *American Economic Review*, **36**, pp. 137-47 (237).

Donnelly, J.H., Berry, L.L. and Thompson, T.W. (1985) *Marketing Financial Services: A Strategic Vision*, Homewood, Illinois, Dow Jones/Irwin (176).

Dow, A and Dow, S.C. (1985) 'Animal Spirits and Rationality', in Lawson, T. and Pesaran, H. (eds) (1985) *Keynes' Economics: Methodological Issues*, London, Croom Helm (38).

Dow, J.C.R. (1964) *The Management of the British Economy 1945-60*, Cambridge, Cambridge Univeristy Press/NIESR (319-20, 326).

Dow, J.C.R. (1987) 'A Critique of Monetary Policy', *Lloyds Bank Review*, No. 166, October, pp. 20-32 (320).

Dow, S.C. (1985) *Macroeconomic Thought: A Methodological Approach*, Oxford, Basil Blackwell (ix, 8).

Dow, S.C. and Earl, P.E. (1982) *Money Matters: A Keynesian Approach to Monetary Economics*, Oxford, Martin Robertson (x, 126, 146, 168, 272).

Duck, S. (1983) *Friends, For Life*, Brighton, Harvester (29).

Duesenberry, J. S. (1949) *Income, Saving and the Theory of Consumer Behavior*, Cambridge, MA, Harvard University Press (55).

Dunning, J.H. and McQueen, M. (1982) 'The Eclectic Theory of the Multinational Enterprise and the International Hotel Industry', in Rugman (ed.) (1982) *New Theories of the Multinational Enterprise*, London, Croom Helm, pp. 79-106 (177).

Earl, P.E. (1983) *The Economic Imagination: Towards a Behavioural Analysis of Choice*, Brighton, Wheatsheaf/Armonk, NY, M.E. Sharpe, Inc. (46).

Earl, P.E. (1984) *The Corporate Imagination: How Big Companies Make Mistakes*, Brighton, Wheatsheaf/Armonk, NY, M.E. Sharpe, Inc. (74, 86, 90, 173, 174).

Earl, P.E. (1986) *Lifestyle Economics: Consumer Behaviour in a Turbulent World*, Brighton, Wheatsheaf/New York, St Martin's Press (21, 23, 40, 46, 48, 50, 74, 307).

Earl, P.E. (1987) 'Scientific Research Programmes, Corporate Strategies and the Theory of the Firm', *Information Research Unit Occasional Paper*, No. 87/1, June, Brisbane, University of Queensland (90).

Earl, P.E. (ed.) (1988) *Behavioural Economics*, Two Volumes, Aldershot, Edward Elgar (37).

Earl, P.E. and Glaister, K.W. (1979) 'Wage Stickiness from the Demand Side', University of Stirling Discussion Papers in Economics, Finance, and Investment, No. 78 (250).

Eatwell, J. (1982) *Whatever Happened to Britain?* London, Duckworth/BBC (318).

Eichner, A.S. (1976) *The Megacorp and Oligopoly*, Cambridge, Cambridge University Press (reissued 1980 by M.E. Sharpe, Inc., White Plains, NY) (65, 73).

Eichner, A.S. (1983) 'Why Economics is not yet a Science', in Eichner A.S. (ed.) (1983) *Why Economics is not yet a Science*, Armonk, NY, M.E. Sharpe, Inc. (4).

Eichner, A.S. (1985) *Toward a New Economics: Essays in Post-Keynesian and Institutionalist Theory*, Armonk, NY, M.E. Sharpe, Inc. (73, 88).

Eichner, A.S. (1987) *The Macrodynamics of Advanced Market Economies*, Armonk, NY, M.E. Sharpe, Inc. (4).

Einzig, P. (1970) *The Case Against Floating Exchanges*, London, Macmillan (124-5).

Eltis, W. A. (1976) 'The Failure of the Keynesian Conventional Wisdom', *Lloyds Bank Review*, No. 122, October, pp. 1-18 (35).

Fama, E. (1980) 'Banking in the Theory of Finance', *Journal of Monetary Economics*, **6**, January, pp. 39-57 (31).

Fama, E. (1983) 'Financial Intermediation and Price Level Control', *Journal of Monetary Economics*, **12**, July, pp. 7-28 (31).

Farrell, M.J. (1959) 'The New Theories of the Consumption Function', *Economic Journal*, **69**, December, pp. 678-96 (54).

Flannery, M.J. (1986) 'Deposit Insurance Creates a Need for Bank Regulation', in Gardener, E.P.M. (ed.) (1986) *UK Banking Supervision: Evolution, Practice and Issues*, London, Allen & Unwin, pp. 257-69 (298).

Ford, J. (1987) *Economic Choice Under Uncertainty: A Perspective Theory Approach*, Aldershot, Edward Elgar (23).

Foster, J. (1987) *Evolutionary Macroeconomics*, London, Allen & Unwin (11, 238, 270).

Foster, J. (1989) 'The Macroeconomics of Keynes: An Evolutionary Perspective', in Pheby, J. (ed.) (1989) *New Directions in Post Keynesian Economics*, Aldershot, Edward Elgar (238).

Friedman, M. (1953) *Essays in Positive Economics*, Chicago, University of Chicago Press (123-6).

Friedman, M. (1957) *A Theory of the Consumption Function*, Princeton, Princeton University Press (55).

Friedman, M. (1968) 'The Role of Monetary Policy', *American Economic Review*, **58**, March, pp. 1-17 (248, 311, 323).

Friedman, M. (1980) 'Evidence to House of Commons Treasury and Civil Service Committee', *Memoranda on Monetary Policy*, Session 1979-80, Vol. 1, HC 720, London, HMSO, July (325).

Galbraith, C.S. and Kay, N.M. (1986) 'Transactions Cost Economics and the Multinational Enterprise', *Journal of Economic Behavior and Organization*, Volume 7, pp. 3-20 (177).

Gart, A. (1985) *Banks, Thrifts and Insurance Companies: Surviving the 1980s*, Lexington, MA, Lexington Books (176).

Godet, M. (1987) *Scenarios and Strategic Management*, London, Butterworths (3).

Goodhart, C.A.E. (1975) *Money, Information and Uncertainty*, London, Macmillan (77, 184, 249).

Goodhart, C.A.E. (1984) *Monetary Theory and Practice: The UK Experience*, London, Macmillan (184, 209, 211, 219).

Goodhart, C.A.E. (1987a) 'Monetary Base', Eatwell, J., Milgate, M. and Newman, P. (eds) (1987) *The New Palgrave: A Dictionary of Economics*, London, Macmillan (213).

Goodhart, C.A.E. (1987b) 'Why do Banks Need a Central Bank?' *Oxford Economic Papers*, **39**, March, pp. 75-89 (291, 299).

Gowland, D. (1985) *Money, Inflation and Unemployment*, Brighton, Wheatsheaf (139).

Graaff, J. de V. (1987) 'Pigou, Arthur Cecil (1977-1959)', Eatwell, J., Milgate, M. and Newman, P. (eds) (1987) *The New Palgrave: A Dictionary of Economics*, London, Macmillan (264).

Grant, A.T.K. (1977) *Economic Uncertainty and Financial Structure*, London, Macmillan (35).

Greenfield, R.L. and Yeager, L.B. (1983) 'A Laissez-Faire Approach to Monetary Stability', *Journal of Money, Credit and Banking*, August, pp. 302-315 (31).

Gruen, F.H. (1985) 'The Federal Budget: How Much Difference do Elections Make?' Discussion Paper No. 120, Centre for Economic Policy Research, Canberra, Australian National University (100).

Gurley, J.G. and Shaw, E.S. (1960) *Money in a Theory of Finance*, Washington, DC, Brookings Institution (263).

Haache, G. and Townsend, J. (1981) 'A Broad Look at Exchange Rate Movements for Eight Countries', *Bank of England Quarterly Bulletin*, December, pp. 489-509 (127).

Hall, R.E. (1982) 'Explorations in the Gold Standard and Related Policies for Stabilising the Dollar', in Hall, R.E. (ed.) *Inflation: Causes and Effects*, Chicago, University of Chicago Press for the National Bureau of Economic Research, pp. 111-122 (31).

Hamilton, A. (1986) *The Financial Revolution*, Harmondsworth, Penguin (151, 158, 176, 206, 293-4, 317).

Harper, I.R. (1984) 'Some Speculation on the Long-Term Implications of Financial Deregulation and Innovation', *Economic Papers*, **3**, December, pp. 1-8 (31).

Harper, I.R. (1986) 'An Application of Contestable Market Analysis to the Australian Banking Industry', *Economic Analysis and Policy*, **16**, March, pp. 50-60 (196).

Harrigan, K.R. (1983) *Strategies for Vertical Integration*, Lexington, MA, Lexington Books (78).

Harrod, R.F. (1939) 'An Essay on Dynamic Theory', *Economic Journal*, **49**, pp. 14-33 (237).

Hart, A.G. (1940) 'Anticipations, Uncertainty and Dynamic Planning', *Journal of Business of the University of Chicago*, **13**, No. 4 (also published separately as a monograph by the University of Chicago Press, Chicago) (23).

Hart, A.G. (1942) 'Risk, Uncertainty and the Unprofitability of Compounding Probabilities', in Lange, O., McIntyre, F. and Yntema, T.O. (eds) (1942) *Studies in Mathematical Economics and Econometrics*, Chicago, University of Chicago Press (reprinted in American Economic Association (1946) *Readings in the Theory of Income Distribution*, Philadelphia, A.E.A.) (23).

Hart, A. G. (1945) '"Model Building" and Fiscal Policy', *American Economic Review*, **35**, September, pp. 531-58 (62).

Hart, A. G. (1947) 'Keynes' Analysis of Expectations and Uncertainty', in Harris, S.E. (ed.) (1947) *The New Economics: Keynes' Influence on Theory and Public Policy*, New York, Knopf (23, 62).

Hart, A.G. (1948) *Money, Debt and Economic Activity*, New York, Prentice-Hall (305).

Hazeldine, T. (1984) *Full Employment Without Inflation*, London, Macmillan (304).

Heathfield, D.F. and Pearce, I.F. (1982) 'A Tract on Sound Money: Why and How', in Hawkins, C. and McKenzie, G. (eds) (1982) *The British Economy: What Will Our Children Think?* London, Macmillan (235).

Heiner, R.A. (1983) 'The Origin of Predictable Behavior', *American Economic Review*, **73**, September, pp. 560-95 (39, 62).

Heiner, R.A. (1986) 'The Economics of Information when Decisions are Imperfect', in MacFadyen, A.J. and MacFadyen, H.W. (eds) (1986) *Economic Psychology: Intersections in Theory and Application*, Amsterdam, North-Holland pp. 293-350 (97).

Hicks, J.R. (1937) 'Mr Keynes and the "Classics": A Suggested Interpretation', *Econometrica*, **5**, April, pp. 147-59 (3).

Hicks, J.R. (1967) *Critical Essays in Monetary Theory*, Oxford, Clarendon Press (23).

Hicks, J.R. (1974) *The Crisis in Keynesian Economics*, Oxford, Basil Blackwell (309, 313).

Hicks, J.R. (1976) 'Some Questions of Time in Economics', in Tang, A.M., Westfield, F.M. and Worley, J.S. (eds) (1976) *Evolution, Welfare, and Time in Economics: Essays in Honor of Nicholas Georgescu-Roegen*, Lexington, MA, Lexington Books (3).

Hicks, J.R. (1980a) *Causality in Economics*, Canberra, Australian National University Press/Oxford, Basil Blackwell (308).

Hicks, J.R. (1980b) 'IS-LM: An Explanation', *Journal of Post Keynesian Economics*, **3**, Winter, pp. 139-54 (3).

Hirsch, F. (1977) *Social Limits to Growth*, London, Routledge and Kegan Paul (34).

Hirschman, A.O. (1958) *The Strategy of Economic Development*, New Haven, CT, Yale University Press (307).

Hodgson, G. (1988) *Economics and Institutions: A Manifesto for a Modern Insitutional Economics*, Cambridge, Polity Press (11, 37).

Hogan, W.P. and Sharpe, I. (1987) 'Some Issues in Prudential Regulation and Examination', in Juttner, D.J. and Valentine, T. (eds) (1987) *The Economics and Management of Financial Institutions*, Melbourne, Longman Cheshire, pp. 386-98 (297).

Horvitz, P.M. (1986) 'The Case Against Risk-Related Deposit Insurance Premiums', in Gardener, E.P.M. (ed.) (1986) *UK Banking Supervision: Evolution, Practice and Issues*, London, Allen & Unwin, pp. 270-81 (298).

Hotson, A.C. (1982) 'The Supplementary Special Deposits Scheme', *Bank of England Quarterly Bulletin*, **22**, March, pp. 74-85 (209).

Hutchison, T. (1977) *Keynes Versus the Keynesians? An Essay on the Thinking of J.M. Keynes and the Accuracy of Interpretation by his Followers*, London, Institute of Economic Affairs (254).

Irwin, H.S. (1937) 'The Nature of Risk Assumption in the Trading on Organised Exchanges', *American Economic Review*, **27**, June, pp. 267-78 (33).

Jackson, L. (1987) 'Country Risk Analysis', in Juttner, D.J. and Valentine, T. (eds) (1987) *The Economics and Management of Financial Institutions*, Melbourne, Longman Cheshire, pp. 329-39 (169).

Jarsulic, M. (ed.) (1985) *Money and Macro Policy*, Boston, Kluwer (184).

Jefferson, M. (1983) 'Economic Uncertainty and Business Decision Making', in Wiseman, J. (ed.) (1983) *Beyond Positive Economics?* London, Macmillan (2).

JMCB (1985) 'Bank Market Studies: A Review and Evaluation', *Journal of Money Credit and Banking*, **16**, November, part 2 (complete issue) (162).

Joaquin, D.C. (1988) 'A Reconsideration of the Focal Outcomes Approach to Portfolio Selection', *Journal of Post Keynesian Economics*, **10**, Summer, pp. 631-45 (46).

Jones, H. (1975) *An Introduction to Modern Theories of Economic*

Growth, London, Nelson (238).

Kahn, R.F. and Posner, M.V. (1977) 'Inflation, Unemployment and Growth', *National Westminster Bank Review*, November, pp. 28-37 (237).

Kaish, S. (1986) 'Behavioral Economics in the Theory of the Business Cycle', in Gilad, B. and Kaish, S. (eds) (1986) *Handbook of Behavioral Economics, Volume B: Behavioral Macroeconomics*, Greenwich, CT, JAI Press, Inc. (275).

Kaldor, N. (1955) *An Expenditure Tax*, London, George Allen & Unwin (337).

Kaldor, N. (1978) *Further Essays in Applied Economics*, London, Duckworth (113, 126-7).

Kaldor, N. (1980) 'Monetarism and UK Monetary Policy', *Cambridge Journal of Economics*, 4, December, pp. 293-318 (325)

Kaldor, N. (1982) *The Scourge of Monetarism*, Oxford, Oxford University Press (31, 184, 325).

Karacaoglu, G. (1984) 'Absence of Gross Substitution in Portfolios and Demand for Finance: Some Macroeconomic Implications', *Journal of Post Keynesian Economics*, 6, Summer, pp. 576-89 (50).

Katona, G. (1975) *Psychological Economics*, Amsterdam, Elsevier (54).

Kay, N.M. (1982) *The Evolving Firm*, London, Macmillan (45, 76, 80, 161, 175, 315).

Kay, N.M. (1983) 'Optimal Size of Firm as a Problem in Transaction Costs and Property Rights', *Journal of Economic Studies*, 10, pp. 29-41 (26).

Kay, N.M. (1984) *The Emergent Firm*, London, Macmillan (11, 76, 80, 161, 175, 177).

Kelly, G.A. (1955) *The Psychology of Personal Constructs*, New York, W.W. Norton & Co. (307).

Keynes, J.M. (1936) *The General Theory of Employment, Interest and Money*, London, Macmillan (3, 23, 34-5, 46, 53, 87, 213, 244-6, 254, 260-2, 264, 272, 276).

Keynes, J.M. (1937a) 'The "Ex Ante" Theory of the Rate of Interest', *Economic Journal*, 47, December, pp. 663-9 (107, 312).

Keynes, J.M. (1937b) 'The General Theory of Employment', *Quarterly Journal of Economics*, 51, pp 209-33 (265, 320).

Keynes, J.M. (1940) *How to Pay for the War*, London, Macmillan (268).

Keynes, J.M. (1973) *The Collected Writings of John Maynard Keynes, Volume XIII: The General Theory and After: Preparation*, London, Macmillan (136).

Keynes, J.M. (1979) *The Collected Writings of John Maynard Keynes, Volume XXIX: The General Theory and After: A Supplement*, London, Macmillan (32, 252).

Killingsworth, C. (1969) 'Full Employment and the New Economics', *Scottish Journal of Political Economy*, **16**, February, pp. 1-19 (254).

Kindleberger, C.P. (1978) *Manias, Panics and Crashes*, London, Macmillan (272)

Kornai, J. (1971) *Anti-Equilibrium*, Amsterdam, North-Holland (37, 303).

Kregel, J.A. (1973) *The Reconstruction of Political Economy*, London, Macmillan (238).

Kregel, J.A. (1980) 'Markets and Institutions as Features of a Capitalistic Production System', *Journal of Post Keynesian Economics*, **3**, Fall, pp. 21-31 (36).

Krugman, P.R. (ed.) (1986) *Strategic Trade Policy and the New International Economics*, Cambridge, MA, MIT Press (136).

Lancaster, K.J. (1966) 'A New Approach to Consumer Theory', *Journal of Political Economy*, **74**, April, pp. 132-57 (42).

Lancaster, K. J. (1971) *Consumer Demand: A New Approach*, New York, Columbia University Press (42).

Lawrence, C. and Shay, R.P. (1986) *Technological Innovation, Regulation, and the Monetary Economy*, Cambridge, MA, Ballinger (181).

Lee, F.S. (1984) 'Full Cost Pricing: A New Wine in a New Bottle', *Australian Economic Papers*, **23**, June, pp. 151-66 (65).

Lee, F.S., Irving-Lessman, J., Earl, P.E. and Davies, J.E. (1986) 'P.W.S. Andrews' Theory of Competitive Oligopoly: A New Interpretation', *British Review of Economic Issues*, **8**, Autumn, pp. 13-39 (65).

Leibenstein, H. (1950) 'Bandwagon, Snob and Veblen Effects in the Theory of Consumers' Demand', *Quarterly Journal of Economics*, **65**, 183-207 (58).

Leibenstein, H. (1976) *Beyond Economic Man*, Cambridge, MA, Harvard University Press (303, 310).

Leijonhufvud, A. (1968) *On Keynesian Economics and the Economics of Keynes*, New York, Oxford University Press (10,

261).

Leijonhufvud, A. (1969) *Keynes and the Classics*, London, Institute of Economic Affairs (312).

Leijonhufvud, A. (1973) 'Effective Demand Failures', *Swedish Journal of Economics*, **75**, pp. 27-48 (311).

Lerner, A.P. (1978) 'A Wage Permit Plan to Stop Inflation', in Okun, A.M. and Perry, G.L. (eds) (1978) *Curing Chronic Inflation*, Washington, DC, Brookings Institution, pp. 255-70 (270, 333).

Lerner, A.P. and Colander, D.C. (1979) 'The Market Anti-Inflation Plan', in Gapinsky, J.H. and Rockwood, C.E., jr (eds) (1979) *Essays in Post-Keynesian Inflation*, New York, Ballinger, pp. 217-29 (270, 333).

Lerner, A.P. and Colander, D.C. (1980) *MAP: A Market Anti-Inflation Plan*, New York, Harcourt Brace Jovanovich (270, 333).

Lewis, M.K. and Wallace, R.H. (eds) (1985) *Australia's Financial Institutions and Markets*, Melbourne, Longman-Cheshire (134).

Lindbeck, A. (1976) 'Stabilisation Policy in Open Economies with Endogenous Politicians', *American Economic Review Papers and Proceedings*, **66**, pp. 1-18 (97).

Llewellyn, D.T. (1979) 'Do Building Societies take Deposits from Banks?' *Lloyds Bank Review*, January, pp. 20-34 (210).

Llewellyn, D.T. (1985) 'The Changing Structure of the UK Financial System', *Three Banks Review*, No. 145, March, pp. 19-34 (317).

Llewellyn, D.T., Dennis, G.E.J., Hall, M.J.B. and Nellis, J.G. (1982) *The Framework of UK Monetary Policy*, London, Heinemann Educational Books (184, 209).

Loasby, B.J. (1976) *Choice, Complexity and Ignorance*, Cambridge, Cambridge University Press (77).

Love, J.F. (1986) *McDonald's: Behind the Arches*, New York, Bantam Books, Inc. (177).

Macrae, D. (1977) 'A Political Model of the Business Cycle', *Journal of Political Economy*, **85**, 239-63 (97).

Maital, S. (1982) *Minds, Markets and Money*, New York, Basic Books (52).

Malcolmson, J.M. (1981) 'Unemployment and the Efficiency Wage Hypothesis', *Economic Journal*, **91**, September, pp. 848-66 (250).

Mariti, P. and Smiley, R.H. (1983) 'Co-operative Agreements and the Organisation of Industry', *Journal of Industrial Economics*,

31, June, pp. 437-52 (81).

Marzouk, G.A. (1987) *The Flow of Funds and Monetary Policy in Australia*, Mosman, NSW, Australian Professional Publications (35, 142).

Mayer, T., Duesenberry, J.S. and Aliber, R.Z. (1984) *Money, Banking, and the Economy*, (2nd edn), New York, Norton (184, 206).

McManamy, J. (1988) *Crash! Corporate Australia Fights for its Life*, Sydney, Pan Books (19).

McWilliams, J.D. (1977) 'Failure Models for Nonfinancial Institutions: Discussion', in Altman, E.I. and Sametz, A.W. (1977) *Financial Crises: Institutions and Markets in a Fragile Environment*, New York, Wiley (202).

Meade, J.E. (1978) *The Structure and Reform of Direct Taxation*, London, Allen & Unwin (337).

Meeks, G. and Whittington, G. (1976) *The Financing of Quoted Companies in the UK: The Significance of Equity Capital and Dividends for Companies of Different Sizes, Sectors and Rates of Growth* (Background Paper No. 1 for Royal Commission on the Distribution of Income and Wealth), London, HMSO (75).

Meiden, A. (1984) *Bank Marketing Management*, London, Macmillan (176).

Menger, K. (1871) *Principles of Economics* (English translation, 1950, Glencoe, Illinois, Free Press) (13, 22).

Miller, E. and Lonie, A. (1978) *Microeconomic Effects of Monetary Policy: The Fallout of Severe Monetary Restraint*, Oxford, Martin Robertson (272).

Miller, M. (1981) 'Monetary Control in the UK', *Cambridge Journal of Economics*, **5**, March, pp. 71-9 (326).

Minsky, H.P. (1975) *John Maynard Keynes*, New York, Columbia University Press (184, 196, 221, 272-3, 303).

Minsky, H.P. (1982) *Inflation, Recession and Ecnomic Policy*, Brighton, Wheatsheaf (221, 272-3)

Minsky, H.P. (1986) *Stabilizing an Unstable Economy*, New Haven, CT, Yale University Press (221, 272-3).

Mises, L. von (1966) *Human Action* (3rd edn), Chicago, Henry Regnery & Company (13).

Modigliani, F. and Brumberg, R. (1955) 'Utility Analysis and the Consumption Function', in Kurihara, K.K. (ed.) (1955) *Post-Keynesian Economics*, London, Allen & Unwin (54).

Mohl, A. (1988) 'Patterns of Financing Post-Deregulation',

Economic Papers, 7, March, pp. 51-64 (317, 327).

Moore, B.J. (1979) 'The Endogenous Money Stock', *Journal of Post Keynesian Economics*, 2, Fall, pp. 49-70 (184).

Moore, B.J. (1983) 'Unpacking the Post Keynesian Black Box: Bank Lending and the Money Supply', *Journal of Post Keynesian Economics*, 5, Summer, pp. 537-56 (184).

Moore, B.J. (1988) *Horizontalists and Verticalists*, Cambridge, Cambridge University Press (184, 196-7, 206).

Moran, M. (1986) *The Politics of Banking*, (2nd edn), London, Macmillan (105, 161, 279, 285, 295).

Morita, A. (1987) *Made in Japan*, London, Collins (17, 128, 314).

Mosley, P. (1976) 'Towards a "Satisficing" Theory of Economic Policy', *Economic Journal*, 86, March, pp. 59-73 (96).

Mosley, P. (1984) *The Making of Economic Policy*, Brighton, Wheatsheaf (98).

Moss, S. (1981) *An Economic Theory of Business Strategy*, Oxford, Martin Robertson (65, 307).

Moss, S. (1984) *Markets and Macroeconomics*, Oxford, Basil Blackwell (307).

Nadler, P.S. and Miller, R.B. (1985) *The Banking Jungle: How to Survive and Prosper in a Business Turned Topsy Turvy*, New York, Wiley (176).

Neild, R.R. (1964) 'Replacement Policy', *National Institute Economic Review*, No, 30, November, pp. 30-43 (88).

Nelson, R.R. and Winter, S.G. (1982) *An Evolutionary Analysis of Economic Change*, Cambridge, MA, Harvard University Press (37, 303).

Nordhaus, W.D. (1975) 'The Political Business Cycle', *Review of Economic Studies*, 42, 169-90 (97).

Pahl, R. (1984) *Disvisions of Labour*, Oxford, Basil Blackwell (29).

Pasinetti, L.L. (1981) *Structural Change and Economic Growth*, Cambridge, Cambridge University Press (238).

Pearce, I.F. (1976) 'Commentary', in Hayek, F.A. (1976) *Choice in Currency: A Way to Stop Inflation*, London, Institute of Economic Affairs (235).

Penrose, E.T. (1959) *The Theory of the Growth of the Firm*, Oxford, Blackwell (79, 182, 274, 309).

Perrin. J.R. (1984) 'A Flow of Funds Framework for Monetary Analysis', paper presented at the 13th Conference of Economists,

Western Australia Institute of Technology, Perth, August (147).

Pheby, J. (ed.) (1989) *New Directions in Post Keynesian Economics*, Aldershot, Edward Elgar (11).

Phelps, E.S. (ed.) (1970) *Microeconomic Foundations of Employment and Inflation Theory*, New York, W.W. Norton & Co. (248, 311).

Pickering, J.F. (1977) *The Acquisition of Consumer Durables: A Cross Sectional Investigation*, London, Associated Business Programmes (54).

Pigou, A.C. (1941) *Employment and Equilibrium*, London, Macmillan (264).

Podolski, T.M. (1986) *Financial Innovation and the Money Supply*, Oxford, Basil Blackwell (295, 326).

Posner, M.V. (1970) 'Technical Change, International Trade and Foreign Investment', in Streeten, P. (ed.) (1970) *Unfashionable Economics: Essays in Honour of Lord Balogh*, London, Weidenfeld and Nicolson, pp. 210-26 (111).

Radcliffe Report (1959) *The Committee on the Working of the Monetary System, Report*, Cmnd. 827, London, HMSO (31, 96, 184).

RBA (1985) 'Prudential Supervision of Banks', *Reserve Bank of Australia Bulletin*, May, pp. 99-101 (185).

RBNZ (1985) 'Abolition of Compulsory Ratio Requirements', *Reserve Bank of New Zealand Bulletin*, **48**, April, pp. 175-8 (207).

Reid, M. (1982) *The Secondary Banking Crisis, 1973-75*, London, Macmillan (168, 285).

Reid, M. (1988) *All Change in the City: The Revolution in Britain's Financial Sector*, London, Macmillan (34, 105).

Reynolds, P.J. (1987) *Political Economy: A Synthesis of Kaleckian and Post Keynesian Economics*, Brighton, Wheatsheaf (65).

Richardson, G.B. (1960) *Information and Investment*, Oxford, Oxford University Press (314).

Richardson, G.B (1969) *The Future of the Heavy Electrical Plant Industry*, London, BEEMA (72).

Richardson, G.B. (1972) 'The Organization of Industry', *Economic Journal*, Volume 82, pp. 883-89 (78).

Robertson, D.H. (1926) *Banking Policy and the Price Level*, London, P.S. King & Son (264).

Robertson, D.H. (1954) *Britain and the World Economy*, London,

Bibliography

George Allen & Unwin (122).

Robinson, J.V. (1937) *Introduction to the Theory of Employment*, London, Macmillan (4).

Robinson, J.V. (1966) *The New Mercantilism: An Inaugural Lecture*, Cambridge, Cambridge University Press, reprinted in Robinson, J.V. (1973) *Collected Economic Papers, Volume IV*, Oxford, Basil Blackwell (117).

Roe, A.R. (1973) 'The Case for Flow of Funds and National Balance Sheet Analysis', *Economic Journal*, 83, June, pp. 399-420 (142, 315).

Rotheim, R.J. (1981) 'Keynes' Monetary Theory of Value (1933)', *Journal of Post Keynesian Economics*, 3, Summer, pp. 568-85 (36).

Rousseas, S. (1985) 'A Markup Theory of Bank Loan Rates', *Journal of Post Keynesian Economics*, 8, Fall, pp. 135-44 (184, 196).

Rousseas, S. (1986) *Post Keynesian Monetary Economics*, Armonk, NY, M.E. Sharpe, Inc. (184, 196)

Seidman, L.S. (1978) 'Tax-Based Incomes Policies' in Okun, A.M. and Perry, G.L. (eds) (1978) *Curing Chronic Inflation*, Washington, DC, Brookings Institution, pp. 65-126 (270).

Shackle, G.L.S. (1938) *Expectations, Investment and Income*, Oxford, Oxford University Press (310).

Shackle, G.L.S. (1949) *Expectation in Economics*, Cambridge, Cambridge University Press (9).

Shackle, G.L.S. (1973) *Epistemics and Economics*, Cambridge, Cambridge University Press (8).

Shackle, G.L.S. (1974) *Keynesian Kaleidics*, Edinburgh, Edinburgh University Press (7, 8, 303).

Shackle, G. L. S. (1979) *Imagination and the Nature of Choice*, Edinburgh, Edinburgh University Press (2, 39).

Shackle, G.L.S. (1982) 'Sir John Hicks' *"IS-LM*: An Explanation": A Comment', *Journal of Post Keynesian Economics*, 4, Spring, pp. 435-8 (4, 13, 241).

Shapiro, H.T. and Angevine, G.E. (1969) 'Consumer Attitudes, Buying Intentions and Expectations: An Analysis of the Canadian Data', *Canadian Journal of Economics*, 2, May, pp. 230-49 (54).

Sheehan, P. (1988) 'Why it Pays to go Broke', *Sydney Morning Herald Magazine*, 27 August, p. 38 (200).

Shiller, R.J. (1988) 'Portfolio Insurance and Other Investor Fashions as Factors in the 1987 Stock Market Crash', in Fischer, S. (ed.)

. (1988) *NBER Macroeconomics Annual 1988*, Cambridge MA, MIT Press (280).

Simon, H.A. (1957) *Models of Man*, New York, Wiley (47).

Simon, H.A. (1959) 'Theories of Decision-Making in Economics and Behavioral Sciences', *American Economic Review*, **49**, June, pp. 253-83 (47, 303).

Simon, H.A. (1969) *The Sciences of the Artificial*, Cambridge, MA, MIT Press (305).

Smith, R.P. (1975) *Consumer Demand for Cars in the USA*, Cambridge, Cambridge University Press (54).

Spero, J. (1980) *The Failure of the Franklin National Bank: Challenge to the International Financial System*, New York, Columbia University Press (285).

Sraffa, P. (1960) *Production of Commodities by Means of Commodities*, Cambridge, Cambridge University Press (305).

Stanford, J.D. and Beale, T. (1987) 'Financial Instability: A Recent Australian Episode', in Juttner, D.J. and Valentine, T. (eds) (1987), *The Economics and Management of Financial Institutions*, Melbourne, Longman Cheshire, pp. 476-99 (286, 290).

Steinbruner, J.D. (1974) *The Cybernetic Theory of Decision: New Dimensions of Political Analysis*, Princeton, NJ, Princeton University Press (94).

Stewart, M. (1983) *Controlling the Economic Future: Policy Dilemmas in a Shrinking World*, Brighton, Wheatsheaf (135).

Strange, S. (1986) *Casino Capitalism*, Oxford, Basil Blackwell (20).

Swan, P.L. (1983) 'The Campbell Report and Deregulation', *Economic Papers*, **2**, Special Edition, April, pp. 177-93 (294, 328).

Thaler, R. and Shefrin, H. (1981) 'An Economic Theory of Self Control', *Journal of Political Economy*, **89**, April, pp. 396-406 (53).

Tobin, J. (1963) 'Commercial Banks as Creators of "Money"', in Carson, D. (ed.) (1963) *Banking and Monetary Studies*, Homewood, Illinois, Richard D. Irwin (184).

Tobin, J. (1980) *Asset Accumulation and Economic Activity*, Oxford, Basil Blackwell (61).

Toffler, A. (1970) *Future Shock*, London, Bodley Head (21, 51, 309).

Townshend, H. (1937) 'Liquidity Premium and the Theory of Value, *Economic Journal*, **47**, March, pp. 157-69 (8, 13, 53).

Tschoegl, A.E. (1982) 'Foreign Bank Entry into Japan and California', in Rugman, A.M. (ed.) (1982) *New Theories of the Multinational Enterprise*, London, Croom Helm, pp. 196-216 (178).

Tschoegl, A.E. (1985) 'Modern Barter', *Lloyds Bank Review*, No. 158, October, pp. 32-40 (29).

Turner, G. (1969) *Busines in Britain*, London, Eyre & Spottiswoode (173).

Tylecote, A. (1981) *The Causes of the Present Inflation*, London, Macmillan (268).

Verzariu, P. (1985) *Countertrade, Barter, and Offsets: New Strategies for Profit in International Trade*, New York, McGraw-Hill (29).

Warr, P.B. (1983) 'Work, Jobs and Unemployment', *Bulletin of the British Psychological Society*, *36*, September, pp. 305-11 (247).

Watts, M.J. and Gaston, N.G. (1982) 'The "Reswitching" of Consumption Bundles: A Parallel to the Capital Controversies', *Journal of Post Keynesian Economics*, 5, Winter, pp. 281-8 (45).

Weintraub, S. (1978) *Capitalism's Unemployment and Inflation Crisis*, Reading, MA, Addison-Wesley (270).

Weintraub, S. (1980) 'Money Supply and Demand Interdependence', *Journal of Post Keynesian Economics*, 2, Summer, pp. 566-75 (184).

Weintraub, S. (1982) 'Hicks on *IS-LM*: More Explanation', *Journal of Post Keynesian Economics*, 4, Spring, pp. 445-52 (4, 308).

Wells, P. (1983) 'A Post Keynesian View of Liquidity Preference and the Demand for Money', *Journal of Post Keynesian Economics*, 5, Summer, pp. 523-36 (36).

Williams, B.R. and Scott, W.P. (1965) *Investment Proposals and Decisions*, London, George Allen & Unwin (310)

Williams, D.J. (1986) 'Shareholder Bonding in Financial Mutuals: An Exploratory Study of the Relative Effects of Altruism and Agency', *Accounting, Organizations and Society*, 11, pp. 271-86 (162, 174).

Williams, K., Williams, J. and Thomas, D. (1983) *Why are the British Bad at Manufacturing?* London, Routledge & Kegan Paul (86).

Williams, R.A. and Defries, L. (1981) 'The Roles of Inflation and Consumer Sentiment in Explaining Australian Consumption and Savings Patterns', *Journal of Economic Psychology*, 1, pp.

105-20 (54).

Williamson, O.E. (1970) *Corporate Control and Business Behavior*, Englewood Cliffs, NJ, Prentice-Hall (84, 173).

Williamson, O.E. (1971) 'Managerial Discretion, Organization Form, and the Multi-division Hypothesis', in Marris, R. and Wood, A. (eds.) (1971) *The Corporate Economy*, London, Macmillan (84, 173).

Williamson, O.E. (1975) *Market and Hierarchies: Analysis and Antitrust Implications*, New York, Free Press (76, 78, 84, 111, 165, 173).

Williamson, O.E. (1985) *The Economic Institutions of Capitalism*, New York, Free Press (76, 78, 161, 165).

Wilson, T. and Andrews, P.W.S. (eds) (1951) *Oxford Studies in the Price Mechanism*, Oxford, Oxford University Press (88-9).

Winter, S.G., Jr. (1964) 'Economic "Natural Selection" and the Theory of the Firm', *Yale Economic Essays*, **4**, Spring, pp. 224-72 (197).

Wood, A.J.B. (1975) *A Theory of Profits*, Cambridge, Cambridge University Press (73).

Wood, A.J.B. (1978) *A Theory of Pay*, Cambridge, Cambridge University Press (309).

Wright, P. (1975) 'Consumer Choice Strategies: Simplifying versus Optimizing', *Journal of Marketing Research*, **12**, February, pp. 60-7 (47).

Yannopoulos, G.N. (1983) 'The Growth of Transnational Banking', in Casson, M. (ed.) (1983) *The Growth of International Business*, London, George Allen & Unwin, pp. 238-57 (178).

Subject Index

363

Subject Index

Experimentation, 65, 302, 321
Exports, 6, 101, 110-23 *passim*,
    221, 313, 321

Finance, 8-9, 24, 35, 107-8, 217-20,
    225, 237, 240-1, 284, 318, 322
    companies, 151-5, 288-90, 327,
    337
Financial intermediaries, 12, 151-83
    passim, 194, 207, 282-3, 293,
    305, 328-32, 335
    rationale for, 152-64
Fire-fighting behaviour, 95
Fiscal policy, 117-19, 306, 319,
    339-42
Flexibility, 16, 21, 37-8, 167, 174,
    251-2, 263-4, 267, 325
Flow of funds analysis, 12, 138-49,
    315
Forecasting, 129-34
Foreign exchange, 20, 30, 142-3,
    313, 327
    controls, 317-18, 339
Franchising, 177-8
Fraud, 168-9, 201-2, 297
Futures, 9, 18-19, 31, 33, 134, 164,
    335-8

General equilibrium theory, 9
Gold, 31, 121, 278, 285
Goodhart's law, 209, 295
Goodwill, 17, 68-70, 74, 97, 111,
    168, 178, 181-2, 197-9, 205-6,
    209, 268-9, 314
Government, 7, 11, 92-109 *passim*,
    115, 123-5, 136-8, 143, 146-9,
    185-6, 208, 212, 223, 226-8,
    232, 235, 249, 253-6, 259, 262,
    265-6, 292-4, 311-13, 318,
    333-4, 337-9
Gross substitution, 29, 252

Hedging, 2, 39, 45, 82-6, 114, 134,

137, 162, 171-2, 183, 278,
    292-3
Hierarchies of wants, 46-51, 278
Hire purchase, 154, 203
    controls over, 96, 319
Hoarding, 230-1, 304
Housing, 43, 58, 231-2, 318,
    331-2

Idiosyncrasy, 16, 27-8
Ignorance, 78, 292, 310
Imagination, 39, 280
Imports, 101, 110-23 *passim*,
    147-9, 212, 221-4, 228,
    233-5, 313, 318, 321,
    325, 327
    controls, 121-2, 136, 145
Incentives, 101-3, 122, 163,
    167, 170-2, 197, 201, 234,
    246-7, 268-70, 287, 298,
    304, 310, 317, 333-4, 340
Income, 6-7, 14, 34-6, 53-6, 59,
    99, 135, 140, 223, 229, 237,
    239, 242, 252-4, 257, 264,
    267, 311, 323, 332
    distribution, 254, 335, 339
Incomes policy, 125, 134, 144,
    147, 244, 268-70, 309
Indeterminacy, 2-3, 12, 183, 216,
    315
Indivisibility, 27
Infinite regress, 39
Inflation, 1, 17, 25, 30, 54, 60-1,
    64, 70, 96, 100-1, 113, 121,
    124-5, 129, 149-50, 175,
    236-7, 263-71, 277-8, 287,
    291-2, 304, 309, 323, 332
Inflationary gap, 259, 266, 268
Information, 22, 41, 83, 94,
    97-9, 152, 161, 166, 169-71,
    177-8, 273, 293, 300, 307,
    314-15, 330, 337
    agreements, 314

366